GUIDE TO BETTER
DUPLICATE BRIDGE

Standard American Edition

The *Guide to Better Duplicate Bridge* is written for the vast majority of bridge players who want to improve their bidding skills beyond the basics. If you have mastered the fundamentals of Standard American bidding methods and wish to consolidate and advance your prowess, then you benefit by reading the *Guide to Duplicate Better Bridge.*

Once you start reaching the best contract regularly, you will want to make sure that your declarer play does not let you down. The *Guide to Better Duplicate Bridge* was designed to improve both declarer skills and defensive technique. It does not contain exotic and rare material. The aim is to make sure you can give yourself the best chance to make the contracts you reach by providing a solid foundation of fundamental declarer play. Information about defense covers the logic and methods needed to defeat contracts. Opening leads, signals, and later plays are all featured.

The *Guide to Better Duplicate Bridge* focuses on improving your tournament technique. Duplicate bridge requires special skills, both in the bidding and in the play. When playing pairs, it may not be enough to make your contract or to defeat their contract. Perhaps you need to make an overtrick. Perhaps in defending you should allow their contract to make as long as you do not give the declarer an undeserved overtrick. Your objective at matchpoints is to outscore the other pairs who will hold the same cards as your partnership. The *Guide to Better Duplicate Bridge* provides the bidding methods and strategy needed to do well at pairs when the bidding involves only your side and when both sides have entered the auction. Bidding today is far more competitive than it was only a decade ago; the player who is not familiar with the best methods will lag behind and not score well as those who know their objectives and have the means to accomplish them.

Declarer play and defense also have special requirements at duplicate. Each of the chapters includes material on declarer technique and defensive strategy appropriate to the pairs game. If you typically play rubber bridge, your thoughts are constantly on making your contract or defeating theirs. You may need to adjust your thinking to pairs strategy, where your objectives are not always as clear. Nine tricks in 3NT will not be enough if the other declares are scoring ten. Similarly, you cannot afford to let your opponents score eleven tricks in four spades if the other pairs are holding the contract to ten tricks.

This book is for you if you are serious about wanting to improve your duplicate skills. If you and your partner adopt the bidding methods recommended in the *Guide to Better Duplicate Bridge* and regularly follow the *Guide*-lines for declarer play and defense geared toward matchpoint thinking, you should see your scores improve significantly. We all like to win, so follow the *Guide* and you should be a winner more often.

Standard American Edition

GUIDE TO
BETTER
DUPLICATE
BRIDGE

RON KLINGER

A Master Bridge Series Title

in conjunction with Peter Crawley

HOUGHTON MIFFLIN COMPANY

Boston   New York   1996

To Suzie, Ari, and Keri,
who were all involved in the production of this book

For information about permission to reproduce selections from this book,
write to Permissions, Houghton Mifflin Company, 215 Park Avenue South,
New York, New York 10003.

For information about this and other Houghton Mifflin trade and reference books
and multimedia products, visit The Bookstore at Houghton Mifflin on
the World Wide Web at http://www.hmco.com.trade/.

Library of Congress Cataloging-in-Publication Data
Klinger, Ron.
Guide to better duplicate bridge / Ron Klinger. — Standard American ed.
p. cm.
Originally published : London : V. Gollancz in association with P. Crawley, 1995.
"A Master bridge series title in conjunction with Peter Crawley."
ISBN 0-395-79149-9
1. Duplicate contract bridge — Bidding.   I. Title.
GV1282.8.D86K57   1996
795.41'5 — dc20   96-8055   CIP

Printed in the United States of America

BP 10 9 8 7 6 5 4 3 2 1

CONTENTS

INTRODUCTION

The *Guide To Better Duplicate Bridge* is geared towards Standard American style bidding but you can adopt and adapt virtually all the recommended methods no matter what system you play. Some of the material may be new to you but it is very likely that the *Guide* methods will be far more widespread in the next ten to twenty years. Some will remember the sixties and seventies when negative doubles and transfers were the province of the expert pairs. Now they are part and parcel of the standard techniques of the competent club tournament player. Roman Key Card Blackwood, introduced only at the start of the eighties, has become the cornerstone of modern slam bidding.

The expert methods today which will probably become routine in the years to come are splinters, 2♣ checkback, Jacoby 2NT, Michaels cue bids, Lebensohl and competitive doubles. A more contentious prediction is that multi-twos will spread through the bridge community as players realise that they can bid many more hands by starting with a multi. Just as transfers vastly expand your bidding capabilities, so multi-openings do the same for weak hands which we would like to open but which do not meet the criteria for one-openings.

How much of the *Guide* should you and your partner adopt? That is naturally your choice but you will not be able to include everything in the *Guide* since at various places you are given choices for your partnership. You may pick and choose among the recommended methods but the more you add to your present methods, the more your tournament results are likely to improve.

Incorporate as much as you can but prefer to do it piecemeal. Too much too soon can overload your mind and your partnership. Cover an area with your partner(s) and cover it thoroughly. When you are confident you have mastered that area, start on something new.

The more modern, advanced and expanded approaches are included in the various chapters under 'Expert Methods'. These are recommended for seasoned partnerships or very enthusiastic pairs.

Should you play 4-card or 5-card majors? This is the question I am asked most often. Despite what many bridge teachers and writers pontificate, the answer is that it matters very little. The facts of life are that at international level about 2/3 of pairs play a system based on 5-card majors. The systems vary but they have in common that major suit openings at the one-level promise 5+ cards.

The reverse side of this coin is that 1/3 of pairs at top level play some 4-card major system. Do these pairs deliberately handicap themselves? Of course not. If you could prove that 5-card majors were superior, everyone would play them and every pair at the top would be playing 5-card majors. The fact that a significant minority of top class players use 4-card major methods is testimony that there is nothing intrinsically defective with that approach.

Personally, I like 5-card majors but that is my own preference. *You* should play the methods with which you are happy. These will usually result from your bridge upbringing, your bridge teacher, your friends, your local club. Whether it is 4-card or 5-card based, if you play it well you will do well. No method will withstand poor application.

One area where 5-card majors tends to have an advantage is competitive bidding at the three-level. You will find in Chapters 17 and 18 that knowing the number of trumps you and partner have together is an important factor in making sensible decisions at the three-level. Players who use 4-card majors and raise freely with 3-card support find much greater difficulty in determining whether the partnership holds seven, eight or nine trumps.

It is naturally important to read the text but do not omit the exercises and the sets of partnership hands for bidding practise. If you can arrange a group of four players, that is ideal for the bidding sets for four and for the 96 set play hands. You can sort out the cards for each player from the lists of hands at the back of the book and when the auction is over, consult the recommended bidding in the text or in the exercise answers also at the back of the book.

Standard terminology is used. LHO = left hand opponent, RHO = right hand opponent, advancer is the partner of the first defensive bidder (overcaller or takeout doubler). The + sign is used to mean 'or more', so that 16+ HCP = 16 high card points *or more*, 5+ suit = 5-card *or longer* suit. Bids in brackets are bids made by the opponents.

Above all, bridge is a game and is meant to be enjoyed. The best slogan for your partnership is *Cheerfulness in the face of adversity.* Keep your sense of perspective and play the game with a chuckle and a sense of humour. Above all, smile at partner, ruefully perhaps, if your partners do not have a smile, give them one of yours. Thus you can make sure that your game is always *happy bridging.*

Ron Klinger, 1996

FOR THE NEW TOURNAMENT PLAYER
HOW DUPLICATE BRIDGE IS PLAYED
(Skip this section if you are a regular duplicate player)

'Duplicate bridge' is the name given to organised bridge tournaments as opposed to social or rubber bridge which involve just four players. The main kinds of competitive bridge are pairs events and teams events.

There are some vital differences between duplicate and ordinary (rubber) bridge in regard to technicalities and strategy. Except at the first table, you will not shuffle and deal the cards. The cards come to you in a tray, called a 'board' and you must put the cards back in the correct slot after the board has been played. The board is marked N, E, S and W, and must be placed properly on the table; the board also states which side is vulnerable and who is the dealer. During the play, the cards are not thrown into the middle of the table. Each player keeps the cards in front of them, turning the card played face down after the trick is over. You may examine the trick just played only while your card remains face up. Tricks won are placed in front of you and perpendicular to the edge of the table ('pointing' towards partner). Tricks lost are placed in front of you and parallel to the edge of the table ('pointing' towards the opponents). After each deal is over, you still have your original thirteen cards in front of you and can see at a glance how many tricks have been won and how many lost.

Each board in tournament bridge is scored independently. In rubber bridge if you make a partscore you have an advantage for the next deal, but in tournament bridge you do not carry forward any scores. You enter the score for the hand played, and on the next board both sides start from zero again.

As each deal is totally unrelated to what happened on the previous deal, there are significant scoring differences at duplicate :
(1) Honors do not count (unless otherwise stated by the tournament rules).
(2) For bidding and making a partscore, add 50 to the trick total.
(3) For bidding and making a game not vulnerable, add 300 to the trick total.
(4) For bidding and making a game vulnerable, add 500 to the trick total.

The result you obtain on the board is entered on the 'travelling score sheet' at the back of the board. You may not look at that until the hand is over, since it contains a record of the hand and also how other pairs fared on the board.

Your score on each board is compared with the scores of every other pair that played the board. If you are North-South, your real opponents are all the other North-South pairs, not the particular East-West pair you play each time. On each board, a certain number of matchpoints is awarded. You receive 2 points for each pair whose score you beat, 1 point for each time you tie with the score of another pair and 0 for each pair whose score beats yours. If your score beats three other pairs, you receive 6 matchpoints. If your score is better than five pairs and ties with three others, you will score 13 matchpoints (5 x 2 plus 3).

The total number of matchpoints available on each deal is usually two less than the number of pairs who play the board. If 13 pairs play a board, the best score receives 24 matchpoints, the next best score receives 22 and so on down to the worst score which receives 0. The best score is called a 'top' and the worst is a 'bottom'. An average score would be 12 matchpoints. (Some countries score in single matchpoints, awarding 1 point for beating another pair and ½ a matchpoint for each score with which you tie.)

The scoring is done once for the N-S pairs and then for the E-W pairs. Obviously, if a N-S pair scores a top, the corresponding E-W pair against whom they played the board gets a bottom. Each pair's points over all the boards are totalled and the pair with the highest number of points wins.

Tactics in pairs events differ from those in rubber bridge. Careful declarer play and defense are the order of the day. Every overtrick and every undertrick could be vital. They make the difference between good scores and bad scores. In rubber bridge, declarer's aim is almost always to make the contract and the defense's aim is to defeat it. At pairs the aim is to obtain the best possible score which may mean from declarer's viewpoint that making the contract is a secondary consideration while from the defenders' viewpoint, the possibility of giving away an overtrick in trying to defeat the contract may be unwarranted.

Being extremely competitive in the bidding is essential. Almost always force the opposition to the three-level on partscore deals, especially if either side is known to have a trump fit. Be quick to re-open the bidding if they stop at a very low level in a suit. In pairs events, re-opening the bidding occurs ten times more often than at rubber bridge.

Minor suit contracts at the game zone should be avoided. Prefer 3NT to 5♣ or 5◊, even if 3NT is riskier, since making an overtrick in 3NT scores more than a minor suit game. On the other hand, it is not necessary to bid borderline games or close slams. The reward for success is not so great in pairs events as to justify 24 point games or 31 point slams. You should be in game or in slam if it has a 50% or better chance. If less, you will tend to score better in the long run by staying out of it.

Chapter 16 deals with the tactics that matter in teams events. Most of the time you will be competing in pairs events. What counts at duplicate pairs is how often a certain strategy will work for you, not the size of the result. If a certain action scores 50 extra points 8 times out of 10, but loses 500 twice, it is sensible at duplicate but ridiculous at rubber bridge.

Penalty doubles are far more frequent at pairs since players are anxious to improve their score. The rule about a two-trick safety margin is frequently disregarded since one down, doubled, vulnerable, may be a top board while one down, undoubled, vulnerable, may be below average.

Safety plays which involve sacrificing a trick to ensure the contract almost never apply in pairs, unless the contract you have reached is an unbelievably good one. In an excellent contract, particularly one that has been doubled, play as safely as you can to make sure of your contract. Overtricks will not matter in such a case.

Much of the time your contract will be similar to that reached by most of the other pairs. On these deals you need to do better than the other declarers in the same contract. Adopt the line of play which will bring in the highest score most of the time. Failing in your contract may not matter. At pairs, each deal carries exactly the same number of matchpoints and each deal is worth about 4% of your maximum possible total. If you foul up one deal, say by losing 800, you can recover all the lost ground on another deal just by making one overtrick if that overtrick gives you a top board.

You and your partner may not have any secret understanding about your bids. That is against the Laws of the game. A bidding system is not a secret code. The opponents are entitled to know as much about what the bidding means as you or your partner. If they ask you what you understand by a certain bid of your partner's, you must tell them truthfully. Of course, partner's bid may be meaningless and if you cannot understand it, all you can do is to be honest and tell the opposition that you do not know what partner's bid means.

Similarly, if you do not understand the opposition's bidding, you are entitled to ask. When it is your turn to bid but before you make your bid, you ask the partner of the bidder 'Please explain the bidding.' You may ask during the auction or after the auction has ended, when it is your turn to play. Unless it affects your making a bid, prefer to wait until the auction is over. After all, the opposition might not understand their bidding either and when you ask, they may well realise their mistake.

If an irregularity occurs at the table, do not be dismayed if the Director is called. That is a normal part of the game and it is the Director's job to keep the tournament running smoothly and to sort out any irregularities.

Duplicate bridge is played internationally. In each odd-numbered year the World Bridge Federation conducts the Bermuda Bowl (World Open Teams) and the Venice Cup (World Women's Teams) for teams representing different geographical zones. The leading teams from each zone compete for the title of world champion. Every four years in the 'Bridge Olympiad' a far greater number of teams compete. In recent years, more than sixty countries have been represented at these Olympiads. In the other even-numbered years the World Bridge Federation holds the World Pairs Championships (open pairs, women's pairs, mixed pairs) as well as the Rosenblum Cup (another World Open Teams).

Each country holds national championships and many tournaments of lower status. There are also tournaments to select the players who will represent their country.

Many clubs run an Individual Championship once a year. In pairs and teams events, you keep the same partner for each session and usually throughout the event. In an Individual you change partners every one, two or three boards. These events are not considered serious events since partnership understandings tend to be minimal. A polite nature, a friendly smile and a calm disposition are prerequisites to surviving an Individual.

Pairs events are more common than any other type of event. The advantage of duplicate is that the element of having good cards or bad cards is reduced to a minimum, since in general all pairs play exactly the same deals. Another advantage is that you can compete against the top players merely by playing in the same tournament. In few other sports could a novice compete against a world champion in a tournament. Duplicate also improves your game, since the hand records are available to check afterwards where you may have gone wrong and to compare your efforts with those of the other pairs.

CHAPTER 1

REVISE YOUR 1 NO-TRUMP OPENING

1NT as 16-18, 15-17 or 15-18?

Opening 1NT simplifies the bidding both for opener and responder. 1NT pinpoints the shape and strength more accurately than opening with a suit bid. The more hands you open with 1NT, the easier the later bidding becomes.

H.C.P.	Frequency %
15	4.4237
16	3.3109
17	2.3617
18	1.6051

If your 1NT range is 16-18, you will open 1NT on 7.2777% of the balanced hands you pick up. Extend the 1NT range to 15-18 and you open 1NT on 11.7014% of your balanced hands. A difference of a bit over 4% may not seem much but the fact that you would open 1NT 50% more often is a huge increase. This is particularly so at duplicate where the frequency of successful action is the critical criterion. The amount you gain is important in rubber bridge and teams. How often you gain is more important at pairs.

Provided you do not sacrifice accuracy, it is clearly superior to play a 4-point range for your opening 1NT. **Extended Stayman** dovetails neatly with a 4-point range for 1NT and also increases your accuracy simultaneously.

The Extended Stayman Convention

After 1NT : 2♣, opener rebids to show the major suits held and also the hand strength, maximum or minimum. The answers are :

2◇	= Both majors, minimum
2♡	= 4 hearts, no 4 spades, minimum
2♠	= 4 spades, no 4 hearts, minimum
2NT	= No 4-card major, minimum
3♣	= No 4-card major, maximum
3◇	= Both majors, maximum
3♡	= 4 hearts, no 4 spades, maximum
3♠	= 4 spades, no 4 hearts, maximum

For a 15-18 1NT opening, 15-16 is minimum and 17-18 is maximum. The memory guide is :

2- level = minimum, 3-level = maximum

Diamonds always = both majors. (Diamonds are a girl's best friend, so the diamond replies are responder's best news.)

As the reply to Extended Stayman can be at the three-level, responder should have 8+ points to use the 2♣ response. The 8 points need not be all HCP —

they could also be 7 HCP plus a 5-card suit — always add 1 point when holding a 5-card suit. When playing extended Stayman, the 2♣ reply is not used as an escape mechanism. To sign off in clubs, use the transfer structure (see Chapter 2).

Responder's strategy

Use 2♣ when you need to know whether opener is minimum or maximum. Typically responder with 8-9 points needs opener to be maximum in order to bid for game, so bid 2♣.

Use 2♣ when you need to know opener's major suit holdings. It pays you to play in a 4-4 major suit game rather than 3NT almost all the time. The major suit game will succeed more often and when both games succeed, the major game produces a higher score more often. Usually, if an overtrick is available in 3NT it is also available in 4♡/4♠ and you score +450 vs. 430 or 650 vs. 630. For example :

WEST	EAST
♠ K 8	♠ A Q 6
♡ A Q 8 7	♡ K J 6 2
◇ A 5 3	◇ 8 7 4
♣ Q J 4 2	♣ K 6 3

WEST	EAST
1NT	2♣
2♡	4♡

3NT will usually make (though it might fail on a diamond lead). 4♡ on the other hand can survive a diamond lead and will usually make 11 tricks (West discarding a diamond on the third spade).

WEST	EAST
♠ A 8 4	♠ 7 3
♡ A J 8 7	♡ K Q 6 2
◇ A 5 3	◇ Q J 10 2
♣ K 3 2	♣ Q J 6

On the likely spade lead, 3NT is in jeopardy but might succeed if the diamond finesse works. If the heart split is the normal 3-2, 4♡ will succeed even if the diamond finesse fails. If the diamond finesse works, 4♡ will usually produce 11 tricks.

This advice to hunt for the 4-4 major fit is valid until the partnership holds about 30 HCP or so. With 30-32 HCP, it is unlikely that there is a danger suit with no stopper or just one stopper. Now two losers are likely and you figure to make 11 tricks whether you play in no-trumps or trumps. Therefore do not use 2♣ with a balanced hand to look for a 4-4 major fit when the partnership is in the 30-32 point range.

Responder's rebids after opener's reply to 2♣

Principle 1
After a three-level reply, all responder's bids below game are forcing.

As responder will have 8 points or more, a reply by opener at the three-level (17-18 points) creates a game-forcing situation. One of the benefits of Extended Stayman is that you can often set a suit as trumps and start a slam auction which would be difficult or impossible with simple Stayman.

1NT : 2♣, 3◊ : 3♡ = Forcing, setting hearts as trumps and showing slam interest. Continue by cue bidding or whatever slam methods your partnership uses (see Chapters 12-15 for suggestions).

1NT : 2♣, 3◊ : 3♠ = Forcing, spades are set as trumps and responder is interested in slam.

After opener's 3♣ or 3♡ or 3♠ reply to 2♣, responder's change of suit below game is natural, forcing and shows a 5-card suit. Opener should support the suit with 3 trumps or better.

Principle 2
Supporting opener's major at the three-level is forcing, sets trumps and shows slam interest.

1NT : 2♣, 2♡ : 3♡ = Forcing, hearts are trumps and slam bidding commences. The raise is *not* an invitation since opener's 2♡ already showed minimum values. If weak, responder would pass. With enough for game, bid 4♡. Although the raise *sounds* invitational, it is in fact stronger than 4♡.

1NT : 2♣, 2♠ : 3♠ = Forcing, the same as the above sequence except that spades are trumps.

Note that using simple Stayman, these slam-going auctions setting opener's major are not available. The raise is needed to invite game.

1NT : 2♣, 2◊ : 3♡ or **1NT : 2♣, 2◊ : 3♠** follows similar logic. Opener has shown a minimum with both majors. If responder does not have enough for game bid 2♡ or 2♠. With enough points for game, bid 4♡/4♠.

It is not worth using 3♡ or 3♠ as an invitation. We are not going to haggle over one point. Thus supporting hearts or spades at the three-level is very strong, forcing and indicates slam aspirations.

Principle 3
After opener's rebid at the two-level to show a minimum, bids by responder at the two-level are weak and should usually be passed. Opener should also pass a 3♣ or 3◊ rebid.

After 1NT : 2♣, 2◊—
2♡ or 2♠ should be passed.
2NT should be passed. Responder was using 2♣ without a major purely to find opener's range.

After 1NT : 2♣, 2♡—
2NT should be passed.

3♣ or 3◊ should be passed. Responder will have a five-card or longer minor and about 7-8 HCP. Responder would have chanced 3NT opposite a maximum. After the minimum, responder aims for the safest partscore. *A decent suit fit at the three-level will succeed more often than 2NT.*
Responder should not be 5-3-3-2 (rebid 2NT).

With 9 HCP plus a 5-card suit, responder should bid game opposite even a minimum 15-18 1NT. Mostly you will succeed. You need not make all your games but you sure have to bid them.

Responder may pass 2♡. With Extended Stayman, you can stop at the two-level when opener is minimum and responder has invitational values.

WEST	EAST
♠ A K 9	♠ Q 10
♡ K Q 5 3	♡ A 8 7 2
◊ A 5 3	◊ Q 7 4
♣ 9 8 7	♣ 6 5 3 2

Playing simple Stayman :

WEST	EAST
1NT	2♣
2♡	3♡
Pass	

3♡ is a poor contract and requires the king of diamonds to be onside as well as a 3-2 trump break.
Playing extended Stayman :

WEST	EAST
1NT	2♣
2♡	Pass

How much better to be in 2♡ than 3♡.

After 1NT : 2♣, 2♠—
2NT should be passed (same as after 2◊ or 2♡).
3♣ or 3◊ should be passed. The logic is the same as rebidding 3♣ or 3◊ after 1NT : 2♣, 2♡ above.
Responder may of course pass 2♠.

After 1NT : 2♣, 2NT—
Responder may pass. A rebid of 3♣ or 3◊ should be passed. A minor suit contract may have even more appeal when opener is known to have no major suit. A rebid of 3♡ or 3♠ over 2NT is forcing and shows a 5-card suit, asking for 3-card support.

1NT : 2♣, 2♡ : 2♠—
This is an unusual rebid as opener does not have four spades. If not using transfers, responder could have 7-8 HCP and five spades. Otherwise, this hand would use a transfer (see Chapter 2). Therefore, 2♠ will be only a 4-card spade suit but not a balanced hand, typically four spades and a long minor. Pass 2♠ with three spades and a 4-4-3-2 pattern. The 4-3 fit is not too bad at the 2-level and should play all right as responder's hand is not balanced. With a doubleton spade or with a 3-4-3-3 pattern, remove 2♠ to 2NT. Responder can then bid the 5-card minor, secure in the knowledge that opener will not hold a doubleton opposite. For example :

WEST	EAST
♠ A 5	♠ K J 3 2
♡ J 7 6 3	♡ 5
◊ A K 3 2	◊ Q 7 4
♣ K J 4	♣ Q 8 6 5 3

WEST	EAST
1NT	2♣
2♡	2♠
2NT	3♣
Pass	

Benefits of playing 1NT as 15-18

1. You can open more hands with 1NT.
2. When opener rebids 1NT (as after 1♣ : 1♡, 1NT), there is no need for responder to invite game with 10 points, as opener's maximum is 14.

Benefits of Extended Stayman

1. Opener's range and 4-card major holdings are known with the reply to 2♣.
2. You can stop at the 2-level when opener is minimum and responder has invitational values.
3. You can often set a major suit as trumps and create a slam-going auction at the 3-level.
4. It is easier to choose the correct game contract.

Extended Stayman gives you a good chance to find the better major suit contract. With a 5-4 fit and a 4-4 fit, choose the 4-4 fit.

WEST	EAST
♠ A K 9 5	♠ Q 10 6 4 3
♡ K Q 5 3	♡ A J 7 2
◊ A 5	◊ 7 4
♣ J 8 7	♣ 3 2

If you play in 4♠, there are only 10 tricks available. You must lose 2 clubs and 1 diamond.

In 4♡, you make 11 tricks if the hearts split 3-2. The extra spade allows you to discard West's diamond loser and ruff one diamond for the overtrick. If hearts are 4-1, you still make 10 tricks.

With the 4-4 fit as the side suit, you can make no more than four tricks in that suit. If the 4-4 fit is the trump suit, more than four tricks may be possible, depending on how many ruffs are available.

With a 4-4 and a 5-4 trump fit available, the 4-4 fit will often give you a better score at pairs.

The 4-4 fit may not be safer (there is a greater risk of a bad trump split) but when the normal 3-2 break occurs you often collect one extra trick. That extra trick means a top board instead of a poor one.

1NT as 15-17

This is a popular range among experts but one consequence is that it commits the partnership to game when opener has 18 points and responder has 6. Sequences like 1♣ : 1♡, 2NT (18-20) are forcing to game. For players below the very top, the practical advice is to retain 18 points within the 1NT opening.

Although the frequency increases as you lower the point range, the price you pay is accuracy in the partscore zone. The 12-14 weak no-trump has a high frequency but often produces the wrong partscore as responder will pass with balanced hands below 11 points. *The lower the point range for 1NT, the more often responder passes 1NT and the more often you play in 1NT instead of a superior partscore.* The 15-18 1NT is a sound compromise between frequency and accuracy.

Expert methods after opener's reply to Extended Stayman to show both majors

After opener shows both majors, 4♣ by responder is a transfer to hearts and 4◊ is a transfer to spades.

1NT : 2♣, 2◊ : 4♣ = 'Please bid 4♡.'
1NT : 2♣, 3◊ : 4♣ = 'Please bid 4♡.'
1NT : 2♣, 2◊ : 4◊ = 'Please bid 4♠.'
1NT : 2♣, 3◊ : 4◊ = 'Please bid 4♠.'

These transfers at the four-level enable the 1NT bidder, the stronger hand, to be declarer. It is often an advantage to have the lead come up to the strong hand. For example :

WEST	EAST
♠ K J 8 3	♠ A Q 10 4
♡ A Q 9 7	♡ K 2
◊ K 3 2	◊ 8 7 4
♣ A 5	♣ Q 6 3 2

WEST	EAST
1NT	2♣
3◊ (1)	4◊ (2)
4♠	Pass

(1) Maximum and both majors
(2) Transfer to spades

If East were declarer in 4♠, a diamond lead could prove fatal. Played by West the ◊K is protected from the opening lead. Without a diamond lead West has the chance to discard a diamond from dummy and so lose at most two diamonds and one club.

Responder is not obliged to transfer. If responder prefers to receive the opening lead, responder simply bids 4♡ or 4♠.

WEST	EAST
♠ A K J 5	♠ Q 8 6 3
♡ Q 8 5 3	♡ K 2
◊ 8 6 2	◊ K 7 4
♣ A Q	♣ K 10 3 2

WEST	EAST
1NT	2♣
2◊ (1)	4♠ (2)

(1) Minimum and both majors
(2) Holding three kings outside the intended trump suit, East chooses to have the lead come up to the kings rather than through them.

4♠ by East might be defeated but it is a better chance than 4♠ played by West.

EXERCISES USING THE 15-18 1NT

A. Partner has opened 1NT. What is your response with each of these hands?

1. ♠ A 9	2. ♠ A J 9	3. ♠ A K 9 2	4. ♠ A K 7	5. ♠ A Q J
♡ Q 7 5 3	♡ K 9 5 3	♡ 9 8 5 3 2	♡ K Q 5 3	♡ K 8 5 2
◊ 8 5 3	◊ 7 5 3	◊ 6 4	◊ K 10 2	◊ K Q 4
♣ 9 8 7 2	♣ 9 8 7	♣ 5 2	♣ Q J 10	♣ J 10 9

B. The bidding has started 1NT : 2♣ (Extended Stayman). What is opener's rebid with these hands?

1. ♠ K 6 3	2. ♠ A K 10 2	3. ♠ J 8 7 3	4. ♠ K Q J	5. ♠ A J 6 4
♡ K J 5 3	♡ K 8 7	♡ A Q 6 4	♡ K Q 8	♡ Q J 9 4
◊ A 5	◊ K Q 5	◊ K Q 6	◊ A K 10	◊ A 4
♣ K J 9 8	♣ Q 10 4	♣ A Q	♣ 9 8 6 3	♣ K 10 6

C. The bidding has started 1NT : 2♣ (Extended Stayman), 2◊ . . . What should responder do next?

1. ♠ J 8 7 3	2. ♠ A J 9	3. ♠ A K 9 2	4. ♠ J 7 5	5. ♠ K 3
♡ A 3	♡ K Q 8 7	♡ 8 6	♡ K Q	♡ J 10 5 4
◊ 8 6 4 2	◊ 7 6 4 2	◊ 6 4 2	◊ Q 8 7 2	◊ K 4 2
♣ K 8 2	♣ 9 7	♣ Q J 8 2	♣ 9 7 6 3	♣ A J 9 3

PARTNERSHIP BIDDING : How should the following hands be bid? West is the dealer each time.

SET 1 — WEST	SET 1 — EAST	SET 2 — WEST	SET 2 — EAST
1. ♠ J 9 3	1. ♠ 8 6	1. ♠ J 9 2	1. ♠ Q 7 4 3
♡ Q 7 5	♡ K 4	♡ A Q J	♡ 5 3
◊ A K 7 3	◊ 8 5 2	◊ A 5 3	◊ K J 2
♣ A Q 3	♣ K J 10 8 7 2	♣ A J 10 3	♣ K 9 8 2
2. ♠ J 8 7 4	2. ♠ A 9 6 2	2. ♠ A 9	2. ♠ J 10 3
♡ K 5	♡ Q 8 4 2	♡ K Q 7 5	♡ 4 2
◊ Q J 10 7 2	◊ A 4	◊ Q 8 5	◊ K J 10 7 6
♣ 6 2	♣ K Q 3	♣ A Q 7 2	♣ K 8 3
3. ♠ K 9	3. ♠ J 8 7 4	3. ♠ A 7 4 3	3. ♠ K 9
♡ A Q 6 2	♡ K 4	♡ 8 6	♡ A K 5 3
◊ K 5 3	◊ Q J 10 7 2	◊ K Q 3	◊ J 5 4
♣ A 7 5 4	♣ 6 2	♣ 8 6 5 3	♣ A Q 10 2
4. ♠ K 9 6 3 2	4. ♠ A 8 5 4	4. ♠ A 9 4 3	4. ♠ K 7 6 2
♡ A 9 6 3	♡ K Q 5 4	♡ K Q 8	♡ A 6 5 2
◊ 8 5	◊ A J	◊ 9 7	◊ A Q
♣ 4 3	♣ K 6 5	♣ J 10 7 4	♣ K Q 2
5. ♠ A K 3	5. ♠ Q 8 6 2	5. ♠ A 7 6 2	5. ♠ K 10 9 4
♡ A 7 6 3	♡ K Q 2	♡ A J 4 2	♡ K 10
◊ 9 7 4	◊ 8 5 2	◊ A 3	◊ Q 8 5 2
♣ K Q 6	♣ A J 5	♣ A 7 2	♣ K J 5
6. ♠ Q 8 7 3	6. ♠ A K 9 2	6. ♠ A K 9 3	6. ♠ Q J
♡ 2	♡ Q 7 5 3	♡ A J 5 3	♡ K Q 10 7
◊ K 6 4 3	◊ A J	◊ 9 6 4	◊ A K Q
♣ A 9 4 2	♣ Q 7 5	♣ A 7	♣ K 5 4 2

PLAY HANDS ON EXTENDED STAYMAN USING A 15-18 1NT OPENING
(These hands can be made up by using pages 160-167)

Hand 1 : Staying low — Opening lead — Trump management

Dealer North : Nil vulnerable

NORTH
♠ K J 7 5
♥ A Q
♦ A Q 10 6
♣ 9 8 3

WEST
♠ 8 3
♥ 10 9 5 4
♦ J 8 5
♣ A 10 5 2

EAST
♠ Q 10 4
♥ J 7 3
♦ K 9 4 3
♣ K Q 7

SOUTH
♠ A 9 6 2
♥ K 8 6 2
♦ 7 2
♣ J 6 4

WEST	NORTH	EAST	SOUTH
	1NT	Pass	2♣
Pass	2♠	Pass	Pass
Pass			

Bidding : North's 2♠ shows a minimum 1NT (15-16) with four spades and without four hearts. Although South can revalue the hand to 9 points, adding 1 for the doubleton, game is likely to be worse than 50% and so a poor bet at pairs. Although you may make game occasionally with such values, perhaps on misdefense, the better bet is to stay low and defeat the pairs in 3♠ when the limit is eight tricks.

Lead : King of clubs. A trump lead is out and to lead from a single honor such as J-x-x or K-x-x-x is dangerous. Better to lead from two honors than from a single honor.

Recommended play : West signals encouragement and East continues with the queen of clubs and a third club. West should then switch to a low diamond, dummy's weak suit. North should finesse the queen, not the 10, as dummy has only a doubleton. East wins and returns a diamond, won by North.

Declarer continues with a spade to the ace and a spade back to the jack, the normal technique with eight trumps missing the queen. The finesse loses to East and declarer makes just eight tricks.

Notes : (1) On a diamond lead, North can make 10 tricks. The diamond loser has vanished and North would cash the A-Q of hearts, cross to the ace of spades and play the king of hearts, discarding a club. Careful play by North from here on would hold the losers to three.
(2) A heart lead gives North an overtrick as North can discard a club loser on the king of hearts, as above.
(3) After winning the third club West should not play the fourth club. North would ruff and discard a diamond from dummy whether East ruffs or not. North can now score nine tricks.

Hand 2 : Choosing the trump suit — Transfer — Opening lead — Card combinations

Dealer East : N-S vulnerable

NORTH
♠ 9 6 2
♥ Q 5
♦ K 10 9
♣ Q 9 7 5 4

WEST
♠ A K Q 4
♥ K J 8 4
♦ A 8 5
♣ 8 6

EAST
♠ 10 7 5 3
♥ A 9 6 3 2
♦ 7 6
♣ K 3

SOUTH
♠ J 8
♥ 10 7
♦ Q J 4 3 2
♣ A J 10 2

WEST	NORTH	EAST	SOUTH
		Pass	Pass
1NT	Pass	2♣	Pass
3♦	Pass	4♠	All pass

3♦ = Maximum, both majors

Bidding : East has just enough to try for game. With invitational values, Extended Stayman is the way to go. After West shows both majors, East has to choose between the 5-4 fit and the 4-4 fit. At pairs, choose the 4-4. In 4♥, only 10 tricks are available.

Lead : 3 of diamonds. Against a suit contact, avoid leading from a suit headed by the ace but no king (so, no club lead). As West has shown both majors, a heart is not attractive. From a 4+ suit headed by Q-J (but no 10, no 9), lead fourth-highest usually, but lead the queen if partner has shown length in the suit.

Recommended play : Take the ace of diamonds and draw trumps. Next comes the ♥A and a heart to the king, normal technique with nine cards missing the queen. Continue with the ♥J and the ♥8, overtaking with ♥9 in hand. On the fifth heart, discard a club from dummy. You lose just one club and one diamond.

Notes : (1) Do not duck the first diamond. North would win with the king and might switch to a club, holding declarer to ten tricks.
(2) If declarer errs by finessing the ♥J on the second round of hearts, the contract can be defeated. North can cash the king of diamonds and, reading South's 2 of diamonds to show five diamonds originally, North switches to a club to give the defense one heart, one diamond and two clubs.
(3) If East fails to unblock ♥J on the third round of hearts, there is no convenient way to reach East's fifth heart.
(4) Note that if hearts are trumps, there is no way to avoid losing one diamond and two clubs as the cards lie.

Hand 3 : Slam decision at pairs — Opening lead — Declarer play in an inferior contract

Dealer South : E-W vulnerable

	NORTH		
	♠ 8 4		
	♡ A K Q 10		
	◊ Q 6 5		
	♣ A K 7 6		
WEST		EAST	
♠ K 9 7 3 2		♠ 10 6 5	
♡ 9 3 2		♡ 6 4	
◊ 10 9 7		◊ 8 4 2	
♣ Q 9		♣ 10 8 4 3 2	
	SOUTH		
	♠ A Q J		
	♡ J 8 7 5		
	◊ A K J 3		
	♣ J 5		

WEST	NORTH	EAST	SOUTH
			1NT
Pass	2♣	Pass	3♡
Pass	4NT	Pass	5♡
Pass	5NT	Pass	6◊
Pass	6♡	All pass	

Bidding : South's 3♡ shows a maximum 1NT (17-18) with four hearts and without four spades. North has enough for slam and checks on aces and kings, intending to take a chance at 7♡ if South produces two aces and two kings. With one king missing, North should bid 6NT. However 6♡ is the contract to be played.

Lead : 10 of diamonds. Against 6NT, avoid leading away from an honor combination. Against 6♡, a spade lead is not so terrible but it is risky to lead from a king into a 1NT opening.

Recommended play : South wins the diamond lead and draws trumps. Diamonds are continued and declarer discards a spade from dummy on the fourth diamond. Next comes the ace of spades followed by the queen of spades. If West plays low, discard a club from dummy. If West covers, dummy ruffs and South's ♠J is a winner. South thus makes thirteen tricks for a probable top board.

Notes : (1) South should realise as soon as dummy appears that North has made a poor decision by choosing 6♡ instead of 6NT. With N-S holding 35 HCP, almost every pair will be in 6NT once a king is found to be missing.
  If the king of spades is with East, everyone in 6NT will make 13 tricks via the repeated spade finesse. South cannot beat those pairs by taking the spade finesse the same way. Therefore South plays for the ♠K to be with West and takes the ruffing finesse line. If this works, South will outscore those in 6NT. If not, the score will hardly be worse. The trouble with obtaining a top this way is that it is unlikely to improve North's bidding.
(2) South could play to ruff two clubs in hand to make 13 tricks but this may not succeed (and does not on the actual deal) and it will not help if the ♠K is with East. South should therefore play for West to hold the ♠K.

Hand 4 : Transfer — Opening lead — Trump management — Power of the 4-4 fit

Dealer West : Both vulnerable

	NORTH		
	♠ Q J 7 3		
	♡ K Q J		
	◊ 10 5 2		
	♣ 8 6 4		
WEST		EAST	
♠ 9 5		♠ A 8 4 2	
♡ 8 6 4 2		♡ A 7 5 3	
◊ A K 9 8		◊ 6 3	
♣ Q J 9		♣ A K 10	
	SOUTH		
	♠ K 10 6		
	♡ 10 9		
	◊ Q J 7 4		
	♣ 7 5 3 2		

WEST	NORTH	EAST	SOUTH
Pass	Pass	1NT	Pass
2♣	Pass	2◊ (1)	Pass
4♡	Pass	Pass	Pass

(1) Minimum, both majors

Bidding : It is all right to open 1NT on the East hand despite the weak doubleton in diamonds. West has enough to bid 3NT but should check whether a 4-4 fit exists in hearts. If East does have four hearts, 4♡ is likely to play better than 3NT. (Although there is no benefit on this layout, West should use the 4♣ transfer to 4♡ if the partnership is using those transfers. West has no holding where being declarer would be an advantage.)

Lead : King of hearts. The sequence lead is the safest and is attractive in trying to protect North's potential spade winners.

Recommended play : Duck the first heart and if North leads a second round, take the next heart. Continue by cashing the ace and king of diamonds followed by a diamond ruff. The 10 of clubs is led to declarer's jack and the fourth diamond is ruffed. If North ruffs, it is with a trump winner anyway. Declarer scores ten tricks, losing just one spade and two trump tricks.

Notes : (1) On some other lead, best technique with such a trump combination is to duck the first round. On regaining the lead, cash ♡A and leave the top trump out. When North leads a trump, declarer adopts the same approach, ducking the first round. Winning the first heart is slightly risky but works on the actual deal.
(2) Playing ace and another heart allows North to draw a third round of trumps and 4♡ would then fail.
(3) Notice the power of the 4-4 fit in hearts. With hearts 3-2, there are eight tricks in no-trumps. Played in hearts, the 4-4 fit generates two extra tricks, even though West has a very weak 4-card suit.

CHAPTER 2

TRANSFERS AFTER 1NT — WEAK HANDS

The 4-Suit Transfer Structure

1NT : 2♣ remains Extended Stayman. The transfer structure does not tamper with 2♣ Stayman and Extended Stayman dovetails neatly with transfers.

1NT : 2◊ = 5 or more hearts

1NT : 2♡ = 5 or more spades

1NT : 2♠ = 5 or more clubs. If responder has a weak hand intending to sign off in 3♣, responder should hold six clubs or more.

1NT : 2NT = 5 or more diamonds. If responder has a weak hand intending to sign off in 3◊, responder should hold six diamonds or more.

While there are other systems of transfers at the two-level, the above 4-suit structure is preferred by most experts. The only loss with transfers is the inability to sign off in 2◊. Just as Stayman prevents a signoff in 2♣, so the 2◊ transfer to hearts prevents a signoff in 2◊. Just as losing a natural 2♣ is a small price to pay for being able to use Stayman to explore major suit contracts, so losing a natural 2◊ is a small price to pay for all the benefits that flow from using transfers. It does mean that responder has to reach the 3-level if wanting to sign off in a minor. Responder may prefer to pass 1NT.

Advantages of Transfers

1. They enable the 1NT opener to be declarer more often, particularly useful when responder is very weak.

2. They enable responder to describe hand types which are difficult or impossible to show when using standard methods. These include :

Hands worth a raise to 2NT plus a 5-card major.

Game invitational hands with a 6-card major.

In addition, all 2-suiters with game or slam potential can be shown below 3NT.

This expansion in bidding vocabulary greatly increases the efficiency of your bidding system. It does so without losing the ability to describe the hands traditionally shown in standard methods :

Weak hands with a 5-card major or 6-card minor.

Game-force hands with a 5-card or longer suit.

3. Opener is able to express degrees of support for responder's suit or degrees of preference when responder reveals a two-suiter.

Allowing the NT opener to be declarer allows the opening lead to come up to the stronger hand. It also keeps the stronger hand concealed from the defenders' prying eyes. Although these are undoubted advantages, the major benefits flow from the vastly expanded flexibility for responder in being able to describe so many hands more accurately.

Transfers to a major when responder is weakish

1. Responder is very weak, not enough to invite game, and has a 5-card or longer major

Transfer to your major and pass when opener bids the major.

WEST	EAST	or	WEST	EAST
1NT	2◊		1NT	2♡
2♡	Pass		2♠	Pass

For example :

WEST	EAST
♠ A 8 4	♠ 7 3
♡ A 9	♡ J 8 7 4 2
◊ A 5 3 2	◊ Q J 6 4
♣ K 6 3 2	♣ 8 7

WEST	EAST
1NT	2◊
2♡	Pass

WEST	EAST
♠ A 4	♠ 9 7 6 5 3 2
♡ Q J 7 2	♡ 8 5
◊ A 6 4	◊ 7 3
♣ K Q 8 7	♣ 6 3 2

WEST	EAST
1NT	2♡
2♠	Pass

There is no suit quality requirement. You may transfer to any 5-card major. The theory is that the weak hand should produce more tricks with the major suit as trumps than in no-trumps. Opposite a worthless hand, the 1NT opener can make usually 4-5 tricks. A 5-card trump suit will generally produce two extra tricks so that you will be better off even if you do not make the contract.

Note that opener is bound to bid responder's suit, even if opener has only doubleton support. Opener has no option to reject the transfer.

2. Responder has enough to invite game and has precisely a 5-card major

Transfer to your major and rebid 2NT when opener bids the major.

WEST	EAST	or	WEST	EAST
1NT	2◊		1NT	2♡
2♡	2NT...		2♠	2NT...

For example :

WEST	W	E	EAST
♠ A J 5	1NT	2◊	♠ Q 7 3
♡ A 9	2♡	2NT...	♡ Q J 7 4 2
◊ A 10 7 6			◊ K 8
♣ K 6 3 2			♣ 8 7 4

Responder will usually have a balanced hand to use the transfer plus 2NT rebid but this need not be so.

WEST			EAST
♠ A J 5			♠ K 9 8 7 3
♡ A 5 4			♡ Q 7 2
◊ A Q 6			◊ K 8 4 2
♣ K 6 3 2			♣ 8

WEST	EAST
1NT	2♡
2♠	2NT ...

While this may not be a perfect way to describe the East hand, it is the best available. It shows the 5-card major and the strength. If opener has 3-card or better support for spades, opener will revert to spades. If opener has a doubleton spade, opener will have length and hopefully strength in the suit in which responder is short. It is not open to East to transfer to spades and rebid 3◊ with the above hand. The transfer-then-new-suit sequence is forcing to game (see Chapter 3).

Opener's options after the 2NT rebid :

Minimum and doubleton in responder's suit : Pass

Maximum and doubleton in responder's suit : 3NT

Minimum and 3-4 cards in responder's suit :
Sign off in 3-of-responder's major.

Maximum and 3-4 cards in responder's major :
Sign off in 4-of-responder's major.

With 3-4 cards in responder's major, remember to add a point for an outside doubleton. Tend to be optimistic if you have 4-card support.

Examples :

WEST	W	E	EAST
♠ A J 5	1NT	2◊	♠ Q 7 3
♡ A 6	2♡	2NT	♡ Q J 7 4 2
◊ A 7 6 3	Pass		◊ K 8 4
♣ Q J 3 2			♣ 8 7

WEST	W	E	EAST
♠ A K 5	1NT	2◊	♠ Q 7 3
♡ A 6	2♡	2NT	♡ Q J 7 4 2
◊ A 7 6 3	3NT	Pass	◊ K 8 4
♣ Q J 3 2			♣ 8 7

WEST	W	E	EAST
♠ A J	1NT	2◊	♠ Q 7 3
♡ A 6 3	2♡	2NT	♡ Q J 7 4 2
◊ A 7 6 3	3♡	Pass	◊ K 8 4
♣ Q 9 3 2			♣ 8 7

WEST	W	E	EAST
♠ K J	1NT	2◊	♠ Q 7 3
♡ A K 6 3	2♡	2NT	♡ Q J 7 4 2
◊ A 7 3	4♡	Pass	◊ K 8 4
♣ 9 6 3 2			♣ 8 7

3. Responder has enough to invite game and has a 6-card or longer major

Transfer to your major and raise your suit to the three-level when opener bids the major.

WEST	EAST	or	WEST	EAST
1NT	2◊		1NT	2♡
2♡	3♡ ...		2♠	3♠ ...

With a 6-card suit, responder should have 6-7 HCP. With 8-9 HCP and a 6-card suit, be prepared to go to game. With a 7-card suit, drop the above HCP requirements by a couple of points.

Opener should pass with a minimum and bid the major suit game with a maximum. Even with a minimum, opener should raise to 4-major with three trumps and an outside doubleton.

Examples :

WEST	W	E	EAST
♠ A 8 5	1NT	2◊	♠ Q 7 3
♡ A 9	2♡	3♡	♡ Q J 8 7 4 2
◊ A J 5 4	Pass		◊ K 8
♣ Q 8 5 2			♣ 7 4

WEST	W	E	EAST
♠ A 8	1NT	2♡	♠ K 9 6 4 3 2
♡ A K 9 2	2♠	3♠	♡ Q J 8
◊ A 9 5 4	4♠	Pass	◊ 8
♣ Q J 2			♣ 9 6 4

WEST	W	E	EAST
♠ Q 8 5	1NT	2♡	♠ K 9 6 4 3 2
♡ A K 9 2	2♠	3♠	♡ Q J 8
◊ 10 9 5 4	4♠	Pass	◊ 8
♣ A Q			♣ 9 6 4

Despite the minimum points, West should raise to game because of the 3-card support and the doubleton outside, giving West potential for an extra trick via a club ruff.

Opener's options after a transfer to a major

Opener has no option to refuse the transfer. Almost all the time opener will simply bid responder's major. This is known as a 'simple accept'. With exceptionally good values, opener may 'super-accept'.

1NT : 2◊	1NT : 2◊
2♡ ...	3♡ ...
Simple accept	Super-accept

There are three key features for opener to consider :
1. 3- or 4-card support for responder's major.
2. A doubleton elsewhere to provide ruffing potential.
3. A maximum 1NT opening.
To super-accept, opener needs all three key features.

After the super-accept, responder may pass with a hand with no hope for game or raise to game with about 6 HCP or better (a shapely 5 count will do). Treat opener's super-accept as showing about 19 points or so in total value. With slam prospects, you may change suit as a cue bid or use Blackwood. These areas are covered in Chapters 12-15.

Transfers to a minor when responder is weakish

1. Responder has a very weak hand : Transfer to your minor and pass when opener bids the minor.

WEST	EAST	*or*	WEST	EAST
1NT	2♠		1NT	2NT
3♣	Pass		3♦	Pass

Use these sequences only with a 6-card or longer minor and less than 7 HCP. You may sign off via a transfer to a major with a 5-card suit but you need at least a 6-card suit to sign off via a transfer to 3-minor. You are committing your side to two extra tricks (from 1NT to 3-minor). With only a 5-card minor you may as well play for 7 tricks in 1NT.

2. Responder has enough values to invite game and has a 5-card or longer minor : Do NOT transfer.

With 1NT : 2NT a transfer, the standard invitational 2NT response is lost. This hand type is shown by bidding 2♣ and following up with a no-trump rebid.

Playing Extended Stayman : With invitational values and a long minor, bid 2♣. Then rebid 2NT over opener's 2-level rebid if you have a 5-card minor and rebid 3-minor over a two-level rebid with a 6-card minor. The 2♣ response has already promised invitational values. Over opener's three-level rebid showing a maximum, bid 3NT.

3. Responder has enough values to invite game with a 4-card major and a longer minor : Do NOT transfer. Use 2♣ Stayman for this hand type.

A transfer followed by a new suit rebid by responder is a game-force (see Chapter 3). You cannot afford such a sequence with only invitational values. Use 2♣ Stayman. If opener bids your major, raise it. If not, rebid 2NT.

With Extended Stayman, you will know the major suit position completely after opener's reply. Over a 3-level reply, bid the appropriate game. After a 2-level reply, rebid 2NT or 3-minor.

Opener's options after a transfer to a minor

Opener is permitted only two bids : the simple accept (bid the minor suit shown) or super-accept the minor (bid the step in-between the transfer and the minor suit shown). No other rebid is available.

1NT : 2♠	1NT : 2♠
3♣ ...	2NT ...
Simple accept	Super-accept

1NT : 2NT	1NT : 2NT
3♦	3♣
Simple accept	Super-accept

To super-accept opener needs a maximum 1NT opening plus support for the minor including a top honor (queen or better). The aim of the super-accept is to reach a sound 3NT where responder's minor will supply the bulk of the tricks. By showing a top honor in the minor, opener enables responder to gauge whether a suit like A-Q-x-x-x-x or K-Q-x-x-x-x is running. If so, prospects for 3NT are rosy.

After the super-accept of a minor suit transfer

With a weakish hand, responder may :

1. Bid 3-minor anyway with a very weak hand and no prospects for game.

2. Rebid 3NT with game-invitational values or with a hand that has improved sufficiently from the fact that opener has a top honor in the long minor.

Responder's options with a strong hand are covered in Chapter 3.

Interference before responder has transferred
After 1NT : (Double) : ?

All suit bids are genuine in standard methods : 2♣ shows clubs and is not Stayman while 2♦/2♥/2♠ show the actual suit bid and are not transfers. Given that their double is for penalties, it becomes important to be able to sign off in a minor at the two-level rather than the three-level.

After 1NT : (Suit Bid) : ?

If they bid a suit over partner's 1NT, transfers no longer apply. A suit bid at the cheapest level is natural and not forcing. For other methods over interference, see Chapter 21.

Expert methods after transfers

After responder's 2NT rebid (e.g., 1NT : 2♦, 2♥ : 2NT), opener may bid a new suit as a long suit trial bid, showing support for responder's major and looking for help in the trial suit. For example :

WEST	W	E	EAST
♠ K Q 6 2	1NT	2♦	♠ 8 4
♥ A K 6	2♥	2NT	♥ Q 9 7 4 2
♦ A 3	3♣	3♥	♦ K Q J
♣ 9 6 4 3	Pass		♣ 8 7 5

West's 3♣ expresses interest in 4♥ and asks for help in clubs. With no useful clubs, East signs off. Swap East's minor suits and East would bid 4♥.

Other ways to super-accept a major suit

1NT : 2♦	1NT : 2♦	1NT : 2♦
2NT ...	3♣ ...	3♥ ...
Super-accept	Super-accept	Super-accept

The 2NT rebid super-accept shows support for responder, a maximum 1NT and a 4-3-3-3 pattern with instant winners in the other suits (such as A-x-x or A-K-x). With such holdings you often make just as many tricks in no-trumps as in the major.

WEST	W	E	EAST
♠ A 9 6	1NT	2♦	♠ K 4
♥ A Q 6	2NT	3NT	♥ K 10 7 4 2
♦ A K 3	Pass		♦ 9 6 2
♣ 9 6 4 3			♣ 8 7 5

3NT is an excellent spot. Had the bidding started 1NT : 2♦, 2♥, East would pass and if West had used 3♥ as the super-accept, East would bid the poor 4♥.

Over 2NT, responder may sign off in the major or try 3NT. Responder may still wish to transfer and to do so, responder can use a rebid of 3♦ over 2NT to ask opener to bid the major suit anyway.

WEST	W	E	EAST
♠ A J 6	1NT	2♦	♠ Q 4
♥ A 9 6	2NT	3♦	♥ J 10 7 5 4 2
♦ A K J	3♥	Pass	♦ 6 2
♣ 10 4 3 2			♣ 8 7 5

Less than delighted by opener's super-accept, East wants to sign off in 3♥ but would still prefer opener to play it. 3♦ = 'Please bid my major anyway.' If East wanted to play in 4♥, East could bid 3♦ to effect the transfer and then raise to 4♥.

A minor suit bid by opener in reply to the transfer is also a super-accept (opener has no option to reject the transfer) and can be played in various ways. One of the best is as a long suit trial, a suit with three or more cards including two or three losers (such as J-x-x-x, A-x-x, x-x-x or similar). If weak, responder can sign off in 3-Major. With good help in the trial suit, bid game.

WEST	W	E	EAST
♠ A J 6 2	1NT	2♥	♠ Q 9 8 5 4 3
♥ A K 6	3♣	4♠	♥ Q 9 7
♦ K Q	Pass		♦ 8 7 2
♣ J 6 4 3			♣ 8

3♣ = super-accept for spades but needs help to reduce losers in clubs.

4♠ = good help in clubs despite the weak hand. If responder treats the super-accept as equal to a total value of 19-20 points, the decision to bid game becomes much easier.

WEST	W	E	EAST
♠ A J 6 2	1NT	2♥	♠ Q 9 8 5 4 3
♥ A K 6	3♣	3♠	♥ Q 9 7
♦ K Q	Pass		♦ 8
♣ J 6 4 3			♣ 8 7 2

This time East has the worst holding in the trial suit and signs off at the three level. Even that may prove too high.

After a minor suit trial bid as the super-accept, responder may still wish to transfer to make opener the declarer. For the transfer into game, responder can bid 4♦. In the above sequence, for example, East can bid 4♦ over 3♣ to have West the declarer in 4♠. To sign off at the three-level, responder can bid 3♦ over a 3♣ trial bid. If opener's trial bid is 3♦, the situation is trickier.

WEST	EAST	If East wants to sign off in 3♥,
1NT	2♦	there is no option other than
3♦	?	bidding 3♥.

WEST	EAST	If East wants to sign off in 3♠,
1NT	2♥	East should simply bid 3♠. It is
3♦	?	better to use 3♥ as a natural and

forcing bid or as a cue bid than as a second transfer.

How should the bidding go on these hands?

WEST	EAST
♠ A K 6 3	♠ Q J 5 4 2
♥ K J 9 6	♥ A Q 4 2
♦ A Q 3	♦ 8 6 2
♣ 9 2	♣ Q

It would be easy enough to hit the second best spot on a sequence like this :

WEST	EAST
1NT	2♥
3♠	4♠
Pass	

4♠ is fine at rubber bridge or teams but at pairs you want to be in 4♥. When the hearts are 3-2, you score one trick more in 4♥ than in 4♠ because of the discard available when the side suit is spades.

It is not satisfactory for East to bid 4♥ over 3♠. Most pairs would not play this as a choice of contract but rather as a cue bid in search of a slam in spades.

It is possible to solve this dilemma by having responder use 2♣ Extended Stayman and that would work well on the hand above. The trouble is that the most common trump fit will be a 5-3 fit in spades. To use 2♣ will often lead to a reply showing no 4-card major and when responder next bids 3♠, a contract of 4♠ will be played by the weaker hand.

It would be worth that loss in order to reach the top spot but it is possible to enjoy the best of both worlds. *When making a super-accept with 4-4 in the majors, opener bids the other major.* So :

WEST	W	E	EAST
♠ A K 6 3	1NT	2♥	♠ Q J 5 4 2
♥ K J 9 6	3♥	4♥	♥ A Q 4 2
♦ A Q 3	Pass		♦ 8 6 2
♣ 9 2			♣ Q

If responder wants to sign off in 3♠, responder just has to bid that over 3♥. If responder wants to play in 4♠, responder can bid 4♠ or transfer to 4♠ via a rebid of 4♦. This allows the opener to be declarer, as usual, whenever the final contract is spades.

The position is similar when responder has four spades and five hearts.

WEST	EAST	West's 2♠ = a super-accept for
1NT	2♥	hearts plus four spades. If East
2♠	?	has four spades as well, East can

raise to 4♠ to sign off. If East has no interest in spades, East can sign off by bidding 3♥ or 4♥. If East wants to transfer opener into a heart contract, East can bid 3♦ as a transfer to 3♥ or 4♦ as a transfer to 4♥.

WEST	EAST	It follows that if opener makes a
1NT	2♦	direct super-accept, opener will not
3♥ ...		have four cards in the other major.

It also follows that opener will not have a holding suitable for a trial bid or a maximum 4-3-3-3 pattern more suited for 3NT.

EXERCISES USING TRANSFERS

A. Partner has opened 1NT. What is your response with each of these hands?

1. ♠ A 9	2. ♠ J 10 9 5 4	3. ♠ 2	4. ♠ 7 4	5. ♠ A J 6 2
♥ 8 7 5 3 2	♥ K 9 5 3	♥ 9 8	♥ 10 3 2	♥ 5 2
◇ 7 2	◇ 7 5	◇ 7 6 3 2	◇ A K 8 7 4 3	◇ 4 3
♣ 9 6 4 3	♣ 9 7	♣ K 9 8 7 5 2	♣ 6 4	♣ Q J 9 6 4

B. The bidding has started 1NT : 2◇ (transfer to hearts). What is opener's rebid with these hands?

1. ♠ K 6 3	2. ♠ A K 10	3. ♠ J 8 7	4. ♠ A K J	5. ♠ A Q 6 4
♥ K J 5 3	♥ 8 7	♥ A Q 6	♥ K Q 8 2	♥ A 9 4
◇ A 5	◇ K Q 5 2	◇ K Q 6 2	◇ A 10	◇ A 4
♣ K J 9 8	♣ K Q 10 8	♣ K Q J	♣ 9 8 6 3	♣ K 10 9 8

C. The bidding has started 1NT : 2◇, 2♥ : 2NT. What should opener do next?

1. ♠ Q J 7 3	2. ♠ A 9 2	3. ♠ A K 9 2	4. ♠ J 10 5 2	5. ♠ A 3
♥ A 3	♥ K Q J 7	♥ 8 6 3	♥ K Q	♥ J 10 5 4
◇ A J 10 2	◇ Q J 4	◇ A K 4 2	◇ A 8 7 2	◇ K Q 2
♣ K Q 9	♣ Q 10 3	♣ K 5	♣ A J 6	♣ A Q 9 3

PARTNERSHIP BIDDING : How should the following hands be bid? West is the dealer each time.

SET 3 — WEST	SET 3 — EAST	SET 4 — WEST	SET 4 — EAST
1. ♠ J 10 9 3	1. ♠ 8 6	1. ♠ J 9 3	1. ♠ 8 6
♥ K 7 5	♥ Q 8 6 4 3 2	♥ K 7 5	♥ 8 4
◇ A K 4	◇ 8 5 2	◇ K Q J 4	◇ 8 5 2
♣ A J 3	♣ 7 2	♣ A Q 3	♣ K J 10 8 7 2
2. ♠ A 7 4	2. ♠ 10 9 6 5 2	2. ♠ 8 5	2. ♠ A J 10 3
♥ A 3 2	♥ K 8 4	♥ 6 3	♥ A 4 2
◇ Q J 7	◇ A 4	◇ Q 8 7 5 4 3 2	◇ A 6
♣ K Q 6 5	♣ J 10 2	♣ 7 4	♣ K J 6 2
3. ♠ 9 4 2	3. ♠ A Q J	3. ♠ A 7 4	3. ♠ 9 5
♥ A K J 8 3	♥ 10 7 2	♥ A 8 6	♥ 9 5 3
◇ 5 4	◇ A 7 2	◇ K 9 3	◇ A Q 10 8 7 5
♣ 8 7 3	♣ K Q J 4	♣ A Q 5 3	♣ 7 2
4. ♠ 9 8 6 4 3 2	4. ♠ A K 7 5	4. ♠ A J 9	4. ♠ K 7 6 2
♥ 2	♥ K Q 5 4	♥ Q 8 4	♥ A 6 5 2
◇ 4 3	◇ 9 6 5	◇ 9 7	◇ A Q 6
♣ 8 5 3 2	♣ A J	♣ J 10 8 7 4	♣ Q 9
5. ♠ J 8 6 2	5. ♠ K Q 9 7 4	5. ♠ 9 4	5. ♠ 8 7 3
♥ K Q 8 2	♥ 6 3	♥ J 8 6 5 3 2	♥ A 10 4
◇ A K	◇ 9 8 5 2	◇ Q 10 9	◇ A K 2
♣ K Q 6	♣ 4 2	♣ A 6	♣ K Q 10 3
6. ♠ 2	6. ♠ A 8 7 3	6. ♠ Q 6	6. ♠ K J 9 7 5 3
♥ Q J 7 5 3	♥ A 9 2	♥ A 7 5 4	♥ 9 3
◇ K Q 4	◇ 6 2	◇ A Q 5	◇ K 6 4
♣ 9 8 7 5	♣ A K J 6	♣ K Q 7 4	♣ 3 2

PLAY HANDS ON TRANSFERS OVER 1NT
(These hands can be made up by using pages 160-167)

Hand 5 : Transfer with a weak hand — Urgent discards — Opportunity to overruff

Dealer North : N-S vulnerable

	NORTH		
	♠ A 9		
	♡ Q 10 2		
	◊ J 7 6 4 3 2		
	♣ J 10		
WEST		EAST	
♠ K 7 6 5 4 2		♠ Q 3	
♡ 8 7 3		♡ J 9 6 4	
◊ 5		◊ A K Q 8	
♣ 9 8 5		♣ A 7 6	
	SOUTH		
	♠ J 10 8		
	♡ A K 5		
	◊ 10 9		
	♣ K Q 4 3 2		

WEST	NORTH	EAST	SOUTH
	Pass	1NT	Pass
2♡	Pass	2♠	All pass

Bidding : West's 2♡ is a transfer to 2♠ and East must accept the transfer. It would be dreadful for West to pass 1NT. The defense against 1NT is routine for two down.

West's pass of 2♠ indicates a weak hand. It often pays to compete in the pass-out seat in such auctions but the weak suit and the vulnerability should convince North to keep quiet.

Lead : Ace of hearts. The ♣K lead is also attractive but leading from an A-K suit has the advantage of retaining the lead, seeing dummy and partner's signal and then deciding whether to continue the suit led or to switch. North encourages and three hearts are cashed. North then switches to the jack of clubs.

Recommended play : East wins with the ♣A and should immediately play the diamond winners to discard dummy's losing clubs. On normal breaks, all of dummy's clubs could be discarded without problem. Then a club could be ruffed in dummy in order to lead a trump towards the queen-doubleton in hand.

Here the diamonds break badly and South ruffs the third round. Should declarer overruff or discard dummy's third club? In such cases it is almost always right to discard the loser and not overruff. After winning with the 8 of spades, South leads a club ruffed in dummy. Declarer now leads a low trump and whether North plays low or rises with the ace, declarer makes eight tricks.

Notes : (1) Had declarer overruffed with the ♠K and then led a trump, the contract can be defeated. North rises with the ace of spades and plays the ten of clubs. South lets North win that trick and then a diamond from North promotes the jack of spades for South and the sixth trick for the defense.

(2) The same could happen if declarer leads the king of spades from dummy. North wins and another diamond from North gives South an extra trump trick.

Hand 6 : Super-accept — Choice of plays

Dealer East : E-W vulnerable

	NORTH		
	♠ 9 8 4		
	♡ A K 10 9 7		
	◊ 10 9 3 2		
	♣ 5		
WEST		EAST	
♠ K Q 10		♠ J 7 6	
♡ 8 4		♡ 6 3 2	
◊ Q 7 6 4		◊ K J 5	
♣ K 9 8 4		♣ 10 7 3 2	
	SOUTH		
	♠ A 5 3 2		
	♡ Q J 5		
	◊ A 8		
	♣ A Q J 6		

WEST	NORTH	EAST	SOUTH
		Pass	1NT
Pass	2◊	Pass	3♡
Pass	4♡	All pass	

Bidding : (1) North has just enough to justify a transfer followed by a rebid of 2NT (despite the singleton).

(2) South is worth the super-accept even though holding only three trumps. The hand is maximum, there is an outside doubleton and the trump support is good. Even if South bids only 2♡, South will jump to 4♡ over North's 2NT rebid.

Lead : King of spades. Second choice : trump lead. It is more attractive to lead an unbid suit which has two or more touching honors than to lead an unbid suit which contains only one honor.

Recommended play : South wins with the ace of spades and has two reasonable lines. Ten tricks are virtually assured by playing ace and another diamond. Declarer plans to ruff two diamond losers in hand with high trumps, returning to dummy once with a trump and once with a club ruff.

The other line is to play the ace of clubs and lead the queen of clubs, discarding a spade from dummy if West plays low. If this were to lose to East, declarer still has ten tricks by ruffing one diamond and discarding one on the jack of clubs. When West has the king of clubs, this line brings in an overtrick most of the time. Say West covers with the ♣K. This is ruffed in dummy, followed by a diamond to the ace and the jack of clubs on which a spade loser is discarded. Next a diamond is conceded and declarer later ruffs two diamonds in hand.

With a choice of plays, choose the line that may yield an extra trick even if that line is slightly riskier.

Hand 7 : Minor suit super-accept — Ruffing finesse — Compulsory duck — Deceptive lead

Dealer South : Both vulnerable

NORTH
♠ J 10 9
♥ 10 8 7 4
♦ K 10 8
♣ A Q 5

WEST
♠ 7 6 4
♥ - - -
♦ Q 7 5 4
♣ J 10 8 7 3 2

EAST
♠ A 5 3 2
♥ K Q J 6
♦ A 2
♣ K 6 4

SOUTH
♠ K Q 8
♥ A 9 5 3 2
♦ J 9 6 3
♣ 9

WEST	NORTH	EAST	SOUTH
			Pass
Pass	Pass	1NT	Pass
2♠	Pass	2NT	Pass
3♣	Pass	Pass	Pass

Bidding : North should not open 3rd-in-hand. To open light in third seat, you should have a strong suit. West's 2♠ = transfer to clubs. East has a maximum 1NT with club support and a top honor in clubs and so bids 2NT, the super-accept. West has no ambitions for game and signs off in 3♣. This can be a loss for the super-accept (that the weaker hand may become declarer) but has its compensation when the super-accept finds the good games and slams on marginal values.

Lead : Jack of spades. Hard to go past top of sequence.

Recommended play : West wins the ♠A and leads the king of hearts. If South plays low, West discards a spade loser. When South plays the ace, West ruffs, crosses to the ♦A and discards two spades on the hearts. Next comes the ♦2 since West wants to ruff at least one diamond in dummy. When South plays low, West should realise North has the ♦K and so West ducks the diamond. North wins and should shift to a trump. With the trump king in dummy a good deceptive move is to lead ace and the low club. West will expect South to have the ♣Q and so rise with the ♣K. A spade is ruffed and a low diamond ruffed in dummy. When the ♦K falls, West's ♦Q is high. West loses two trumps and a diamond for +130.

Notes : If West tackles trumps before going for the diamond ruff (say, ruff a spade at trick 6 and lead a trump), the defense can draw dummy's trumps before West can negotiate a diamond ruff. If West mispicks the trump position, this would hold West to nine tricks.

Hand 8 : Minor suit transfer — Opening lead — Pairs technique after a favorable lead

Dealer West : Nil vulnerable

NORTH
♠ A Q 7
♥ A 6 5 4
♦ K 8 4
♣ A J 8

WEST
♠ J 6
♥ Q J 10 8
♦ Q J 10
♣ 10 9 5 4

EAST
♠ K 10 8 3 2
♥ K 9 3 2
♦ 7
♣ Q 6 2

SOUTH
♠ 9 5 4
♥ 7
♦ A 9 6 5 3 2
♣ K 7 3

WEST	NORTH	EAST	SOUTH
Pass	1NT	Pass	2NT
Pass	3♣	Pass	3NT
Pass	Pass	Pass	

Bidding : (1) South is borderline for the transfer sequence. It would not be unreasonable to bid 2♣, planning to rebid 3NT after a maximum (North would bid 3♥ and South 3NT).
(2) South's 2NT shows diamond length, North's 3♣ shows a maximum with diamond support and a top honor in diamonds.
(3) South has no sensible way to check on the heart position (as 3 no-hearts is still not a legal bid) and should brazen it out with 3NT. *When in doubt, choose 3NT and not a 5-minor contract.*

Lead : 3 of spades. The long suit is the normal choice. You need a strong reason to avoid the lead likely to be the field's choice.

Recommended play : West plays the jack and North wins with the queen. North notes at once that the spade was a lucky lead. A heart would have been much more damaging.

North tackles the diamonds : king of diamonds and another diamond. When East shows out, declarer may as well duck the diamond to West. The rest of the diamonds in dummy are now winners.

Should West now return a spade or switch to the ♥Q (which works well if North's hearts are K-6-5-4)? To solve this West should note East's discard on the second diamond. A defender who discards from the suit led originally is not interested in having that suit returned. Thus, if East discarded a spade, West should switch to ♥Q. East should discourage the heart shift as a spade lead from West will set up East's spades. If West returns a spade, North wins and cashes the diamonds. The question then is whether to take the club finesse : East should hold on to ♣ Q-x-x and spade winners (and West signals with ♥Q so that East can pitch hearts). As the opening lead was so favorable, North should reject the club finesse and settle for ten tricks.

Notes : If West does shift to the ♥Q, North should duck this, win the second heart (discarding a club), cash the ace of spades and run the diamonds. This gives North 11 tricks as East is caught in a spade-club squeeze.

CHAPTER 3

TRANSFERS AFTER 1NT — STRONG HANDS

Transfers to a major when responder is strong
1. Responder has game values with a 5-card major and no second suit

Transfer to your major and rebid 3NT.

WEST	EAST	*or*	WEST	EAST
1NT	2♦		1NT	2♥
2♥	3NT...		2♠	3NT...

Opener should pass with a doubleton and almost always revert to the major with 3-4 card support. With 3-card support and a 4-3-3-3 hand, opener may pass 3NT if every outside suit is doubly stopped.

2. Responder has game values with a 6+ major and no interest in any other suit

Transfer to your major and then jump to game.

WEST	EAST	*or*	WEST	EAST
1NT	2♦		1NT	2♥
2♥	4♥		2♠	4♠
No			No	

There is another way to transfer to your major suit game if you are using four-level transfers.

1NT : 4♣ = 'Please bid 4♥.'
1NT : 4♦ = 'Please bid 4♠.'

Four-level transfers are definitely preferable to reserving 1NT : 4♣ for Gerber, asking for aces. There are other (and better) ways to check on aces. Using four-level transfers may prevent a cheap lead-directing entry to the auction :

WEST	NORTH	EAST	SOUTH
1NT	Pass	2♦	2♠
Pass	Pass	3NT	Pass
4♥	Pass	Pass	Pass

This auction has allowed South to indicate a lead to North. This might be vital to the defense.

WEST	NORTH	EAST	SOUTH
1NT	Pass	4♣	?

While South may venture a two-level overcall, it is far less likely that South will come in over 4♣. Now when West bids 4♥, North has no clues suggesting a spade lead might be useful.

When you transfer, next player may double your artificial bid to indicate a lead to partner. That may influence your choice of which transfer route to take. If you want to reach 4♠, but a possible lead-directing double of 4♦ would be unwelcome, you may choose the 1NT : 2♥, 2♠ : 4♠ path instead.

It is not compulsory for responder to transfer. If it appears that the lead coming to responder's hand is preferable, responder may bid 1NT : 4♥ or 1NT : 4♠. Such situations are rare. Responder would have a long weak suit and holdings such as K-x, K-J-x and A-Q in the outside suits.

3. Responder has game values with both majors and at least a 5-4 pattern

Transfer to the longer major and then bid the other major. Only the first two-level response is a transfer. The next suit bid is genuine.

WEST	EAST	*or*	WEST	EAST
1NT	2♦		1NT	2♥
2♥	2♠...		2♠	3♥...
Opener has at least			Opener has at least	
5 hearts and 4 spades			5 spades and 4 hearts	

Change of suit after a transfer is forcing to game.

Showing a 5-5 pattern

WEST	EAST	*or*	WEST	EAST
1NT	2♥		1NT	2♥
2♠	4♥...		2♠	3♥
			3NT	4♥...

In both auctions, East is showing at least 5-5 in the majors. What is the difference? The principle known as 'Fast Arrival' says that the immediate jump to game is the weaker action. Thus, the jump to 4♥ over 2♠ shows game interest only. West should pass or give preference to spades. Where East bid 3♥ and then 4♥, this is 'Slow Arrival'. East has some ambitions for slam, particularly if West has useful help in the majors and instant winners in the minors.

4. Responder has a 5+ major and a 4-card minor

Unless you have ambitions for slam, it is better not to show the minor suit. Basic pairs strategy is not to play in a 5-minor contract unless there is no other possibility. Therefore, if you have game values only, do not show the minor. Opener's raise of the minor suit would be unwelcome.

WEST	W	E	EAST
♠ A 10 8 4	1NT	2♦	♠ 7 2
♥ J 6	2♥	3NT	♥ A Q 10 4 2
♦ A Q 3 2	Pass		♦ K J 6 4
♣ K Q 3			♣ 8 7

With no ambitions for slam, East should not introduce the diamonds. 5♦ may make but 3NT has reasonable chances for 10 tricks, thus outscoring 5♦ even if that makes an overtrick. 4♥ is a good spot but always tough to reach on a 5-2 fit.

With a 5-4 pattern, responder needs about 14 HCP before introducing a minor. With less than that, slam prospects are not great for the minor suit. With a 5-5 pattern, 11-12 HCP would be enough to show the minor if the two 5-card suits are strong.

♠ 8 6   ♥ A Q 10 7 4   ♦ K Q 10 5 3   ♣ 7

This is certainly enough for a 3♦ rebid after a transfer to 2♥.

Transfers to a minor when responder is strong

1. Responder is worth 3NT and has both minors or is one-suited with a long minor

Do NOT transfer. Just raise to 3NT.

WEST	
♠ 5	East has opened 1NT and
♡ J 5 4	South has passed.
◇ 9 8 6	What action should West
♣ A K Q 6 3 2	take?

It is tempting to transfer to clubs and then rebid 3NT but that does not really solve your problem. What you need to know is whether partner is strong enough in spades. Showing the clubs does nothing to indicate your area of concern. Resign yourself to the fact that you cannot solve this problem in standard methods and take the percentage action (bid 3NT and avoid minor suit games). Pairs bridge can be a health hazard for those with pacemakers.

2. Responder has values for game but not for slam and has a 4-card major with a longer minor

Do NOT transfer. Use 2♣ to try to find the major suit fit. If that is not forthcoming, rebid 3NT and take your chances.

WEST	
♠ 5	East has opened 1NT and
♡ A J 5 4	South has passed.
◇ 9 8 6	What action should West
♣ K Q 6 3 2	take?

West has enough for game but nowhere near enough for a slam. West should bid 2♣. If East shows hearts, the partnership will reach 4♡. If East does not show hearts, West should rebid 3NT. If you fail, you fail . . . so what else is new?

3. Responder has enough for game and some prospects for slam, plus a two-suiter, at least 5-4, with the minor suit as the longer suit

Transfer to the long minor and then bid the second suit. We have seen that responder shows slam ambitions by a transfer to a major followed by a minor suit rebid. The same applies if responder transfers to a minor and then shows a 4-card major. Without slam ambitions, responder would have travelled via 2♣.

WEST	EAST
1NT	2♠
3♣	3♡ . . .

East is showing 5+ clubs and 4 hearts and some hopes for slam if a trump fit exists.

WEST	EAST
1NT	2NT
3♣	3♡ . . .

East is showing 5+ diamonds and 4 hearts and some hopes for slam if a trump fit exists. Even though West's 3♣ was a super-accept for diamonds, East's 3♡ bid is still natural. There could be a heart fit as well as a diamond fit.

Opener's options after responder has shown a two-suiter

Opener has five basic paths :
* Bid 3NT to deny support for either suit.
* Show weak support for responder's first suit.
* Show strong support for responder's first suit.
* Show weak support for responder's second suit.
* Show strong support for responder's second suit.

Where responder has shown a 5-card major, opener should support with 3+ trumps.

* Weak support for opener's first suit is shown by supporting that suit at *game level*.

WEST	EAST	West's 4♠, bidding the first
1NT	2♡	suit at game level, shows
2♠	3♡	weak support ('fast arrival').
4♠ . . .		

* Strong support for opener's first suit is shown by supporting that suit *below game level*.

WEST	EAST	West's 3♠, bidding the first
1NT	2♡	suit below game level, shows
2♠	3♡	strong support.
3♠ . . .		

What is weak support? What is strong support?

In Chapter 2 it was noted that there are three key features for opener to consider when responder transfers :

1. 3- or 4-card support for responder's suit.
2. A doubleton elsewhere to provide ruffing potential.
3. A maximum 1NT opening.

When responder has transferred to a major and opener has accepted the transfer, opener will not have all three of these features. With that, opener would already have given a super-accept. Therefore when responder shows a second suit and opener supports the original major :

Strong support = 2 of the 3 key features

Weak support = 0 or 1 of the 3 key features

* Weak support for opener's *second* suit is shown by raising that suit (to game level if it is a major, to the four-level if it is a minor).

WEST	EAST	West's 4♡, raising the
1NT	2♡	second suit to the four-level,
2♠	3♡	shows weak support for the
4♡ . . .		second suit.

* Strong support for opener's *second* suit is shown by a cue bid, bidding an ace in an unbid suit.

WEST	EAST	West's 4♣, a new suit, is a
1NT	2♡	cue bid, showing strong
2♠	3♡	support for hearts plus the ace
4♣ . . .		of clubs.

When showing support for the second suit, 2 or 3 key features = strong support, 0 or 1 key feature = weak support. If you have strong support for the second suit but no ace available for a cue bid, you will just have to raise the second suit.

When showing both majors, responder may have no slam ambitions. If so, even if opener shows strong support for either major, responder can simply sign off in game. Where responder has shown a minor suit, that in itself indicates slam interest.

WEST	EAST	Opener's support of diamonds,
1NT	2♡	while denying the ability to cue
2♠	3◇	bid 3♡ or 4♣, shows willingness
4◇ . . .		to co-operate with East's slam
		ambitions in diamonds.

The next move is up to responder who may choose a cue bid or use 4NT to ask for aces.

What if opener can support both suits?

If responder has shown both majors, support the major in which you have more cards. In particular, you should generally prefer a 4-4 fit to a 5-3 fit.

If responder has shown a major-minor two-suiter, prefer to show the support for the major. Opener's raise of the minor suit denies support for the major and denies the ability to cue bid an outside ace.

Slam-going auctions
The 1NT : 3♣/3◇/3♡/3♠ sequences

A transfer sequence does not cope well with a one-suiter and slam prospects, especially for a major. This hand type is shown by a jump to the three-level. The suit bid is genuine, not a transfer. It promises a one-suiter and shows slam interest. With a two-suiter and slam interest, you would *definitely* adopt a transfer sequence, since opener can then show weak support or strong support for either suit. Without slam interest, there is always a convenient auction without needing the jump to the three-level.

After responder's jump to the three-level, opener rebids 3NT if holding only a doubleton in responder's suit (e.g., 1NT : 3♡, 3NT), raises the suit with weak support (0 or 1 key feature) or bids an outside ace with strong support (2 or 3 key features). For example, 1NT : 3♠, 4◇ shows good spade support, the ace of diamonds but no ace of clubs : with more than one ace, bid the cheaper. After receiving support, responder can make a cue bid or use 4NT to ask for aces or key cards. (For another approach here, see Chapter 13)

If opener bids 3NT, denying support, a new suit by responder is a cue bid with the original suit set as trumps. Responder has a strong 6-card or longer suit. For example, 1NT : 3♠, 3NT : 4◇ . . . spades are set as trumps and responder is keen on slam. Responder has shown the ◇A and denied the ♣A.

What does this sequence mean :
1NT : 3♡, 3NT : 4NT ?
And what about :
1NT : 2◇, 2♡ : 4NT ?

It makes sense to play one of them as quantitative and the other as asking for aces. It does not matter much which way you play them provided you and partner have a clear understanding which is which.

After a transfer to a major

After opener has accepted the transfer a jump in a new suit is not needed as a natural bid since a simple change of suit would be forcing. One method is to play this as a cue bid with responder's major set as trumps. For example, 1NT : 2♡, 2♠ : 4♣ sets spades as trumps, indicates slam ambitions and shows the ace of clubs.

Why did responder not simply bid 1NT : 3♠? Because opener may then have bid 4♠ or cue bid 4♡ or 4◇, cutting out the 4♣ bid. The transfer and then jump-as-a-cue-bid may save valuable bidding space.

The jump-shift cue does not apply to the sequence 1NT : 2♡, 2♠ : 4♡. Here responder has shown 5-5 in the majors and no slam interest (see page 22). The jump to 4♡ is not a cue bid. The jump-shift cue does apply to 1NT : 2◇, 2♡ : 3♠ (♠A and 6+ hearts).

Another way to play the jump-shift after a transfer is as a splinter. Thus 1NT : 2♡, 2♠ : 4♣ would show a 6-card or longer spade suit, a shortage in clubs and slam interest. It is in the nature of a short suit try for slam. If opener has no wasted values in responder's short suit opener should be keen to head for slam. Holdings with the king, queen or jack are usually wasted opposite responder's shortage.

After a transfer to a minor

Raising the minor suit to the four-level sets the minor suit as trumps and asks partner to start cue bidding. For example, 1NT : 2♠, 3♣ : 4♣ . . .

The same applies if opener made a super-accept. For example, 1NT : 2♠, 2NT : 4♣ = clubs are trumps.

When responder rebids 3NT, the meaning will depend on whether opener gave a simple accept or a super-accept.

WEST	EAST	*or*	WEST	EAST
1NT	2♠		1NT	2NT
3♣	3NT		3◇	3NT

After a simple accept, responder's 3NT shows a hand close to slam values. If opener had given a super-accept, responder would have moved towards slam. Opener should push on with a maximum 1NT, particularly with Q-x or stronger in responder's suit.

WEST	EAST	*or*	WEST	EAST
1NT	2♠		1NT	2NT
2NT	3NT		3♣	3NT

After a super-accept, responder's 3NT shows a hand barely worth game. It is only because the hand has improved with the super-accept that responder is taking a shot at 3NT. Had opener given a simple accept, responder would have passed.

WEST	EAST	Where responder has shown
1NT	2♠	two suits and opener rebids 3NT,
3♣	3♡	responder's rebid of the minor at
3NT	4♣ . . .	the 4-level sets the minor suit as
		trumps and asks opener to start cue

bidding. This applies whether opener gave a simple accept or a super-accept.

Expert methods
Bidding after a super-accept of a major

After a super-accept of a major, a new suit would be a cue bid.

WEST	EAST	Responder's 4◇ shows interest
1NT	2♡	in slam plus the ace of diamonds
3♠	4◇	and denies the ace of clubs.

It also makes sense to treat 3NT as Blackwood after a super-accept of a major. Having received super support for the major, responder would have no reason to suggest 3NT as an alternative contract.

WEST	EAST	Responder's 3NT offers opener
1NT	2♡	a choice of contracts. Opener has
2♠	3NT	not shown spade support.

WEST	EAST	Responder's 3NT can be used as
1NT	2♡	an ace ask as opener has shown
3♠	3NT	excellent support for responder.

Where opener has used a different form of super-accept such as a new suit (see page 17) :

1NT : 2♡   If 3♣ is used as a long suit trial
3♣ ...   for game responder's options are :

Bid the major at the three level : Sign-off.
Bid the major at game level : Sign-off.
New suit = cue bid with the major suit trumps.
3NT = asking for aces as above.

WEST	EAST	*or*	WEST	EAST
1NT	2♡		1NT	2◇
2NT			2NT	

Here opener is showing a maximum 1NT in a hand more suitable for no-trump play : a 4-3-3-3 pattern and aces in the outside suits. Here 3NT by responder would not be asking for aces but rather acceding to opener's suggestion to play in no-trumps despite the major suit fit. If that does not appeal, responder may sign off in 3-Major or 4-Major. It makes sense to use a change of suit here as a cue bid. It is thus possible to play both cue bids and splinters after the 2NT super-accept : a change of suit is a cue bid and a jump-shift is a splinter.

Bidding after a super-accept of a minor

After a super-accept of a minor, a new suit is played as natural and not as a cue bid.

WEST	EAST	Even though opener has shown
1NT	2♠	excellent support for clubs and a
2NT	3♡	maximum 1NT responder's 3♡ still

shows a 4-card heart suit. There may be a fit in hearts as well as in clubs. If East wants to start cue bidding East can bid 4♣ over 2NT.

3NT over the super-accept of a minor is to play so that if responder simply wants to ask for aces after the super-accept, bid 4NT to ask or raise the minor to start the cue bidding and continue with 4NT to ask for aces. As opener has already shown a maximum 1NT it would not make sense here to use 4NT as a quantitative try for 6NT.

What does it mean if responder transfers to a minor and then jumps to game in a major?

WEST	EAST	*or*	WEST	EAST
1NT	2♠		1NT	2♠
2NT	4♡/4♠		3♣	4♡/4♠

Are these natural bids or are they cue-bids or perhaps splinters? Because there are always memory risks when a jump to game (which sounds natural) is used in a conventional sense it is recommended that these jumps are used as natural bids whether opener gave a simple accept or a super-accept. The hand type for responder would be a weakish 6-5 with no slam interest (5-7 HCP would be enough for such a freak hand).

With a strong 6-5 and hopes for slam responder should transfer and then bid the major at the three level. After a super-accept responder knows that slam is likely in the minor anyway. After a simple accept responder can suggest a slam or start cue bidding by setting the minor suit :

WEST	EAST	If responder bids 4♡ over 3NT
1NT	2♠	responder is showing a 6-5 and
3♣	3♡	suggesting slam. Opener may pass
3NT	?	4♡ or convert to 5♣, particularly

with poor holdings (such as K-Q-x or K-Q-J opposite responder's short suits). Aces in the short suits would make a move towards slam attractive.

If responder bids 4♣ over 3NT this sets clubs as trumps and asks opener to start cue bidding.

Interference after the transfer

If they bid a suit over the transfer :
Opener passes unless worth a super-accept. After opener's pass, further action is up to responder. If responder bids the suit shown originally, this is not forcing. A *new* suit by responder is still a game-force.

If they double the transfer bid :
The double of a transfer bid usually shows a strong holding in the suit doubled. One of the problems for the opening side is whether they should compete to the three-level if fourth player bids the suit shown by the doubler. This will often depend on the number of trumps opener holds.
Bid the major shown = doubleton only and no desire to compete to the three-level.
Pass = 3+ support and prepared to compete to three. If this comes back to responder, redouble asks opener to accept the transfer anyway.
Redouble = 4-card support and maximum values. Definitely wants to compete and invites game. This would show a maximum 1NT with two key features.
Super-accept = usual values (all 3 key features).

If they bid responder's major :
Pass = weak support and no desire to compete at the three-level. Double = 3+ support and desire to bid further. Super-accept = usual values.

EXERCISES USING TRANSFERS

A. Partner has opened 1NT. What is your response with each of these hands?

	1.	2.	3.	4.	5.
♠	A 9	A 9	2	7 4	K J 2
♥	K J 5 3	K J 5 3	9 8 6	A K Q 8 2	J 8 7 5 4 3 2
♦	7 2	7 2	A Q 3 2	A K 8	K 3
♣	A Q J 4 3	A 8 6 4 3	K J 8 7 5	9 6 4	4

B. The bidding has started 1NT : 2♥, 2♠ : 3♥. What is opener's rebid with these hands?

	1.	2.	3.	4.	5.
♠	K 6 3	K 10	J 8 7	K J	A Q 6 4
♥	K J 5 3	A K 9 2	A Q 6	K 8 2	A 4
♦	A 5	A K 3	K Q 6 2	A 10 9 2	A 9 4
♣	K J 9 8	8 7 6 3	K J 9	A J 9 6	J 10 9 8

C. The bidding has started 1NT : 2♠, 3♣ : 3♥. What should opener do next?

	1.	2.	3.	4.	5.
♠	9 7 3	A K 2	A K 9 2	A 9 5 2	K Q J
♥	A J	K Q J 7	8 6 3	K Q 7 5	J 5 2
♦	A K J 2	Q 8 4	A K 4 2	A 8 7	A K J
♣	K 9 7 2	J 6 3	K 5	A 6	J 9 3 2

PARTNERSHIP BIDDING : How should the following hands be bid? West is the dealer each time.

	SET 5 — WEST	SET 5 — EAST	SET 6 — WEST	SET 6 — EAST
1. ♠	A Q 9 6 5	K 7 2	A 10 3 2	K Q 6 4
♥	K 3	A 7	K 10 6 2	A 9 7 5 3
♦	J 8 4 2	Q 10 5 3	A 7 4	8 6
♣	7 6	A K 9 4	A 3	5 4
2. ♠	K Q 5 2	6	A K 5 2	7 4 3
♥	A 5 2	K J 10 7 4 3	A Q J 6	8
♦	Q J 6	A K 3	6 5	A K Q 9 8 7
♣	A 10 5	4 3 2	K 8 3	J 5 2
3. ♠	A 9 3	K J 4 2	K 7 4 2	A Q 8 5 3
♥	K Q 10	5	A 8 6	9
♦	K 5	A Q 10 9 7 2	K 9	A Q 8 7 5
♣	A J 8 4 3	7 6	A Q 5 3	7 2
4. ♠	7 2	A K 7 5	J 9	K Q 6 2
♥	9 2	K Q 5 4	K Q 8 4 3	J 6 5 2
♦	A K 4 3	9 6 5	9	A K J
♣	K 9 5 3 2	A J	A 10 8 7 4	Q 9
5. ♠	A K 4	8 2	8 7 4 3	K Q 10 5 2
♥	Q 3	A J 10 5 4	K J 2	3
♦	A 9 8 3	K Q 7	A K Q	8 2
♣	K 10 7 2	9 8 3	K 8 4	A J 10 6 3
6. ♠	A K 5 4 2	Q 7 3	K 3	A Q J 6 4
♥	Q 9 8 4	A K 2	K 4 2	A 8 5
♦	J 3 2	A Q 9	A J 9 7	5
♣	5	J 6 4 3	A J 6 4	K Q 3 2

PLAY HANDS ON STRONG TRANSFERS OVER 1NT
(These hands can be made up by using pages 160-167)

Hand 9 : Transfer then new suit — Choosing the better trump suit

Dealer North : E-W vulnerable

NORTH
- ♠ A K 7 6
- ♥ K 8 6 2
- ♦ Q 7 2
- ♣ A 6

WEST
- ♠ 9 8
- ♥ 10 5 4
- ♦ K 9 5
- ♣ K Q 10 8 5

EAST
- ♠ 10 3
- ♥ 9 7
- ♦ A J 10 6 3
- ♣ J 4 3 2

SOUTH
- ♠ Q J 5 4 2
- ♥ A Q J 3
- ♦ 8 4
- ♣ 9 7

WEST	NORTH	EAST	SOUTH
	1NT	Pass	2♥
Pass	2♠	Pass	3♥
Pass	4♥	All pass	

Bidding : South's sequence (transfer to spades and then 3♥) is a game force with at least 5 spades and 4 hearts. At rubber bridge or teams North might choose the 5-4 fit which is often safer than the 4-4 fit. At pairs North should choose the 4-4 fit even though the spade support is stronger and the partnership may hold more spades than hearts. The 4-4 fit may not be safer (a terrible trump split is more likely when five trumps are missing) but it will often produce an extra trick, perhaps the overtrick which gives you a great score rather than just an average.

Lead : King of clubs. The strong unbid suit is normal.

Recommended play : South wins with the ♣A (it would be a serious error to duck since ten tricks would then be the limit) and should draw trumps. Next the spades are cashed starting with the ace and king and on the fifth spade declarer discards dummy's club loser. Ruff a club and concede two diamonds for 11 tricks. +450.

Notes : (1) If spades are trumps the heart suit produces only four tricks. With hearts as trumps declarer can use the spades to obtain a vital discard and the club ruff means the heart suit has produced five tricks.
(2) If hearts were 4-1 (28% of the time) only ten tricks would be made, the same as having spades as trumps. 4♥ is slightly riskier than 4♠ since a 5-0 break would defeat 4♥ while a 4-0 break would not beat 4♠. The chance of a 5-0 break is about 4%. When hearts are 3-2 (68%) there are frequent opportunities for the overtrick.

Hand 10 : When to transfer when to avoid it — Catering for a bad break

Dealer East : Both vulnerable

NORTH
- ♠ A 9
- ♥ K 8 5 4
- ♦ J 10 9 6
- ♣ J 6 3

WEST
- ♠ J 3 2
- ♥ 9
- ♦ A K Q 5 3
- ♣ 9 5 4 2

EAST
- ♠ Q 8 7 4
- ♥ A Q 6
- ♦ 7 4 2
- ♣ A K Q

SOUTH
- ♠ K 10 6 5
- ♥ J 10 7 3 2
- ♦ 8
- ♣ 10 8 7

WEST	NORTH	EAST	SOUTH
		1NT	Pass
3NT	Pass	Pass	Pass

Bidding : Despite the singleton West should bid 3NT. At pairs do not play in 5♣ or 5♦ if 3NT is feasible. The test is : 'Might 3NT make?' If the answer is 'Yes, it might' take your chances in 3NT. It would be wrong to transfer to diamonds and rebid 3NT. Firstly this does not highlight the problem (short hearts) and it also suggests slam values. The West hand has no tangible prospects for slam. If 3NT happens to go sour, what you desperately need is a partner who will not only be philosophical about the loss but will also console you and agree with your action. What a partner!

Lead : 3 of hearts. After 1NT : 3NT a major suit is usually best and the longer suit is the normal choice.

Recommended play : East captures North's king and leads a diamond to the ace. East returns to hand with a club and leads a second diamond. When South shows out the diamond is ducked to North. East wins the expected heart return, cashes the clubs and crosses to dummy in diamonds. With clubs 3-3 declarer scores an overtrick.

Notes : (1) At rubber or teams East would win the heart lead and duck a diamond at trick 2. This secures the contract even if diamonds are 4-1. At pairs you play for the normal 3-2 break (68% chance) since this gives you an overtrick. However East should not simply start cashing diamonds. The 4-1 break would mean that there are only three diamond tricks and if the clubs were not 3-3 declarer would fail. The recommended play loses nothing if diamonds are 3-2 and caters for a 4-1 break with South having the singleton.
(2) After East returns to hand with a club and leads a diamond, if South were to follow declarer would win with a top diamond in dummy. If diamonds were 3-2, declarer would then cash the top clubs (in case they were 3-3) and the ♥A followed by the diamond winners. If it turns out that South began with four diamonds declarer would then have to switch to clubs and hope they were 3-3.

Hand 11 : Choice of transfers — Discarding losers

Dealer South : Nil vulnerable

	WEST	NORTH	EAST	SOUTH
				Pass
	1NT	Pass	2♡	Pass
	2♠	Pass	4♠	All pass

NORTH
♠ K 7 6 4
♡ 10 9 5
♦ A 7 2
♣ 10 7 4

WEST
♠ 5 3 2
♡ A Q 4 3
♦ K 8 5
♣ A K Q

EAST
♠ A Q J 10 9 8
♡ K
♦ 9 6 4
♣ J 6 5

SOUTH
♠ - - -
♡ J 8 7 6 2
♦ Q J 10 3
♣ 9 8 3 2

Bidding : East has the choice of jumping to 4♠ or transferring to 4♠. (3NT works well here but could be fatal if the spade finesse lost.) There is no benefit having the East hand as declarer and so East should transfer. East could choose 1NT : 4◊ (four-level transfer) but this might be doubled and a diamond lead could be unwelcome from East's point of view. A double of the 2♡ transfer is much less likely to be damaging.

Lead : 10 of hearts. North has no attractive lead. As the hearts contain a short sequence the heart lead is preferable to the club lead. It is normal to choose the stronger holding.

Recommended play : The ♡K wins trick 1. Declarer comes to hand with a club and cashes two more heart winners to discard two diamond losers from dummy. Next comes the spade finesse. That works but North is marked with all the spades. Come to hand with a club, repeat the spade finesse, return to hand with a club and take the spade finesse again. The ace of spades drops North's king and declarer has 12 tricks +480.

Notes : (1) Not every transfer yields a tangible benefit. On this hand however, the transfer is worth two extra tricks. If East were declarer South would lead the queen of diamonds and the defense would take the first three tricks. Declarer would now score only +420.
(2) If North happened to lead a club West should make only 11 tricks +450. Win the club, cross to ♡K, return with a club and pitch two diamonds on the hearts. Declarer now lacks the entries to take the spade finesse three times and North will score the ♠K.
(3) If the ♠K were with South then 4♠ by East would fail but 4♠ by West would make 11 tricks.
(4) Do not take the spade finesse before discarding dummy's diamonds. If it failed, declarer might go one down.

Hand 12 : Transfer with two suits and a shortage — Urgent discards

Dealer West : N-S vulnerable

	WEST	NORTH	EAST	SOUTH
	Pass	1NT	Pass	2♡
	Pass	2♠	Pass	3NT
	Pass	4♠	All pass	

NORTH
♠ J 9 2
♡ A K Q 3
♦ Q 9 5
♣ A 9 3

WEST
♠ A 6 5
♡ J 8 6 2
♦ 7 6 4
♣ K 8 4

EAST
♠ 8 7
♡ 10 9 5 4
♦ A 8 2
♣ Q J 10 2

SOUTH
♠ K Q 10 4 3
♡ 7
♦ K J 10 3
♣ 7 6 5

Bidding : South has enough for game and should travel via a transfer to spades. After North bids 2♠ South should not show the diamonds. South is not interested in playing in 5◊ at pairs and to introduce the diamonds would indicate some interest in slam. South has only borderline values for game.

South's 3NT offers North the choice of playing in 4♠ or in 3NT. With the 3-card support North should choose 4♠ even with the flat shape. For all North knows, South might have a singleton in diamonds or clubs and 3NT could be very risky.

Lead : Queen of clubs. Top-of-sequence is almost always best.

Recommended play : North should win trick 1 with the ace of clubs and shift to hearts, cashing the ace, king and queen to discard dummy's club losers. Next comes the jack of spades. Upon regaining the lead North draws trumps and then forces out the ace of diamonds. This makes 11 tricks for +450.

Notes : (1) 3NT could be defeated on a club lead. Even if you were to escape the club lead, a club switch after the defenders take their first ace would leave North-South with a terrible score.
(2) There is no reason to duck the opening lead. That would hold declarer to ten tricks (as two aces have to be lost) and +420 would be an awful score, possibly a bottom.
(3) It would be a dreadful error to tackle trumps before playing out the heart winners. After winning the ♠A the defenders could cash two clubs and the ace of diamonds for one down.
(4) After discarding dummy's clubs start on trumps and do not ruff a club or a heart in dummy. This could be fatal if trumps happened to be 4-1. Avoid shortening the long trump hand without a specific reason.

CHAPTER 4

BIDDING AFTER A 2NT OPENING

The 2NT range
Goren 2NT : 22-24 points
Problem : Responder with 2 points will usually pass and game could be missed.
Acol 2NT : 20-22 points
Problem : Responder with 4 points will usually pass and game could be missed.

A 3-point range for 2NT is awkward as responder has no invitational bid. Having a 2-point range for 2NT means that responder will always know the combined total within one point.

Recommended 2NT : 21-22 points
With more than 22, open 2♣ or 2◊ (your game force opening) and rebid in no-trumps.

2NT : 3♣
There are two basic conventions that are popular :
Stayman 3♣, asking for opener's major suits. With no major, opener bids 3◊.
Baron 3♣, asking for 4-card suits up-the-line. If opener's only suit is clubs, opener rebids 3NT.

At pairs it is definitely superior to use Stayman. The Baron Convention often means that the weaker hand becomes declarer in a major suit game. With the great disparity in strength, it is a significant loss to have the weaker hand declarer frequently.

WEST	Stayman		EAST
♠ A K 8 4	W	E	♠ Q 9 7 2
♡ K 6 5	2NT	3♣	♡ 9 8 2
◊ A Q 3 2	3♠	4♠	◊ K J 6
♣ A Q	Pass		♣ 8 7 3

Here West is declarer and 4♠ is a good chance.
Playing Baron the bidding would go :

W	E
2NT	3♣
3◊	3♠
4♠	Pass

With East declarer a heart lead could produce a result one trick worse than with West declarer.

WEST	Stayman		EAST
♠ A Q 8 4	W	E	♠ K 9 7 2
♡ A J 6 5	2NT	3♣	♡ K 2
◊ K Q 7	3♡	3NT	◊ J 10 5 4
♣ A Q	4♠	Pass	♣ 8 7 3

Playing Baron the bidding would go :

W	E
2NT	3♣
3♡	3♠
4♠	Pass

With West declarer, a heart or a club lead is a benefit. With East declarer, a heart or a club lead may result in an extra trick lost.

The advantage of Baron is that it is easier to find minor suit slams on a 4-4 fit. This tiny plus is greatly outweighed by the drawback of the weaker hand becoming declarer in the far more common major suit games.

Note how responder when playing Stayman rebids 3NT over 3♡ when holding four spades. The 3♣ response promises a major and so when opener bids 3♡, responder's 3NT says, 'That was not the major I wanted.' If opener has four spades opener can now bid 4♠ and become declarer.

After the 3♡ response, 3♠ by responder does show four spades but indicates slam interest. With slam potential and four spades, responder cannot afford to bid 3NT in case opener passes. As transfers to the minors are not generally used over 2NT, the 3♠ bid may be the beginning of a sequence where responder intends to show a minor suit next if opener does not have spade support.

WEST		E	EAST
♠ A J 9 4	2NT	3♣	♠ K 10 7 2
♡ A K 5 3	3♡	3♠	♡ 2
◊ A Q 2	4♣	4NT	◊ K J 6
♣ A 10	5♣	6♣	♣ K J 9 8 3

4♣ = cue bid with spade support. 5♣ = 0 or 4 aces.
If West did not have spade support and rebid 3NT over 3♠, East would have continued with 4♣.

After 2NT : 3♣, 3◊ . . .
A major suit now by responder shows a 5-card major. Since 3◊ denied a major there would be no point in responder now showing a 4-card major. Responder's choice of 3♣ rather than a transfer suggests responder is at least 5-4 in the majors.

WEST	Stayman		EAST
♠ A K 8	W	E	♠ Q 9 7 5 2
♡ Q 10 5	2NT	3♣	♡ K 9 8 2
◊ K J 2	3◊	3♠	◊ 6 4
♣ A K J 3	4♠	Pass	♣ 8 7

If stronger, West would cue bid with spade support.

Playing Baron you need a 2NT : 3♠ response to show the East hand. You cannot afford to use Baron 3♣ when 5-4 in the majors.

After any reply to Stayman, a bid of 4♣ or 4◊ by responder is natural and shows a 5-card suit. Opener can support via a raise or a cue bid, and deny support by 4NT.

Note that after 2NT, there is no Extended Stayman sequence. You do not want to reach the four level unnecessarily. Some play that 2NT : 3♣, 3◊ shows no major and that 2NT : 3♣, 3NT shows both majors. There is no significant benefit in this.

Bidding structure after 2NT

2NT : 3♣ = Stayman
2NT : 3◊ = Transfer to hearts
2NT : 3♡ = Transfer to spades
2NT : 3♠ = Optional. See later.
2NT : 3NT = To play
2NT : 4♣/4◊ = 6+ suit, slam values
2NT : 4♡/4♠ = To play
2NT : 4NT = Invitation to 6NT

After 2NT : 3◊ . . . *or* 2NT : 3♡ . . .

Opener will usually bid the major shown but may super-accept by jumping to game in the major. With 4-4 in the majors, opener should bid the other major to preserve the chance of the 4-4 fit.

WEST	W	E	EAST
♠ A Q 7 2	2NT	3◊	♠ K 9 6 3
♡ K Q 8 5	3♠	4♠	♡ A 6 4 3 2
◊ A J	Pass		◊ 6 4
♣ A J 4			♣ 8 7

4♠ will often produce 12 tricks, 4♡ will rarely bring in more than 11 tricks. If East had no interest in spades, East could sign off in 4♡ or, preferably, repeat the transfer to hearts via 4◊.

After 2NT : 3◊, 3♡ . . . *or* 2NT : 3♡, 3♠ . . .

Responder may pass, bid 3NT to offer a choice of contracts, raise to game in the major with a 6+ suit or bid a new suit below game as forcing.

WEST	W	E	EAST
♠ A Q 7 2	2NT	3◊	♠ 6 3
♡ A 5	3♡	Pass	♡ J 8 6 4 3 2
◊ A K J			◊ 6 4 3
♣ A 9 6 4			♣ 8 7

Transfers allow responder to bail out in a partscore, something not possible in standard methods. West would be very lucky to come to seven tricks in 2NT. In 3♡ there are reasonable chances for nine tricks.

2NT : 3♠ . . .

With 4 spades - 5 hearts, there is no problem in using transfers. Both suits can be shown below 3NT. When responder has 5 spades - 4 hearts, it is not appropriate to use a transfer sequence. After the transfer to spades you cannot afford to bid 4♡ with a 4-card suit. Opener may not have support for either suit. The sequence 2NT : 3♡, 3♠ : 4♡ shows responder has at least a 5-5 pattern in the majors.

The 5 spades - 4 hearts hand can be solved by using Stayman or by an immediate response of 3♠. Many partnerships use 2NT : 3♠ in this way. It is forcing to game and does not deny slam interest.

Another possible use for 2NT : 3♠ is to show a hand with both minors and slam interest. Opener can rebid 3NT to deny decent support for either minor (over 3NT, responder can still bid 4♣ or 4◊ to show a 5+ minor) or bid 4♣ or 4◊ to show support for the minor. Responder can continue via a cue bid or 4NT to check on controls.

After 2NT : 4♣ or 4◊

These responses are natural and show a 6-card or longer suit with slam interest. Opener should cue bid the cheapest ace. Responder will continue with a cue bid or 4NT asking.

Expert methods

Many top pairs will open 2NT with a 5-card major if their methods do not provide some other way of showing the balanced 21-22 with a 5-major. If so, 2NT : 3♣ should be used to ask for a 5-card major.

Opener's replies are :

3◊ = No 5-card major, but one or two 4-card majors
3♡ or 3♠ = 5-card major
3NT = no 5-card major, no 4-card major

Over 3◊, responder can fossick for a 4-4 major fit. 2NT : 3♣, 3◊ : 3♡ or 3♠ = 4-card suit, forcing.

After 2NT : 3♣, 3◊ : 3♡ opener would bid 3♠ if holding four spades.

The drawback to this approach is that responder will be declarer in many major suit games.

Puppet Stayman over 2NT

This structure locates all the 5-3 and 4-4 fits and ensures opener becomes declarer as often as possible. Opener's rebids after 2NT : 3♣ are the same as above for 5-card major Stayman. Over opener's 3◊, if responder wishes to explore a 4-4 fit, responder bids the major in which there is no interest :

2NT : 3♣, 3◊ : 3♡ = 4 spades
2NT : 3♣, 3◊ : 3♠ = 4 hearts
2NT : 3♣, 3◊ : 4◊ = 4-4 majors (opener has a major)

Over any rebid, opener can easily select the contract. With extras, responder can push on to slam.

Responder should choose the 3♣ response when holding a 4-card major or 3-card support for either major (unless wishing to stay in no-trumps with some 4-3-3-3). With a 5-card major, including 5-3 in the majors, responder should use a transfer.

2NT : 3◊ = transfer to hearts, showing 5+ hearts (and could have four spades also). Opener will usually bid 3♡ and bidding proceeds normally as after a transfer. Opener will refuse the transfer and bid 3♠ with 5 spades and 2 hearts. Responder may raise to 4♠, rebid 3NT or transfer to 4♡ via 4◊.

2NT : 3♡ = transfer to spades with 5+ spades but denying four hearts. Opener will almost always bid 3♠ and the bidding proceeds normally as after a transfer. Opener may reject the transfer and bid 3NT when holding five hearts and two spades. Responder may pass 3NT, bid 4♡ or transfer to spades via 4◊. (In this method 4◊ always transfers to responder's major.)

2NT : 3♠ = responder has 5 spades and 4 hearts, forcing. Opener chooses the contract. Responder may push on for slam after opener's rebid.

The only loss in the above structure is the rare occasion when opener is 5-2 in the majors and the partnership cannot stop in a 3-Major signoff.

EXERCISES FOR BIDDING AFTER A 2NT OPENING

A. Partner has opened 2NT. What is your response with each of these hands?

1.	♠ J9	2.	♠ J9	3.	♠ J984	4.	♠ J9843	5.	♠ 987532
	♡ KJ53		♡ KJ532		♡ K9862		♡ K982		♡ 2
	◇ 762		◇ 762		◇ 32		◇ 32		◇ 632
	♣ 8742		♣ 874		♣ 75		♣ 64		♣ 874

B. The bidding has started 2NT : 3♣, 3♡. What should responder do next?

1.	♠ K63	2.	♠ K874	3.	♠ K874	4.	♠ K874	5.	♠ K4
	♡ K853		♡ K962		♡ Q6		♡ A2		♡ KQ94
	◇ 75		◇ 63		◇ 962		◇ A1052		◇ A4
	♣ 9842		♣ 763		♣ 8753		♣ 1096		♣ Q10982

C. The bidding has started 2NT : 3◇, 3♡ : 3♠. What is opener's rebid with these hands?

1.	♠ K73	2.	♠ AK2	3.	♠ AJ52	4.	♠ AK52	5.	♠ AK92
	♡ AJ		♡ KQJ7		♡ KQ75		♡ Q5		♡ AJ3
	◇ AKJ2		◇ QJ4		◇ A8		◇ AQJ		◇ AK42
	♣ KQ72		♣ KQ3		♣ AK4		♣ KQ84		♣ K5 ‚

PARTNERSHIP BIDDING : How should the following hands be bid? West is the dealer each time.

SET 7 — WEST	SET 7 — EAST	SET 8 — WEST	SET 8 — EAST
1. ♠ QJ9653	1. ♠ AK	1. ♠ K1032	1. ♠ Q764
♡ 93	♡ KQJ	♡ AJ10	♡ K74
◇ 84	◇ A965	◇ AKQ4	◇ J86
♣ 762	♣ KQ43	♣ A3	♣ 542
2. ♠ KQ8	2. ♠ 52	2. ♠ AK52	2. ♠ 8743
♡ A63	♡ J87542	♡ AQ96	♡ 84
◇ AKQ2	◇ 74	◇ AJ	◇ Q987
♣ QJ5	♣ 862	♣ A83	♣ QJ2
3. ♠ KQ8	3. ♠ 52	3. ♠ Q853	3. ♠ K74
♡ AK63	♡ J87542	♡ 97532	♡ A8
◇ AK82	◇ 74	◇ A5	◇ KQ2
♣ K5	♣ 862	♣ 76	♣ AKQ32
4. ♠ J987432	4. ♠ A5	4. ♠ KJ92	4. ♠ AQ4
♡ 92	♡ AQ5	♡ KQ843	♡ AJ52
◇ ---	◇ A9653	◇ 9	◇ KJ7
♣ 9632	♣ AK4	♣ 1084	♣ KQJ
5. ♠ K4	5. ♠ QJ2	5. ♠ A8	5. ♠ K10652
♡ Q8732	♡ A4	♡ KJ82	♡ Q763
◇ 983	◇ KQJ72	◇ AKQ3	◇ 2
♣ 872	♣ AKJ	♣ KQ4	♣ 1063
6. ♠ K82	6. ♠ Q9753	6. ♠ J8632	6. ♠ KQ4
♡ AKJ4	♡ Q62	♡ Q10642	♡ A85
◇ KQJ	◇ 9742	◇ 97	◇ AQ32
♣ A42	♣ 3	♣ 4	♣ AQ6

PLAY HANDS ON TRANSFERS OVER 2NT
(These hands can be made up by using pages 160-167)

Hand 13 : Bailing out of 2NT — When to discard first, when to tackle trumps first

Dealer North : Both vulnerable

NORTH
♠ A 2
♡ A 7 5 4
♢ A 8 4 3
♣ A K Q

WEST
♠ K 10 7
♡ J 10
♢ K J
♣ 10 8 7 6 3 2

EAST
♠ Q 9
♡ K Q 9 8
♢ Q 9 6 5 2
♣ J 5

SOUTH
♠ J 8 6 5 4 3
♡ 6 3 2
♢ 10 7
♣ 9 4

WEST	NORTH	EAST	SOUTH
	2NT	Pass	3♡
Pass	3♠	All pass	

Bidding : South has an almost hopeless hand. Without transfers, South would pass since a bid of 3♠ would be forcing. Playing transfers, South is able to bid 3♡ showing 5+ spades and pass when North accepts the transfer with 3♠.

The transfer-then-pass sequence is best reserved for a 6-card major. With a 7-card suit, even with no points, it is worth taking a shot at game. With a 5-card suit it is usually best to pass 2NT.

Lead : King of hearts. Against no-trumps East would choose a diamond but against a suit contract it is more attractive to lead from a K-Q combination than from a suit with only one honor. To lead from ♣J-x holds no appeal.

Recommended play : North wins with the ♡A. It would not cost to duck but there is no benefit either. North should continue with ace and another spade. East wins with the queen and can continue with the hearts but the defense can take only two hearts and two spades. When North regains the lead, North can cash the clubs and discard a diamond loser from dummy.

Notes : (1) It would be an error for North to start on clubs at trick 2. There is no urgency for a discard since North still has the ♢A and can discard a diamond loser from dummy later. If North were to play the clubs at once East will ruff the third round. If dummy overruffs, declarer should lose two spades, two hearts and a diamond, while if dummy discards, declarer should lose two tricks in the red suits, the club ruff and two spades.
(2) Note that nine tricks are available in spades while in no-trumps North has only six tricks available.

Hand 14 : Treatment of a two-suiter — Judging which honor to play with K-J opposite junk

Dealer East : Nil vulnerable

NORTH
♠ 9 6 4
♡ 10 5
♢ Q J 10 8 7
♣ Q 5 4

WEST
♠ A Q J 5
♡ A Q J 9
♢ A 4
♣ K J 6

EAST
♠ K 8 3 2
♡ K 7 6 4 2
♢ 3 2
♣ 8 3

SOUTH
♠ 10 7
♡ 8 3
♢ K 9 6 5
♣ A 10 9 7 2

WEST	NORTH	EAST	SOUTH
		Pass	Pass
2NT	Pass	3♢	Pass
3♡	Pass	3♠	Pass
4♠	Pass	Pass	Pass

Bidding : East has shown 5 hearts and 4 spades. West should choose spades as trumps even though this means the weaker hand will be declarer. *Being in the best contract is 90% of your task. Having it played from the right side is 10%. Do not sacrifice the contract for the sake of having the stronger hand as declarer.* If you can be in the best contract and have it played from the right side, that is a bonus. If not, still choose the best spot.

Lead : 5 of diamonds. It is usually better to lead from an unbid suit headed by the king than one headed by the ace.

Recommended play : East wins the diamond lead with dummy's ace and draws trumps. Next come the hearts. East overtakes the fourth round and cashes the fifth heart on which dummy's diamond loser is discarded. East continues with a club. If South rises with the ace, East has 12 tricks. South should play low and East has to guess whether to finesse the jack or the king. If dummy's jack is played, East makes 11 tricks while if East calls for dummy's king, East scores 12 tricks.

Notes : (1) On the first diamond North should play the ♢Q. If North can later signal South the count in diamonds, South will know East began with two diamonds only and so it is safe to duck the club lead.
(2) There is a tiny clue which might guide East into picking the clubs correctly. South led a diamond rather than a club. With ♣A South would be reluctant to lead a club. Without the ♣A South might have chosen a club lead rather than the diamond. As South chose a diamond, perhaps holding the ♣A was the reason.
(3) In hearts, East-West can make only 11 tricks even if the clubs are picked correctly. In spades East-West can make 12 tricks. Note that if East uses Stayman West bids 3♡. It would be very tough then to reach 4♠.

Hand 15 : Choice of transfers — Discarding losers

Dealer South : N-S vulnerable

NORTH
♠ K 10 9 6 3
♡ Q 8 7 2
◇ 9 5
♣ 7 4

WEST
♠ Q 4 2
♡ 5
◇ A 10 8 7 6
♣ Q 8 6 3

EAST
♠ J 8 5
♡ J 10 9 6 4
◇ K 2
♣ 10 9 5

SOUTH
♠ A 7
♡ A K 3
◇ Q J 4 3
♣ A K J 2

WEST	NORTH	EAST	SOUTH
			2NT
Pass	3♠	Pass	3NT
Pass	Pass	Pass	

Bidding : 3♠ shows 5 spades and 4 hearts. With no fit for either major, South chooses 3NT.

North might bid this hand type via Stayman as follows :

WEST	NORTH	EAST	SOUTH
			2NT
Pass	3♣	Pass	3◇
Pass	3♠	Pass	3NT
Pass	Pass	Pass	

3◇ = no major and then 3♠ = five spades.

Lead : 7 of diamonds. The long suit is the normal choice.

Recommended play : East wins with the ◇K at trick 1 and returns the ◇2. South plays an honor, captured by West who plays a third diamond. South wins in hand and discards a heart from dummy (a tough decision). With eight tricks on top, there is no rush to try the club finesse for the ninth trick. Best is to play the ace of spades and duck the next spade into the East hand (safe as East is known to be out of diamonds). Win the return from East, cash one top club in case the queen drops and then play off the hearts, ending in dummy. Test the spades by cashing the ♠K. When spades turn out to be 3-3, you have ten tricks without needing the club finesse.

Notes : (1) Knowing from the bidding that South figures to have only two spades, a thoughtful West might play the ♠Q on the second round of spades. If that persuades South that West has Q-J-x in spades, South might switch to the club finesse and so fail.
(2) If declarer discards a club from dummy on the third diamond, East should play a club when in with the ♠J. Now South has to guess whether the club finesse is necessary before finding out how the majors break. If you decide to discard from a major, keep the length in spades where if things go well you score more tricks.

Hand 16 : Transfer with a weak hand — Coping with a bad break

Dealer West : E-W vulnerable

NORTH
♠ J 10 8 4 3
♡ - - -
◇ 10 7 6 4
♣ Q 7 5 2

WEST
♠ K Q
♡ A K 6 2
◇ A K Q J
♣ 9 8 3

EAST
♠ 9 7 6
♡ J 10 9 5 4 3
◇ 8 2
♣ 10 6

SOUTH
♠ A 5 2
♡ Q 8 7
◇ 9 5 3
♣ A K J 4

WEST	NORTH	EAST	SOUTH
2NT	Pass	3◇	Pass
4♡	Pass	Pass	Pass

Bidding : West should open 2NT despite the weakness in clubs. There is no other opening bid which can describe the shape and the strength as accurately as 2NT. Take your chances!

East transfers to hearts with the intention of passing 3♡. East should not pass 2NT. On a spade lead and return West has no more than seven tricks against competent defense.

After the 3◇ transfer, West should super-accept with 4♡. West has a maximum 2NT, 4-card heart support and a doubleton outside as ruffing potential.

Lead : Jack of spades. Prefer the top of a near sequence to leading from a suit headed by one or two honors.

Recommended play : East might well wish West loads of luck as dummy is revealed. South wins the ace of spades and should cash the top clubs. If South plays a third club, this is ruffed in dummy. A heart to the ace reveals the bad news. Needing to return to dummy to take the heart finesse, declarer plays ◇A, ◇K and ruffs the third diamond. The jack of hearts is led and if South plays low, so does declarer.

Notes : (1) At trick 1 it is clear West began with ♠ K-Q. Even if West did not drop an honor, South should shift to clubs. If South fails to cash the clubs early, West can discard club losers on the diamond winners.
(2) Normally 4♡ would be child's play. If trumps were 2-1 (about 78% of the time), declarer could just draw trumps and claim. If South cashed two clubs and then led a diamond or a spade, West would reach dummy by ruffing a club. If South had five diamonds and two clubs, making declarer ruff the club in dummy would almost certainly defeat the contract.

CHAPTER 5

2♣ CHECKBACK

One of the most severe problems in standard methods is the lack of invitational bids after a 1NT rebid. In most systems the only invitation is 2NT whether or not the hand is suitable for no-trumps. Take a sequence such as :

WEST	EAST
1◇	1♠
1NT	?

In most systems a rebid of 2♣/2◇/2♡/2♠ here is not forcing and not necessarily even encouraging. Jumps to the three-level are forcing and that leaves just 2NT for the invitational range. Thus responder's new suit rebids have a wide range, c. 6-11 points. After the above start, what should East do with :

(a)	♠ J 10 8 7 6	or	(b)	♠ A J 8 7 6
	♡ A J 8 5			♡ K Q 5 4
	◇ 9 3			◇ 7 2
	♣ 4 2			♣ 9 8

On (a) you figure 2♡ or 2♠ should be a decent partscore. On (b) you have genuine game prospects if a fit in either major exists and partner is not a hopeless minimum. If you rebid 2♡ with both of these, when does opener know when to give up and when to push on? The range for a 2♡ rebid of 6-11 is just too wide. If opener has a fit in hearts and raises to 3♡, you may be too high on (a) and if opener passes 2♡, you may miss a game on (b).

It is not satisfactory to rebid 2NT with (b). With a minimum opener may pass and you may miss a better and safer spot in either major. The answer is that hand (a) wants to sign off at the two-level and hand (b) wants to make an invitational bid and show both majors.

Even when responder does not have a second suit a raise to 2NT can leave you in an inferior spot.

WEST	W	E	EAST
♠ Q J 8	1◇	1♠	♠ K 9 7 5 2
♡ A 6 4	1NT	2NT	♡ Q 5
◇ K 8 7 2	?		◇ Q J 5
♣ Q J 3			♣ K 8 7

Where West has enough to bid on to game, West can bid 3♠ en route to show the 3-card support and give East the choice of 3NT or 4♠. When West is minimum, West passes 2NT. That is what West should do on the given hand with just 13 points and flat distribution.

Which contract would you like to reach with these cards? A spade partscore is best, making nine tricks most of the time. It is not too hard to imagine 2NT failing. On a heart lead, even if the ♡Q scores, you could easily lose three heart tricks and three aces. Even if 2NT makes, spades will usually score better.

The 2♣ Checkback

A useful solution to this problem is responder's 2♣ rebid after opener's 1NT. The 2♣ rebid says, 'I have invitational values. Tell me more about your hand.' Even if the opening bid was 1♣, responder's 2♣ rebid is 'checkback' and not a mere preference.

Other suit bids at the two-level are weak and deny the values to invite game. For example :

WEST	EAST	2♣ = checkback
1♣	1♠	2◇ = choice of partscores
1NT	?	2♡ = choice of partscores
		2♠ = sign off

Jumps to the three-level are still game forcing.

Replying to 2♣ Checkback

There are two popular methods :

1. Bids at the two-level show a minimum opening, bids at the three-level show a maximum. Opener bids the cheapest feature in each case.

2. Opener is given three divisions for the 1NT rebid :

   2◇ = absolutely minimum, a rock-bottom opening
   2♡/2♠/2NT = reasonable values
   3-level rebids = maximum values

For a 1NT rebid in the 12-14 zone, this would translate into :

   2◇ = 12 points (and 11s, if that is your whim)
   2♡/2♠/2NT = 13 points (and very good 12s)
   3-level rebids = 14 points

Method 1 works well after a 1◇ opening as 2◇ allows opener to show a minimum with five diamonds. Other than that, method 2 works better as long as the partners' memory can manage the three ranges.

Examples featuring Method 2 :

WEST	W	E	EAST
♠ Q J 8	1◇	1♠	♠ K 9 7 5 2
♡ A 6 4	1NT	2♣	♡ Q 5
◇ K 8 7 2	2◇	2♠	◇ Q J 5
♣ Q 6 3	Pass		♣ K 8 7

2◇ = absolutely minimum 1NT rebid.

WEST	W	E	EAST
♠ Q J 8	1◇	1♠	♠ K 9 7 5 2
♡ A 8 6 4	1NT	2♣	♡ Q 5
◇ K 8 7 2	2♡	2♠	◇ Q J 5
♣ Q J	Pass		♣ K 8 7

2♡ = 13 points with 4 hearts.

WEST	W	E	EAST
♠ Q J 8	1◇	1♠	♠ K 9 7 5 2
♡ A 6 4	1NT	2♣	♡ Q 5
◇ K 8 7 2	2♠	Pass	◇ Q J 5
♣ Q J 3			♣ K 8 7

2♠ shows 13 points and three spades, and denies four hearts.

WEST	W	E	EAST
♠ A 8 3	1◇	1♠	♠ K 9 7 5 2
♡ K 10 4 2	1NT	2♣	♡ Q 5
◇ K 8 7 2	3♡	3♠	◇ Q J 5
♣ A 4	4♠	Pass	♣ K 8 7

3♡ shows 14 points and four hearts.

If responder wants to go to game after a two-level rebid, responder needs to jump to the three-level :

WEST	W	E	EAST
♠ Q J 8	1◇	1♠	♠ K 9 7 5 2
♡ A 6 4 2	1NT	2♣	♡ K 5
◇ K 8 7 2	2♡	3♠	◇ Q J 5
♣ Q J	4♠	Pass	♣ K 8 7

2♡ = 13 points and 4 hearts. 3♠ = 5 spades and forcing, offering opener the choice of 4♠ or 3NT. 2♠ over 2♡ would have been droppable.

♠ A 4	W	E	♠ K 9 7
♡ J 9 8	1♣	1♡	♡ Q 5 4 3
◇ A 10 2	1NT	2♣	◇ Q J 5
♣ A J 9 4 2	3♣	3NT	♣ K 8 7

3♣ = 14 points with 5 clubs.

Given that responder will always invite game with 11 points, opener need not upgrade such 14-point hands to open a 15-18 1NT.

Jumps to the three-level

Responder's jump rebid to the three-level in a new suit shows a 5-4 pattern and is forcing to game. This allows opener to show weak support or strong support for either suit (as indicated in Chapter 3).

The jump rebid in opener's minor suit shows support but perhaps only a 4-card major.

WEST	EAST	
1♣	1♡	East's 3♣ is forcing to game
1NT	3♣ ...	and shows 4+ clubs. East may have 4 hearts or 5 hearts.

Opener's first priority is to show 3-card support for the hearts with 3♡. If responder does not wish to play in hearts, responder can now rebid 3NT or revert to opener's minor.

Without support for hearts, opener may bid 3NT with strength in the unbid suits, make a stopper bid in one of the unbid suits or pursue a slam in clubs with a raise to 4♣ or a cue bid of 4◇.

The jump rebid in responder's suit

WEST	EAST	
1♣	1♠	East's 3♠ is a game-force with
1NT	3♠ ...	a 5+ suit. Opener supports with three spades, else rebids 3NT.

Responder's 2NT rebid

Responder's 2NT requires opener to bid 3♣

This enables responder to sign off in clubs :

WEST	W	E	EAST
♠ Q 8	1♣	1♠	♠ K 9 7 5
♡ A 6 4 3	1NT	2NT	♡ 8
◇ K Q 2	3♣	Pass	◇ 7 6 3
♣ Q 9 7 2			♣ K 8 6 4 3

You may fail in 3♣ but it is a better bet than 1NT.

The loss of playing in 2♣ is an illusion. The opponents would not have sold out to 2♣ and it is hard to imagine that you would be able to defeat 2♡.

WEST	W	E	EAST
♠ 8 3	1◇	1♠	♠ K Q 7 5
♡ A J 4	1NT	2NT	♡ 8
◇ K Q 7 6 2	3♣	Pass	◇ 5 4
♣ Q 9 7			♣ J 8 6 4 3 2

You may fail in 3♣ but what better spot is there?

Expert methods

Since the 2NT rebid is not needed to invite game (all invitations travel through 2♣), responder can use the 2NT rebid for other game-going hands. If responder does not pass 3♣, the auction becomes game-forcing. Rebidding in responder's suit shows a 6-card or longer suit. This allows responder to check whether opener rebid 1NT with a singleton.

WEST	W	E	EAST
♠ 3	1♣	1♠	♠ A J 8 7 5 2
♡ Q 9 4 2	1NT	2NT	♡ K 5
◇ A K Q	3♣	3♠	◇ 7 4 3
♣ Q 9 7 4 2	3NT	Pass	♣ A K

3♠ = game force with 6+ spades
3NT = singleton spade

Over 3♠, opener should rebid 3NT with a singleton spade, raise to 4♠ with a weak hand and make a cue bid with a decent hand. Over 3NT, responder may choose to pass or sign off in 4♠. If still interested in slam, a new suit by responder over 3NT is a cue bid and asks opener to cue bid in return.

After responder's 2NT rebid and opener's forced 3♣ reply, a new suit rebid shows a 5-card suit.

WEST	W	E	EAST
♠ J 3	1◇	1♠	♠ K Q 7 5 2
♡ A 9	1NT	2NT	♡ K 8 6 3 2
◇ A Q 7 6 2	3♣	3♡	◇ 5
♣ J 10 7 4	3NT	Pass	♣ A Q

3♡ = 5-5 at least in the majors

Opener would choose a major suit with 3+ support.

Responder's new suit rebid at the two-level in a higher-ranking suit

WEST	EAST	
1◇	1♡	East's 2♠ is best played as
1NT	2♠ ...	forcing to game and suggests a three-suited hand.

Opener will not have four spades to support and the best rebid is usually 2NT. Responder can then rebid 3♣ or 3◇ to show the third suit, thereby highlighting the problem for 3NT as responder will have a singleton or a void in the remaining suit. Opener bids 3NT if strong in the short suit, else chooses one of responder's suits. Of course, if responder continues with 3♠ over 2NT, responder is showing a 6-5 pattern in hearts-spades.

EXERCISES FOR 2♣ CHECKBACK

A. WEST : 1◊, EAST : 1♠, WEST : 1NT. What should East rebid with each of these hands?

1. ♠ A J 9 7 2	2. ♠ A J 9 7 2	3. ♠ Q J 9 7 3 2	4. ♠ Q J 9 7 3 2	5. ♠ J 10 3 2
♡ Q J 5 3	♡ A Q 5 3	♡ K 9 8	♡ K 9 8	♡ A J 5
◊ 7	◊ 7 6	◊ 3 2	◊ 3 2	◊ K Q 3 2
♣ 8 7 4	♣ 8 7	♣ 7 5	♣ A 4	♣ A 4

B. The bidding has started 1♣ : 1♡, 1NT : 2♣. What should opener do next?

1. ♠ A Q J	2. ♠ 6 2	3. ♠ K 8 7	4. ♠ K 8 7	5. ♠ 9 8 2
♡ 8 5 3	♡ Q 7 4	♡ Q J 2	♡ A 2	♡ J 9
◊ K 5	◊ A 5 3	◊ A K 2	◊ A K 5	◊ A J 3
♣ Q 9 8 4 2	♣ K Q J 10 2	♣ 8 7 5 3	♣ 10 9 6 3 2	♣ A K J 9 2

C. The bidding has started 1◊ : 1♠, 1NT : 3♡. What should opener do next with these hands?

1. ♠ 7 3	2. ♠ A 7	3. ♠ J 5	4. ♠ A K 5	5. ♠ 9 7 6
♡ 6 4 2	♡ A Q 7 5	♡ K Q 7 5	♡ K 9 2	♡ K 3
◊ K Q J 9	◊ A 10 9 2	◊ K J 8 2	◊ A 10 4 3	◊ K Q 8 7
♣ A K J 2	♣ 8 7 3	♣ Q J 4	♣ 10 9 4	♣ K Q 6 5

PARTNERSHIP BIDDING : How should the following hands be bid? West is the dealer each time.

SET 9 — WEST	SET 9 — EAST	SET 10 — WEST	SET 10 — EAST
1. ♠ 9 7 4	1. ♠ 10 6 5 3 2	1. ♠ A 10 3	1. ♠ K Q 4 2
♡ K 8 6 3	♡ A 7 5 2	♡ A J 10	♡ K Q 7 4 2
◊ A Q	◊ K 8	◊ K Q 4	◊ J 8 6
♣ A 7 6 2	♣ 4 3	♣ 9 7 5 3	♣ 2
2. ♠ K Q 8	2. ♠ A 7 5 2	2. ♠ A K 5	2. ♠ 7 4
♡ 9 6 3	♡ Q 2	♡ 6 2	♡ K 9 7 5 3
◊ A 9 8 7	◊ K Q 6 4	◊ A J 9	◊ K Q 2
♣ Q J 5	♣ 10 6 2	♣ J 10 6 4 2	♣ A Q 5
3. ♠ 8 6	3. ♠ K 5 2	3. ♠ 8 5 3	3. ♠ A Q 10 7
♡ A K 6 3	♡ Q 8	♡ A Q 7 2	♡ 6 3
◊ 8	◊ A Q 7 4 3	◊ Q 8 5	◊ 4
♣ 8 7 5 4 3 2	♣ K 9 6	♣ A J 4	♣ 10 9 7 6 5 2
4. ♠ J 9 8 7 4	4. ♠ A 5 2	4. ♠ 10 5 3	4. ♠ A 4 2
♡ J 9 2	♡ K 7 5	♡ Q 7 3	♡ K J 8 2
◊ K Q 8 7	◊ J 5 3	◊ A 6 2	◊ Q J 9 7 5
♣ 2	♣ A Q 8 4	♣ K Q J 3	♣ 4
5. ♠ A 5 2	5. ♠ J 9 8 7 4	5. ♠ A 3	5. ♠ Q J 9 7 4 2
♡ K 7 5	♡ A 9 2	♡ K 6 2	♡ A Q 8 4 3
◊ K 5 3	◊ A Q 8 7	◊ A J 7 3	◊ 9
♣ A 9 8 4	♣ 2	♣ 9 8 6 3	♣ 4
6. ♠ K J 8 6 2	6. ♠ A 3	6. ♠ Q 8 6	6. ♠ A 7 5 3
♡ K J 9 7 5	♡ Q 6 2	♡ Q 10 6 4	♡ 5
◊ 8	◊ K Q J 2	◊ A J	◊ K 3 2
♣ Q 2	♣ 9 8 6 4	♣ K J 5 3	♣ A Q 6 4 2

PLAY HANDS ON 2♣ CHECKBACK
(These hands can be made up by using pages 160-167)

Hand 17 : Discarding losers — Card combination technique

Dealer North : Nil vulnerable

	NORTH			
	♠ A K 3			
	♡ 10 3			
	◇ A K 8 6 2			
	♣ 7 5 4			

WEST		EAST
♠ Q 7		♠ J 10 6 5 2
♡ K 8 7 5		♡ Q
◇ J 9 4 3		◇ 10 7 5
♣ Q J 8		♣ K 10 6 3

	SOUTH
	♠ 9 8 4
	♡ A J 9 6 4 2
	◇ Q
	♣ A 9 2

WEST	NORTH	EAST	SOUTH
	1◇	Pass	1♡
Pass	1NT	Pass	2♣
Pass	3◇	Pass	4♡
Pass	Pass	Pass	

Bidding : With a poor 11 HCP, South is not strong enough to insist on game and so uses 2♣ Checkback. North's 3◇ shows 14 points and five diamonds. South can now be confident that North has at least two hearts. With a 3-1-5-4, North would have rebid 3♣. A rebid of 3♠ by North is also feasible on the actual deal. This denies three hearts, shows a spade stopper (not four spades since North would have bid 1♠ over 1♡ with that) and indicates concern about the clubs.

Lead : Queen of clubs. The other choices are far more dangerous.

Recommended play : South wins with the ♣A, cashes the queen of diamonds and crosses to dummy with a spade. Two clubs are discarded on the ace and king of diamonds. Now it is time to tackle trumps. The 3 of hearts is led from dummy and South captures East's queen. A low heart is played from hand towards dummy's ten. If West wins this and leads a spade, take the ace, ruff a club and draw trumps.

If West ducks the second heart, ruff a club and lead the jack of hearts. Later ruff a club to hand and draw the last trump with your 9 of hearts. You make 11 tricks, losing one trump and one spade.

Notes : (1) It is an error to lead the 10 of hearts on the first round of trumps and on this layout would create an extra trump loser. (Do not feel bad if you did this. A world famous international made this very mistake in a world championship and thus lost a makeable slam.)
(2) If East were to follow low on the first heart, finesse the 9. If this loses, later cross to dummy with a spade and lead the 10 of hearts for a second trump finesse.

Hand 18 : Reply to 2♣ with a maximum — Catering for the normal break

Dealer East : N-S vulnerable

	NORTH
	♠ J 10 8 4
	♡ A 9 5 4
	◇ J 9 2
	♣ J 3

WEST		EAST
♠ A K Q 7 2		♠ 6 5
♡ Q 7		♡ J 8 2
◇ 6 5		◇ A K Q 4
♣ 10 7 4 2		♣ A 9 8 6

	SOUTH
	♠ 9 3
	♡ K 10 6 3
	◇ 10 8 7 3
	♣ K Q 5

WEST	NORTH	EAST	SOUTH
		1◇	Pass
1♠	Pass	1NT	Pass
2♣	Pass	3NT	All pass

Bidding : West's 2♣ Checkback invites game and East's 3NT shows 14 points without 4 hearts and without 3 spades. East might bid 3♣ rather than 3NT as the hearts are not so strong but it rarely pays to tell the opponents too much. With a singleton spade or no high card at all in hearts, 3♣ would be the preferred rebid.

Lead : 3 of hearts. It is true that the heart lead does not work out well for the defense as it sets up a heart trick for declarer. Nevertheless it is normal to lead an unbid suit and it is usually preferable to lead an unbid major to an unbid minor.

Recommended play : North wins with the ♡A and returns the 4 of hearts. South wins with the king and plays a third heart. It should be clear to East from the cards played by South and North that the hearts are breaking 4-4. East can therefore guard against a 4-2 break in spades by ducking a spade at trick 4. North wins and a heart is cashed but declarer has nine tricks.

Notes : East must decide whether to cash the spades from the top and hope that they are 3-3 or duck a spade to ensure the contract if the spades are 4-2. Playing for spades 3-3 (36%) makes ten tricks and a top about 1/3 of the time, and fails, for a bottom, about 2/3 of the time. Ducking a spade works better when spades are 4-2, about 50% of the time. In a normal contract if the chance for an overtrick is below 50%, take the line which offers the best chance to make your contract.

Hand 19 : Discarding losers — Playing for overtricks

Dealer South : E-W vulnerable

NORTH
♠ A K J 9 6
♡ 8 6 2
◇ 5
♣ K J 3 2

WEST
♠ 7 2
♡ 10 5 4
◇ K Q 10 6
♣ 10 8 7 5

EAST
♠ Q 8 5
♡ K Q J 7
◇ J 9 3
♣ 9 6 4

SOUTH
♠ 10 4 3
♡ A 9 3
◇ A 8 7 4 2
♣ A Q

WEST	NORTH	EAST	SOUTH
			1◇
Pass	1♠	Pass	1NT
Pass	2♣	Pass	3◇
Pass	3♠	Pass	4♠
Pass	Pass	Pass	

Bidding : North has a strong hand and it would not be a serious error to insist on game. However, there are plenty of unsuitable minimum hands for opener which would make game unattractive. If South bid 2◇ over 2♣, North could still bid 3♠ as a strong invitation to game.

3◇ shows 14 points with 5 diamonds. 3♠ shows five spades.

Lead : King of hearts. Wouldn't it be nice if all our opening leads were as easy as this?

Recommended play : Win with the ♡A, cash ♣A and ♣Q, followed by ◇A and a diamond ruff. The ♣K is cashed and a heart discarded from dummy. Next comes the jack of clubs. If East ruffs with the queen of spades or does not ruff at all, discard the last heart from dummy. You can ruff a diamond to hand, ruff a heart, play a spade to hand and ruff your last heart. This line brings in twelve tricks.

Notes : (1) At rubber bridge you would win ♡A and tackle trumps at once. Playing on clubs could cost the contract if a defender ruffs the first or second round of clubs.
(2) If trumps are played early and East comes in with the ♠Q, two hearts are cashed and declarer makes just ten tricks. At matchpoints this would be almost certainly a bottom score. If overtricks are readily available, you must take them.
(3) If East dares to ruff the fourth club with the 5 of spades, declarer may make just eleven tricks. If declarer overruffs with the ten and concedes a heart, East wins and plays a third diamond. North ruffs a heart in dummy and may misguess spades for a second loser. Declarer also loses two tricks if declarer discards dummy's last heart instead of overruffing East. The diamond return is ruffed, a heart is ruffed, a spade to hand is followed by another heart ruff, but the fourth diamond from dummy promotes East's ♠Q.

Hand 20 : Game try with a flat 12 count — Card combination — Timing

Dealer West : Both vulnerable

NORTH
♠ K 7
♡ 9 7 5 3
◇ K 8 3
♣ 8 7 4 3

WEST
♠ 8 4 3
♡ Q 8 6 4
◇ J 6
♣ A K Q J

EAST
♠ J 9 6 2
♡ A K 10
◇ A 7 2
♣ 9 6 2

SOUTH
♠ A Q 10 5
♡ J 2
◇ Q 10 9 5 4
♣ 10 5

WEST	NORTH	EAST	SOUTH
1♣	Pass	1♠	Pass
1NT	Pass	2♣	Pass
2♡	Pass	3NT	All pass

Bidding : East's flat 12 would be worth an invitational 2NT in standard methods. Using 2♣ Checkback with three divisions for opener's rebid, East plans to rebid 2NT opposite a 2◇ absolute minimum. West's 2♡ shows the middle range, 13 points, with four hearts. It does not deny three spades. Opposite 13, East should be prepared to take a shot at game. You will not always be successful but with 25 HCP together, 3NT is about a 50% chance and that makes it acceptable.

Lead : 3 of diamonds. Second choice, a club. Diamonds is the only unbid suit but West's clubs need not be genuine.

Recommended play : Win with the ace of diamonds and cash the ace and king of hearts. When the jack of hearts drops, cash the 10 of hearts, come to hand with a club and cash the ♡Q, followed by the clubs.

Notes : (1) It is mildly risky to duck the first diamond, although if North has led from K-Q-x-x, you would score the jack of diamonds. On the actual deal, South would win with the queen of diamonds and if South switched to the 5 of spades, the defense could collect four spade tricks.
(2) It would be an error to cash the clubs before testing the hearts. After four rounds of clubs, there is no way to unravel the hearts to make four tricks when the jack falls singleton or doubleton.
(3) If the jack of hearts did not fall on the first two rounds of hearts, declarer can then run the clubs and hope the hearts are 3-3 or that an opponent discards a heart on the clubs.

CHAPTER 6

SPLINTERS

How do you treat the sequence 1♡ : 4◇? Or 1♣ : 3♠? In standard methods these are played as pre-empts but such a treatment is not very profitable. Firstly, the occurrence is rare and to pre-empt after partner has opened is seldom useful and rarely necessary. To pre-empt beyond 3NT can be downright foolish.

For these reasons many tournament players have assigned a different meaning to the double jump in a new suit after partner has opened the bidding. Known as 'splinters' because they indicate the tiniest part of the hand, these jumps show good trump support (normally at least four trumps), sufficient high card values for game and a singleton or a void in the suit bid. The strength will vary according to what has been shown so far.

Responder's immediate splinters to a major
1♡ : 3♠/4♣/4◇ and 1♠ : 4♣/4◇/4♡

Expectancy is 4+ trumps, 11+ HCP and a void or a singleton in the suit bid. Opener should consider the splinter as a short suit try for a slam. Opposite a singleton, the ace is a good card but the other honors are wasted ('duplication'). For the following layouts, imagine that a major suit is trumps.

Situation (1)		Situation (2)	
◇ J x x	◇ K Q x	◇ J x x	◇ A x x
♣ x	♣ A x x	♣ x	♣ K Q x

In (1) the singleton is opposite the ace and no other high cards. The partnership should lose only one trick in the minors. In (2), with the singleton opposite K-Q-x the partnership could easily have three minor losers if the defenders start on the diamonds early.

Opposite a void, even the ace is often wasted.

Situation (3)		Situation (4)	
◇ K Q J x	◇ A x x	◇ K Q J x	◇ x x x
♣ - - -	♣ x x x	♣ - - -	♣ A x x

In (3) with nothing useful opposite the void, there are no minor suit losers. In (4) you have to lose a diamond. The ♣A contributes almost nothing.

The best holding facing the short suit is three or four low cards. That allows you to ruff two or three times to eliminate two or three losers. A doubleton facing the singleton is not so great since you can ruff only once and a singleton facing a singleton is no asset at all. Again, this is known as 'duplication'. A 5-card holding facing the singleton can also have problems. There may not be enough trumps in dummy to ruff all the losers in a long suit, particularly if the opponents start leading trumps. Opposite a singleton A-x-x, A-x-x-x, x-x-x and x-x-x-x are excellent holdings and opposite a void, x-x-x or x-x-x-x are best.

After responder's immediate splinter, opener should sign off in game with a minimum opening hand unless you have one of the excellent holdings opposite responder's short suit. Opener should look for slam with a minimum opening if opener has an excellent holding facing the shortage, or with sufficient extra values to compensate for the duplication opposite the shortage.

WEST	W	E	EAST
♠ A Q 8 6 3	1♠	4◇	♠ K 9 7 5 2
♡ A 6	?		♡ K 5 3
◇ K 7 6			◇ 5
♣ 6 3 2			♣ A Q 8 4

West should sign off in 4♠. West has a minimum opening and the ◇K is wasted. If the club finesse fails, there are three losers.

WEST	W	E	EAST
♠ A Q 8 6 3	1♠	4◇	♠ K 9 7 5 2
♡ A 6	?		♡ K 5 3
◇ 6 3 2			◇ 5
♣ K 7 6			♣ A Q 8 4

West should move towards 6♠ which is an excellent slam. Although holding only a minimum opening, West has an excellent holding opposite the diamond shortage. When bidding for slam, you may ask with 4NT or cue bid (see chapters 12-15).

WEST	W	E	EAST
♠ A Q 8 6 3	1♠	4◇	♠ K 9 7 5 2
♡ A 6	?		♡ K 5 3
◇ K Q 2			◇ 5
♣ K 6 3			♣ A Q 8 7

West should move on to 6♠. Although there is severe duplication in diamonds, West has much more than a minimum opening. In such cases, ask yourself 'If I remove the wasted high cards opposite the shortage, would I be looking for a slam?' If after removing the duplication you still have a decent opening hand, the answer should be yes. Here if West considers the ◇K-Q-x as ◇x-x-x, West still has a sound opening and with an ideal diamond holding, would certainly be looking for slam.

WEST	W	E	EAST
♠ A Q 8 6 3	1♠	4◇	♠ K 9 7 5 2
♡ A 6	4♠...		♡ K J 3
◇ K 7 6			◇ 5
♣ 9 3 2			♣ A K Q 8

Even if opener signs off, responder may push on with sufficient extra values. The minimum would be 16 HCP or a 5-loser hand. If worse than that, responder should respect opener's signoff. Here with great support, 16 HCP and 5 losers, East should continue with 4NT and finish in 6♠.

Responder's immediate splinter to a minor
1♣ : 3◊/3♡/3♠ *and* 1◊ : 3♡/3♠/4♣

Expectancy is 5+ trumps, no 4-card major, at least 13 HCP and a singleton or void in the suit bid.

With strong support for a major, you want to play in the major suit game. With strong support for a minor, there remains the question of whether you would be better off in 3NT. Except for the rarely used 1◊ : 4♣ sequence, the splinter responses to a minor do not commit the partnership to a minor suit contract. If opener is very strong in responder's short suit (at least a double stopper), opener should choose 3NT.

WEST	W	E	EAST
♠ Q 6 3	1♣	3♡	♠ A 7 5
♡ K Q J 2	?		♡ 8
◊ J 2			◊ A K 5 4
♣ A 7 5 4			♣ K 8 6 3 2

With such strong hearts facing the shortage, West should choose 3NT which is not only more likely to succeed than 5♣ but also scores more.

If opener does not fancy 3NT, opener may treat the splinter as a short suit try for slam. Again with an ideal holding opposite the shortage, slam is a good bet.

WEST	W	E	EAST
♠ K Q 3	1♣	3♡	♠ A 7 5
♡ 9 7 3 2	?		♡ 8
◊ J 2			◊ A K 5 4
♣ A Q J 4			♣ K 8 6 3 2

With the ideal holding in hearts, West bids 4♣ indicating no desire for no-trumps and slam interest in clubs. It is best to treat the splinter as game-forcing and not treat 4♣ here as a signoff. With good controls, East here should bid 4NT and finish in 6♣.

It is even possible to suggest a contract in some other suit :

WEST	W	E	EAST
♠ K Q 6 3	1♣	3♡	♠ A 7 5
♡ K 5 2	?		♡ 8
◊ Q 3			◊ A K 5 4
♣ Q J 5 4			♣ K 8 6 3 2

Sometimes one stopper opposite the singleton will do for 3NT but most of the time it is too risky. Here West can bid 3♠ to suggest 4♠ on a 4-3 fit and East should raise to 4♠. The 4-3 fit is reasonable if the short hand is doing the ruffing. Here 5♣ is safe enough but 4♠ will succeed most of the time for a better score.

Opener's splinter rebid after a major response

When opener has enough to raise responder's major to game, opener can also use the splinter structure. For example :

WEST	EAST	
1♣	1♠	West has enough for 1♣ : 1♠,
4◊ . . .		4♠ and has a singleton or void in diamonds.

The same would apply to sequences like 1♣ : 1♡, 3♠ or 1◊ : 1♠, 4♡, and so on. Responder can sign off in game or head for a slam.

With a balanced hand of 19-20 points with support for responder's major, opener should travel via the 2NT rebid. For example :

WEST	W	E	EAST
♠ A 4 3	1♣	1♡	♠ K 9
♡ K Q 9 8	2NT	3NT	♡ A 5 4 3
◊ A 2	4♡	Pass	◊ J 5 3
♣ A Q 9 4			♣ 8 7 5 2

Opener's 2NT shows 19-20 points and is forcing to game. Removing 3NT to 4♡ shows the 4-card support. Naturally if East rebid other than 3NT opener would show the heart support then.

It thus follows that sequences like 1♣ : 1♡, 4♡ or 1◊ : 1♠, 4♠ will be neither balanced nor have a singleton or a void. The pattern must be 5-4-2-2.

WEST	W	E	EAST
♠ A 4	1♣	1♡	♠ K 9 7
♡ K Q 9 8	4♡	Pass	♡ A 5 4 3
◊ 10 2			◊ J 5 3
♣ A K J 9 4			♣ 8 7 2

After the auction has started 1♠ : 2♡, a rebid of 3♣ or 3◊ by opener is forcing and so it is sensible to use a jump to 4♣ or 4◊ as a splinter raise of hearts. The same would apply after responder's jump-shift. Opener's jump in a new suit would be a splinter.

It is also conceivable for opener to make a splinter with the second rebid.

WEST	W	E	EAST
♠ K Q 6 3	1♡	2♣	♠ A 7 5 4
♡ A K 9 8 3 2	2♡	2♠	♡ 6
◊ 2	4◊...		◊ J 8 7
♣ J 8			♣ A K Q 3 2

Too weak to reverse, West rebids 2♡ but over 2♠, West shows the good support and diamond shortage with the jump to 4◊. East-West should now reach 6♠.

Opener's splinter rebids after a minor response

After 1♣ : 1◊, opener's jump rebid to 3♡ or 3♠ has little value as a natural bid and can be harnessed as a splinter with 4-card diamond support.

After a two-level response in a minor, you need to weigh up the value of a jump shift as a natural rebid or as a splinter. For example :

WEST	EAST	
1♠	2♣	In all standard systems, change
3♡ . . .		of suit is played as forcing after a two-level response.

After 1♠ : 2♣ a rebid of 2♡ is therefore forcing and a natural jump to 3♡ is used to show a good hand with 5-5 in the majors. The splinter jump to 3♡ would show at least 4-card support for the minor, 16+ HCP and a singleton or void in hearts. You cannot have both and must decide which method to play. These 3-level splinters avoid the jump to 4-minor on hands too good for 3-minor and still leave open the option for 3NT.

Responder's splinter rebid

Where opener has rebid with a change of suit, the only suit left will be the fourth suit. A simple bid of the fourth suit is played as conventional and forcing. A jump in the fourth suit is played as natural and game forcing.

WEST	EAST	
1◊	1♠	East's 3♡ shows game values
2♣	3♡ ...	and 5-5 in the majors. As East has no natural 2♡ bid available, it is

important to use the jump here as natural and not as a splinter.

Where opener's rebid is in the suit opened, change of suit is natural and forcing and so a jump in a new suit can sensibly be played as a splinter. If opener's suit is a major, the splinter will show just 3-card support. With better support responder could have splintered on the first round.

WEST	W	E	EAST
♠ A 6 3	1♡	2♣	♠ J
♡ K Q 6 5 4 2	2♡	?	♡ A 7 3
◊ K 6 3			◊ A Q 8 4
♣ 2			♣ A K 10 8 5

How should East continue? The splinter jump to 3♠ expresses East's values well : 3-card support for hearts, short in spades and too strong for a mere jump to 4♡. After the 3♠ splinter East-West have a firm basis to reach 7♡.

If opener's suit is a minor, responder may have genuine support for the minor :

WEST	W	E	EAST
♠ 3	1♣	1♠	♠ K Q 7 5 2
♡ K 5 2	2♣	3◊	♡ Q 8 4
◊ A K 3	3NT		◊ 2
♣ Q J 5 4 3 2			♣ A K 8 6

East's 3◊ shows club support, short diamonds and game values. With strong diamonds, West chooses 3NT. Although 5♣ will make, 3NT has no problems and will often score an overtrick.

Expert methods

Splinters after overcalls

Just as you can splinter after an opening, so you splinter after an overcall to show good high card strength as well as the support and shortage requirements. A slam is unlikely after the opponents have opened but it is not impossible if there is no duplication facing the shortage.

WEST	EAST
♠ K Q J 6 3	♠ A 7 5 4
♡ K 5 2	♡ Q J 8
◊ 3	◊ A K 5 4 2
♣ A 8 5 4	♣ 2

SOUTH	WEST	NORTH	EAST
1♣	1♠	Pass	4♣
Dble	4NT	Pass	5♡
Pass	6♠	All pass	

With a strong overcall and an ideal holding in East's known short suit, West heads for slam.

Splinters after powerful two openings

This is a very fruitful area for splinters. After a negative response to an artificial strong opening of 2♣ or 2◊, responder can show useful values in support of opener's suit rebid plus the shortage. This may often be enough to encourage opener to head for a slam.

WEST	W	E	EAST
♠ A K Q 6 3 2	2♣	2◊	♠ 8 7 5 4
♡ - - -	2♣	4♣	♡ 8 6 4 3 2
◊ K Q J 3	4♡	5◊	◊ A 7 4
♣ A Q 4	7♠	Pass	♣ 2

After West rebids 2♠, East has a great hand with the 4-card support, the singleton and the ace as well. The jump to 4♣ shows the shortage and now West can see there are no club losers. West cue bids 4♡ to show first round control in hearts and East's 5◊ shows first round control there (see Chapters 14-15 for cue bidding). That is enough for West to bid the grand slam.

WEST	EAST	
2♣	2◊	It follows that if a weak responder
2♠	3♠ ...	simply raises opener's suit, then

either responder has no short suit (the more likely explanation) or has inadequate trump support.

Splinters after a 1NT opening
1NT : 3♣/3◊/3♡/3♠

These sequences are commonly used to show one-suiters with slam interest (see Chapter 2). Some partnerships prefer to use the jumps to the three-level as splinters, indicating concern about 3NT as the best spot. The splinter jump here shows enough for game with a singleton or void in the suit bid. The splinter would deny a 5-card major and the 1NT : 3♠ splinter ought to deny four hearts.

With the short suit well-stopped, opener can bid 3NT without any interest in a major suit contract.

With the danger suit stopped and major suit interest, opener can bid the major first. Without support, responder makes a natural bid. Having already shown the shortage, responder can bid 3NT without support for opener's major.

WEST	W	E	EAST
♠ A K 7 2	1NT	3♡	♠ Q 5
♡ J 8 7	3♠	3NT	♡ 4
◊ A K 3	4♣	5◊	◊ Q J 8 7 6 2
♣ Q 9 5	Pass		♣ A J 8 6

3♡ = 0 or 1 heart, 3♠ suggests spades, 3NT = no support for spades, 4♣ = no interest in 3NT (a bid of 4◊ by West would be sensible, asking East to choose the contract) and East has an easy 5◊.

Playing splinters, the strong single-suiters can be shown via a transfer and raise to the four-level (for the minors) or a 4NT rebid (for the majors). The sequence transfer-to-a-major followed by a jump to 4♣ or 4◊ can be used either as a splinter or for the single-suiter with slam interest.

EXERCISES ON SPLINTERS

A. West has opened 1♡. North passes. What should East bid with each of these hands?

1.	♠ A J 10 7	2.	♠ J 9 7 2	3.	♠ 2	4.	♠ 8	5.	♠ A K Q
	♡ Q J 5 3 2		♡ A Q 5 3		♡ A K 9 8 4		♡ K 9 8		♡ A J 7 5 4
	◇ 7		◇ A K 4 3		◇ A 3 2		◇ K 8 4 3		◇ - - -
	♣ 8 7 4		♣ 7		♣ 9 8 7 5		♣ A K 7 6 3		♣ 10 9 4 3 2

B. The bidding has started 1♠ : 4♣ (splinter). What should opener do next?

1.	♠ A Q J 6 2	2.	♠ A Q J 6 2	3.	♠ A Q J 6 2	4.	♠ K J 8 7 4	5.	♠ A J 9 8 2
	♡ 8 5 3		♡ A 2		♡ 6 2		♡ A 2		♡ K J 9
	◇ K 5		◇ K Q 3		◇ A K		◇ 9 7 3 2		◇ A J 3 2
	♣ Q 9 8		♣ Q J 2		♣ 9 8 6 2		♣ K Q		♣ 2

C. The bidding has started 1♡ : 2◇, 2♡. What should responder do next with these hands?

1.	♠ 7	2.	♠ Q 7 2	3.	♠ 4	4.	♠ 5	5.	♠ 6
	♡ 6 5		♡ Q J 5		♡ K Q 7		♡ K 9 2		♡ K 8 3
	◇ K Q J 9 3		◇ A Q 9 7 6 2		◇ K Q 7 6 2		◇ A K Q J 4		◇ Q J 7 4 2
	♣ A K J 7 2		♣ 5		♣ A 7 6 2		♣ K 10 9 4		♣ A J 6 5

PARTNERSHIP BIDDING : How should the following hands be bid? West is the dealer each time.

SET 11 — WEST	SET 11 — EAST	SET 12 — WEST	SET 12 — EAST
1. ♠ A J 7 4 2	1. ♠ 10 8 6 5 3	1. ♠ A J 5 2	1. ♠ 4
♡ K 8 6 3	♡ A Q 2	♡ K Q 7 5 4	♡ J 9 8 3 2
◇ 3	◇ A K 4 2	◇ A K	◇ Q 8
♣ A 7 6	♣ 5	♣ 8 2	♣ K 9 7 4 3
2. ♠ A J 7 4 2	2. ♠ 10 8 6 5 3	2. ♠ 6	2. ♠ A K 9 7 5
♡ K 8 6 3	♡ A Q 2	♡ 8 5 3	♡ Q
◇ 3	◇ A K 4 2	◇ A K 5	◇ Q 7
♣ K Q 6	♣ 5	♣ A J 10 6 4 2	♣ K 8 7 5 3
3. ♠ K 6	3. ♠ A 9 5 2	3. ♠ 5 3	3. ♠ A K J 7 4
♡ A Q 6 3	♡ K 8 5 4 2	♡ A J 7 2	♡ K Q 8 6 3
◇ A K 5 4 3 2	◇ 8	◇ 5	◇ 9 4
♣ 3	♣ 7 4 2	♣ A K 10 9 7 4	♣ 2
4. ♠ K 6	4. ♠ A 9 5 2	4. ♠ A K Q 6 2	4. ♠ 7 3
♡ A Q 6 3	♡ J 7 5 2	♡ K Q 6 4 3	♡ A J 9 7 2
◇ A K 5 4 3 2	◇ 8	◇ Q 9 2	◇ A 8 4
♣ 3	♣ K 9 8 4	♣ - - -	♣ J 7 4
5. ♠ K J 8 6	5. ♠ A Q 7 4	5. ♠ A K Q 6 2	5. ♠ 7 3
♡ K J	♡ Q 6 2	♡ K Q 6 4 3	♡ A J 9 7 2
◇ A 9 4	◇ 8 7 2	◇ Q 9 2	◇ J 8 4
♣ A Q J 7	♣ K 4 3	♣ - - -	♣ A 7 4
6. ♠ K J 8 6	6. ♠ A Q 7 4 3	6. ♠ A K Q 8 6 3	6. ♠ 9 7 5 2
♡ K 9	♡ Q 6 2	♡ A K Q J	♡ 5 3 2
◇ A 9	◇ J 8 2	◇ - - -	◇ K 9 8 3 2
♣ A Q J 7 2	♣ K 4	♣ A 5 3	♣ 2

PLAY HANDS ON SPLINTERS
(These hands can be made up by using pages 160-167)

Hand 21 : Judging game or slam potential — Setting up a winner for a discard

Dealer North : N-S vulnerable

WEST	NORTH	EAST	SOUTH
	Pass	1♡	Pass
4◊	Pass	4♡	All pass

```
                NORTH
                ♠ 9764
                ♡ ---
                ◊ A9873
                ♣ A1095
WEST                          EAST
♠ A83                         ♠ K52
♡ K9852                       ♡ AJ764
◊ 6                           ◊ QJ42
♣ KJ72                        ♣ Q
                SOUTH
                ♠ QJ10
                ♡ Q103
                ◊ K105
                ♣ 8643
```

Bidding : West's 4◊ splinter shows a strong hand (normally 11 HCP or more) with 4+ support for opener and a singleton or void in diamonds. The splinter is best considered as a short suit try for slam. East has a poor holding in the splinter suit with the Q-J of diamonds wasted opposite the singleton. The ace is the only good card opposite a singleton. The diamond duplication effectively reduces East's opening bid from 13 HCP to 10 HCP including a singleton queen and so East signs off in 4♡. If West had a very powerful hand, West could still bid on.

Lead : Queen of spades. Top of sequence is always attractive. A trump lead also appeals on splinter auctions but not from Q-10-x.

Recommended play : Win with the ♠K in hand and lead a low heart to the king. The bad break reveals a loser in trumps. A low club is led from dummy. If North rises with the ♣A and returns a spade, win with dummy's ace and discard a spade loser on the king of clubs. Cash the ♡A and concede just three tricks, a heart, a diamond and a club.

Notes : (1) If North ducks the club from dummy (and it could be right to do so . . . suppose East were void in clubs), East wins with the queen. Now declarer can score an overtrick. Play a diamond to make dummy void. Win the spade return with the ace and lead the king of clubs. When North plays the ace, you ruff, cash the ace of hearts and ruff a diamond in dummy. Discard your spade loser on the jack of clubs and cross ruff from there. The defense comes to just one heart and one diamond.

(2) If North does duck the first club, it is important that declarer does not cash the ace of hearts before giving up a diamond. Otherwise, South could cash the ♡Q and draw a third round of trumps. This would prevent declarer scoring three ruffs in dummy and three in hand and restrict declarer to ten tricks.

Hand 22 : Card valuation opposite a shortage — Ruffing in dummy vs. establishing a long suit

Dealer East : E-W vulnerable

WEST	NORTH	EAST	SOUTH
		Pass	1♠
Pass	4♣	Pass	4NT
Pass	5◊	Pass	6♠
Pass	Pass	Pass	

```
                NORTH
                ♠ KQ73
                ♡ K73
                ◊ A8642
                ♣ 3
WEST                          EAST
♠ 96                          ♠ 52
♡ Q1052                       ♡ J984
◊ Q975                        ◊ J10
♣ Q96                         ♣ AK1054
                SOUTH
                ♠ AJ1084
                ♡ A6
                ◊ K3
                ♣ J872
```

Bidding : After North's splinter, South should be enthusiastic about slam prospects. South has only a minimum opening but the club holding is ideal. Three or four useless cards opposite the shortage means that no significant high cards are wasted. South checks on aces and bids the slam when just one ace is missing. Using 4NT Roman Key Card Blackwood, North's reply would be 5♠ (2 key cards plus the trump queen — see Chapter 12.) South would then be more confident about bidding the slam.

Lead : 6 of spades. After a splinter auction, lead a trump.

Recommended play : South wins the trump lead in hand and leads a club. If the defenders do not lead a second trump, declarer can ruff the three club losers in dummy. The defenders should play a second trump and now declarer can score only two ruffs in dummy. Declarer should tackle the diamonds next : king of diamonds, diamond to the ace and ruff a diamond, heart to the king and ruff another diamond. This establishes dummy's fifth diamond as a winner and declarer can now ruff two clubs in dummy and discard the other club loser on dummy's diamond winner.

Notes : (1) When leading a trump, it is standard to lead lowest from an even number.
(2) If the opening lead is not a trump (a heart, the suit with two honors, would be next choice), declarer wins and concedes a club. Now the defense cannot stop declarer ruffing three club losers in dummy.

Hand 23 : Second round splinter — Cue bid to suggest a slam

Dealer South : Both vulnerable

NORTH
- ♠ A 10 9 6
- ♡ - - -
- ◊ 10 7 6 4 3
- ♣ J 7 5 4

WEST
- ♠ J 3 2
- ♡ A K 10 9 6 5
- ◊ A 8
- ♣ 8 6

EAST
- ♠ 5
- ♡ Q 8 3
- ◊ K Q 5 2
- ♣ A K 9 3 2

SOUTH
- ♠ K Q 8 7 4
- ♡ J 7 4 2
- ◊ J 9
- ♣ Q 10

WEST	NORTH	EAST	SOUTH
			Pass
1♡	Pass	2♣	Pass
2♡	Pass	3♠	Pass
4◊	Pass	4NT	Pass
5♡	Pass	6♡	All pass

Bidding : With only three trumps, East should not splinter at once. East changes suit and when West rebids 2♡, East can now splinter with 3♠ to show a singleton or void in spades, 3 hearts and the values for at least game. West has an ideal spade holding opposite the singleton and so suggests slam possibilities with the cue bid of 4◊. East checks on aces and bids the slam. (With 4NT RKCB, West would bid 5♣ to show 0 or 3 key cards — see Chapter 12.)

Lead : 4 of diamonds. Spades or clubs are less appealing.

Recommended play : Win with the king of diamonds and concede a spade. If a diamond is returned, win with the ace and ruff a spade. Next comes the queen of hearts and when North shows out, finesse the 10 of hearts and draw trumps. The other spade loser is discarded on the queen of diamonds.

Notes : (1) Note how easy it can be to make a slam with just 26 HCP and a decent trump fit when there are no wasted high cards opposite a short suit.

(2) If North had J-x-x-x in trumps, the defense would prevail by starting with two rounds of spades.

(3) If North-South were sure 6♡ would make, the sacrifice in 6♠ would be worth taking but how to find it?

(4) West could try for an overtrick by hoping clubs are 3-3, but this risks failing in the slam when North has fewer than three clubs and can overruff West on the third round. As the 3-3 club break is only 36%, the risk is not worth taking. The slam is an excellent contract which many may miss, and so the overtrick is not as important as giving yourself the best chance of making the slam.

Hand 24 : Splinter by a very weak hand — Cue bidding to slam

Dealer West : Nil vulnerable

NORTH
- ♠ A K Q J 8 2
- ♡ K Q 3
- ◊ - - -
- ♣ A Q 7 2

WEST
- ♠ - - -
- ♡ J 10 9 8 6 5
- ◊ A K 6
- ♣ 9 8 6 3

EAST
- ♠ 9 7 6
- ♡ - - -
- ◊ Q J 10 7 4 2
- ♣ K J 10 5

SOUTH
- ♠ 10 5 4 3
- ♡ A 7 4 2
- ◊ 9 8 5 3
- ♣ 4

WEST	NORTH	EAST	SOUTH
Pass	2♣	Pass	2◊
Pass	2♠	Pass	4♣
Pass	4◊	Pass	4♡
Pass	7♠	All pass	

Bidding : South's 4♣ splinter shows spade support and a singleton or void in clubs. The 4◊ cue bid shows the ace of diamonds or a void there and 4♡ shows first round control of hearts (certainly the ace, given the splinter in clubs). That is enough for North to bid the grand slam.

If playing Benjamin Twos, North would open 2◊, South would give a 2♡ negative and the rest of the auction would be the same.

Lead : 7 of spades or queen of diamonds. Against a grand slam a trump lead is often the safest.

Recommended play : On a trump lead, win in hand, cash ♣A and ruff a club, ruff a diamond, ruff a club, ruff a diamond and ruff your last club. Return to hand with a diamond ruff and draw trumps.

Notes : (1) If declarer tries to come to hand with a heart, East ruffs and the grand slam is defeated. That is very unlucky for North but even such a tiny risk is unnecessary. It is quite safe to come to hand each time via a diamond ruff.

(2) If a diamond is led, ruff, cash ♣A, ruff a club, ruff a diamond, ruff a club, ruff a diamond, ruff the last club and then lead a trump to draw trumps.

(3) If East intervenes with 2◊, South passes and West might raise to 3◊. North would bid 3♠ and if East passes, South can then splinter with 5♣. North would cue bid 5◊, South 5♡ and North again jumps to 7♠. If the East-West interference is more violent, North-South may be unable to find the grand slam.

CHAPTER 7

THE JACOBY 2NT CONVENTION

Raising opener's major

There are four basic raises which responder wishes to convey :

(1) The weak raise, 6-9 points
(2) The pre-emptive raise, less than 10 HCP, 4+ trumps and an unbalanced hand
(3) The invitational raise, 10-12 points
(4) The game-forcing raise, 13+ points

Different approaches show these hand types in different ways. Obviously you and partner need to decide which of these methods you wish to adopt.

Jump-raise as a game-force

1♡ : 2♡ or 1♠ : 2♠ = 3+ support, 6-9 points
1♡ : 3♡ or 1♠ : 3♠ = 4+ support, 13+ points. If playing splinters (see Chapter 6), these raises deny a singleton or a void.
1♡ : 4♡ or 1♠ : 4♠ = the pre-emptive raise

The invitational 10-12 point raise is shown by changing suit and supporting opener on the next round, usually at the three-level.

Limit Raises

1♡ : 2♡ or 1♠ : 2♠ = 3+ support, 6-9 points
1♡ : 3♡ or 1♠ : 3♠ = 4+ support, 10-12 points

The invitational raise figures to be a balanced hand. With 10-12 points, 4+ support and a singleton or a void you have enough for game. With an unbalanced hand with 4+ trumps and below 10 points, you should use :

1♡ : 4♡ or 1♠ : 4♠ = the pre-emptive raise

That leaves the 13+ raise. You could change suit and continue with a jump to game when you are in the 13-15 range (the 'delayed game raise'). With 16+ points, rebid game if opener's rebid shows a minimum, but use fourth-suit after a new suit rebid.

Growing in popularity is a response of 2NT to cover the 13+ raise. This is known as :

The Jacoby 2NT Response

This shows :
● 4+ support for opener's major,
● 13+ points, and
● a balanced or semi-balanced hand.

With a void or a singleton, use a splinter response. With only 3-card support, use a change of suit auction. With a natural 2NT response, change suit and follow up with 2NT (10-12 points) or 3NT (13-15 points).

The Jacoby 2NT response has several significant advantages. It creates a much cheaper game-force than 1-major : 3-major and thus provides more room for slam exploration. It sets opener's suit as trumps at once in contrast to the possibly awkward change-suit-and-support-opener-later approach.

Splinters are a very effective way to bid slams on modest values when responder has good support and a singleton or void (see Chapter 6). Where responder has strong support but opener has the short suit, this may not be easy to discover using standard methods. For example :

WEST	W	E	EAST
♠ A 9 8 6 4 3	1♠	3♠	♠ K Q 5 2
♡ A 6 2	?		♡ K 5 3
◇ K J 6			◇ Q 2
♣ 6			♣ A 8 4 3

6♠ is a great spot but after this beginning, with a minimum opening, West may well bid just 4♠ and East has no reason to go further. If the bidding started 1♠ : 2♣, 2♠, East can do little more than 4♠.

However, after 1♠ : 2NT Jacoby, opener shows a singleton and would bid 3♣ on the above hand to show the shortage. East can now see the slam potential and could continue with 3♠ (good hand for slam) or 4♣ (cue bid, slam interest):

Opener's rebids after 2NT Jacoby

1. A new suit at the three-level shows a singleton or void in the suit bid.
2. Repeating the major shows around 14-15 points, not dreadful but not fantastic. It denies any singleton or void.
3. 3NT shows a hand with no singleton or void but with 16+ HCP, a hand with slam potential.
4. A jump in a new suit shows a 5-card suit headed by K-Q, A-Q or A-K. Opener will have a 5-5 or 6-5 pattern but this is the only case where opener does not show the singleton or void first.
5. Jump to 4-opener's-major shows a minimum opening, 12-13 points, and no short suit.
6. 4NT is Blackwood.

After opener's reply, responder can—
● Sign off in opener's major at the four-level with a minimum or with unsuitable values opposite opener's short suit.

Bid a new suit as a cue bid to start a slam auction.
● Bid 3NT, if available, or 4NT as Blackwood.
● Bid 3-of-opener's-major, if available, as the most convenient start of a slam auction.

WEST	W	E	EAST
♠ 3	1♡	2NT	♠ 9 4 2
♡ A 6 4 3 2	3♠	3NT	♡ K Q 8 5
◇ A J 6 2	4♠	6♡	◇ K 5
♣ A 4 3	Pass		♣ K Q J 6

3♠ = singleton or void, 3NT = Blackwood. (Over 4♠, East could make an asking bid of 5♠ to check whether West has the spade void.)

Pre-emptive jump raises in the majors

W	E	EAST (1)	EAST (2)
1♠	?	♠ Q 8 6 5 3	♠ K 10 5 3
		♡ 6 2	♡ 2
		◇ 9 7 2	◇ A 7 4 2
		♣ J 8 4	♣ 6 5 3 2

Hand (1) has no suitable action in standard methods. With no short suit, a jump to 4♠ is not recommended and the strength is not close to a single raise to 2♠. Few would want to pass, however, with such excellent support. Hand 2 is very strong for a single raise, given the 4-card support and the singleton.

Some partnerships have adopted two pre-emptive raises. This is one such structure for 5-card majors:

1♡ : 2♡ or 1♠ : 2♠ = 6-9 points, 3-card support
1♡ : 3♡ or 1♠ : 3♠ = pre-emptive, 0-5 points, 4+ support (less than two defensive tricks) : Hand 1
1♡ : 4♡ or 1♠ : 4♠ = standard pre-empt, 7 losers

To cover the stronger hand types, some use :

Bergen Raises

1♡/1♠ : 3♣ = 6-9 points and 4+ support (Hand 2)
1♡/1♠ : 3◇ = 10-12 points and 4+ support
1♡/1♠ : 2NT = Jacoby 2NT raise

One advantage of this structure is that some scope exists for trial bids over the 3♣ and 3◇ replies. The theory underlying the 3♣ response is that strong players are sure to compete over 1♡ : 2♡ or 1♠ : 2♠. When you have at least nine trumps, it is worthwhile for your side to compete to the three-level. Therefore, if you know that you have nine or more trumps, you may as well commit your side to the three-level at once. There is also some pre-emptive value in the 3♣ response.

Raising opener's minor

The Jacoby 2NT response can be harnessed to the minor suits as well. A basic structure could be :

1♣/1◇ : 2♣/2◇ = 6-9 points
1♣/1◇ : 3♣/3◇ = 10-12 points, not forcing
1♣/1◇ : 2NT = Jacoby raise, 13+ points, no singleton or void (no splinter) and forcing to game

The 2NT response denies a 4+ major. Over the 2NT response, opener bids :

● New suit at the three-level = singleton or void.
● 3NT = minimum balanced opening.
● Rebidding the opened minor at the three-level shows extra strength but denies a singleton or void.
● Rebidding the opened minor at the four-level starts a slam bidding sequence.

WEST	W	E	EAST
♠ A 7 5 4	1◇	2NT	♠ K 9 6
♡ 9	3♡	3NT	♡ K Q J
◇ K J 7 3	Pass		◇ A Q 9 8
♣ A 4 3 2			♣ J 8 6

3♡ = singleton or void, 3NT = well covered in hearts. Interchange East's hearts and clubs and East would be heading for a slam over 3♡.

After opener has shown a singleton, responder can sign off in 3NT or start a slam auction by bidding opener's minor at the four-level or by bidding a new suit as a cue bid. If responder bids 3NT, opener can still start a slam auction, either by bidding the minor at the four-level or by a new suit cue bid.

After opener bids 3NT over 2NT, responder can still commence a slam sequence by bidding opener's minor at the four-level or a new suit as a cue bid.

After 1♣ : 2NT, 3♣ or 1◇ : 2NT, 3◇ a new suit at the three-level is a stopper probe for 3NT. To start a slam auction, support opener's minor at the four-level (sooner or later) or bid a new suit at the four-level as a cue bid.

Inverted minor suit raises

Although the preceding structure works pretty well, hands can arise where it is not best to have responder as declarer in no-trumps.

WEST	W	E	EAST
♠ K 7	1♣	2NT??	♠ 6 4
♡ 9 3 2	3NT	Pass	♡ A 8
◇ K Q 6			◇ A 8 3
♣ A J 4 3 2			♣ K Q 9 8 6 5

It is easy to see the folly of 3NT by East which could fail on a spade lead whereas there are at least ten tricks in 3NT if played by West.

To cater for such situations, many top pairs play inverted raises, where the jump-raise to the three-level is weak and the raise to the two-level strong and forcing for at least one round. In this approach:

1♣/1◇ : 3♣/3◇ = 6-9 points, not forcing
1♣/1◇ : 2♣/2◇ = 10+ points, forcing for one round
1♣/1◇ : 2NT = Jacoby raise

Responder is at liberty to choose the single minor raise or the 2NT response according to the nature of the hand. After the forcing minor raise to the two-level, suit bids at the two-level show stoppers. If either partner rebids 3-of-the-opened minor, that shows a minimum hand and is droppable. If either partner bids beyond 3-of-the-opened-minor, this commits the partnership to game. Inverted minors is an excellent structure and is highly recommended.

Playing this method, the bidding on the above hand would go 1♣ : 2♣ (forcing), 2◇ (stopper) : 2♡ (stopper), 2NT : 3NT and the right hand is playing it.

Pre-emptive minor suit raises

The highly competitive nature of the modern game has led to the use of the jump-raise as a pre-empt :

1♣/1◇ : 3♣/3◇ = 0-5, pre-emptive raise
1♣/1◇ : 2♣/2◇ = 6+ points *and forcing for one round*. The theory is that the opponents will not let you play at the two-level after a weak single raise and you will be pushed to 3-minor anyway. Rebids of 3-minor by either partner show a minimum. Two-level new suit shows extra values. A rebid at the three-level beyond 3-of-opener's minor commits the partnership to game.

1♣/1◇ : 2NT = Jacoby raise

EXERCISES ON THE JACOBY 2NT RESPONSE

A. Partner has opened 1♡, pass on your right. Playing Jacoby 2NT, what would you respond?

1. ♠ K 6 3	2. ♠ K 6 3	3. ♠ 7	4. ♠ J	5. ♠ A K
♡ K J 5 3	♡ K J 5 3 2	♡ Q 6 5 3 2	♡ K Q 8 2	♡ K 6 5 3 2
◇ A 5	◇ 9 5 2	◇ 6 2	◇ A K 4	◇ 6
♣ 9 8 6 2	♣ A K	♣ K 10 8 7 3	♣ 9 8 6 3 2	♣ K Q J 10 3

B. You opened 1♠ and partner replied 2NT (Jacoby raise). What is your rebid?

1. ♠ Q J 7 3 2	2. ♠ A J 7 3 2	3. ♠ A 9 7 4 2	4. ♠ A 10 7 5 2	5. ♠ A J 7 4 2
♡ A Q 4 3	♡ A Q 4 3	♡ 3	♡ K Q	♡ Q 4
◇ 2	◇ 2	◇ A K J 4 2	◇ Q 7 2	◇ K Q 2
♣ K 9 2	♣ A K 2	♣ Q 5	♣ J 10 6	♣ A Q 9

C. The bidding has started 1♡ : 2NT (Jacoby raise), 3◇ (singleton or void). What is responder's rebid?

1. ♠ Q J 7	2. ♠ A 2	3. ♠ 8 2	4. ♠ K Q 5	5. ♠ K J 8
♡ A Q 4 3	♡ A Q 4 3	♡ A Q 4 3	♡ K Q 7 4 3	♡ Q J 9 8 3
◇ K Q	◇ 9 7 6	◇ J 7 6	◇ 9 7 2	◇ K Q 2
♣ 9 7 6 2	♣ K Q 7 2	♣ A K 7 2	♣ K 2	♣ A 9

PARTNERSHIP BIDDING : How should the following hands be bid? West is the dealer each time and you are using the Jacoby 2NT response over majors (Set 15) and over minors (Set 16).

SET 13 — WEST	SET 13 — EAST	SET 14 — WEST	SET 14 — EAST
1. ♠ A J 7 4 2	1. ♠ K Q 8 6	1. ♠ A Q 4	1. ♠ K 8 3
♡ K Q 3	♡ A J	♡ K Q 3	♡ A J
◇ K 8 4 3	◇ A 5 2	◇ K 8 7 2	◇ A Q 9 6
♣ 5	♣ 8 7 4 2	♣ 9 5 3	♣ 8 7 4 2
2. ♠ A J 7 4 2	2. ♠ K Q 8 6	2. ♠ A J 7 4	2. ♠ K Q 8
♡ K Q 3	♡ 8 7 4 2	♡ 3	♡ Q 6 2
◇ K 8 4 3	◇ A 5 2	◇ K Q 8 4 3	◇ A 9 7 5 2
♣ 5	♣ A J	♣ K 8 3	♣ A J
3. ♠ A K 7 4 3 2	3. ♠ Q 9 8 6	3. ♠ A J 7 4	3. ♠ Q 6 2
♡ 9 6	♡ A K 3	♡ 3	♡ K Q 8
◇ K 8 3	◇ A 7 5	◇ K Q 8 4 3	◇ A 9 7 5 2
♣ A K	♣ 7 5 2	♣ K 8 3	♣ A J
4. ♠ J	4. ♠ A 7 6 2	4. ♠ 9 7	4. ♠ 6 2
♡ Q 8 4 3 2	♡ A K 9 6 5	♡ A Q	♡ K 9
◇ Q 7	◇ A 6	◇ Q J 7	◇ A K 4 2
♣ A K J 7 4	♣ Q 9	♣ A J 7 4 3 2	♣ K 9 8 6 5
5. ♠ 4	5. ♠ A 7 6	5. ♠ K 5	5. ♠ 7 6
♡ Q 8 4 3 2	♡ A K 9 6 5	♡ A Q J 2	♡ 6 5
◇ K 7	◇ A 3	◇ 7 3	◇ A K 8 6
♣ A K 8 7 4	♣ Q J 3	♣ K 8 7 4 3	♣ A Q J 6 2
6. ♠ K Q 8 4 2	6. ♠ A J 9 7	6. ♠ K Q J	6. ♠ A 7
♡ Q J 7	♡ A 3	♡ 9 3	♡ A K 4
◇ K 4	◇ A Q J 3	◇ A K 8 6 4 3	◇ J 10 7 5 2
♣ Q 7 5	♣ 8 3 2	♣ K 4	♣ A 8 3

PLAY HANDS ON RESPONDER'S STRATEGY
(These hands can be made up by using pages 160-167)

Hand 25 : Jacoby 2NT — Locating a missing queen

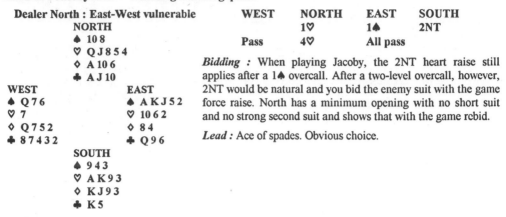

Dealer North : East-West vulnerable

	NORTH		
	♠ 10 8		
	♥ Q J 8 5 4		
	◊ A 10 6		
	♣ A J 10		
WEST		**EAST**	
♠ Q 7 6		♠ A K J 5 2	
♥ 7		♥ 10 6 2	
◊ Q 7 5 2		◊ 8 4	
♣ 8 7 4 3 2		♣ Q 9 6	
	SOUTH		
	♠ 9 4 3		
	♥ A K 9 3		
	◊ K J 9 3		
	♣ K 5		

WEST	NORTH	EAST	SOUTH
	1♥	1♠	2NT
Pass	4♥	All pass	

Bidding : When playing Jacoby, the 2NT heart raise still applies after a 1♠ overcall. After a two-level overcall, however, 2NT would be natural and you bid the enemy suit with the game force raise. North has a minimum opening with no short suit and no strong second suit and shows that with the game rebid.

Lead : Ace of spades. Obvious choice.

Recommended play : West signals encouragement and East continues with the ♠K and a third spade ruffed by North. Trumps are drawn in three rounds, followed by the ♣K, ♣A and the ♣J ruffed in dummy. Declarer plays West for the queen of diamonds : cash the ◊K followed by the ◊J, letting the jack run if West plays low. When the diamond finesse works, declarer scores an overtrick.

Notes : (1) North's 4♥ is absolutely safe but the overtrick is essential to secure a good score.
(2) There is no benefit in taking a club finesse either way. Even if this succeeds there is no useful discard.
(3) It may seem attractive to play East, the bidder, for the ◊Q. North can place East with five spades for the overcall, three hearts (discovered when drawing trumps) and ♣ Q-x-x (discovered on the play of the clubs). East therefore cannot hold more than two diamonds and so West began with 4+ diamonds. East could have ◊ Q-x but you need a powerful reason to counter the 2-1odds in favor of West holding the queen.
(4) On the hearts, West should discard two clubs. One diamond discard is safe but looks suspicious.

Hand 26 : Jacoby 2NT — Setting up an endplay — Passive defense

Dealer East : Both vulnerable

	NORTH		
	♠ A 6		
	♥ 6 5 3 2		
	◊ A 9 7 5 3		
	♣ Q 2		
WEST		**EAST**	
♠ J 8 5 3 2		♠ K Q 10 9 7	
♥ K 8		♥ A Q	
◊ K J 2		◊ 6 4	
♣ K J 10		♣ A 7 5 4	
	SOUTH		
	♠ 4		
	♥ J 10 9 7 4		
	◊ Q 10 8		
	♣ 9 8 6 3		

WEST	NORTH	EAST	SOUTH
		1♠	Pass
2NT	Pass	3NT	Pass
4♠	Pass	Pass	Pass

Bidding : Although 2NT normally shows 13+ points, West should choose 2NT, given the excellent trump support. It would be far too timid to treat West as a limit raise. In standard Jacoby 3♠ by East = 14-15 points and 3NT = 16+ HCP. East is entitled to upgrade to 16 because there are no wasted honors, the shape is semi-balanced and East has only 5½ losers. West is keen to sign off at the first opportunity and East has nothing to spare.

Lead : Jack of hearts. The other suits are much riskier.

Recommended play : Win ♥A and play a heart to the king. Then lead the ♠J from dummy. If North plays low, continue with a second spade. North has to give declarer a ruff and discard or solve the diamond or club position.

Notes : (1) The hearts are cashed at once in order to endplay North if North began with singleton ♠A.
(2) If ♠J is led from dummy, it is hard for North to rise with the ♠A (South might have ♠Q or ♠K bare). If North takes the first spade (e.g., the spade is led from the East hand), North should exit with a spade. Declarer should then tackle clubs. The normal play with this club combination is a first round finesse but even if South has the ♣Q, there is no useful discard on the fourth club. Here East should cash ♣A and then finesse ♣J. The second round finesse gives you a better chance to endplay North. In with the ♣Q, North has to give East a ruff and discard via a third heart or eliminate East's guess in diamonds. If East takes a first round club finesse, North should exit with the second club and let East guess the diamonds.

Hand 27 : Jacoby 2NT — Slam technique

Dealer South : Nil vulnerable

NORTH
- ♠ A 2
- ♡ A Q 7 4
- ◊ K 7 2
- ♣ 9 7 6 2

WEST
- ♠ J 10 9 7
- ♡ 2
- ◊ J 10 8 6
- ♣ A Q 10 5

EAST
- ♠ 8 6 5 4
- ♡ 8 6 5
- ◊ Q 9
- ♣ K J 8 3

SOUTH
- ♠ K Q 3
- ♡ K J 10 9 3
- ◊ A 5 4 3
- ♣ 4

WEST	NORTH	EAST	SOUTH
			1♡
Pass	2NT	Pass	3♣
Pass	4NT	Pass	5◊
Pass	6♡	All pass	

Bidding : If you appreciate the value of splinters, you must also appreciate Jacoby 2NT which allows opener to show a short suit. If the bidding had started 1♡ : 3♡ (forcing), South would probably rebid 4♡ and it would be very tough to reach 6♡.

3♣ showed a singleton or void in clubs and with only one club loser and 4 outside losers, North could see the slam potential. Playing Roman Key Card Blackwood (Chapter 12) South would answer 4NT with 5♡ (two key cards but no trump queen).

Lead : Jack of spades. Prefer the stronger sequence.

Recommended play : South should win with the king of spades and lead the singleton club at once. Win any return, say a spade taken by the ace. Draw two rounds of trumps with ♡K and ♡J, cash ♠Q and discard a diamond from dummy, followed by ◊K, ◊A and a diamond ruffed with a top trump in dummy. Ruff a club to hand and ruff the last diamond in dummy. South has only trumps left.

Notes : (1) The slam is excellent with just 26 HCP and many pairs will stop in game. It is important to play the hand as safely as possible. You could ruff three clubs in hand but this line has no superiority unless the opponents start with two rounds of clubs, thus helping your entry position.
(2) You could win ♠A, cash ♠K and ♠Q discarding a diamond, and follow with ◊K, ◊A, third diamond ruffed high in dummy. If you ruff low, you will be overruffed. However, it is slightly safer to draw two rounds of trumps before playing to ruff the diamonds as long as you keep two top trumps in dummy.
(3) You must not start with three spades, ♡K, ♡J, ◊K, ◊A, diamond ruff because then you have no easy way back to hand. East can win the club exit and lead a third trump. Playing the club first solves this.

Hand 28 : Rebid with a weak hand after Jacoby 2NT — Playing it safe

Dealer West : N-S vulnerable

NORTH
- ♠ 10 9 7 2
- ♡ 8 4
- ◊ 9 8 1
- ♣ K J 9 5

WEST
- ♠ Q J 6
- ♡ K Q 9 6 5
- ◊ Q J
- ♣ Q 10 2

EAST
- ♠ A 4
- ♡ A J 7 2
- ◊ A K 10 7
- ♣ 8 7 4

SOUTH
- ♠ K 8 5 3
- ♡ 10 3
- ◊ 6 5 3 2
- ♣ A 6 3

WEST	NORTH	EAST	SOUTH
1♡	Pass	2NT	Pass
4♡	Pass	Pass	Pass

Bidding : West may have to check twice to ensure that this is worth an opening bid. It sure looks like 13 low card points. Over 2NT, West is anxious to bid 4♡. If ever there was a minimum opening, this is it. Although East has a strong hand, East has too many losers to push on over 4♡ which will usually be an 11-13 point 5-3-3-2 hand.

Lead : 10 of spades. A near-sequence is usually better than leading from a suit with broken honors or from a rag suit.

Recommended play : West rises with dummy's ♠A, draws trumps and then runs the diamonds, discarding two club losers. A spade is played and declarer makes eleven tricks, losing one spade and one club.

Notes : (1) A club lead would give the defense three tricks but North has no way of telling.
(2) North's lead might be from K-10-9-x but it would be foolish for declarer to take the first round spade finesse. Firstly, it is not likely that North has led from the ♠K. Secondly, declarer has eleven safe tricks by rising with the ♠A. It is silly to jeopardise a normal contract when an overtrick is perfectly safe. Thirdly, other tables might receive a club lead and be held to ten tricks. Therefore, make sure of eleven.
(3) If declarer received a trump lead or a diamond lead, declarer would draw trumps, cash the diamonds and discard two clubs. Later declarer could safely try the spade finesse for an extra trick.

CHAPTER 8

STRATEGY FOR OPENER & RESPONDER

The Suit Quality Test

> **Number of Cards in Suit**
> **+ Number of Honors in Suit**
> **= Suit Quality**

For example :

K Q 8 7 4 3 = Suit Quality of 8
(6 cards + 2 honors)

When assessing suit quality, the jack and ten are counted only if the suit also contains a higher honor (ace, king or queen). Thus :

J 8 6 4 3 = SQ 5

5 cards but do not count the jack as the suit does not contain a higher honor.

K J 8 6 3 = SQ 7 (5 cards + 2 honors)

The Suit Quality Test is useful when the quality of a suit is relevant to your bidding decision. For example, for a pre-empt you should have a decent suit. How decent? The SQ should equal the number of tricks for which you are bidding. Thus a weak two opening should have a suit quality of 8 (6-card suit and at least two honors), a 3-level pre-empt should have a suit quality of 9, and so on.

Suit quality is not relevant to opening bids of one in a suit, but can be useful when rebidding. With a suit quality of ten, you can insist on your suit as trumps. SQ 10 = 6-card suit with four honors or a 7-card suit with three honors. For example :

WEST	EAST	
1♠	2♦	After East has responded 2♦ to
?		West's 1♠ opening, what should
		West rebid with these hands?

(1)	(2)	(3)
♠ K Q 8 4 3 2	♠ K Q 8 4 3 2	♠ K Q J 10 3 2
♡ A J 8	♡ A J 8	♡ A 8 2
◇ 5 3	◇ 5 3	◇ 5 3
♣ K 3	♣ A K	♣ A K

(1) This is only a minimum opening. Bid 2♠.

(2) 17 HCP = a strong opening. Bid 3♠.

(3) This has the same strength as (2) but your suit has a Suit Quality of 10. You can show this with a rebid of 4♠. Thus the jump to game shows the same strength as a jump rebid but promises a better suit. SQ of 10 means the suit is playable opposite a singleton, and even opposite a void, the suit may have only one loser.

K-Q-x-x-x-x opposite a singleton will have three losers most of the time. K-Q-J-10-x-x opposite a singleton will usually play for just one loser. One advantage of being able to show such suit quality is that responder is able to head for a slam, even with the barest support because of the knowledge that the trump suit should be all right.

Suit Quality Test for Responder

Just as the Suit Quality Test is useful for overcalls, pre-empts and opener's rebid, so it can be used for responses and responder's rebids.

WEST	EAST	
1♣	4♡	Responder's immediate jump to game should be based on a hand with seven playing tricks, about
1◇	4♠	6-9 HCP and a 7+ suit which has a Suit Quality of 10+.

Beware of the 1♠ : 4♡ sequence if you are using that as a splinter raise of spades.

With a single-suiter (6+ suit) and 10 HCP or more, prefer to start with a simple change-of-suit response.

WEST	EAST	
1♣	1♡	Jump-rebid your suit to the three-level with 10-12 points and
1♠	3♡	a suit quality below 10.

WEST	EAST	
1♣	1♡	Jump-rebid to game in your major with 10-12 points and a
1♠	4♡	suit quality of 10+.

W	E	EAST (1)	EAST (2)
1◇	1♠	♠ K Q 8 6 5 3	♠ K Q J 10 5 3
2♣	?	♡ A 6 2	♡ A 6 2
		◇ 8 2	◇ J 2
		♣ Q 7	♣ 6 3

With (1), rebid 3♠. The suit quality of the spades is only 8. With (2), you have a suit quality 10 and should therefore rebid with a jump to 4♠.

Once you hit 13 HCP or more with a strong single-suiter, your rebid will depend on whether opener made a narrow range rebid (e.g., rebid of suit opened) or with a wide-range rebid (change of suit). After opener has rebid the suit opened, it is sensible to play that a jump rebid by responder is forcing. For example :

W	E	EAST (1)	EAST (2)
1◇	1♠	♠ K Q 8 6 5 3	♠ K Q J 10 5 3
2◇	?	♡ A 6 2	♡ A 6 2
		◇ A 2	◇ A 2
		♣ Q 7	♣ 6 3

With (1), it could be very silly to jump to 4♠ (which might fail if opener is void or singleton in spades, with 3NT laydown). Jump to 3♠, forcing after opener's rebid in the suit opened. With (2) your spades have SQ 10 and you should rebid 4♠.

When opener rebids with a change of suit, you can use fourth-suit forcing with strong hands. This allows the jump-rebid to be used for the 10-12 point hands and fourth-suit forcing for the stronger hands. For example :

W	E	EAST (1)	EAST (2)
1◇	1♠	♠ A Q 8 6 5 3	♠ A Q J 10 5 3
2♣	?	♡ A 6 2	♡ A 6 2
		◇ A 2	◇ A 2
		♣ 7 2	♣ 7 2

Both of these are too strong for a rebid of 3♠. As opener may yet have a strong hand, you do not want to give up on slam chances. Use 2♡ fourth-suit forcing. Over opener's next bid of say, 2NT, 3♣ or 3◇, follow up with 3♠ on (1) and 4♠ on (2). The 3♠ rebid will be forcing : after fourth-suit, responder's next bid below game is forcing.

The same principle can apply after a jump-shift :

W	E	EAST (1)	EAST (2)
1◇	2♠	♠ K Q 8 6 5 3	♠ A Q J 10 5 3
3♣	?	♡ Q 6 3	♡ Q 6 3
		◇ A K	◇ A K
		♣ A J	♣ K 2

With (1), bid 3♠ while with (2), you should rebid 4♠, showing the self-sufficient suit. That may enable opener to bid on to a slam. If not prepared to stop in game, rebid 3♠ even with a suit of SQ 10.

Fourth-Suit Forcing

WEST	EAST	Where the fourth-suit bid
1♠	2♣	comes at the three-level, it is
2♡	3◇	sensible to play the sequence as
?		forcing to game.

Where the fourth-suit bid occurs at the two-level, it is standard to play that a minimum rebid by opener can be passed but any rebid by responder below game is forcing.

WEST	EAST	At this point, 2♠, 2NT, 3♣ or
1◇	1♠	3◇ by opener is not forcing. Over
2♣	2♡	any of these, responder's 3♠ or
?		minor-suit support is forcing.

WEST	EAST	Opener's jump-rebid in the
1◇	1♠	fourth suit is played as natural,
2♣	3♡	showing at least 5-5 in the suits
?		bid and forcing to game.

There is only one sequence where the fourth suit rebid occurs at the one-level.

WEST	EAST	This sequence is played as
1♣	1◇	natural and 1♠ is forcing,
1♡	1♠	showing 4+ spades but only 6+
?		points (like 1♣ : 1♠ at once).

To create a fourth-suit auction, you need to make a jump-rebid to 2♠ :

WEST	EAST	The jump to 2♠ *denies* four
1♣	1◇	spades, but shows 10+ points.
1♡	2♠	Bidding continues as in a normal
?		fourth-suit auction.

Opening in third seat

It is permissible to open light in third seat and it is not unusual to open with 10-11 HCP in third seat. However, the light opening bid should be used only when the suit you are opening is strong. Do not open on a weak hand just for the sake of opening. Open despite your weak points if you are indicating a good lead for your partner.

Once partner has passed and you have 12 HCP or less, chances for game for your side are remote. Unless you can make a pre-emptive bid, opening the bidding on light values will often help your opponents. If they win the contract, declarer may be able to place the missing cards because of your opening bid. Better to pass in third seat unless your bid has some constructive purpose.

Tricks and therefore matchpoints are often thrown away with the opening lead. If you can stop partner from the usual rotten opening lead, you will see a significant improvement in your duplicate scores.

A good test for opening light in third seat is this : Would you be happy to overcall in the suit you are opening? If yes, you are worth an opening bid in third seat. If not, do not open light.

Another good test is this : Does the suit you are opening third-in-hand have Suit Quality of 7? If so, it is worth opening light. If not, prefer to pass.

If you play 5-card majors, you should be prepared to open 1♡ or 1♠ in third seat on a strong 4-card suit, a suit with a SQ of 7. For example :

♠ A K Q 8	After two passes, unless you are
♡ 7 3	going to open 1♠ with this hand,
◇ 9 6 3	don't bother. Rather pass than
♣ J 8 4 2	open 1♣.

1♠ shows partner what to lead and forces the opponents to start bidding their suits at the two-level. 1♣ has no lead-directing value and no hindrance value either.

Having opened light in third seat, you are expected not to bid again. On the above hand, you would pass any response from partner. If you open in third seat and do bid again, you are showing full opening values, normally 13 HCP or more.

If you have a good 5-card major (SQ 8 or better), be prepared to open with a weak two, even though you are normally expected to have a 6-card suit.

♠ 8	After two passes, open 2♡,
♡ K Q J 7 3	weak, or do not open at all. If
◇ 9 7 4	you open 1♡, you have no good
♣ Q J 4 2	action if partner responds 1♠.

Another advantage is partner will usually pass 2♡.

The Drury 2♣ Convention

Because it is common to open light in third seat, it is easy for responder to bid too high. The Drury Convention is designed to check whether opener's third seat opening is genuine.

After a major suit opening, the 2♣ response by a passed hand is 'Drury' and asks : 'Is your third seat opening full value?'

In reply :

2◊ = 'No, I have opened light.'

All others = Natural and genuine opening bid. The failure to bid 2◊ usually leads to game at least.

The standard Drury 2♣ response normally has support for opener's major. After 2◊, responder can sign off in opener's major at the two-level. This avoids the three-level with two 10-11 point hands.

Drury not promising support

In this approach, the 2♣ response by a passed hand does not guarantee support for opener's major but merely a maximum pass. Opener's reply to show a minimum or sub-minimum opening is 2◊.

Any reply other than 2◊ is natural and forcing to game. Responder can show support for opener with the rebid whether opener rebids 2◊ or not.

WEST	EAST	The jump to 3♡ after opener's
	Pass	2◊ negative shows 5+ hearts and
1♠	2♣	spade support as well. With only
2◊	3♡	four hearts, rebid 2♡.

One plus for this approach is that a passed hand reply of 2◊ or 2♡ guarantees a 5+ suit. The 2NT response by a passed hand is not needed as a natural bid and can be used for 5-5 in the minors.

In both versions of Drury, the maximum pass with support travels through 2♣. The jump raise by a passed hand can then be played as pre-emptive (excellent support but less than 6 points).

Double Drury

Another approach to passed hand bidding :

2♣ = Maximum pass, no support or poor support for opener's major

2◊ = Maximum pass plus decent support for opener's major

Over 2♣, the negative response is 2◊ and over 2◊, the negative action is the signoff in the major. Over 2◊, opener can jump to game with suitable values without disclosing anything further to the opponents. If responder has a maximum pass and long diamonds, responder can bid 2♣ and pass opener's 2◊ reply.

This approach enjoys the best of both Drury methods and has very few drawbacks. Also, the passed hand 2NT response can show both minors.

Opening in fourth seat

There is less pressure to open in fourth seat since you can simply pass out the bidding. In fourth seat, by all means open all 13-point or stronger hands but be conservative below 13 points. This is a good approach for 10-12 point hands in fourth seat :

Add your HCP to the number of spades you hold. If the total is 15 or more, be prepared to open.

When each side has about 20 points, each side can usually make eight tricks in its trump fit. Owning the spade suit is therefore very important. It means you can bid up to 2♠ and the opponents will have to bid to the three-level to prevent your making 2♠. Therefore be reluctant open with 10-12 points if short in spades but by all means open with length and strength in spades.

In fourth seat, weak twos are played as 8-12 points (since you will hardly have less than 8 HCP in fourth seat) and a good 5-card suit (SQ of 8) is fine for a weak two in fourth seat.

Suit rebids at the 1-level

WEST	EAST	Is 1♠ forcing or not?
1♣	1♡	In theory, a one-level rebid is
1♠	?	not forcing but responder should
		pass only with less than 6 HCP.

The logic is that if East is strong enough to answer the 1♣ opening, then East would have been strong enough to answer a 1♠ opening. In that case East is also strong enough to answer a 1♠ rebid. Only if East fudged the original response, say with just 3-4 points, then East may pass 1♠ with 3-4 card support. Otherwise East should find some rebid.

Showing 16-18 HCP and a 5-card major

If your 1NT opening can include a 5-card major, then that solves your problem. If not, then to show a 16-18 point 5-3-3-2 hand with a 5-card major, open with the major and rebid 2NT (e.g., 1♡ : 2♣, 2NT or 1♠ : 1NT, 2NT). Open your major and jump rebid to 3NT (e.g., 1♠ : 2◊, 3NT) to show the 19-20 point 5-3-3-2 type.

After a two-level response, you can rebid 2NT with 15-18 points. With 12-14 points, show your minimum opening by rebidding your major. This does not promise a 6-card suit after a 2-level reply.

Weak Jump Shift Responses

If your system does not need strong jump shifts, you can use the jump shift for awkward weak hands. The jump shift to the two-level shows 0-5 points and a 6+ suit while the jump shift to the three-level shows a 7+ suit (or a 6-card suit with a SQ of 9) and 5-8 HCP. In each case, responder denies support for opener. A two-level response followed by a rebid of that suit (1♡ : 2♣, 2◊ : 3♣) would then show 9-11 HCP and a 6+ suit.

EXERCISES

A. West : Pass, North : Pass. What should East do with each of these hands?

1. ♠ A J 9 7	2. ♠ A 2	3. ♠ A K J 6 2	4. ♠ J 6 3 2	5. ♠ A K J 9
♡ Q J 5 3	♡ K Q J 3	♡ 7 4	♡ 9 8 4 3	♡ Q 7 5
◇ 7	◇ 7 5 3 2	◇ 8 4 2	◇ A K Q	◇ 8 3 2
♣ Q 8 7 4	♣ 8 4 3	♣ 7 6 2	♣ 8 4	♣ J 6 4

B. There have been three passes to South. What should South do with each of these hands?

1. ♠ A Q J 3	2. ♠ 4	3. ♠ K 8 7	4. ♠ 7	5. ♠ A K Q 9 8 2
♡ 8 5	♡ A 6 2	♡ A Q J 9 8 2	♡ 9 2	♡ - - -
◇ K 5	◇ K Q J 3	◇ J 8 4	◇ Q J 7 5	◇ 8 3
♣ Q 9 8 4 2	♣ Q 7 5 4 2	♣ 3	♣ A K J 9 8 4	♣ Q J 7 4 2

C. Partner 1◇ : You : 1♡ : Partner 2♣. What is your rebid with each of these hands?

1. ♠ A 9	2. ♠ K 5 4	3. ♠ A J 7 2	4. ♠ A 7 2	5. ♠ A 7 2
♡ K J 9 8 7 3	♡ K Q J 10 8 2	♡ A Q 8 4	♡ A Q 8 4 2	♡ A Q 8 4 3 2
◇ Q 2	◇ Q 5	◇ Q 2	◇ Q 2	◇ Q 2
♣ 6 4 2	♣ J 4	♣ 7 5 4	♣ J 5 4	♣ J 5

PARTNERSHIP BIDDING : How should the following hands be bid? West is the dealer each time and you are playing Drury not guaranteeing support for opener's major.

SET 15 — WEST	SET 15 — EAST	SET 16 — WEST	SET 16 — EAST
1. ♠ 3	1. ♠ A 8 6	1. ♠ 7 3	1. ♠ K Q 10 4 2
♡ K 7 5	♡ Q 8 6 4 3	♡ A 9 5 3	♡ Q J 7 2
◇ A J 4 3 2	◇ K 9	◇ Q J 6 2	◇ K 4
♣ A Q 3 2	♣ K 7 5	♣ A 6 3	♣ 7 5
2. ♠ Q 7	2. ♠ A K J 6 5 2	2. ♠ 9 7 4	2. ♠ 10 6 5
♡ A 9 7 3 2	♡ 8	♡ K 8 6 3	♡ A Q J 5 2
◇ A 7	◇ K Q 3	◇ K 6	◇ A 2
♣ K 6 5 3	♣ Q J 2	♣ A 7 6 2	♣ 8 5 3
3. ♠ 9 4 3 2	3. ♠ A 8 7 5	3. ♠ 8 6	3. ♠ J 7 5 2
♡ A K J 8	♡ 7 2	♡ J 8 7 6 3 2	♡ A K Q 4
◇ 4	◇ K J 7 5 2	◇ 8	◇ 7 5 4 3
♣ K J 6 2	♣ 8 4	♣ A K 4 2	♣ 6
4. ♠ A J 9	4. ♠ 7 5 2	4. ♠ A J 5 3	4. ♠ K Q 10 7 4
♡ K J 6 2	♡ Q 5	♡ A Q 7 2	♡ K J 6 3
◇ 4 3	◇ A K 9 6 5	◇ 8 5	◇ A 4
♣ A 8 5 3	♣ K J 4	♣ 7 6 4	♣ 9 3
5. ♠ 8	5. ♠ 7 5 2	5. ♠ J 2	5. ♠ A K 10 9
♡ A K 8 2	♡ Q 5	♡ A Q J 7 3	♡ 8 6 5
◇ J 7 3	◇ A K 9 6 5	◇ Q 10 6 2	◇ K 7 5
♣ A 8 6 3 2	♣ K J 4	♣ 7 4	♣ 9 6 5
6. ♠ A 8 7 4	6. ♠ 6 5 2	6. ♠ K 10 3 2	6. ♠ 8 7 5
♡ - - -	♡ A 8 5 3	♡ 7 6	♡ 9 8 4
◇ K Q 8 6 3	◇ J 5 2	◇ J 6 3 2	◇ A K Q
♣ K Q 5 3	♣ J 8 4	♣ Q 9 5	♣ 8 6 4 2

PLAY HANDS ON OPENER'S STRATEGY
(These hands can be made up by using pages 160-167)

Hand 29 : Opening in third seat — Drury Convention — Card reading

Dealer North : Both vulnerable

NORTH
♠ K 7 6 4
♡ A Q
♦ 10 7 5
♣ Q 10 8 3

WEST
♠ Q 9 2
♡ 9 5 3 2
♦ A J 8 6 3
♣ 5

EAST
♠ 8
♡ 10 8 6 4
♦ Q 9 2
♣ A K J 9 4

SOUTH
♠ A J 10 5 3
♡ K J 7
♦ K 4
♣ 7 6 2

WEST	NORTH	EAST	SOUTH
	Pass	Pass	1♠
Pass	2♣	Dble	2♦
Pass	2♠	All pass	

Bidding : North's 2♣, Drury, asks about South's opening and 2♦ indicates a light opening. North therefore signs off in 2♠. Without Drury, North might well jump to 3♠, which is hopeless as the cards lie and might go two down. East's double of 2♣, an artificial bid, asks partner to lead a club.

If not vulnerable, East might chance a takeout double of 2♠ and East-West would then land in 3♦ or 3♡. At adverse vulnerability, the risk is not worthwhile.

Lead : 5 of clubs. Without East's double, West might well have led a heart and that may have turned out better for the defense.

Recommended play : East takes the first three club tricks and West signals for a diamond switch. East shifts to the 2 of diamonds (showing an honor). South plays low and West wins with the jack followed by the ace of diamonds. If West continues with a third diamond, South ruffs, cashes the ace of spades and leads the jack of spades, letting it run if West plays low. South thus scores eight tricks.

Notes : (1) After East has turned up with A-K-J in clubs, South knows West has the ace of diamonds, as East would have opened with 12 HCP. If East also turns up with the ♦Q, that marks West with the ♠Q.
(2) If East continues with a club at trick 4, South should discard a diamond, as West will have the ♦A. West ruffs and now declarer has no problem with the trump suit. If South ruffs the fourth club, West makes a trump trick and declarer will fail after losing two diamond tricks later.
(3) If West wins ♦A, cashes ♦J and switches to a heart, declarer can play dummy's third diamond to locate the ♦Q (although that is risky if West discarded diamonds on the clubs). Even without that, declarer should figure East has the ♦Q and play West for the ♠Q. With ♦ A-Q-J-x-x, West would almost certainly have doubled South's artificial 2♦.

Hand 30 : Opening in third seat — Competitive bidding

Dealer East : Nil vulnerable

NORTH
♠ A J 10 7 5
♡ A 10 2
♦ 10 8 3
♣ A J

WEST
♠ 9 3
♡ Q 9 7 3
♦ A K Q
♣ 7 6 4 3

EAST
♠ 6 2
♡ K J 8 5 4
♦ J 7 6 2
♣ 9 2

SOUTH
♠ K Q 8 4
♡ 6
♦ 9 5 4
♣ K Q 10 8 5

WEST	NORTH	EAST	SOUTH
		Pass	Pass
1♦	1♠	Dble	3♠
Pass	4♠	All pass	

Bidding : West should not open 1♣ or 1♡. If not prepared to open 1♦, do not open at all. With 5-3 in the majors, North should overcall 1♠ rather than double. Prefer the double if you are 4-3, 4-4 or 5-4 in the majors. East's double shows 4+ hearts and 6+ points. If playing the jump to 3♠ as pre-emptive, South could bid 2♦ to show the strong passed hand or jump to 3♣ to show a maximum pass with spade support. If South did bid 2♦, West should double to insist on a diamond lead.

Lead : 2 of diamonds. Definitely after a third-in-hand opening.

Recommended play : West wins and cashes two more diamonds. West would then switch to a heart. North wins and draws trumps. The heart losers can be ruffed in dummy or discarded on the clubs. 10 tricks.

Notes : (1) If West opened 1♣, East would lead a club. If West passes originally, East might well lead a club, a trump or even a heart. On anything but a diamond lead, North can make thirteen tricks : draw trumps, discard the diamond losers on the clubs and ruff two hearts in dummy. Once you see how rotten partner's usual leads are, you will be eager to indicate a good lead with your third seat opening.
(2) Even though the diamond lead does not defeat 4♠, East-West will score very well by holding the contract to ten tricks. At many tables, North will be allowed to make thirteen tricks.

Hand 31 . Opening in third seat — Competitive bidding

Dealer South : N-S vulnerable

NORTH
- ♠ A K J 9
- ♥ 6 5
- ♦ 8 7 3
- ♣ Q 8 4 3

WEST
- ♠ 8 7 2
- ♥ Q J 2
- ♦ K 10 6 5
- ♣ A 10 5

EAST
- ♠ 6 5 4
- ♥ A K 10 9 7
- ♦ A 9 2
- ♣ K 9

SOUTH
- ♠ Q 10 3
- ♥ 8 4 3
- ♦ Q J 4
- ♣ J 7 6 2

WEST	NORTH	EAST	SOUTH
			Pass
Pass	1♠	2♥	2♠
4♥	Pass	Pass	Pass

Bidding : If North is not prepared to open 1♠, North should pass. It would not be worth opening 1♣. West has a tough decision whether to bid 3♥ or 4♥. On the actual layout, 4♥ is not much of a contract but West would expect East to be shortish in spades (at most a doubleton) on the North-South bidding. If West did bid 3♥, East should pass, even though East might think West is short in spades.

Lead : 3 of spades. One usually leads partner's suit. When partner has opened in third seat and the opponents win the contract, it is even more important to lead partner's suit.

Recommended play : North wins the lead with the king of spades and cashes the ace. North continues with a third spade, won by South. When South exits safely with a trump, declarer has no way to avoid losing a diamond trick. This defense holds the contract to nine tricks. Even if East-West stopped in 3♥, this figures to give North-South a respectable score.

Notes : (1) Had North passed, South would have a tough lead, with a trump or the ♦Q as the recommended choices. A trump lead gives declarer nothing but on the ♦Q lead, declarer can make eleven tricks (win ♦A, draw trumps ending in hand, finesse ♦10 and discard a spade on the thirteenth diamond).
(2) On a trump lead, if declarer wins and plays a diamond to the 9, South would have to find the spade switch to hold declarer to nine tricks.
(3) A club lead, unattractive from J-x-x-x, would also give declarer eleven tricks. Declarer captures North's queen, plays a heart to the queen and a heart back to the ace, finesses the 10 of clubs, discards a diamond on the ♣A, plays ♦A, ♦K and ruffs a diamond, plays a trump to dummy to draw the last trump and cashes the thirteenth diamond for a spade discard.

Hand 32 : Opening in fourth seat — Competitive bidding

Dealer West : East-West vulnerable

NORTH
- ♠ K J 4 2
- ♥ 9 5 3
- ♦ A 9 6
- ♣ J 8 6

WEST
- ♠ 9 3
- ♥ K J 10 7 2
- ♦ J 10 4
- ♣ K Q 5

EAST
- ♠ 10 8 7
- ♥ A Q 8
- ♦ 8 5 3
- ♣ A 9 7 2

SOUTH
- ♠ A Q 6 5
- ♥ 6 4
- ♦ K Q 7 2
- ♣ 10 4 3

WEST	NORTH	EAST	SOUTH
Pass	Pass	Pass	1♦
1♥	Dble	2♥	2♠
3♥	Pass	Pass	Pass

Bidding : East has no suit strong enough to justify a light third-seat opening. In fourth seat, with a borderline opening, add the number of spades to your HCP. If the total comes to 15 or more, it is worth opening. Here South has 15 on the fourth seat count and makes the normal opening. West has a routine overcall and North's negative double shows four spades (if not using the negative double in that way, North would bid 1♠). East raises to 2♥ and South is worth 2♠. It is important not to sell out at the two-level in such auctions and so West competes to 3♥.

Lead : 2 of spades. No reason to select a different suit.

Recommended play : South should win with the ace of spades and switch to the king of diamonds. North encourages and a low diamond goes to North's ace. North cashes the king of spades and leads a third diamond to South's queen, defeating the contract by one trick.

Notes : (1) South can tell that there are no more than two spade tricks for the defense and so starts setting up extra tricks in diamonds. If the defense starts with three rounds of spades, West can make 3♥.
(2) If East-West had passed out 2♠, North-South would have no trouble making eight tricks.
(3) Note the importance of the spade suit. Swap the majors and South should pass the hand in (11 HCP and only two spades = 13). With the majors reversed, if South did open, East-West could make 2♠ and North-South would need to compete to 3♥, one down.

CHAPTER 9

WEAK TWOS

In the beginning, all twos were forcing to game (Goren Twos). Then came Acol Twos where game force hands are opened 2♣ and the 2◇ / 2♡ / 2♠ openings showed a strong 5-card or longer suit and usually 8-9½ playing tricks. The major problem with these methods is the rarity of such powerful hands.

Modern systems are concerned with frequency of occurrence. You need to be able to deal with the hands that come up again and again, not with those that occur relatively rarely. Consequently, most duplicate partnerships have adopted weak twos which allow you to enter the bidding more often. The more action you generate, the better. Used in a disciplined fashion, weak twos enable partner to judge further action accurately and still make life tough for the opponents who usually have to start their auction at the three-level.

Standard American Style
2◇ / 2♡ / 2♠ = weak two in the suit bid
2♣ = artificial opening, 23+ points, game-forcing

Benjamin Twos Style
2♡ / 2♠ = weak two in the major suit bid
2◇ = artificial opening, 23+ points, game-forcing
2♣ = artificial opening, showing 8½-9½ playing tricks, about one trick short of game

Most pairs use weak twos in the majors. Very few use a weak 2◇ opening which has little pre-emptive or constructive value. It is better to adopt the Benjamin Twos structure which deals more effectively with the strong hands. Another choice gaining in popularity is to use the Multi-2◇ opening (see Chapter 23).

WEAK TWOS IN THE MAJORS
To open with a weak two, you should have :
1. A 6-card suit, headed by the queen or better and containing at least two honors. Suit Quality should be 8+. It might be fun to open a weak two on J-8-6-4-3-2, but it can do untold harm. If partner leads from A-x or K-x, this can easily cost a trick.

When vulnerable, you may open a weak two with a 7-card suit if the hand is not worth a 3-opening.
2. 6-10 HCP. With 11 HCP and a good 6-card suit, choose a 1-opening.
3. 7-8 losers. A minimum weak two has 8 losers and a maximum has 7.
4. No 4-card major. Do not to open a weak two with a 4-card holding in the other major. You may miss your best spot.
5. No freak shape. 6-3-2-2 and 6-3-3-1 patterns are normal. 6-4-2-1 is acceptable if the 4-card suit is a minor. 6-4-2-1s may be 6-loser hands.

One singleton is permitted for a weak two but not two singletons and not a void. Hands with such extreme shape have too much playing strength and partner will often be unable to appreciate the value of the combined hands. With these freak shapes, if you are unable to start with a 1-opening or a 3-opening, prefer to pass than open a weak two.

Weak Twos in third or fourth seat
Once partner has passed and you have no more than 10 points, prospects for game are poor. The above requirements therefore become more flexible. In third seat, the range expands to 6-12 HCP and it is not taboo to have a 7-card or 5-card suit rather than the normal 6-card holding. If it is a 5-card suit, it should contain three honors (e.g. A-K-J-x-x). In fourth seat, the range is played as 8-12 HCP, partly because it is so unlikely that there would be no opening bid ahead of a 7-point or weaker hand in fourth seat and partly because with 7 HCP or less, you are probably far better off to pass the hand in. A weak two in third or fourth seat may contain a void.

Some players open a weak two in first or second seat on a strong 5-card suit. Although it increases the frequency of opening, this practise cannot be recommended. In order to compete effectively at the three-level and to find decent sacrifices, partner needs to know the combined trump length. Opening weak twos on 5-card *and* 6-card suits makes it nigh impossible for partner to gauge the combined trump length correctly.

Examples

♠ A Q 8 7 6 3	♠ A Q 8 7 6 3	♠ K J 10 5 4 2
♡ 9 6	♡ 9 6	♡ 3
◇ 7 3 2	◇ 7 3 2	◇ A J 8
♣ 6 3	♣ K 6	♣ 7 4 2
Open 2♠	Open 2♠	Open 2♠
Minimum	Maximum	Maximum

Even though the third hand has 8 losers, it is treated as a maximum because of the 9 HCP and strong spade suit. A minimum weak two usually has two high card winners and a maximum will usually have three.

♠ 6 3	♠ 6 3	♠ 5
♡ Q J 10 9 6 2	♡ A K Q 9 6 2	♡ A K 8 6 3 2
◇ K 3 2	◇ 7 3	◇ 10 8 5 3
♣ 6 3	♣ 9 6 5	♣ Q 2
Open 2♡	Open 2♡	Open 2♡
Minimum	Maximum	Maximum

♠ 6 3	♠ - - -	♠ A 9 8
♡ J 8 7 6 4 2	♡ K J 10 8 6 2	♡ A Q J 9 3 2
◇ K 3 2	◇ 8 7 6 3	◇ 5 3
♣ A 3	♣ A 4 2	♣ 7 2
Pass.	Pass in 1st or	Open 1♡.
Suit quality	2nd seat. Open	Hand too
too poor for 2♡.	2♡ in 3rd seat.	strong for 2♡.

♠ K Q J 10 7 3	♠ A Q 8 7 6 4 3	♠ K Q J 10 5
♡ 6	♡ 6	♡ 3
◇ Q J 9 8 4	◇ 7 3 2	◇ J 8 5 3
♣ 2	♣ 6 4	♣ 7 4 2
Open 4♠.	Open 2♠ if vul,	Open 2♠ in
Too freakish	3♠ if not vul.	3rd seat. Pass
for 2♠.		1st or 2nd seat.

When are you maximum, when minimum?

6-7 HCP is normally a minimum, 9-10 = maximum.
8 losers = minimum, 7 losers = maximum.
6-4-2-1 : 7 losers = minimum, 6 losers = maximum.
Three cover cards = maximum.
Two cover cards = minimum.
'Cover card' = ace, guarded king (K-x or better) or guarded queen (Q-10-x or better).

Bidding structure after a weak two

(1) Raises of opener's suit are pre-emptive, not invitational. Opener is not to bid again.

(2) Change of suit is forcing. A new suit is a good 5-card or longer suit and a very strong hand. Opener should raise with 3 trumps or with Q-x or better support. The change of suit normally indicates a singleton or void in opener's suit.

(3) The OGUST 2NT Response

2NT asks opener to describe the strength of the hand and the strength of the 6-card major. Opener bids 3♣ / 3◇ with a minimum and 3♡ / 3♠ / 3NT if maximum. *Minors minimum, majors maximum.*

Opener's reply also indicates whether opener holds one, two or three of the top honors (A, K or Q) in the major. The cheapest reply in each case shows just one top honor.

After 2♡ : 2NT or 2♠ : 2NT —

3♣ = Minimum, 1 top honor	*Memory guide*	
3◇ = Minimum, 2 top honors	*for honors :*	
3♡ = Maximum, 1 top honor	1-2, 1-2-3	
3♠ = Maximum, 2 top honors		
3NT = 3 top honors (A-K-Q-x-x-x in the major)		

After the reply to 2NT, 3-of opener's-major is to play and any game bid is a signoff, too. 4NT is Blackwood and a new suit is played as a cue bid with opener's major agreed as the trump suit.

If they double the weak two for takeout : Redouble is strong, looking for penalties. 2NT is still Ogust while a new suit is genuine but is a rescue bid which opener should pass.

If they overcall with 2NT or a suit : If they bid 2♠ over 2♡, 2NT is still Ogust. In other cases, 3-of-opener's-major becomes an invitation to game. A new suit is forcing and double is for penalties.

If they overcall after responder has bid 2NT Ogust:
Make your normal reply if still available. If your normal reply is not available, pass.

Responder's strategy after a weak two

Singleton or void in opener's suit

Below 16 HCP : Pass. Your side does not have the values for game. With no fit with opener's suit, you are high enough already.

16 HCP or more : Bid a new suit (forcing) with a strong 5-card or longer suit or use the Ogust Convention (2NT — see later). With 16-18 HCP and no long, strong suit, bid 2NT and if opener shows a maximum, try 3NT, but opposite a minimum, sign off in 3-of-opener's major.

With 19 HCP or more, you should be in at least game, even opposite a minimum weak two. Bid a new suit or bid 3NT. If the quality of opener's suit is relevant, you can use the Ogust 2NT response.

If responder bids 3NT, that is to play and opener should normally pass. However, with a major which has a suit quality of 10 (6-card suit with 4 honors), it is better to remove 3NT to 4-Major. Such a suit plays well enough opposite a singleton or a void.

With 2+ cards in opener's suit

A maximum weak two can have six playing tricks. With tolerance (doubleton) or support (3+ trumps) for opener's major, responder should therefore try for game with four winners, and even better than three sure tricks may justify a move towards game.

Counting your tricks in support of opener :
A, K or Q of trumps = 1 trick
Outside suits : Count only your quick tricks, the winners in the first two rounds of a suit :
A-K = 2, A-Q = 1½, A = 1, K-Q = 1 and K-x = ½
With support for opener, you can count one trick for an outside singleton and two tricks for a void.

With 3 trumps and less than 2½ tricks : Raise to three level as a pre-empt.

With 4+ trumps and up to 3 tricks : Raise to game pre-emptively.

With 3½-4 tricks : Use the Ogust 2NT Convention. Bid game opposite a maximum, but sign off at the three-level in opener's major opposite a minimum.

With 4½-5½-tricks : Bid game, expecting to make. Whether opener has 5 or 6 tricks, game should be a reasonable bet.

With 6 or more tricks : Use the Ogust 2NT response and explore slam possibilities.

EXERCISES USING WEAK TWOS IN THE MAJORS

A. You are the dealer, neither side vulnerable. What do you do with each of these hands?

1. ♠ 9 7 3	2. ♠ A K 9 7 6 2	3. ♠ A K	4. ♠ K 9 5 2	5. ♠ A Q J 9 8 7
♡ A J 9 8 5 4	♡ K J 7	♡ 1 0 9 8 6 3 2	♡ A J 7 5 4 3	♡ 2
◊ K J 2	◊ 8 4	◊ Q 9 7	◊ 8 7	◊ J 2
♣ 7	♣ 5 2	♣ 9 5	♣ 6	♣ J 9 3 2

B. Partner has opened 2♡. What is your response with each of these hands?

1. ♠ A 9 2	2. ♠ A 9 7 4	3. ♠ K Q 9 8	4. ♠ 7 4 3 2	5. ♠ K J 10 2
♡ K J 5 3	♡ K 3	♡ 6	♡ A 9 2	♡ 2
◊ 7	◊ Q J 7 2	◊ A Q 9 6 2	◊ A K 8 6	◊ A K 9 3
♣ Q J 7 4 3	♣ 8 6 4	♣ J 8 7	♣ K 4	♣ K Q J 4

C. The bidding has started 2♠ : 2NT. What is opener's rebid with these hands?

1. ♠ K Q 9 6 3 2	2. ♠ A K Q 6 4 2	3. ♠ A J 8 7 4 2	4. ♠ Q J 7 6 4 2	5. ♠ A Q 9 6 4 3
♡ 5 3	♡ 2	♡ 6 4	♡ 8 2	♡ 4
◊ J 8 5	◊ 8 6 3	◊ K Q	◊ 10 6	◊ J 7 4
♣ 9 7	♣ 7 4 3	♣ 9 6 2	♣ A 5 4	♣ K 8 2

PARTNERSHIP BIDDING : How should the following hands be bid? West is the dealer each time.

SET 17 — WEST	SET 17 — EAST	SET 18 — WEST	SET 18 — EAST
1. ♠ K 3	1. ♠ 9 5 2	1. ♠ 7	1. ♠ A Q 9 4
♡ K Q 9 7 5 3	♡ A 6 2	♡ A Q J 6 4 3	♡ 7
◊ 8 6 4	◊ A K J 3	◊ 9 7 2	◊ K Q 6 4 3
♣ 7 2	♣ K Q 4	♣ J 10 3	♣ K 8 4
2. ♠ K Q 5 3	2. ♠ 6 4	2. ♠ Q 2	2. ♠ A K 4 3
♡ A 5	♡ K J 10 7 4 3	♡ K Q 8 6 5 3	♡ 2
◊ J 6	◊ K 3	◊ 6 5	◊ A K 9 8
♣ 9 8 5 4 2	♣ J 6 3	♣ 9 8 3	♣ K Q J 10
3. ♠ A K 8 6 3 2	3. ♠ Q 9 7 5	3. ♠ 5 2	3. ♠ A K 4 3
♡ 5 3 2	♡ 8	♡ K Q J 10 9 6	♡ 2
◊ 5	◊ A 9 7 2	◊ 6 5	◊ A K Q 9 8
♣ 6 4 3	♣ A J 5 2	♣ 9 8 3	♣ K Q J
4. ♠ A J 9 6 4 3	4. ♠ K 8 7 5 2	4. ♠ A Q 10 7 6 5	4. ♠ J 4 2
♡ 9 7 2	♡ 5 4	♡ 7 3	♡ A K 5 2
◊ 8 3	◊ 9	◊ 9 5 2	◊ A Q 4 3
♣ K 9	♣ Q 8 5 4 2	♣ K 8	♣ 9 5
5. ♠ A 9 7 4 2	5. ♠ K Q J 8 3	5. ♠ A K 8 7 4 3	5. ♠ Q 10 5 2
♡ Q 3	♡ 10 5 4	♡ 5 4 2	♡ A 9 3
◊ A 9 8 3	◊ 2	◊ 3 2	◊ A 8 5
♣ 7 2	♣ A 9 6 4	♣ 8 6	♣ A 10 4
6. ♠ 9 6 2	6. ♠ A K 5 4	6. ♠ A K Q 8 7 3	6. ♠ 9 6 4 2
♡ A J 7 6 4 2	♡ 8 5	♡ 7 2	♡ A 8 5
◊ 7	◊ A J 3 2	◊ 9 7	◊ K Q J
♣ Q 8 7	♣ K J 2	♣ 6 4 3	♣ A 7 2

PLAY HANDS ON WEAK TWO OPENINGS
(These hands can be made up by using pages 160-167)

Hand 33 : 3NT vs. 4-Major — Establishing a long suit

Dealer North : Nil vulnerable

WEST	NORTH	EAST	SOUTH
	2♡	Pass	4♡
Pass	Pass	Pass	

NORTH
♠ 6
♡ A K J 9 8 3
♢ J 10
♣ 7 4 3 2

WEST
♠ Q 10
♡ 6 4
♢ 7 6 5 4 3
♣ K Q 10 9

EAST
♠ K J 9 7
♡ 7 5 2
♢ K Q 9 2
♣ J 6

SOUTH
♠ A 8 5 4 3 2
♡ Q 10
♢ A 8
♣ A 8 5

Bidding : South has four clearcut winners (three aces and the queen of trumps plus good potential for an extra trick — a potential ruff in diamonds and a spade suit that might be established). That justifies bidding game rather than checking on opener's strength. If South did use 2NT (Ogust), North would bid 3♠ (maximum points and two top honors in hearts). South could see that 3NT would be available but should still choose 4♡ where there would be better chances for overtricks.

Lead : King of diamonds. J-x is usually a poor lead. Better to choose the suit where the honors are touching (diamonds) than the suit where the honors are split (spades).

Recommended play : North wins with the ♢A and should immediately set about establishing the spades. Ace of spades, ruff a spade, heart to the ten, ruff a spade, heart to the queen, ruff a spade. Two spade winners are now set up in dummy. Draw the last trump and then cross to the ♣A to cash the spades. 11 tricks.

Notes : (1) If trumps are drawn at once, declarer is relying on clubs 3-3, less than a 40% chance.
(2) A better plan is to ruff a club with one of dummy's top trumps : win ♢A and play ace and another club. The opponents can thwart this plan by switching to trumps and eliminating dummy's ruffing power.
(3) When setting up a long suit, use the trump entries to dummy before using the outside entries.
(4) Note how much better you do in 4♡ (450) than in 3NT (400). The possibility of overtricks is a vital consideration at pairs.

Hand 34 : Using Ogust 2NT — Establishing a long suit

Dealer East : N-S vulnerable

WEST	NORTH	EAST	SOUTH
		2♠	Pass
2NT	Pass	3♠	Pass
4♠	Pass	Pass	Pass

NORTH
♠ 5 3
♡ 6 6 4 2
♢ K Q 10
♣ J 9 6 5

WEST
♠ K 9 2
♡ J 10
♢ A J 2
♣ A Q 10 8 7

EAST
♠ A Q J 10 6 4
♡ Q 9
♢ 7 5 4
♣ 3 2

SOUTH
♠ 8 7
♡ A K 8 7 3
♢ 9 8 6 3
♣ K 4

Bidding : West can count 3½ tricks in support of spades. Add the heart shortage and the club length and there is enough potential to try for game. East has 9 HCP but 8 losers. Because of the strong spades (Suit Quality 10), East should bid 3♠ to show maximum points and two top honors in spades. The jack and the ten are not conisdered 'top' honors.

Lead : Ace (or king) of hearts. Most top players prefer to lead the ace from A-K-x or longer. After cashing two hearts, South should switch to a diamond. From the bidding and play so far, South can tell that North has diamond strength.

Recommended play : East should take the ace of diamonds at once, cross to hand with a trump to the ace and lead a club. When South plays low, finesse the queen. If that lost, declarer would be two down. When the ♣Q wins, cash the ♣A and ruff a third club high. Play a low spade to dummy's 9 and ruff a fourth club. Dummy's last club is now a winner. Cross to the king of spades, cash the club and discard a diamond loser.

Notes : (1) If two rounds of trumps are drawn before starting on the clubs, declarer is one entry short to set up the clubs if they divide 4-2.
(2) If East ruffs the third round of clubs low, South overruffs. Two down.
(3) With only two clubs in hand, finesse the queen of clubs, not the ten.
(4) Declarer succeeds even if the first round of diamonds is ducked. The advantage of taking the first diamond comes when clubs are 3-3 with the ♣K with South. After finessing ♣Q, cashing the ♣A and ruffing a club, there are two club winners established in dummy and both diamond losers can be discarded.

Hand 35 : Action after a weak two — Card reading — Playing for the overtrick

Dealer South : E-W vulnerable

	WEST	NORTH	EAST	SOUTH

NORTH
♠ 7 4
♡ J 10 9 8
◇ K Q 9
♣ K J 6 5

WEST	NORTH	EAST	SOUTH
			Pass
2♠	Pass	Pass	Pass

WEST
♠ A K 10 6 5 3
♡ 7 4 2
◇ J 7 2
♣ 9

EAST
♠ 9 8 2
♡ Q 5 3
◇ A 6 4
♣ A Q 7 4

SOUTH
♠ Q J
♡ A K 6
◇ 10 8 5 3
♣ 10 8 3 2

Bidding : East has less than three quick tricks and so prospects for game are poor. If the opposition compete, East would be worth a push to 3♠ as East knows the partnership has 9 trumps.

Most club players would pass out 2♠ on the South cards but many top players would compete with a double. This is not so risky as South is a passed hand. North may well bid 3♡ which would not play well (2 spades, 2 clubs, 2 club ruffs and a diamond to be lost) but it may push East-West to 3♠.

Lead : Jack of hearts. Choose the sequence that is solid (hearts) rather than the suit where there are only two honors in sequence (diamonds) or the suit with no sequence (clubs).

Recommended play : Declarer plays low in dummy and so does South. After three rounds of hearts, South shifts to the 3 of diamonds. Declarer plays low and North's 9 forces the ace. Trumps are drawn in two rounds and the contract is now secure.

Should declarer take the club finesse to try for an overtrick? If the finesse works, declarer can discard a diamond loser and make nine tricks. If the finesse fails, the opponents can probably cash two diamonds and defeat the partscore.

Notes : (1) Deciding whether to jeopardise the contract for an overtrick is a common problem at pairs. If your contract is excellent and the finesse is 50%, it is not worth the risk. If your contract is poor, you should take any reasonable risk to try to improve your score. If your contract is normal as here, it usually does not pay to risk the contract if the chance for an overtrick is 50% or worse.

(2) Here the club finesse is almost a certainty. South passed as dealer but has turned up with A-K in hearts and Q-J in spades. That makes 10 points. If South had the king of clubs, that would make 13 HCP and South would almost certainly have opened despite the poor spade holding. Therefore take the club finesse.

Hand 36 : Weak two in fourth seat — Card reading — Discovery play

Dealer West : Both vulnerable

NORTH
♠ J 10 8
♡ A 9 8
◇ A Q 10
♣ 10 7 5 4

WEST	NORTH	EAST	SOUTH
Pass	Pass	Pass	2♡
Pass	Pass	Pass	

WEST
♠ A K 7 2
♡ 7 5 4
◇ 9 6 2
♣ A 6 3

EAST
♠ Q 9 6 4
♡ K
◇ 8 7 5 4
♣ Q J 9 8

SOUTH
♠ 5 3
♡ Q J 10 6 3 2
◇ K J 3
♣ K 2

Bidding : In fourth seat, the weak two is usually played as 8-12 HCP. With less, pass the deal in. With 3 hearts, West's shape does not justify coming in over 2♡. With only 2½ tricks, North has no reason to push higher. With the shortage in hearts and four cards in each other suit, East has the right shape to compete. Again, most club players would pass while most experts would compete with a double. West would bid 2♠, which makes easily, and North would compete to 3♡. Do not sell out at the two-level when your side has a trump fit.

Lead : Ace of spades. East encourages and West continues with the king of spades and a third spade.

Recommended play : South ruffs the third spade and the natural inclination is to tackle trumps next. However, South should cross to dummy with a diamond and lead a club to the king. West wins and may return a club. South ruffs the third club and leads a heart to the ace. When the king drops singleton, South makes nine tricks and the vital overtrick.

Notes : (1) The standard play in hearts is to lead the queen and let it run if West plays low.

(2) Since the club finesse has to be taken some time, there is little risk in taking it early. If East has the ace of clubs, South can later play the hearts in the normal fashion.

(3) When West turns up with the ace of clubs as well as the A-K of spades, that makes 11 HCP. As West passed as dealer, West cannot hold the king of hearts as well. Since the finesse must lose, play the ace. Playing on clubs early is a 'discovery' play. Locating the ace of clubs helps you in the play of the hearts.

CHAPTER 10

THE BENJAMIN 2♣ OPENING

A sound approach for those who play weak twos is the use of 2♣ and 2♦ for strong hands. The Benjamin Twos structure uses 2♦ for game-going hands and 2♣ for hands about one trick short of game. The 2♣ opening caters for the 19-21 point hand with a 6+ suit, a hand that cannot be shown in standard methods. The typical problem :

♠ A K 2	Suppose you open 1♦ and
♥ A 6	partner responds 1♥?
♦ A K J 9 8 4	What now?
♣ 6 2	

You are too strong for 3♦, which shows 16-18 points and is not forcing. 3NT is just a gamble with nothing in clubs and to bid 1♠ with a 3-card suit should leave you cold.

The Benjamin 2♣ opening solves the problem. You open 2♣ and rebid 3♦ showing the strength and the good suit.

♠ A Q	Similarly, suppose you open 1♣
♥ A K 4	on this hand. What is your rebid
♦ 6 2	if partner bids 1♥? What about
♣ A K 10 9 8 4	after a 1♠ response?

You are strong enough for game but which game? Over 1♥, there is no satisfactory rebid. Over 1♠, many would choose a 2♥ reverse, but this does not come risk-free. Opening 2♣ Benjamin and rebidding 3♣ shows the strength and the nature of the hand.

As the popularity of the Benjamin 2♣ increased, the problems began when players used it on unsuitable hands, on any 19-21 point hands. 2♣ is fine for the 19-21 point hand with a 6-card or longer suit. It may be used for other powerful hands but it does not work well if you open 2♣ willy-nilly on any 19-21 point hand.

The playing strength for the 2♣ opening should be about 8½-9½ tricks. You should open 2♣ when you are worried that partner may pass your 1-opening and you may still miss a game. In general, an 8-trick hand (5 losers) is not strong enough. Opposite that, you need two tricks to make 4♥ or 4♠ a good bet. With two tricks or even 1½ tricks, partner will have enough to respond to a 1-opening. When just one ace or one useful king in partner's hand is all you need for game, it is sensible to start with 2♣. In other words, open 2♣ when you are about one trick short of game.

Open 2♣ with an unbalanced hand and 8½-9½ playing tricks. The HCP strength should be 16-22 if not balanced. Below 16 HCP, start with a 1-opening, or a pre-empt if below 10 HCP. The 2♣ opening may also be used for balanced hands of 23-24 points. If stronger, choose the 2♦ opening (see Chapter 11).

Another sensible guide : Open 2♣ with —
1. **23-24 HCP and a balanced hand**
2. **21-22 HCP and an unbalanced hand**
3. **21-22 HCP and a 5-3-3-2 with a 5-card major**
4. **18-20 HCP and a 6+ suit.** 18 HCP is borderline.

With poor short suit holdings (J-x, Q-x), choose the jump-rebid sequence such as 1♥ : 1NT, 3♥ . . .
5. **16-18 HCP and a 7+ suit.** 16 HCP is borderline.

Avoid opening 2♣ with a two-suiter below about 21-22 HCP. Strong two-suiters that are not worth insisting on game can be shown via a 1-opening followed by a jump-shift, such as 1♥ : 1NT, 3♣.

Do not open 2♣ with a balanced 19-20 points. Opposite this strength and shape, you need partner to have 6 points or more to make game a good bet. With that, partner will respond to your 1-opening. If partner cannot respond to a 1-opening, you are better off being passed out at the 1-level than reaching 2NT with 19-20 HCP opposite nothing or just one or two points. With a balanced 21-22, open 2NT.

As a rough guide, then, open 2♣ with —

23-24 HCP and a balanced hand
21-22 HCP and a 5+ suit
19-20 HCP and a 6+ suit
17-18 HCP and a 7+ suit

RESPONDING TO 2♣

2♦ = Artificial negative response, 0-7 HCP and less than 1½ quick tricks.

All other responses = positive responses, 8+ HCP or 1½ quick tricks or better.

Quick tricks : A-K = 2, A-Q = 1½, A = 1, K-Q = 1 and K-x = ½.

CHOOSING YOUR POSITIVE RESPONSE

It is playable for a 2-Major response to be based on just a 4-card suit but it is recommended that any suit reply shows a 5-card or longer suit and that the 2NT response is a balanced hand of 8 HCP or more.

What should you do with a positive response and a 4-4-4-1 pattern? The good news is that this is a rare shape. You should bid your cheapest 4-card suit and hope for the best. Partner will expect a 5-card major but it is not worth changing your whole bidding structure to cater for one infrequent pattern. Almost always a 2-Major response is a 5-card or longer suit and it pays to treat it as such.

With a two-suiter, bid your longer suit first and bid the higher suit first with a 5-5 or 6-6 pattern.

OPENER'S REBID

(a) After the 2◊ negative response

Any rebid by opener can be passed. Opener should choose :

2♡ / 2♠ = 5+ suit, 8½ tricks or 21-22 HCP. If you have opened 2♣ with a 4-4-4-1 and 21-22 HCP, bid your cheaper 4-card major.

3♡ / 3♠ = 6+ suit and exactly 9 playing tricks

4♡ / 4♠ = 6+ suit and 9½ playing tricks

3♣ / 3◊ = 8½-9½ tricks, usually 6+ suit (it may be a 5-card suit occasionally)

4♣ / 4◊ = 9½-10 tricks, 6+ suit, unsuitable for a try at 3NT

5♣ / 5◊ = 10½ tricks, 7+ suit, unsuitable for 3NT

3NT = long, solid minor suit with at least two outside suits stopped and nine running tricks or thereabouts. A typical 3NT rebid might look like one of these :

♠ A 3	♠ 8 2
♡ 9 6 4	♡ A K
◊ A K Q J 8 7 2	◊ A 5 2
♣ A	♣ A K Q J 9 2

While 3NT may not be a certainty, you are more likely to take nine tricks in no-trumps than eleven tricks in your minor opposite a negative response where responder has less than 1½ quick tricks.

It is reasonable to take a chance on one unguarded suit with a 3NT rebid but it is sensible to have at least two cards in such a suit. With a void or a singleton, a rebid of 3NT is too risky. Prefer a rebid in your minor suit.

2NT = the balanced 23-24 point hand. This rebid is not forcing but responder would pass only with a very weak hand. With two points or more, it is worth trying for game. After the 2NT rebid, bidding proceeds as after a 2NT opening, with 3♣ Stayman, 3◊ and 3♡ transfers, and so on (see Chapter 4).

(b) After a positive response

Any positive response is forcing to game and so any bid below game is forcing. Opener's rebid is natural. Bid your longer suit first and the higher suit with a 5-5 or 6-6 pattern. With a 4-4-4-1 and a singleton in responder's suit, rebid in no-trumps.

Responder's suit may be supported with 3-card or better support but it will often work out better to show your own long suit first and support responder on the next round. This will help responder assess the fit for slam purposes. Particularly if you have only 3-card support, prefer to describe your hand first (e.g., with a 2NT rebid) and show the support for responder later.

A jump rebid after a positive response is best played as a splinter : 4+ support for responder and a singleton or void in the suit bid. For example,

♠ A K 6 3	Open 2♣. If partner bids 2♡,
♡ A Q 2	bid 3♣ and support the hearts
◊ 2	later. If partner bids 2♠, jump to
♣ A K J 7 3	4◊ (splinter).

After a 2NT positive response, it is sensible to play 3♣ as Stayman.

RESPONDER'S REBID

(a) After the 2◊ negative response

You may pass any rebid by opener but you are not obliged to pass. You should certainly bid again with one sure winner in your hand or with 5-7 HCP. You may raise opener's suit with three trumps or better support. Where opener's rebid is in a major, you should be eager to raise the major. Where opener's rebid is 3♣ or 3◊ and you have enough to bid, angle towards 3NT if possible rather than raise the minor. A risky 3NT will usually result in a better score than a minor suit game.

A new suit by responder will be a 5+ suit while a no-trump rebid would show about 5-7 points and no 5+ suit of your own. A no-trump rebid is acceptable with a 4-4-4-1.

A jump rebid by responder is a splinter (4+ support for opener and a singleton or void in the suit bid).

♠ 9 8 7 3 2	In reply to 2♣, you bid 2◊
♡ 2	negative. If opener rebids 2♡,
◊ A 8 3 2	bid 2♠, but if opener's rebid is
♣ 9 6 4	2♠, you are worth 4♡ (splinter).

After the negative 2◊ response, it is more useful to treat responder's jump rebid in a new suit, such as 4♡ here, as a splinter than as natural. With long hearts, bid 3♡ over 2♠ and then rebid 4♡ if you wish.

If the bidding has started 2♣ : 2◊, 3♡ or 3♠, you may raise the major suit with doubleton support or better and the slightest chance for a trick. A king or better would be enough.

(b) After a positive response

The partnership is committed to game at least. As opener's hand is limited, even though very strong, it is usually up to responder to initiate slam auctions.

A rebid of 3NT by responder indicates a minimum positive response and insufficient for a slam. Other game rebids by responder including supporting opener's suit to game also suggest slam is unlikely.

Raising opener's suit below game shows slam prospects. As opener has around four losers or about nine winners, responder should envisage slam potential with three winners or more if a trump fit exists. With 12 HCP or more or four winners or better, slam figures to be a good bet anyway.

EXERCISES FOR THE BENJAMIN 2♣ OPENING

A. You are the dealer, neither side vulnerable. What do you do with each of these hands?

1. ♠ 9 7 3	2. ♠ A K Q 9 7 6 2	3. ♠ A K Q	4. ♠ A Q J 7 2	5. ♠ A Q 8
♡ A K J 8 5 4	♡ J 3	♡ 10 9 8 6 3	♡ 8	♡ 2
◇ A K J	◇ 8	◇ A K Q 3	◇ A Q J	◇ A K 2
♣ 7	♣ K Q J	♣ J	♣ A K J 9	♣ A K 9 8 4 2

B. Partner has opened 2♣. What is your response with each of these hands?

1. ♠ K J 8 7 4	2. ♠ K J 8 7 4	3. ♠ K J 8 7	4. ♠ 9 2	5. ♠ K J 10 2
♡ 6 3	♡ 7	♡ 7 5	♡ Q J 9 3	♡ 2
◇ 7 2	◇ A 7 6 4	◇ J 7 4	◇ A K 9 8 6 2	◇ Q J 8 4
♣ Q 7 4 3	♣ 8 6 4	♣ A J 8 7	♣ 4	♣ K 8 4 2

C. The bidding has started 2♣ : 2◇. What is opener's rebid with these hands?

1. ♠ A 4 3	2. ♠ A 4 3	3. ♠ A K	4. ♠ A K J 8	5. ♠ A Q 9 6 4
♡ A K Q 8 5 3	♡ 6 2	♡ 6	♡ A K	♡ K Q 7
◇ A K	◇ A K	◇ A Q 4 2	◇ Q 8 2	◇ A 6
♣ 6 2	♣ A K Q 8 5 3	♣ A K 9 8 6 2	♣ A Q J 4	♣ A K 8

PARTNERSHIP BIDDING : How should the following hands be bid? West is the dealer each time.

SET 19 — WEST	SET 19 — EAST	SET 20 — WEST	SET 20 — EAST
1. ♠ A K 3	1. ♠ 8 6 5 2	1. ♠ J 3	1. ♠ K Q 10 9 4 2
♡ A K Q 8 7 3 2	♡ 10 4	♡ 5 2	♡ K 8 4
◇ 9 2	◇ J 8 7 3	◇ A K Q	◇ 7 5 2
♣ 8	♣ 10 7 4	♣ A K Q J 8 6	♣ 3
2. ♠ A K 3	2. ♠ 8	2. ♠ 2	2. ♠ A K J 8 3
♡ A K Q 8 7 3 2	♡ 10 4	♡ K Q 5 3 2	♡ 6
◇ 9 2	◇ J 7 5 4 3	◇ K 6 5	◇ A Q J 2
♣ 8	♣ 9 7 5 4 2	♣ 9 7 4 2	♣ K Q J
3. ♠ 6 3	3. ♠ A K Q J 9 4 2	3. ♠ A Q J 8 7 3	3. ♠ K 5 2
♡ 5 4 2	♡ 8 3	♡ 6 3	♡ Q J 8 7 2
◇ Q 7 4 3	◇ A 2	◇ K 9	◇ Q J 4
♣ 8 6 5 2	♣ K Q	♣ A K Q	♣ J 9
4. ♠ 7 6	4. ♠ A K Q J 9 4 2	4. ♠ Q 9 6 4 2	4. ♠ 3
♡ A 7 4 2	♡ 8 3	♡ A 3	♡ K Q J
◇ 7 6 4 3	◇ A 2	◇ 9 7 5 2	◇ A K Q J 4 3
♣ 6 5 2	♣ K Q	♣ A 10	♣ K J 5
5. ♠ 7 6 3 2	5. ♠ A 8	5. ♠ K Q	5. ♠ 8 6
♡ J 8 7 2	♡ 5 4 3	♡ A 10 9 8 7 5 3	♡ K Q 6 2
◇ 7 6 4 3	◇ A	◇ A K Q	◇ J 5
♣ 6	♣ A K Q J 9 8 2	♣ 5	♣ A K 8 7 3
6. ♠ K Q	6. ♠ A 5 4 3	6. ♠ Q 10 5 4 2	6. ♠ A K 8 7
♡ A K J 7 6 4	♡ 8 5 3 2	♡ A 8 3 2	♡ 9 4
◇ A K	◇ J 8 3 2	◇ 9 5	◇ A K Q
♣ 8 7 4	♣ 2	♣ 8 4	♣ A K J 6

PLAY HANDS ON THE BENJAMIN 2♣ OPENING

(These hands can be made up by using pages 160-167)

Hand 37 : Rebidding to show nine tricks — Competitive action

Dealer North : N-S vulnerable

NORTH
♠ K Q 9 8
♡ 10
♢ Q 9 3 2
♣ K 7 6 4

WEST
♠ 7
♡ 6 4 2
♢ 10 8 7 5
♣ J 9 8 3 2

EAST
♠ A 4 2
♡ A K Q 9 8 7 3
♢ A 4
♣ Q

SOUTH
♠ J 10 6 5 3
♡ J 5
♢ K J 6
♣ A 10 5

WEST	NORTH	EAST	SOUTH
	Pass	2♣	Pass
2♢	Pass	3♡	Pass
4♡	Pass	Pass	Pass

Bidding : East has a strong hand but not enough to insist on game. After West's 2♢ negative, showing 0-7 points, East's jump to 3♡ shows a good 6-card or longer suit and exactly nine playing tricks. Had East's rebid been 2♠ or 3♠, West would have passed, but the heart support and the singleton spade is certainly enough to raise to 4♡. Note that if East would have opened 1♡, West should pass this and an excellent game might be missed.

Lead : 5 of spades. South has no attractive lead. The bidding suggests a trump lead, but J-x in trumps can be risky. A spade lead here is the least of evils.

Recommended play : The play is much the same regardless of the lead. On a spade lead, win the ace of spades, ruff a spade, play a heart to the ace, ruff a spade, play a diamond to the ace and draw trumps. Making 11 tricks. On a trump lead, win ace of hearts, cash ace of spades, ruff a spade, diamond to the ace and ruff the last spade, leading to the same result.

Notes : It is difficult for North-South to enter the auction but 4♠ is an excellent spot for North-South. After East wins the first heart and say, switches to the ♣Q, taken by the ace, declarer leads a spade to the king. If East wins and returns a spade, take this in the North hand and led a diamond to the king. Cross back to the North hand with a trump and lead a second diamond. East's ace does not capture an honor and declarer can discard the club loser on the ♢Q later. This line is available no matter how the defenders wriggle.

At any other vulnerability, North might make a delayed takeout double of 4♡ (on the auction, it cannot sensibly be a penalty double by a passed hand) and South would bid 4♠. After West passes 4♠, East cannot see four tricks in defense and so should push on to 5♡ which makes. At adverse vulnerability, it is very, very tough for North to risk the double of 4♡.

Hand 38 : Rebidding with a solid minor

Dealer East : E-W vulnerable

NORTH
♠ 10 6 5 4
♡ 8 6 3
♢ 5 3
♣ J 8 6 4

WEST
♠ K Q 8 7 2
♡ K 4 2
♢ 9 8 4
♣ 7 5

EAST
♠ A 9
♡ Q J 10 7 5
♢ 10 6
♣ Q 10 9 2

SOUTH
♠ J 3
♡ A 9
♢ A K Q J 7 2
♣ A K 3

WEST	NORTH	EAST	SOUTH
		Pass	2♣
Pass	2♢	Pass	3NT
Pass	Pass	Pass	

Bidding : South has 22 HCP and four losers, not enough to choose a game-force opening. After the negative response, South's best shot is 3NT. Without a spade lead, nine tricks are almost certain and a spade lead will be fatal only if the opponents can take five or more tricks at once. Certainly 3NT is more likely to succeed than 5♢. With four losers, South can hardly expect partner to cover two of those losers after the 2♢ negative response. Note that North would pass a 3♢ rebid.

Lead : 7 of spades. There is no reason to choose other than the normal long suit lead.

Recommended play : East wins with the ace of spades and may well try a switch to the queen of hearts (hoping for K-x with South and A-x-x with West). South wins and has nine tricks on top.

Notes : (1) When South runs the diamonds East cannot afford to discard two clubs. Otherwise declarer makes four club tricks and eleven tricks in all.
(2) If East returns a spade, West can cash two more spades. A fourth spade (or a cunning 8 of spades at trick three) would give declarer ten tricks. East should signal with the queen of hearts on the third spade.

Hand 39 : Rebids by opener and responder — Defensive technique

Dealer South : Both vulnerable

NORTH
- ♠ J 5 4
- ♡ K Q J 6 4 2
- ◇ Q 3
- ♣ J 2

WEST	NORTH	EAST	SOUTH
			2♣
Pass	2♡	Pass	3♣
Pass	3♡	Pass	4♡
Pass	Pass	Pass	

WEST	EAST
♠ A Q 7 6 2	♠ K 10 9
♡ 5 3	♡ A 10 9
◇ 8 7 6 4	◇ J 10 9 5 2
♣ 10 3	♣ 6 5

SOUTH
- ♠ 8 3
- ♡ 8 7
- ◇ A K
- ♣ A K Q 9 8 7 4

Bidding : Even with only 16 HCP, South has nine playing tricks and should open 2♣ rather than 1♣. Opening 1♣ and rebidding with a jump to 3♣ shows a 6+ suit, 16-18 points and 5-6 losers. A 4-loser hand is too strong for that sequence. North's 2♡ shows 8+ points and a 5-card or longer suit. Repeating the hearts then shows a 6+ suit, allowing South to raise with just a doubleton. Note that if 2♡ could be just a 4-card suit, the 3♡ rebid might be just five hearts, making life very tough for opener.

Lead : Jack of diamonds. Nothing else has greater appeal.

Recommended play : Declarer wins in dummy and should lead a spade, hoping to ruff a spade in dummy.

Notes : (1) If declarer leads a spade and the defense tries to counter the threat of the ruff by playing ace and another heart, declarer makes twelve tricks. The defense should switch to a trump but not play the ace. Then if declarer leads a second spade, the defense can win, cash the ace of hearts and a third spade.
(2) If declarer leads a spade and the defense does not switch to a trump, the contract cannot be beaten.
(3) If declarer leads a heart to the king at trick two and East wins with the ace, the contract cannot be defeated. If East fails to switch to a spade, declarer makes twelve tricks and if East does switch to a spade, the contract can be held to ten tricks.
(4) East can see that there are no tricks for the defense in the minors and the only hope to beat the contract is to take four tricks in the majors. If East lets the king of hearts hold, the defense can later win the ace of hearts to draw dummy's last trump and cash their spade tricks.

Hand 40 : Slam bidding — Playing for an overtrick

Dealer West : Both vulnerable

NORTH
- ♠ 8 7 6 5
- ♡ K 3
- ◇ K Q 10 9
- ♣ 8 7 3

WEST	NORTH	EAST	SOUTH
2♣	Pass	3♣	Pass
3♡	Pass	4NT	Pass
5♣	Pass	5NT	Pass
6◇	Pass	6♡	All pass

WEST	EAST
♠ A K 3	♠ J
♡ A Q J 10 8 7	♡ 9 5 4 2
◇ A J 8	◇ 7 6 3
♣ 6	♣ A K Q J 5

SOUTH
- ♠ Q 10 9 4 2
- ♡ 6
- ◇ 5 4 2
- ♣ 10 9 4 2

Bidding : As West has shown 8+ tricks, East with 4+ winners should look for slam once the heart fit is located. East might splinter with 4♠ over 3♡, but given West's known strength, it is unlikely that the diamond suit is wide open.

5NT, the king ask, is either a grand slam try or aimed at reaching 6NT. If East-West are using 4NT Roman Key Card Blackwood (see Chapter 13), West's reply would be 5♣ (showing 0 or 3 key cards) and East would bid 6♡ at once since one key card is known to be missing.

Lead : King of diamonds. No reason for any other lead.

Recommended play : Declarer wins with the ace of diamonds. Declarer should continue by playing three top clubs and discarding the diamond losers. Next comes the heart finesse, losing. West wins any return, draws the last trump and ruffs the spade loser in dummy. Making twelve tricks.

Notes : (1) At teams or rubber bridge where safety first is vital and overtricks are usually of little significance, the best play is to cash the ace of hearts at trick two and if the king of hearts has not dropped, tackle the clubs next. The standard play in hearts is to lead the nine and let it run if South plays low.
(2) At pairs duplicate, the overtrick may be vital since 6♡ figures to be found by most pairs. Taking the heart finesse is far more likely to avoid a heart loser than playing for the drop. There is a slight risk in playing the clubs first but the risk is worthwhile in giving you a better chance to avoid a loser in trumps. As it happens, both lines bring in twelve tricks.

CHAPTER 11

THE BENJAMIN 2◇ OPENING

Playing Benjamin Twos, the 2♣ opening caters for hands about one trick short of game, while the 2◇ opening covers hands which are forcing to game.

Open 2◇ with :

(a) Any balanced hand of 25 HCP or more.

(b) Any non-balanced hand of 23 HCP or more

(c) Any hand of 16-22 HCP with 10 playing tricks or better (3 losers or fewer) and a long major.

(d) Any hand of 16-22 HCP with 10½ playing tricks or better (2½ losers or fewer) with a long minor as the dominant suit.

Hands just short of a 2◇ opening should start with 2♣ (see Chapter 10), or 2NT if 21-22 balanced.

RESPONDING TO 2◇

2♡ = Artificial negative response, 0-7 HCP and less than 1½ quick tricks.

Quick tricks : A-K = 2, A-Q = 1½, A = 1, K-Q = 1 and K-x = ½.

Any hand of 0-5 HCP should give the negative response. Most hands of 6-7 HCP should also bid 2♡ negative but holdings such as A-K (2 tricks), an ace plus a king in another suit (1½ tricks) or an A-Q suit (1½ tricks) are worth a positive response.

All other responses = positive responses, 8+ HCP or 1½ quick tricks or better.

Any positive response indicates slam is likely. Opener has 23+ points and responder has 8+, or opener has 10+ tricks and opener has 1½ or better. In each case, the slam potential is good.

The function of the negative response is to deny values suitable for a slam. If opener has three losers and responder has less than 1½ quick tricks, slam is not likely to be a good bet.

The sequence 2◇ : 2♡, 2NT shows a balanced hand of 25-27 HCP and is forcing to game. Further bidding follows the same structure as after a 2NT opening (3♣ Stayman, transfers, etc.). For details, see Chapter 5. Use 2◇ : 2♡, 3NT for 28-30 HCP. Responder can raise no-trumps to invite slam.

CHOOSING YOUR POSITIVE RESPONSE

With positive values, it is best to play that any suit reply shows a 5-card or longer suit. The 2NT response is a balanced hand of 8 HCP or more. If your suit is hearts, you will have to bid 3♡ over 2◇, as 2♡ is the negative reply. With a 4-4-4-1, bid your cheapest 4-card suit and hope for the best. With a two-suiter bid your longer suit first, and with a 5-5 or 6-6 pattern, start with the higher-ranking suit.

OPENER'S REBID

(a) After the 2♡ negative response

(i) Opener has a balanced hand

23-24 points : Rebid 2NT (not forcing). Further bidding is the same as after a 2NT opening (see Chapter 4).

25-28 points : Rebid 3NT. Then, 4♣ by responder is Stayman, 4◇ is natural and forcing. Any suit game is to play. Jumps to 5♡ or 5♠ invite slam. 4NT shows 5-6 points balanced and invites 6NT while 5NT shows 7 points balanced and invites 6NT.

29-30 points : Rebid 4NT (not asking for aces)

31-32 points : Rebid 5NT

33-34 points : Rebid 6NT (you should be so lucky!)

(ii) Opener has an unbalanced hand

Rebid in a suit, *forcing to game.* Responder will treat the suit bid as a 5+ suit. With a huge 4-4-4-1, bid your cheapest 4-card suit and bid naturally later. With a two-suiter, bid your longer suit first. Start the higher-ranking suit with a 5-5 or 6-6 pattern. Opener's jump rebid in a suit below game (for example, 2◇ : 2♡, 3♠) shows a solid suit. This sets opener's suit as trumps and asks responder to bid any ace. With no ace, responder bids opener's suit.

(b) After a positive response

After a 2NT response, 3♣ is Stayman and any other suit promises a 5+ suit (there are no transfers by the strong opener). 3NT over 2NT = the 23-24 point balanced opening.

After a suit response, opener may raise responder's suit with 3+ trumps. Raising responder below game (e.g. 2◇ : 2♠, 3♠) sets responder's suit as trumps and asks responder to bid the cheapest ace (see Chapter 14 on Cue Bidding). If opener changes suit, the first suit bid will be a 5+ suit and responder should support if possible. Opener's second bid suit may be only a 4-card suit. Opener's 3NT rebid shows 23-24 balanced and leaves slam bidding to responder.

RESPONDER'S REBID

After a negative response, unless opener rebid 2NT, the bidding must continue until game is reached, no matter how weak responder's hand. Support opener if possible. If not, bid your own long suit (5+ cards) or bid no-trumps with no long suit.

After a positive response, bidding is natural and most auctions should lead to a slam. Try to agree on a trump suit before asking for aces and try to allow opener, the stronger hand, to do the asking. You should play that a positive response followed by a suit raise, even to 4♡ or 4♠, is forcing.

EXERCISES FOR THE BENJAMIN 2◊ OPENING

A. Partner has opened 2◊. What is your response with each of these hands?

1. ♠ 9 7 3	2. ♠ K 7 6 2	3. ♠ 3	4. ♠ Q J 7 2	5. ♠ 8
♡ 8 2	♡ 6 3 2	♡ 6 3	♡ K 8 5 2	♡ A 9 8 2
◊ 9 7 5 3 2	◊ 8 4	◊ A Q 9 4 3	◊ Q J 4	◊ Q 8 5 2
♣ 7 6 3	♣ K 8 4 2	♣ K J 7 4 2	♣ 9 2	♣ K 9 8 4

B. The bidding has started 2◊ : 2♡. What should opener rebid with each of these hands?

1. ♠ A Q 8 7 4	2. ♠ 7 4	3. ♠ A K Q J 8 7 2	4. ♠ A K 6 2	5. ♠ K Q J
♡ 6	♡ A K J 10 7 2	♡ K Q J	♡ K Q	♡ A K 9 4
◊ A K Q	◊ A K	◊ ---	◊ A K J 8	◊ A K Q
♣ A K Q 3	♣ A K Q	♣ K Q 7	♣ K Q J	♣ A K J

C. The bidding has started 2◊: 2♡, 2♠. What is responder's rebid with these hands?

1. ♠ 4 3	2. ♠ K 7 6 2	3. ♠ 8 7 4 2	4. ♠ Q 8 7 2	5. ♠ 3
♡ K Q 7 6 3	♡ 6 3 2	♡ J 6 4	♡ 6 4	♡ Q 7 4 3
◊ 8 6 4 2	◊ 8 4	◊ 8	◊ 9 7 4 2	◊ 8 6 5 3
♣ 6 2	♣ K 8 4 2	♣ A 9 7 3 2	♣ 7 4 2	♣ 7 4 3 2

PARTNERSHIP BIDDING : How should the following hands be bid? West is the dealer each time.

SET 21 — WEST	SET 21 — EAST	SET 22 — WEST	SET 22 — EAST
1. ♠ A K 6 3	1. ♠ J 8 5 2	1. ♠ J 8 3	1. ♠ A K Q
♡ A J	♡ 9 5	♡ K 5 2	♡ A 6
◊ A Q J 10	◊ K 6 3	◊ K J 10	◊ A Q 5 2
♣ K Q J	♣ 8 5 4 3	♣ 8 7 6 3	♣ A K 4 2
2. ♠ 7 3	2. ♠ A K J 6 2	2. ♠ K Q J 8	2. ♠ A 3
♡ 8 7 5 3	♡ A K 6 2	♡ K Q J 6 2	♡ A 9 3
◊ 9 6 4	◊ A K Q	◊ A K	◊ 7 2
♣ 8 5 3 2	♣ 7	♣ A 3	♣ K 9 7 6 5 2
3. ♠ A K Q J 9 4	3. ♠ 8 7 3	3. ♠ A Q J 8	3. ♠ K 5 2
♡ 8 3	♡ K Q 6	♡ K Q	♡ A 8 7 2
◊ A J	◊ 9 8 6 4 2	◊ A 9 5	◊ K J 4
♣ A K Q	♣ 7 2	♣ A K Q 2	♣ J 9 5
4. ♠ A 6 3 2	4. ♠ K Q J 8 5 4	4. ♠ 4 2	4. ♠ A K Q 6 3
♡ 8 7 3 2	♡ A K Q	♡ A 8 4 3	♡ K Q J 9 2
◊ 9 8 7 2	◊ A	◊ 9 8 5 2	◊ A K
♣ 8	♣ A Q 4	♣ 10 6 3	♣ A
5. ♠ 10 9 6 5 2	5. ♠ A Q	5. ♠ K Q 7 2	5. ♠ J 9 6
♡ 8 7 5 2	♡ A K 6 3	♡ A J	♡ K Q 6
◊ Q J 2	◊ A K 5 3	◊ A K Q	◊ 7 5 4
♣ 6	♣ K Q 5	♣ A K Q J	♣ 8 6 3 2
6. ♠ A K Q 7 3 2	6. ♠ ---	6. ♠ 5 2	6. ♠ A K J 7 4
♡ A 9 6	♡ 8 7 5 4 3 2	♡ K 9 6 3 2	♡ A 10
◊ A K	◊ J 7 5 2	◊ A 7 3	◊ K Q J
♣ A J	♣ 8 4 3	♣ Q 4 2	♣ A K 6

PLAY HANDS ON THE BENJAMIN 2◊ OPENING

(These hands can be made up by using pages 160-167)

Hand 41: No-trumps versus minor suit games — Entries

Dealer North : E-W vulnerable

	WEST	NORTH	EAST	SOUTH
		2◊	Pass	2♡
	Pass	3◊	Pass	3♠
	Pass	4♣	Pass	5◊
	Pass	Pass	Pass	

```
                 NORTH
                 ♠ 2
                 ♡ K Q
                 ◊ A Q J 9 8 6
                 ♣ A K Q J
    WEST                      EAST
    ♠ A 10 8 7                ♠ K Q 9
    ♡ A 6                     ♡ J 10 9 8 3
    ◊ K 5 2                   ◊ 7
    ♣ 10 9 5 3                ♣ 8 7 4 2
                 SOUTH
                 ♠ J 6 5 4 3
                 ♡ 7 5 4 2
                 ◊ 10 4 3
                 ♣ 6
```

Bidding : North is borderline between a 2♣ and a 2◊ opening. If the decision is close, prefer to insist on game. North's 3◊ over 2♡ commits the partnership to game. South's 3♠ shows a 5+ suit but does not promise any values. North might consider 3NT but with only one stopper in the suit likely to be led and diamonds not solid, it is preferable to aim for a suit contract. If North's diamonds were A-K-Q-x-x-x, 3NT would be the choice. South supports diamonds over 4♣ and 5◊ is less encouraging than 4◊.

Lead : Jack of hearts. Obvious choice.

Recommended play : West wins with the ace of hearts and might as well return a heart. There is no rush to switch to a spade (which could help declarer with K-x in spades). North wins and should tackle the trumps. It is normal to finesse for the king but to do this declarer needs to reach dummy. Therefore North continues with the ace of clubs and the jack of clubs ruffed in dummy, followed by the 10 of diamonds. If West plays low, the ◊10 is run. When it wins, declarer leads dummy's remaining diamond, again finessing, and then draws trumps. Making 11 tricks.

Notes : (1) Note the likely outcome in 3NT. East leads the jack of hearts and a heart is returned. With no entry to dummy, declarer can do no better than make six tricks.
(2) In 5◊, if North leads the low diamond from dummy and finesses the jack, the finesse wins but, unable to take a second finesse, North will lose a trump trick to West.

Hand 42 : Positive response — Choosing the right slam

Dealer East : Both vulnerable

	WEST	NORTH	EAST	SOUTH
			2◊	Pass
	3♣	Pass	3♡	Pass
	3♠	Pass	4NT	Pass
	5◊	Pass	6♣	All pass

```
                 NORTH
                 ♠ Q 10 7 5
                 ♡ 10 9
                 ◊ 10 9 8 6 5 3
                 ♣ 5
    WEST                      EAST
    ♠ A K J 2                 ♠ 8
    ♡ 3                       ♡ A K Q J 2
    ◊ 4 2                     ◊ A Q J
    ♣ 10 9 8 7 6 3            ♣ K Q J 2
                 SOUTH
                 ♠ 9 6 4 3
                 ♡ 8 7 6 5 4
                 ◊ K 7
                 ♣ A 4
```

Bidding : West chooses 3♣, long suit first, when giving a positive. Although East has club support, East should try to find a fit in hearts before agreeing on the minor. West's 3♠ shows four spades, five clubs and denies three hearts. Playing simple Blackwood, East asks for aces and settles for 6♣ when one ace is missing. If playing Roman Key Card Blackwood, 4NT would set spades as trumps, so that East should bid 4♣ over 3♠ to set the trump suit. West can then cue bid 4♠ and East can then use 4NT to check on the key cards. With one ace missing, East again settles for 6♣.

Lead : 10 of diamonds. Normal unbid suit and top of sequence.

Recommended play : Win ◊A, cash two top hearts and discard the diamond loser, then lead trumps.

Notes : (1) If you take the diamond finesse at trick 1, you fail quickly.
(2) If you win ◊A and lead trumps at once, you fail almost as quickly.
(3) The best spot on these cards is 6NT played by East. Over 3♠, East could bid 4NT and follow up with 5NT asking for kings. After finding one ace and one king, East could take a chance and bid 6NT. The risk is that West has the ace of clubs and the king of diamonds and a spade lead might defeat 6NT. However, unless the player on lead holds A-K of spades, a spade lead would be unlikely. Using 4NT RKCB over 3♠ locates two key cards and again it is reasonable, although no certainty, to play in 6NT rather than 6♣.

Hand 43 : Locating the trump fit — Card reading in defense

Dealer South : Nil vulnerable

	WEST	NORTH	EAST	SOUTH
				2◇
	Pass	2♡	Pass	3♣
	Pass	3♡	Pass	3♠
	Pass	4♠	All pass	

NORTH
- ♠ Q 10 5 3
- ♡ J 9 8 6 4
- ◇ 6 2
- ♣ 10 8

WEST
- ♠ 9 8 2
- ♡ K Q 7 5 2
- ◇ 10 9 8 7 4
- ♣ ---

EAST
- ♠ 7 4
- ♡ 10 3
- ◇ A K J
- ♣ 9 7 6 5 4 2

SOUTH
- ♠ A K J 6
- ♡ A
- ◇ Q 5 3
- ♣ A K Q J 3

Bidding : With 24 HCP, South should start with the 2◇ game force opening. After the 2♡ negative, South bids longer suit first and 3♣ commits the partnership to game. North bids 3♡, showing 5+ hearts but not promising any significant values. South now shows the second suit with 3♠ and North raises. As the cards lie, 3NT would make but the more common result would be 3NT failing while 4♠ makes eleven tricks.

Lead : 10 of diamonds. Top of sequence. You need a strong reason to choose other than the unbid suit.

Recommended play : The contract should be defeated. East wins with the king of diamonds and returns the 2 of clubs for West to ruff. West plays another diamond to East's ace and the next club ruff beats 4♠.

Notes : (1) On the bidding East knows South started with five clubs and with two clubs in dummy and six in hand, East can tell that West is void in clubs.
(2) If West leads anything but a diamond, declarer has a comfortable eleven tricks by drawing trumps.
(3) If East wins the lead and cashes the other diamond, the contract can no longer be defeated. If East then fails to find the club ruff, declarer comes to eleven tricks.
(4) On the North-South cards, even without a diamond lead, there are only ten tricks in no-trumps. Playing in 4♠ will almost always produce eleven tricks (even if trumps were 4-1). It is only the vile club break that takes 4♠ down.

Hand 44 : Slam bidding — Finding the right fit

Dealer West : N-S vulnerable

WEST	NORTH	EAST	SOUTH
2◇	Pass	2♡	Pass
2♠	Pass	3♡	Pass
4NT	Pass	5◇	Pass
7♡	Pass	Pass	Pass

NORTH
- ♠ J 9 5 4 3
- ♡ ---
- ◇ 10 9 8 5 4
- ♣ K J 9

WEST
- ♠ A K Q 8 7 6
- ♡ A K Q 9 3
- ◇ 2
- ♣ A

EAST
- ♠ 2
- ♡ J 7 6 5 4
- ◇ A 7 3
- ♣ 8 7 6 2

SOUTH
- ♠ 10
- ♡ 10 8 2
- ◇ K Q J 6
- ♣ Q 10 5 4 3

Bidding : West has only one loser and thus twelve playing tricks. After the 2♡ negative, West rebids in the longer suit first. East's 3♡ rebid shows 5+ hearts but does not promise any points. West should insist on hearts as trumps and now has enough to bid 6♡. It costs nothing to check whether East has the missing ace and when East does show up with the ace of diamonds, West can confidently bid the grand slam in hearts. As East is declarer and bound to be somewhat anxious, West should reveal the good trumps first.

Lead : King of diamonds. The obvious choice.

Recommended play : The play is routine. Win the lead, draw trumps and then start on the spades. East needs to ruff spades twice to establish the sixth spade as a winner.

Notes : (1) West should not consider 7NT which would require a 3-3 break in spades. If West's spades were as good as A-K-Q-J-x-x, it would be reasonable to expect the suit to run at no-trumps, even opposite a void but the same cannot be said for A-K-Q-x-x-x.
(2) Although it does not affect the outcome, North should not discard a spade as trumps are drawn. 'Keep length with dummy' is a sound principle when deciding what to keep and what to discard.
(3) After drawing trumps, East should not play for ruffs in dummy. When the choice is to set up a long suit or to take ruffs, play first to set up the long suit.
(4) It would be a sharp lesson if East elected to play two top spades before drawing trumps.
(5) A minor flaw in using the Benjamin 2◇ is that a negative response of 2♡ leads to the weak hand being declarer in heart contracts. That does not matter on this deal. It is a loss one is prepared to accept in exchange for the many benefits that flow from using the strong 2♣ and 2◇ openings.

CHAPTER 12

ROMAN KEY CARD BLACKWOOD (1)

In the constant quest for greater accuracy, one of the great products of the 1980s was Roman Key Card Blackwood (RKCB), popularised by Eddie Kantar. There are many who are happy to stick with the same bridge they have been playing for years, but for those who are ambitious, slam bidding without RKCB is like bidding your hand with your eyes shut. Once you are used to RKCB, you will not want to return to the good ol' Black. Obviously both partners will need to know RKCB.

In reply to 4NT *simple* Blackwood, the answers are 5♣ = 0 or 4 aces, 5◊ = 1 ace, 5♡ = 2 aces and 5♠ = 3 aces. After the reply, 5NT asks for kings and the replies are in similar vein : 6♣ = 0, 6◊ = 1, 6♡ = 2, 6♠ = 3 and 6NT = all four.

Simple Blackwood may still be relevant if no trump suit has been agreed. After a trump suit has been set, 4NT = RKCB.

Roman Key Card Blackwood

4NT asks for five cards : the four aces *and* the king of trumps. These five cards are called the key cards. Not every king is a key card, only the king of trumps. The standard replies to 4NT RKCB are :

5♣ = 0 or 3 Key Cards
5◊ = 1 or 4 Key Cards
5♡ = 2 Key Cards, but no queen of trumps
5♠ = 2 Key Cards plus the queen of trumps

Recently Eddie Kantar has recommended transposing the 5♣ and 5◊ replies. Wise though this may be, the above replies are pretty well ingrained into bridge thinking. If you wish to amend the above with your partner, by all means do so.

There are five key cards and in theory, one player could hold all five. It would be even rarer, though possible, for the other player to have a hand which would justify asking for key cards. The replies to show all the key cards are :

5NT = 5 Key Cards, but no queen of trumps
6♣ = 5 Key Cards plus the queen of trumps

If partner is asking and hears 5NT or 6♣, that should be enough to jolt the memory. There can hardly be any more that partner needs to know (but a six-level asking bid is still possible — see Chapter 13).

Note :

(1) The answers of 5♡ and higher include the location of the queen of trumps.
(2) The answers of 5♣ and 5◊ give no information about the location of the queen of trumps. An extra asking bid is necessary if you need to find out whether partner holds the trump queen.

WHICH SUIT IS TRUMPS?

1. If a suit is bid and supported, that suit is trumps :

WEST	EAST	WEST	EAST	WEST	EAST
1♠	2◊	1♠	2♡	1♠	2◊
2♡	4♠	4♡	4NT	2♡	3♣
4NT				3◊	4NT
♠s are trumps		♡s are trumps		◊s are trumps	

2. If no suit has been supported, the RKCB ask refers to the last bid suit as trumps.

WEST	EAST	WEST	EAST	WEST	EAST
1♠	2◊	1♠	2♡	1♡	1♠
4NT		3♣	4NT	3NT	4NT
◊s are trumps		♣s are trumps		♠s are trumps	

3. If no genuine suit has been bid, 4NT is simple Blackwood.

WEST	EAST	
1NT	2♣	The 3♣ reply to Extended Stayman = maximum points and no major. As no genuine suit has been shown, 4NT is just simple Blackwood.
3♣	4NT	
?		

The importance of the king of trumps

WEST	W	E	EAST
♠ J 7 6	1♡	3♠	♠ 2
♡ A Q 8 6 3	4NT	5◊	♡ 9 7 5 2
◊ A K 10 6	5♠	Pass	◊ Q J 9 3
♣ 6			♣ A K Q 4

East's 3♠ is a splinter raise, short in spades. With little wasted in spades, West sees slam prospects. East's 5◊ reply shows 1 or 4 key cards, obviously only one as West has two. West knows that either two aces are missing or one ace and the trump king. 6♠ figures to be a poor bet in either case. On the actual cards, 6♠ needs South to have the doubleton king in hearts, about a 21% chance.

WEST	W	E	EAST
♠ J 7 6	1♡	3♠	♠ 2
♡ A Q 8 6 3	4NT	5♡	♡ K 7 5 2
◊ A K 10 6	6♠	Pass	◊ Q J 9 3
♣ 6			♣ A Q 4 3

This time East bids 5♡ showing two key cards but no trump queen. With just one key card missing and a singleton spade opposite, West can bid the small slam with fair confidence. 6♡ is a 90% chance.

Note that East has the same pattern, same HCP, the same losers on each of the above hands. Using simple Blackwood East shows one ace each time. If West now pushes on, the poor slam is reached on the first hand. If West signs off in 5♡ over 5◊, then the excellent slam is missed. Simple Blackwood does not solve this sort of problem. RKCB does.

WEST	W	E	EAST
♠ A Q 8 6 3	1♠	4◇	♠ 9 7 5 2
♡ K Q 6	4NT	5♡	♡ A J 5
◇ A K 7 6	6♠	Pass	◇ 5
♣ 6			♣ A K 8 4 2

East's 4◇ is a splinter raise, short in diamonds. 5♡ showed two key cards without the queen of trumps. West has two key cards and knows that one key card is missing, either an ace or the king of trumps. Either way, 7♠ will not be a good contract.

As it is, 7♠ needs South to have the doubleton king of spades, about a 21% chance. Poor odds.

WEST	W	E	EAST
♠ A Q 8 6 3	1♠	4◇	♠ K 7 5 2
♡ K Q 6	4NT	5♣	♡ A J 5
◇ A K 7 6	7♠	Pass	◇ 5
♣ 6			♣ A 8 5 4 2

East's 5♣ shows 0 or 3 key cards. From East's 4◇ bid and the West cards, West can tell that it must be three. East could not have enough for the 4◇ splinter with no key cards. Knowing East has at least K-x-x-x in trumps, ♡A, ♣A and a singleton diamond, West is able to bid the grand slam.

East again has the same pattern, the same HCP, the same losers on each of the above hands. Using simple Blackwood East shows two aces each time and one king in reply to 5NT. But which king?

Not knowing which king East holds, West cannot judge whether the grand slam is a sensible risk or a foolish one. Playing RKCB will eliminates this kind of guesswork.

The importance of the queen of trumps

Where the reply to 4NT RKCB is 5♡ or 5♠, the asker will know whether the trump queen is held or not.

WEST	W	E	EAST
♠ A J 6 4 3	1♠	4◇	♠ K 7 5 2
♡ A K Q 6	4NT	5♡	♡ J 10 3
◇ A 7 6	6♠	Pass	◇ 5
♣ 6			♣ A K 8 4 2

5♡ shows two key cards but no queen of trumps. West knows that East holds the ♠K and the ♣A but no ♠Q. The grand slam will therefore be a poor bet and West settles for 6♠. With nine trumps missing the queen and jack, the chance for no loser (the 2-2 split) is 42%. Even with the jack of trumps, the chance for no trump loser is only a bit over 50%.

WEST	W	E	EAST
♠ A J 6 4 3	1♠	4◇	♠ K Q 5 2
♡ A K Q 6	4NT	5♠	♡ J 10 3
◇ A 7 6	7♠	Pass	◇ 5
♣ 6			♣ A J 8 4 2

5♠ shows two key cards plus the queen of trumps. With those cards and a singleton diamond opposite, West can see that all losers are covered. Although not a certainty, the grand slam should be a good chance. Simple Blackwood has no provision for finding the trump queen or finding the trump king.

Locating the trump queen after a 5♣ or 5◇ reply

Over 5♣ or 5◇, if you need to know whether partner holds the queen of trumps, bid the cheapest suit outside trumps. This asks : "Do you have the queen of trumps?" If no, partner makes the cheapest bid possible ('Step 1'). If yes, partner bids one more than the cheapest bid ('Step 2').

If clubs are trumps

Over the 5♣ reply, 5◇ asks for the ♣Q.
Answers : 5♡ = No, 5♠ = Yes.
Over the 5◇ reply, 5♡ asks for the ♣Q.
Answers : 5♠ = No, 5NT = Yes.

If diamonds are trumps

Over the 5♣ reply, 5◇, the agreed trump suit, would be a signoff. Therefore, over 5♣ or 5◇, 5♡ asks for the ◇Q.
Answers : 5♠ = No, 5NT = Yes.

If hearts are trumps

Over the 5♣ reply, 5◇ asks for the ♡Q.
Answers : 5♡ = No, 5♠ = Yes.
Over the 5◇ reply, 5♠ asks for the ♡Q since 5♡, the agreed suit, would be a signoff.
Answers : 5NT = No, 6♣ = Yes.

If spades are trumps

Over the 5♣ reply, 5◇ asks for the ♠Q.
Answers : 5♡ = No, 5♠ = Yes.
Over the 5◇ reply, 5♡ asks for the ♠Q.
Answers : 5♠ = No, 5NT = Yes.

Strategy for small slams

Assuming that the values for a small slam exist :
1. If two key cards are missing, stay out of slam.
2. If one key card is missing but the trump queen is held, bid the small slam.
3. If one key card *and* the trump queen are missing, bid six with ten or more trumps, and also with nine trumps if you hold the trump jack. The slam will be better than 50%. With fewer than nine trumps or with nine trumps but not holding the trump jack, stay out of the slam. Slam figures to be below 50%.

Strategy for grand slams

Assuming the losing trick count or other assessment method indicates the potential for thirteen tricks :
1. If you hold ten trumps or more, the partnership should have all five key cards but need not have the trump queen.
2. With nine trumps or fewer, you need all five key cards plus the queen of trumps to make seven a good bet. If you can count thirteen tricks, bid seven. With thirteen winners in top cards, bid 7NT. With a strong trump fit and no losers in the first three rounds of any suit, seven should be a good contract.
3. If you need to know about partner's holding in a suit outside trumps, you can ask for kings (if 5NT is available) and you can also make a Control Asking Bid. These are both covered in Chapter 13.

EXERCISES FOR ROMAN KEY CARD BLACKWOOD

A. Hearts have been set as trumps and partner bids 4NT RKCB. What is your reply with these hands?

1. ♠ K Q 7 3	2. ♠ K 8 7 3	3. ♠ Q 8 7 3	4. ♠ 7 4 3	5. ♠ A 8
♥ A 8 6 2	♥ A Q 6 2	♥ A K 6 2	♥ A K Q 2	♥ A K Q 2
◊ J 3 2	◊ J 3 2	◊ J 3 2	◊ K J 2	◊ A 8 5 2
♣ A K	♣ A K	♣ A K	♣ A 6 4	♣ A J 4

B. Diamonds are trumps and in reply to 4NT partner has shown one key card. What should you do next?

1. ♠ K Q 2	2. ♠ A K Q	3. ♠ K Q J	4. ♠ A K	5. ♠ A
♥ 6	♥ 6	♥ 7	♥ A	♥ A
◊ A K 7 6 4	◊ A Q 7 6 4	◊ A K Q 7 4 2	◊ A K 1 0 8 4	◊ A Q J 9 6 2
♣ K Q 8 3	♣ K Q J 5	♣ A K J	♣ K Q J 4 2	♣ A K Q J 10

PARTNERSHIP BIDDING : How should the following hands be bid? West is the dealer each time.

SET 23 — WEST	SET 23 — EAST	SET 24 — WEST	SET 24 — EAST
1. ♠ A Q J 7 2	1. ♠ 8 6 5 4	1. ♠ A Q	1. ♠ 4
♥ A K Q J	♥ 9 8	♥ A 8 7 3	♥ K J 10 6 2
◊ A K Q	◊ J 5 3	◊ 7 2	◊ A K Q 5 4
♣ 7	♣ K 8 6 3	♣ Q 9 8 4 2	♣ A K
2. ♠ A Q J 7 2	2. ♠ K 6 5 4	2. ♠ A 7	2. ♠ 4
♥ A K Q J	♥ 9 8	♥ A Q 7 3	♥ K J 10 6 2
◊ A K Q	◊ J 5 3	◊ 7 2	◊ A K Q 5 4
♣ 7	♣ 8 6 3 2	♣ Q 9 8 4 2	♣ A K
3. ♠ 8 6 5 4	3. ♠ A Q J 7 2	3. ♠ A K J 8 2	3. ♠ 9 5 4
♥ 9 8	♥ A K Q J	♥ A K Q 6	♥ J 7
◊ J 5	◊ A K Q	◊ 9 5 4	◊ A K J 3 2
♣ A K 8 6 3	♣ 7	♣ Q	♣ K J 9
4. ♠ K 6 5 4	4. ♠ A Q J 7 2	4. ♠ A K J 8 2	4. ♠ Q 5 4
♥ 9 8	♥ A K Q J	♥ A K Q 6	♥ 7 2
◊ J 5	◊ A K Q	◊ 9 5 4	◊ A K J 3 2
♣ A 8 6 3 2	♣ 7	♣ Q	♣ K 7 3
5. ♠ K Q J	5. ♠ A 6	5. ♠ K 8 7 3	5. ♠ A J 10 6 4
♥ Q 9 8 7 5	♥ A 6 3 2	♥ A K	♥ 6
◊ A K Q 3	◊ 8 7 2	◊ A J 8 6 2	◊ K 5
♣ 3	♣ K Q 6 4	♣ 4 3	♣ A K Q 5 2
6. ♠ K Q J	6. ♠ A 6	6. ♠ K Q 7 3	6. ♠ A J 10 6 4
♥ Q 9 8 7 5	♥ A K 3 2	♥ A J	♥ 6
◊ A K Q 3	◊ 8 7 2	◊ A J 8 6 2	◊ K 5
♣ 3	♣ Q 8 6 4	♣ 4 3	♣ A K Q 5 2
7. ♠ A 9 6 5	7. ♠ Q 8 7 4 3 2	7. ♠ A	7. ♠ 10 9 6
♥ A K	♥ 8	♥ A K 8 7 5 2	♥ 9 6 3
◊ 8 3	◊ A K Q 7	◊ K Q J 2	◊ A 5 4
♣ A 8 7 4 2	♣ K 6	♣ A K	♣ Q 9 7 6
8. ♠ A K 6 5	8. ♠ Q 8 7 4 3 2	8. ♠ A	8. ♠ 10 9 6
♥ A 9	♥ 8	♥ A K 8 7 5 2	♥ Q 6 3
◊ 8 3	◊ A K Q 7	◊ K Q J 2	◊ A 5 4
♣ A 8 7 4 2	♣ K 6	♣ A K	♣ 9 7 6 2

PLAY HANDS ON ROMAN KEY CARD BLACKWOOD

(These hands can be made up by using pages 160-167)

Hand 45 : Precaution play — Catering for a bad break

Dealer North : Both vulnerable

WEST	NORTH	EAST	SOUTH
	1♠	Pass	4NT
Pass	5♠	Pass	7♠
Pass	Pass	Pass	

NORTH
- ♠ K Q 10 6 3
- ♡ A J 8 7
- ◇ K 6 4
- ♣ 8

WEST
- ♠ - - -
- ♡ K Q 10 5
- ◇ 9 8 5 3 2
- ♣ 10 7 4 2

EAST
- ♠ J 8 7 5
- ♡ 9 4 3 2
- ◇ Q J 10
- ♣ J 3

SOUTH
- ♠ A 9 4 2
- ♡ 6
- ◇ A 7
- ♣ A K Q 9 6 5

Bidding : With a solid suit, excellent support and control in hearts and diamonds, South has the values for slam and should take control of the bidding by asking for key cards at once. If the bidding started 1♠ : 3♠ (forcing), North should cue bid 4♡ to show slam interest and then South would bid 4NT. 5♠ shows two key cards plus the queen of spades. South need not be concerned about a parking spot for the diamond loser. Even if North had no kings outside trumps, the club suit should provide North with all the discards needed for any red suit losers.

Lead : Queen of diamonds. Routine.

Recommended play : North should win the lead in hand and tackle the trumps. Missing J-x-x-x, it is correct to leave one top trump in each hand. Start with the king of spades. When the bad break appears, lead a low spade towards dummy and insert the 9 when East plays low. Cash the ace and king of spades to draw East's trumps and then start on the clubs. You need to ruff the fourth round of clubs to set up the suit. Cash your red suit winners ending with the ace of diamonds in dummy, and dummy is high.

Notes : (1) If North starts trumps by leading a spade to the ace, there is a trump loser. One down.
(2) If the first diamond is won in dummy, the timing is a little different. At trick 2, a trump to the king reveals the bad break. Continue with a club to the ace, ruff a club, cash the queen of spades, finesse the nine of spades and draw East's last trump with the ♠A. Dummy needs an entry after the clubs are set up.

Hand 46 : Catering for a bad break — Handling a tenace combination

Dealer East : Nil vulnerable

WEST	NORTH	EAST	SOUTH
		1♠	Pass
2♡	Pass	4NT	Pass
5♡	Pass	7♡	All pass

NORTH
- ♠ J 8 7 5
- ♡ - - -
- ◇ K Q 5 3
- ♣ J 7 6 4 2

WEST
- ♠ 3
- ♡ K J 7 6 2
- ◇ 10 7 2
- ♣ A Q 9 3

EAST
- ♠ A K Q 6 4 2
- ♡ A 9 5 4 3
- ◇ A
- ♣ 8

SOUTH
- ♠ 10 9
- ♡ Q 10 8
- ◇ J 9 8 6 4
- ♣ K 10 5

Bidding : Do not open 2♣ or 2◇ with a huge two-suiter unless you have loads of HCP. If the opponents intervene, it can become awkward to show both suits economically. Here East opens 1♠, planning to jump shift in hearts next. After 2♡, East knows that there is a huge fit in hearts. With only one loser outside, East asks at once with 4NT. 5♡ showed two key cards but no ♡Q. Even though the ♡Q is missing, East knows that there are at least 10 trumps between the two hands and the odds are almost 80% that the missing trumps will split 2-1.

Lead : King of diamonds. The other choices are much worse.

Recommended play : Win the ace of diamonds and start on trumps at once. Even though the normal break is 2-1, you should still guard against a 3-0 break whenever possible. Your K-J in hearts is a tenace and allows a finesse later if necessary. When holding a tenace in one hand, best technique is to cash the winner(s) opposite the tenace first. Here, this means that you should start with the ace of hearts. When North shows out you can finesse the jack of hearts on the next round. Draw the last trump and set up the spades next by ruffing the fourth round.

Notes : (1) It would be an error to play the king of hearts first. Here this costs you the grand slam. If North has the Q-10-8, you can do nothing to capture the queen. Since you can deal only with Q-10-8 with South, you cater for that possibility by playing the ace of hearts first.
(2) After drawing trumps you should not start ruffing losers in dummy. When you have a choice of setting up winners or ruffing losers, setting up winners comes first. Here that means that after trumps have been drawn you should set up the spades.

Hand 47 : Setting up the right secondary suit — Minimising the risks

Dealer South : N-S vulnerable

NORTH
- ♠ 10 8 5 2
- ♡ 10 9 7 2
- ◇ Q 10 3
- ♣ J 8

WEST
- ♠ K Q 7 3
- ♡ A J
- ◇ A J 8 6 2
- ♣ 4 3

EAST
- ♠ A J 9 6 4
- ♡ 4
- ◇ K 5
- ♣ A K Q 5 2

SOUTH
- ♠ - - -
- ♡ K Q 8 6 5 3
- ◇ 9 7 4
- ♣ 10 9 7 6

WEST	NORTH	EAST	SOUTH
			Pass
1◇	Pass	1♠	Pass
3♠	Pass	4NT	Pass
5♣	Pass	5◇	Pass
5♠	Pass	7♠	All pass

Bidding : With a void, South should not open 2♡. In reply to 4NT, 5♣ = 0 or 3 key cards. Checking the unseen HCP, East can tell it must be three. West could not have the values to jump rebid 3♠ with no key cards. Having found the ♠K, ♡A and ◇A, East next asks for the trump queen via 5◇ and 5♠ says 'I have the ♠Q'. That covers all of East's losers in the first three rounds of every suit and so East bids the grand slam.

Lead : King of hearts. The obvious choice.

Recommended play : Declarer wins and starts on the trumps with the ♠K. When the 4-0 break appears, East must not draw all North's trumps. Best is to continue with ♣A, ♣K and ruff a low club with the ♠Q. Next lead a spade and finesse the 9, followed by the ace and jack of spades to draw North's trumps.

Notes : (1) When trumps are played, South should discard low hearts and keep the clubs and diamonds.
(2) Drawing four rounds of trumps relies on clubs 3-3, or diamonds 3-3 with the ◇Q onside. If South does not discard a club, declarer should fail if declarer starts by drawing all of North's trumps.
(3) After ♠K reveals the bad break, it would work, as the cards lie, to play ◇K, ◇A and ruff a diamond. However, this line requires diamonds 3-3. Playing on clubs works if clubs are 3-3 or 4-2.
(4) If declarer ruffs the third club low in dummy, North overruffs. Declarer can afford to ruff high.

Hand 48 : Handling a tenace combination — Making the maximum number of tricks

Dealer West : E-W vulnerable

NORTH
- ♠ A K Q 9 5 4
- ♡ A J 9 5
- ◇ A 4
- ♣ 2

WEST
- ♠ 8 6
- ♡ Q 10 8 7
- ◇ K J 3
- ♣ J 10 8 4

EAST
- ♠ J 10 7 3
- ♡ - - -
- ◇ 9 8 6 5 2
- ♣ Q 7 6 5

SOUTH
- ♠ 2
- ♡ K 6 4 3 2
- ◇ Q 10 7
- ♣ A K 9 3

WEST	NORTH	EAST	SOUTH
Pass	1♠	Pass	2♡
Pass	4NT	Pass	5♡
Pass	6♡	All pass	

Bidding : Although North has excellent spades, North should make hearts the trump suit. The spades will provide South with discards for any minor suit losers. North has four losers, South's 2♡ should have eight losers or fewer, so North can recognise slam potential. In addition, a strong trump fit plus a running suit is a sign that slam is likely. With control in each suit, North is well placed to ask with 4NT. South's 5♡ = two key cards but no queen of trumps. As the trump queen is missing, North should give up on any ambitions for a grand slam.

Lead : Jack of clubs. Almost a sequence.

Recommended play : Win with the ace of clubs and start on trumps. As dummy's A-J is a tenace, you should *cash the winner opposite the tenace first*. Start trumps with the king of hearts. When East shows out, lead a low trump and cover West's card. If West plays the 5 or 7, finesse the 9. Cash the ace of spades and ruff a spade to return to your own hand. Cash the other top club while you are in hand to discard the diamond loser. Then repeat the trump finesse. Draw West's last trump and dummy is high. Although the grand slam is not a good bet, the recommended line brings in thirteen tricks thanks to the heart position.

Notes : (1) With four trumps missing including the queen, the chance for no loser is only a touch above 50%. You need better odds to justify a grand slam. With ten trumps, missing three including the queen, the chance for no loser is much better, almost 80% and that would make a grand slam worthwhile if that is the only problem on the deal.
(2) If declarer starts by leading a low heart to the jack, there will be a trump loser. You can still make the slam, but you will not score well as thirteen tricks are available.
(3) If you fail to cash the ♣K after ruffing a spade, there is no later entry to reach the ♣K and you will again hold yourself to twelve tricks. You must make the most tricks possible to score well at pairs.

CHAPTER 13

ROMAN KEY CARD BLACKWOOD (2)

10 trumps = the trump queen

When the partnership holds ten trumps including the ace and king but no queen and no jack, the chance for no loser (the 2-1 break) is 78%, almost 4 out of 5. When ten trumps are held missing the queen, but including the ace and king plus the jack in the same hand as a higher honor, such as :

K-J-x-x-x opposite A-x-x-x-x, or

A-K-J-x-x-x opposite x-x-x-x

or equivalent holdings, the chance for no loser is 89%, about nine times out of ten (either a 2-1 break or the queen onside if trumps are 3-0). As the chance of a loser is so low in these cases, it pays you to *show the trump queen if you know that the partnership holds at least ten trumps*.

WEST	W	E	EAST
♠ A 8 7 6 3	1♠	2♡	♠ 2
♡ A J 8 6 3	4♣	4NT	♡ K 9 7 5 2
◇ A 8	5♣	5◇	◇ K J
♣ 6	5♠	7♡	♣ A K J 7 2

4♣ = splinter, strong raise of hearts, short in clubs
5♣ = 0 or 3 key cards, clearly three on the bidding
5◇ asks for the trump queen

5♠ says 'I have the queen of hearts'. As West knows the partnership holds ten trumps at least, West 'shows' the trump queen. East can then bid the grand slam with reasonable confidence.

5NT asking for kings

After the answer to 4NT, a rebid of 5NT asks for kings outside the trump suit. Since the trump king was already included as a key card in reply to 4NT, it is not shown again in reply to 5NT.

Replies to the 5NT king ask :

6♣ = No king
6◇ = 1 king
6♡ = 2 kings
6♠ = 3 kings

These king answers are the same as the answers to 5NT simple Blackwood.

The 5NT king ask also applies if it is available after the reply to the trump queen ask.

Suppose hearts are trumps :

WEST	EAST	4NT = RKCB
...	...	5♣ = 0 or 3 key cards
4NT	5♣	5◇ = Ask for the trump queen
5◇	5♠	5♠ = I have the trump queen
5NT ...		5NT = Asking for kings

The king ask may be necessary if looking for a grand slam or for playing in 6NT rather than in a suit small slam (or 7NT rather than a suit grand slam).

Other Asking Bids

While the 5NT ask for kings can be useful, it may be necessary to find a king or queen in a specific suit. The king in one suit may be useless, in another suit (opposite A-Q-J-x, for example), it may be gold. Once you are familiar with RKCB, you may wish to add extra asking bids. The principles are :

After the reply to 4NT :
Cheapest suit (excluding trumps) = Trump queen ask
Any other suit bid (excluding trumps) = Control Ask
5NT = Asking for kings (excluding the trump king)

After the reply to the trump queen ask :
Any suit except trumps = Control Ask
5NT if available = Asking for kings outside trumps

Replies to the Control Ask
The ace is known from the reply to the RKCB ask.

Step 1 = No king, no queen in the asked suit
Step 2 = Queen in asked suit but no king
Step 3 = King in asked suit but no queen
Step 4 = King and queen in the asked suit
Step 5 = King + queen + jack in the asked suit

WEST	W	E	EAST
♠ A K J 7 2	2◇	2♡	♠ Q 6 5 4
♡ A K Q	2♠	3♠	♡ 9 8 2
◇ A Q J 9 3	4NT	5♣	◇ K 5
♣ - - -	5◇	5♠	♣ 9 8 6 4
	6◇	6NT	
	7♠	Pass	

2◇ = artificial game force, 2♡ = artificial negative, 5♣ = 0 or 3 key cards, clearly none, 5◇ = ask for trump queen, 5♠ = 'I have the trump queen', 6◇ = 'What is your diamond holding?' and 6NT = 'I have the king of diamonds but not the queen.' West has found the cards necessary to bid the superb 7♠. Had East bid 6♡ (no diamond honor), West would have settled for 6♠. Note that 5NT asking for kings would not have helped West. If East had shown one king, West would be unable to tell whether it is the king of diamonds (gold) or the king of clubs (dross).

WEST	W	E	EAST
♠ K Q 8	1♡	2NT	♠ A 7 2
♡ A Q J 6 3	3◇	4♡	♡ K 9 7 5
◇ 6	4NT	5♣	◇ A 9 7
♣ A K J 8	6♣	6♡	♣ Q 6 2
	7NT	Pass	

Even though West's singleton (3◇) is useful, East is so minimum that the signoff in 4♡ is best. West has more than enough to push on. 5♣ showed 0 or 3 key cards (West can tell it must be three). 6♣ asked for East's holding in clubs and 6♡ showed the queen of clubs but no king. West now knows enough to bid the grand slam in no-trumps.

Ambiguity with the 5♣ and 5◊ replies

When you hear a 5♣ reply to 4NT you can usually tell whether it is no key cards or whether it is three. If you hold 3+ key cards yourself, obviously partner has none. Even when you hold two key cards or fewer, you can usually tell. You will know partner's minimum HCP from the bidding and by looking at your own high cards, you work out what partner could hold with no key cards at all. For example :

♠ K Q	Partner opens 1♣, you bid 1♡
♡ A Q J 6 3 2	and partner raises to 2♡. When
◊ A K 4	you later bid 4NT, partner bids
♣ J 2	5♣, 0 or 3 key cards. Which is it?

For partner to have zero key cards, the most partner could hold would be ♠J, ◊Q-J and ♣K-Q. That is 9 HCP, inconsistent with the opening bid and so partner must have the three missing key cards.

The same applies when the answer is 5◊, one or four key cards. For example :

♠ A Q J 7 3	You open 1♠, partner bids
♡ K Q J 6 3	2NT, Jacoby (13+ points). Later
◊ K Q	you bid 4NT and partner bids 5◊.
♣ J	Is it one key card or four?

Suppose partner holds just one key card. The most partner could have would be one ace, K-Q in clubs and the ◊J. That is only 10 HCP, too weak for a Jacoby 2NT reply. Except for chronic overbidders, partner must have four key cards and you are worth a shot at 7NT.

There are still occasions when you will not be certain whether partner has the lower number of key cards or the higher. In that case, assume the worst and sign off in the trump suit. *If partner has the higher number of key cards, partner must bid on.* The asker should not need more than three cards (or four) for the slam to be reasonable. So, pass the signoff with the lower number, bid on with the higher number.

WEST	WEST	EAST
♠ K 9 6 4 3 2		1◊
♡ 2	1♠	3♠
◊ A 9 5 3	4NT	5♣
♣ K 2	?	

Has East three key cards or none? East might have either of these hands :

EAST 1	EAST 2
♠ Q J 8 5	♠ A J 8 5
♡ K Q J	♡ A 8
◊ K Q J 6 2	◊ Q 7 6 4 2
♣ 8	♣ A 8

With East 1, slam is ridiculous, but with East 2, 6♠ is a good bet, although not a certainty.

West should sign off in 5♠. East 1 will pass, but East 2 will bid again.

When bidding on with the higher number of key cards, treat the signoff bid as the ask for the queen of trumps. So, Step 1 = No queen, Step 2 = Queen. East 2 above bids 5NT : 3 key cards but no ♠Q.

Using RKCB below 4NT

If you and partner use 4♣ Gerber for aces, you can adapt RKCB and play Roman Key Card Gerber. The basic replies to the 4♣ ask would be :

4◊ = 0 or 3 key cards
4♡ = 1 or 4 key cards
4♠ = 2 key cards, no queen of trumps
4NT = 2 key cards plus the queen of trumps

Gerber 4♣ is not recommended, particularly because it conflicts with splinters and is not compatible with cue bidding (see Chapters 14-15) and most experts strongly prefer splinters and cue bidding to Gerber.

There is good news. You can play RKCB at a level even lower than Gerber.

If a major suit is bid and supported to the three-level, 3NT should be used as RKCB rather than as a natural attempt to play in 3NT.

Where a primary major suit fit has been found, the likelihood that 3NT is superior *and* that you can tell that 3NT *is* superior is remote. It is therefore sensible to treat 3NT in auctions such as these as RKCB :

WEST	EAST	WEST	EAST	WEST	EAST
1◊	1♠	1♠	2♡	2◊	2♡
3♠	3NT	3♡	3NT	2♠	3♠
				3NT	

3NT RKCB should be used only after major suit agreement and then only after a direct raise. 3NT in these auctions in not RKCB :

WEST	EAST	WEST	EAST	WEST	EAST
1♠	2♣	1♣	1◊	1♠	2◊
3♠	3NT	3◊	3NT	2♡	2NT
No major suit		No major suit		3♣	3♠
agreement		agreement		3NT	

In the final auction, East's 3♠ is belated support and West's 3NT should be suggestion of contract.

Naturally, you and partner need to agree on using 3NT as RKCB. It would certainly help East 1 in the previous column :

WEST	W	E	EAST
♠ K 9 6 4 3 2		1◊	♠ Q J 8 5
♡ 2	1♠	3♠	♡ K Q J
◊ A 9 5 3	3NT	4♣	◊ K Q J 6 2
♣ K 2	4♠	Pass	♣ 8

No-one wants to reach 5♠ off three aces. A similar benefit applies to this example :

WEST	W	E	EAST
♠ A Q 8 7 2	2◊	2♡	♠ 10 6 5 4
♡ A K Q J	2♠	3♠	♡ 8 7 3
◊ A K Q	3NT	4♣	◊ 6 4 2
♣ 6	4♠	Pass	♣ K Q 4

Better to stop in 4♠ than to reach 5♠ and complain about your wretched luck when North has ♠K-J-x.

Using 3NT RKCB follows the same structure as for 4NT RKCB but all bids are one level lower. 3NT RKCB can also be used after 1NT where opener gives a super-accept of a transfer and after the Jacoby 2NT reply to a major suit opening.

RKCB after minor suit agreement

After minor suit agreement at the two-level or three-level, 3NT is to play. After minor suit agreement at the four-level, 4NT RKCB can push the partnership overboard when two key cards are missing, especially when the trump suit is clubs.

One way to overcome this problem is to treat a minor suit raise to the four-level as starting a key card auction. This structure allows you both to ask for key cards and to show key cards. For example,

WEST	EAST	
		4◊ = RKCB Asking
1♡	2♣	4♡ = offer to play in 4♡
4♣	?	4♠/4NT/5♣ =RKCB replies
		(0 or 3 / 1 or 4 / 2 key cards)

The same would apply to auctions featuring a raise of diamonds to the four-level. For example :

WEST	EAST	
		4♡ = RKCB
1◊	1♠	4♠/4NT/5♣/5◊ = RKCB replies
3◊	4◊	(the usual four replies). Here 4♠
?		is not needed as natural.

Thus, after minor suit agreement at the four-level, Step 1 is the RKCB ask. The other bids up to 5-of-the-agreed-minor are normally the RKCB replies as though partner had asked. To sign off, bid Step 1 (RKCB ask) and sign off after the reply.

This method is incompatible with cue bidding after minor suit agreement (see Chapters 14-15), but the RKCB asking approach has much merit.

Expert Methods

Showing kings simultaneously with your answer to the trump queen ask

WEST	EAST	
		4NT = RKCB
...	...	5◊ = 1 or 4 key cards
4NT	5◊	5♡ = Ask for the trump queen
5♡	?	East : 5♠ = No, 5NT = Yes

Without the trump queen, you must bid Step 1, but when you have the trump queen you can give partner extra information. In the above sequence, what would 6♣ mean over 5♡? Or 6◊? Some play these bids to show the trump queen plus a very good suit. The occasions for this use would be rare. A better idea is to use these bids to show kings. Thus, 6♣ shows the trump queen plus the king of clubs, 6◊ would show the trump queen plus the king of diamonds and no king of clubs.

This approach does lose the chance to make a control ask for the queen in a particular suit. If you wish to overcome this, you use the extra steps only when you lack the queens in the suit bypassed. Thus, 6♣ would show the queen of trumps, the king of clubs but no queen of clubs. Likewise, 6◊ = trump queen plus the king of diamonds but denies the king of clubs, queen of clubs and queen of diamonds. Naturally, you do not bypass your agreed trump suit at the six-level.

WEST	W	E	EAST
♠ Q 8 2	1♣	2♠	♠ A K J 6 5 3
♡ A 7 3	3♠	3NT	♡ 5
◊ K Q 2	4◊	4♡	◊ A J 6 3
♣ K 5 4 2	5♣	5◊	♣ A 3
	6♣	7NT	

3NT = RKCB

4◊ = 1 or 4 key cards (East knows it is one)

4♡ = Asking for the queen of trumps

5♣ = I have the trump queen plus the king of clubs but no queen of clubs.

5◊ = Control Ask in diamonds

6♣ = Step 4, showing the king + queen of diamonds, but no jack of diamonds (see page 75)

East knows virtually all of West's hand and can count thirteen tricks. Note how economical the bidding is after starting with 3NT RKCB and how helpful it was for West to show the ♣K with 5♣.

RKCB after a pre-empt by partner

After partner's pre-empt, there is little merit in changing suit to a minor. It is useful to play :

3◊/3♡/3♠ : 4C = RKCB

3♣ : 4◊ = RKCB. 3♣ : 3◊ may be seeking 3NT.

Weak Key Card Responses

When partner has a very limited hand (such as a negative reply to a 2♣ or 2◊ opening), partner cannot have very many key cards. It can be useful to use a different set of replies for a poor hand :

Step 1 = No key card, no queen of trumps

Step 2 = Queen of trumps but no key card

Step 3 = One key card, no queen of trumps

Step 4 = One key card + the queen of trumps

Step 5 = Two key cards, no queen of trumps (if this is possible for the weak hand)

Showing key cards in other auctions
After 1NT : 3♣/3◊/3♡/3♠ (see page 24)

Where these response show a 5+ suit, opener bids 3NT without support, but with support, opener can show key cards at once. For example, after 1NT : 3♠ —

3NT = Doubleton spade only

4♣ = spade support, 0 or 3 key cards

4◊ = spade support, 1 or 4 key cards

4♡ = spade support, 2 key cards, no trump queen

4♠ = spade support, 2 key cards + trump queen

When responder sets a major a suit after Extended Stayman (see page 10)

After 1NT : 2♣, 2♡ : 3♡ or 1NT : 2♣, 2◊ : 3♠ or similar auctions, responder has indicated slam ambitions. Opener can show key cards by steps in the usual order.

After a demand opening

If opener supports responder after a game-force opening, treat the raise as RKCB. Responder shows key cards by steps at once. It is better for the strong hand to receive the key card information.

EXERCISES ON ROMAN KEY CARD BLACKWOOD (2)

A. Spades are trumps. West bids 4NT, East 5◊, West rebids 6♣. What is East's next bid on these hands?

1. ♠ A K 4 2	2. ♠ K 8 7 3	3. ♠ 9 8 7 3	4. ♠ 7 4 3	5. ♠ A 8 7 2
♥ Q 9 8 2	♥ K Q 6 2	♥ A K 6 2	♥ K 8 2	♥ Q 2
◊ A 3	◊ J 3	◊ K Q	◊ K J 5 2	◊ K 8 5 2
♣ A 6 3	♣ K 6 5	♣ J 7 4	♣ A Q 9	♣ K Q 8

B. Hearts are trumps. In reply to 4NT, you bid 5♣. What next if partner bids (a) 5♥ *or* (b) 5NT?

1. ♠ A 8 7 3	2. ♠ K Q 5	3. ♠ A J 4	4. ♠ 5	5. ♠ 5
♥ K Q 6 2	♥ J 6 4 3	♥ A 8 7 3 2	♥ A K 3 2	♥ A K Q 6 2
◊ J 3	◊ K Q J 6 4	◊ A 7	◊ A 1 0 8 4	◊ A 6 2
♣ A 6 5	♣ 3	♣ 9 6 4	♣ K J 4 2	♣ K 8 7 5

PARTNERSHIP BIDDING : How should the following hands be bid? West is the dealer each time.

SET 25— WEST	SET 25 — EAST	SET 26 — WEST	SET 26 — EAST
1. ♠ A 9 7 3 2	1. ♠ K 6 5 4	1. ♠ K Q 6	1. ♠ A J 8 7 3 2
♥ 3	♥ K Q 8	♥ Q 8 4	♥ A K J 2
◊ A K Q 6 2	◊ 4	◊ Q 7 2	◊ A
♣ K 9	♣ A 8 6 3 2	♣ J 9 4 2	♣ A K
2. ♠ A 9 7 3 2	2. ♠ K 8 6 5 4	2. ♠ Q 10 9 7 2	2. ♠ A K 6 4 3
♥ 3	♥ K Q 8	♥ A	♥ K Q J 10 2
◊ A K Q 6 2	◊ 4	◊ A K 3	◊ 7
♣ K 9	♣ A 8 6 3	♣ 9 7 4 2	♣ A 6
3. ♠ 3	3. ♠ A 9 7	3. ♠ 8 6 4 3	3. ♠ K Q J 7 5 2
♥ A J 7 6 4	♥ K 8 3 2	♥ 6 2	♥ A K Q
◊ K Q J	◊ A 8 4 3 2	◊ K 5 4	◊ A Q J
♣ A J 6 2	♣ 7	♣ K 8 7 2	♣ A
4. ♠ 3	4. ♠ A 9 7	4. ♠ A K J 8 2	4. ♠ Q 5 4 3
♥ A J 7 6 4	♥ K 9 8 3 2	♥ K 8 6 3	♥ A Q 7
◊ K Q J	◊ A 8 4 3	◊ A 4 3	◊ K Q 5
♣ A J 6 2	♣ 7	♣ 2	♣ A 7 3
5. ♠ K Q J	5. ♠ 3	5. ♠ A K Q 8 2	5. ♠ J 5 4 3
♥ Q J 8 7	♥ A 10 9 5 2	♥ K 8 6 3	♥ A Q 7
◊ A	◊ K Q J 5 3	◊ A 4 3	◊ K Q 5
♣ Q 10 8 7 3	♣ K J	♣ 2	♣ A 7 3
6. ♠ A 6 2	6. ♠ 3	6. ♠ K Q 7 3	6. ♠ A J 10 6 4
♥ K 8 7 3	♥ A 10 9 5 2	♥ A K	♥ 6
◊ A	◊ K Q J 5 3	◊ J 8 6 4 2	◊ A 5
♣ A 6 5 4 2	♣ K J	♣ Q 3	♣ A K J 10 2
7. ♠ A 6	7. ♠ 3	7. ♠ 5	7. ♠ A 9 6
♥ 9 6 2	♥ A K Q	♥ K Q 7 5	♥ A 9 6 4 3 2
◊ A 4	◊ K Q 8 5 3	◊ A K 8 6 3 2	◊ Q
♣ A Q J 5 4 2	♣ K 9 6 3	♣ K 9	♣ A 5 4
8. ♠ Q J 6 4 2	8. ♠ K	8. ♠ A J	8. ♠ 10 9 5
♥ K	♥ 5 2	♥ A Q J	♥ K 3 2
◊ A K	◊ Q 8 5 2	◊ K Q J 6	◊ A 5
♣ K J 5 4 2	♣ A Q 8 7 6 3	♣ A K 6 4	♣ Q J 9 7 2

PLAY HANDS ON ROMAN KEY CARD BLACKWOOD (2)
(These hands can be made up by using pages 160-167)

Hand 49 : Asking bids — Endplay

Dealer North : Nil vulnerable

NORTH
- ♠ K 7 5 4 2
- ♡ A K 5 2
- ◊ A K Q
- ♣ A

WEST
- ♠ Q 10 9
- ♡ J 10
- ◊ 8 7 4
- ♣ J 9 6 4 2

EAST
- ♠ 6
- ♡ Q 9 8 6
- ◊ J 10 9 2
- ♣ Q 10 5 3

SOUTH
- ♠ A J 8 3
- ♡ 7 4 3
- ◊ 6 5 3
- ♣ K 8 7

WEST	NORTH	EAST	SOUTH
	2◊	Pass	2NT
Pass	3♠	Pass	4♠
Pass	4NT	Pass	5◊
Pass	5♡	Pass	5♠
Pass	5NT	Pass	6◊
Pass	6♡	Pass	6♠
Pass	Pass	Pass	

Bidding : 5◊ = one key card. Over 5♠ (no queen of trumps), North was worth 6♠ but tried to find whether 6NT was playable. 6◊ showed one king, 6♡ asked in hearts and 6♠ = no king, no queen in hearts. If South had ♠A, ♣K and ♡Q, North should be prepared to play in 6NT.

Lead : Jack of diamonds. Prefer the solid sequence.

Recommended play : Win with the ace of diamonds and cash the king of spades. Unblock the ace of clubs and then lead a low spade. When East shows out, win with dummy's ace, cash the ♣K and ruff a club. Play off your diamond winners, followed by the ace and king of hearts. Then throw West in with the third spade. With no hearts left, West has to give you a ruff-and-discard.

Notes : (1) If North fails to play off the ace of clubs before the second round of trumps, North will have no way to complete the elimination of the minor suits.

(2) When East shows out on the second spade, it seems that a trump loser and a heart loser are inevitable. The only hope is for the hand with the spade winner to be short in hearts.

(3) 6NT would make if there were no spade loser, about a 50% chance. From North's point of view, when the bidding shows that there are not twelve tricks on top, 6♠ looks safer, especially as South need not have the jack of spades and might have a doubleton heart.

Hand 50 : Asking bids — Dummy reversal

Dealer East : N-S vulnerable

NORTH
- ♠ 8 7 2
- ♡ 10 9 8 7
- ◊ K J 9 6
- ♣ 10 2

WEST
- ♠ K Q 5
- ♡ J 5 4 3
- ◊ A 8 5
- ♣ A K 7

EAST
- ♠ A 4 3
- ♡ A K Q 6 2
- ◊ 2
- ♣ Q 8 6 3

SOUTH
- ♠ J 10 9 6
- ♡ - - -
- ◊ Q 10 7 4 3
- ♣ J 9 5 4

WEST	NORTH	EAST	SOUTH
		1♡	Pass
2NT	Pass	3◊	Pass
3NT	Pass	4♣	Pass
4◊	Pass	4♠	Pass
5♣	Pass	5♡	Pass
7♡	Pass	Pass	Pass

Bidding : 2NT = Jacoby (game force raise). 3◊ = short in diamonds. 3NT = RKCB. 4♣ = 0 or 3 key cards (West can tell it must be three). 4◊ = ask for the trump queen. 4♠ = 'Yes, I have it.' 5♣ = Control Ask. 5♡ = ♣Q, no ♣K. West can now see the first three rounds of every suit covered and so has enough to bid the grand slam. West can count only 12 tricks in no-trumps.

Lead : Jack of spades. Choose the solid sequence.

Recommended play : Win the lead and play the ace of hearts. If everybody had followed, the rest would be child's play after drawing trumps. With trumps 4-0, you can hope for clubs 3-3 or that North has four or more clubs so that you can ruff the fourth round in dummy. Neither of those lines has a high chance of success. Far better is to switch to a diamond to the ace and ruff a diamond, club to the ace and ruff a diamond. Then cash the king and queen of hearts, cross to dummy. With only six spades and seven clubs, it is slightly safer to cross to dummy with the second round of spades. Draw North's last trump with the ♡J, discarding your club loser. This play, ruffing in the long trump hand, is known as a dummy reversal.

Notes : (1) It would be wrong for East to draw four rounds of trumps at the start. If East does this, South should discard diamonds, given East showed a singleton diamond in the bidding.

(2) If East plays clubs before drawing trumps, North ruffs the third round.

Hand 51 : Opening lead — Playing for the overtrick

Dealer South : E-W vulnerable

NORTH
♠ A 7 6 4
♡ 4
♢ K Q 8
♣ A 8 6 3 2

WEST
♠ Q J 10
♡ J 9 3
♢ A J 7 6 2
♣ Q 4

EAST
♠ 3
♡ 10 8 7 5
♢ 10 9 5 4
♣ J 10 7 5

SOUTH
♠ K 9 8 5 2
♡ A K Q 6 2
♢ 3
♣ K 9

WEST	NORTH	EAST	SOUTH
			1♠
Pass	4♡	Pass	4NT
Pass	5♡	Pass	5♠
Pass	Pass	Pass	

Bidding : 4♡ = splinter, strong raise in spades and short in hearts. With only four losers, South must try for a slam. As North has a singleton heart and at least four trumps, South sees that the heart losers can be ruffed in dummy and can envisage a grand slam opposite three aces and the queen of spade. North's 5♡ reply shows that one ace is missing as well as the ♠Q and so South signs off.

Lead : Queen of spades. A solid trump sequence will not give away a trick but as will be seen later, West has a better lead.

Recommended play : Declarer wins and cashes a second round of spades. There is no problem making 5♠, but South should try for an overtrick. Continue with the top hearts, discarding two diamonds from dummy. Then lead your fourth heart. If West ruffs, the other diamond loser is discarded. West will probably discard and the heart is ruffed in dummy. A club to the king is followed by the fifth heart, now a winner. Whether West ruffs or not, dummy's last diamond is discarded and South's diamond loser is ruffed in dummy. 12 tricks.

Notes : (1) South could also try for an overtrick, hoping that clubs are 3-3 and so South's diamond could be discarded on an established club winner. Given that West has three spades and East one, the club play is not as good as playing hearts. The hearts figure to be 4-3 most of the time and clubs figure not to be 3-3.
(2) Against 6♠, West would lead the ace of diamonds but there is a strong case for leading the ◊A even against 5♠. At pairs, it is vital to hold declarer to the minimum number of tricks. As North has shown a strong hand and South has tried for slam, West with 11 HCP should realise that East will have almost nothing. Therefore West should try for a diamond trick at once by leading the ace.

Hand 52 : Handling a tenace combination — Making the maximum number of tricks

Dealer West : Both vulnerable

NORTH
♠ Q 9 5 4 3
♡ 9 8 5 3 2
♢ K Q 8
♣ - - -

WEST
♠ - - -
♡ A K Q 6 4
♢ 10 9 7 4 2
♣ A 7 6

EAST
♠ A J 7
♡ J 10
♢ A J
♣ K Q 10 9 5 2

SOUTH
♠ K 10 8 6 2
♡ 7
♢ 6 5 3
♣ J 8 4 3

WEST	NORTH	EAST	SOUTH
1♡	Pass	2♣	Pass
2♢	Pass	2♠	Pass
3♣	Pass	4♣	Pass
4NT	Pass	5♡	Pass
6♢	Pass	7NT	All pass

Bidding : 2♠ = fourth suit and 3♣ shows a 1-5-4-3 or 0-5-5-3 pattern. 4♣ sets clubs as trumps and 4NT = two key cards for clubs. (Over 4♣, 4◊ = RKCB — 'I want to ask', 4♡ = 0 or 3, 4♠ = 1 or 4, 4NT = 2 key cards, no ♣Q and 5♣ = 2 key cards + ♣Q.) Over 4NT, 5♣ = signoff and 5◊ = ask in diamonds. 5♡ is a Control Ask in hearts and 6◊ shows the K + Q but no J. East can count to 13 tricks with six clubs, five hearts and two aces.

Lead : King of diamonds. Clearcut against 7NT.

Recommended play : Win ◊A and cash ♣K. If everyone followed to this, the rest would be easy : cash jack and ten of hearts, cross to ♣A, cash the hearts to discard the ◊J and the spade losers, and claim. When the clubs are 4-0, the situation is awkward. You run the 10 of clubs but you cannot afford to cash ♡J-10 as there is no entry back to dummy's clubs. So, run ♣10, then cash ♣A, cross to ♡10 and run the clubs and cash the ♠A. In the ending, declarer has ♡A K Q 6 and East has ♠J-7, ♡J and ◊J. North is squeezed and with four cards left cannot hold on to four hearts and the ◊Q. If the ◊Q is thrown, dummy's ◊J is high and if North throws a heart, play the ♡J and overtake it. West's ♡6 will be a winner.

Notes : (1) If North had started with J-x-x-x in clubs, the play would be much easier.
(2) If East-West reached 7♣, the play should follow the recommended line. After a heart lead against 7♣, East should return to hand via the ◊A and not a heart after ♣K, ♣10 and club to the ace.

CHAPTER 14
CUE BIDDING (1)

Cue bidding is a method of exploring slams by showing precisely which aces and which kings are held. It is also able to locate singleton and void holdings. It is thus superior to simple Blackwood or the Gerber Convention. It works well when used in conjunction with Roman Key Card Blackwood.

What is a cue bid?

A cue bid is a change of suit after suit agreement in a game-forcing auction. East's last bid in each of these auctions would be taken as a cue bid :

WEST	EAST	WEST	EAST	WEST	EAST
1♣	2♠	1♦	1♥	1♠	2♥
3♠	4♦	3♥	3♠	3♥	4♣

Where the suit agreed is a minor suit and the raise is to the three-level, new suit bids at the three-level are stopper bids, angling for 3NT.

WEST	EAST	
1♣	2♣	3♦ is a stopper bid, not a cue bid.
3♣	3♦...	The partnership needs to agree whether 3♦ *shows* a stopper or *asks* for a stopper.

Most play that 3♦ shows a stopper and the focus is on whether a heart stopper is held. Some play that 3♦ asks partner to bid 3NT if a stopper in diamonds is held. Partnership agreement is needed here. If you have no preference, stopper *asks* are recommended.

After minor suit agreement at the four-level, change of suit is played as a cue bid in standard methods. In the previous chapter, it was suggested that using RKCB rebids at that point is valuable. You and partner will need to settle this.

After cue bidding has begun, there are no cue bids in the trump suit itself. A bid in the agreed trump suit is a signoff, saying : 'I have no further cue bid to make. I am unable or unwilling to go higher.'

When should you choose to cue bid?

A cue bid is appropriate when the bidding reveals slam potential and a key card ask is unsuitable. The most common situations for cue bidding are :
1. You hold a void, OR
2. You lack control in a suit (you do not have the ace, king or a singleton in that suit).

What does a cue bid show?

Cue bids aim to reveal control of suits outside trumps. To say that you have 'control' of a suit generally refers to first- and second-round control and means that the opponents are unable to cash the first two tricks in that suit (rather important for a slam, isn't it?). To have control, you need to hold the ace or king or void or singleton in that suit.

First-round control = ace or void

Second-round control = king or singleton

When does cue bidding start?

The first cue bid usually occurs at the four-level. If hearts are trumps (e.g., 1♣ : 1♥, 3♥ . . .) 3♠ will be the first cue bid. Where a minor suit has been raised to the four-level, it will be assumed for Chapters 14 and 15 that cue bidding is used.

PRIMARY CUE BIDS

A primary cue bid shows first round control of the suit bid. The first cue bid made is a primary cue. A new suit cue bid will also be a primary cue unless the ace or void in that suit has already been shown or denied.

Rule 1 : Do not differentiate between an ace or a void when making a primary cue.

Rule 2 : With more than one primary cue available, bid the cheapest possible. If you bypass a suit other than trumps, you deny first round control in that suit.

WEST	EAST	
1♦	1♥	3♠ is a primary cue. It promises the ace of spades or a void in spades.
3♥	3♠...	

WEST	EAST	
1♦	1♥	4♣ is a primary cue, showing ace or void in clubs *and denying* ace or void in spades.
3♥	4♣...	

WEST	EAST	
1♦	1♥	4♦, a primary cue, shows ace or void in diamonds *and denies* ♠A or void *and denies* ♣A or void.
3♥	4♦...	

WEST	W	E	EAST
♠ A K Q J 8 7	2♦	2♥	♠ 9 5 4 3
♥ ---	2♠	3♠	♥ 9 7 4 2
◊ K Q J 3	4♣	4◊	◊ A 5
♣ A K Q	7♠	Pass	♣ 7 4 2

4♣ and 4◊ are primary cues. Note that asking for key cards would not solve West's problem (does East have an ace and if so, which one?).

WEST	W	E	EAST
♠ A K Q J 8 7	2♦	2♥	♠ 9 5 4 3
♥ ---	2♠	3♠	♥ A 7 4 2
◊ K Q J 3	4♣	4♥	◊ 6 5
♣ A K Q	6♠	Pass	♣ 7 4 2

4♥ denied the ◊A and so West knows to reject the grand slam.

WEST	W	E	EAST
♠ A K Q J 8 7	2♦	2♥	♠ 9 5 4 3
♥ K Q J 5	2♠	3♠	♥ A 7 4 2
◊ A K Q	4♣	4♥	◊ 6 5
♣ ---	7♠	Pass	♣ 7 4 2

4♣ and 4♥ are primary cues. Note the void in clubs, the cheaper bid, is shown ahead of the ◊A.

WEST	W	E	EAST
♠ A K Q J 8 7	2♦	2♥	♠ 9 5 4 3
♥ - - -	2♠	3♠	♥ K J 4 2
◇ K Q J 3	4♦	4♠	◇ 6 5
♣ A K Q	6♠	Pass	♣ 7 4 2

4♠, the return to the trump suit, denied the ♥A and the ◇A and therefore West knows there is no grand slam.

SECONDARY CUE BIDS

A secondary cue bid shows second round control of the suit bid. It promises either the king or a singleton in that suit.

A secondary cue bid means that you can win the second round of the suit bid, either with the king or by ruffing when you have the singleton. If you are known to have a balanced hand, then the secondary cue bid must be based on the king.

A cue bid is a secondary cue if —

(a) It is a bid in a suit in which a primary cue has already been made, *OR*

(b) It is a bid in a suit which the bidder previously bypassed and thus denied first round control.

Rule 3 : Do not make a secondary cue if you can still make a primary cue. A secondary cue normally denies first round control in any unbid suit outside the trump suit. Show your primary controls first. Only when your primary controls are exhausted, start on your secondary controls.

Rule 4 : Do not differentiate between a king and a singleton when making a secondary cue bid.

Rule 5 : With two or more secondary cue bids available, bid the cheapest possible. Bypassing a suit to make a secondary cue denies second round control in each suit bypassed other than trumps.

WEST	EAST	
1◇	1♥	3♠ and 4♣ are primary cues. 4♠ is a secondary cue, showing ♠K
3♥	3♠	or a singleton spade. 4♠ denies
4♣	4♠ ...	first round control of diamonds as 4◇ was bypassed. (Rule 3)

WEST	EAST	
1◇	1♥	3♠ and 4♣ are primary cues. 5♣ is secondary (♣K or singleton),
3♥	3♠	*and denies* first round diamond
4♣	5♣ ...	control (Rule 3) and second round spade control (as 4♠ was bypassed — Rule 5).

WEST	EAST	
1◇	1♥	4♣ and 4◇ are primary cues. 4♠, a secondary cue, shows ♠K or a
3♥	4♣	singleton spade. 4♠ is secondary
4◇	4♠ ...	as 4♣, bypassing 3♠, denied first round spade control.

WEST	EAST	
1◇	1♥	4♣ and 4◇ are primary cues. 5◇ is secondary, (◇K or a singleton
3♥	4♣	diamond) and, bypassing 4♠ and
4◇	5◇ ...	5♣, denies second round in spades and clubs.

WEST	W	E	EAST
♠ A K Q 8 6 5	2◇	3♥	♠ 9 4 3
♥ - - -	3♠	4♣	♥ Q 10 9 8 2
◇ K Q 8 3	5♣	5◇	◇ A 4
♣ A Q 3	5♥	6♣	♣ K 8 4
	7♣	Pass	

East raises to 4♠ in order to allow the stronger hand to take control of slam bidding. The strong hand has fewer losers and can usually judge the final contract better than the weaker hand. After a game force opening and a positive reply, supporting partner's suit should be played as forcing.

5♣, 5◇ and 5♥ are primary cues. 6♣ = secondary cue as 5♣ was a primary cue.

WEST	W	E	EAST
♠ A K Q 8 6 5	2◇	3♥	♠ J 4 3
♥ - - -	3♠	4♠	♥ Q J 10 8 6
◇ K Q 8 3	5♣	5◇	◇ A 4
♣ A Q 3	5♥	5♠	♣ J 10 4
	6♠	Pass	

5♠, the return to the trump suit, denies the ability to make another cue. Therefore, East has no ♣K, no club singleton and so West rejects the grand slam which figures to be 50% at best.

With a major suit as trumps

Situation A : Suit agreement at the three-level, two or three primary cues followed by a signoff in 4-Major.

Message : Only mild slam interest. Slam not clearcut.

WEST	EAST	
1♠	3♠	4♣ and 4◇ are primary cues. 4♠ is a signoff indicating that
4♣	4◇	West has no more than a modest
4♠ ...		interest in slam.

WEST	EAST	
1♠	2◇	4♣, 4◇ and 4♥ are primary cues. 4♠ is a signoff by East,
3♣	3♠	indicating that East has no
4♣	4◇	significant extra values. West
4♥	4♠ ...	may still bid on, of course.

Situation B : Suit agreement at the four-level. Two primary cues followed by a signoff in 5-Major.

Message : Strong slam interest but no control in the unbid suit. Partner is asked to bid six with control in the missing suit, or pass with no control.

WEST	EAST	
1♠	2♥	4♠ and 5◇ are primary cues. The 5♥ signoff = no club control.
3♣	3♥	This asks West to bid 6♥ with
4♥	4♠	club control and to pass 5♥
5◇	5♥ ...	without club control.

Situation C : Primary and secondary cues in two suits only, followed by signoff in 5-Major.

Message : Pass with no control in the unbid suit, bid on if you have control.

WEST	EAST	
1♠	2♥	4♣/4♠ are primary cues. 5♣ is a secondary cue. The 5♥ signoff
3♥	4♣	= 'I have no diamond control.
4♠	5♣	Pass if you also cannot control
5♥ ...		diamonds, bid 6♥ if you can.'

EXERCISES ON CUE BIDDING (1)

A. The bidding has started 1◊ : 1♡, 3♡. What should responder bid next bid with these hands?

1. ♠ A Q 4 2	2. ♠ J 7	3. ♠ 9	4. ♠ 7	5. ♠ Q 8 7 2
♡ Q J 9 8 2	♡ K Q 8 6 4 2	♡ A K J 6 4 2	♡ A Q 7 5 2	♡ A K Q 2
◊ A 3	◊ 3	◊ A 8 3	◊ K 8 2	◊ A 2
♣ 9 6	♣ A 6 5 2	♣ K Q 3	♣ K Q 9 3	♣ J 8 2

B. W : 1♡, (N : 3♠), E : 4♡, (S : No), W : 5♣. What should East bid now with these hands?

1. ♠ J 8	2. ♠ Q 8	3. ♠ A J 7	4. ♠ 8 5	5. ♠ 6
♡ K Q 6 2	♡ K 6 4 3 2	♡ A 9 6 3 2	♡ Q J 7 6 4	♡ A 8 7 5 2
◊ J 3 2	◊ A 6 4 3 2	◊ A 5	◊ A 8 4 2	◊ A 6 2
♣ K Q 6 5	♣ 3	♣ 9 7 4	♣ J 4	♣ K Q 5 4

PARTNERSHIP BIDDING : How should the following hands be bid? West is the dealer each time.

SET 27— WEST	SET 27 — EAST	SET 28 — WEST	SET 28 — EAST
1. ♠ A K Q J 3 2 ♡ - - - ◊ K Q J 2 ♣ A K Q	1. ♠ 9 7 5 4 ♡ 8 7 6 2 ◊ A 4 ♣ 5 4 2	1. ♠ J 10 2 ♡ K J 2 ◊ A J 8 5 ♣ K 3 2	1. ♠ A K Q 7 5 ♡ A Q 7 6 3 ◊ 3 ♣ A 6
2. ♠ A K Q J 3 2 ♡ - - - ◊ K Q J 2 ♣ A K Q	2. ♠ 9 7 5 4 ♡ A 7 6 2 ◊ 6 4 ♣ 5 4 2	2. ♠ A J 8 7 2 ♡ A ◊ 9 6 3 2 ♣ K 7 4	2. ♠ K 6 4 3 ♡ K Q J ◊ 7 ♣ Q J 8 6 2
3. ♠ A K Q J 3 2 ♡ - - - ◊ K Q J 2 ♣ A K Q	3. ♠ 9 7 5 4 ♡ K Q J 2 ◊ 6 4 ♣ 5 4 2	3. ♠ K 9 7 4 3 2 ♡ 3 ◊ K Q 4 ♣ A 7 2	3. ♠ A Q J 8 ♡ K 9 6 5 ◊ A J 9 5 ♣ 9
4. ♠ 9 7 5 4 ♡ 8 7 6 2 ◊ A 5 3 2 ♣ 5	4. ♠ A K Q J 8 3 2 ♡ - - - ◊ K Q J ♣ A Q 2	4. ♠ A K J 8 6 2 ♡ - - - ◊ A K 7 4 ♣ 9 8 6	4. ♠ Q 7 5 4 3 ♡ A K 7 ◊ Q J 5 2 ♣ 2
5. ♠ 9 7 5 ♡ 8 7 6 3 2 ◊ A 5 ♣ 8 5 4	5. ♠ A K Q J 8 3 2 ♡ - - - ◊ K Q J ♣ A Q 2	5. ♠ A K J 8 6 2 ♡ - - - ◊ A K 7 4 ♣ 9 8 6	5. ♠ Q 7 5 4 3 ♡ K Q J 3 ◊ Q J 5 2 ♣ - - -
6. ♠ 9 7 5 ♡ Q J 10 7 3 ◊ A 7 ♣ K 7 3	6. ♠ A K Q J 8 3 2 ♡ - - - ◊ K Q J ♣ A Q 2	6. ♠ Q J 7 3 2 ♡ A 4 2 ◊ J 8 6 ♣ K Q	6. ♠ 6 4 ♡ K Q J 9 7 ◊ A K Q 7 5 ♣ J
7. ♠ J 5 3 ♡ K 8 4 ◊ A K Q 8 ♣ 5 4 3	7. ♠ A K Q 6 2 ♡ Q ◊ 6 4 2 ♣ A K J 6	7. ♠ Q J 7 3 2 ♡ A 4 2 ◊ J 8 6 ♣ A Q	7. ♠ 6 4 ♡ K Q J 9 7 ◊ A K Q 7 5 ♣ J
8. ♠ K 9 4 2 ♡ Q J 5 ◊ 7 ♣ A K Q 9 6	8. ♠ A Q 10 6 3 ♡ 7 6 2 ◊ A K Q ♣ J 8	8. ♠ A J 7 3 2 ♡ A 4 2 ◊ J 8 6 ♣ A 4	8. ♠ 6 4 ♡ K Q J 9 7 ◊ A K Q 7 5 ♣ J

PLAY HANDS ON CUE BIDDING (1)

(These hands can be made up by using pages 160-167)

Hand 53 : Suit without control — Squeeze play

Dealer North : N-S vulnerable

NORTH
♠ J 5 3
♡ K 8 4
◇ A K Q 8
♣ 5 4 3

WEST
♠ 7 4
♡ A J 3
◇ J 10 7 3
♣ Q J 10 9

EAST
♠ 10 9 8
♡ 10 9 7 6 5 2
◇ 9 5
♣ 7 2

SOUTH
♠ A K Q 6 2
♡ Q
◇ 6 4 2
♣ A K 8 6

WEST	NORTH	EAST	SOUTH
	1◇	Pass	1♠
Pass	1NT	Pass	3♣
Pass	4♠	Pass	5♣
Pass	5◇	Pass	6♠
Pass	Pass	Pass	

Bidding : 4♠ = weak preference (3♠ would have been stronger). Over 4♠, South should be concerned about the diamond position. Perhaps North has no diamond control. Therefore South cue bids 5♣ and when North can bid 5◇, South takes a shot at 6♠ which figures to be a reasonable chance.

Lead : Queen of clubs. Even though South bid clubs, this is safe. The ♡A is all right, but South must have heart control to jump to 6♠ over 5◇.

Recommended play : On the ♣Q lead, win with the ♣A and draw trumps. Play a diamond to the ace and lead a low heart from dummy. West captures the queen and plays a second club. South wins, crosses to the ◇K, cashes the ♡K to discard a club and then ruffs a heart. West is down to ◇ J-10-7-3 ♣ 10. South now leads the last trump and West is squeezed in diamonds and clubs.

Notes : (1) It would work if South wins the lead, crosses to ◇A and leads a heart to the queen at once, but there is a slight risk of a club ruff.
(2) On the third spade, West can safely discard a club or a heart but should hang on to the diamonds ('keep length with dummy').
(3) South leads a heart from dummy in the hope that East might have the ♡A and might play low.
(4) If West switches to a diamond after winning ♡A, the play goes the same way. South needs to keep track of the club spots. If South's ♣8 is not high, then South has to hope that the diamonds will provide four tricks. Note South's play of the last trump before playing off the diamonds. If the diamonds are 3-3, that can wait. The last trump may squeeze somebody.

Hand 54 : Lack of control in side suit — Play it as safe as you can

Dealer East : E-W vulnerable

NORTH
♠ A Q 10 6 3
♡ 7 6 2
◇ A K Q
♣ J 8

WEST
♠ - - -
♡ 10 9 4
◇ J 8 6 5
♣ 10 7 5 4 3 2

EAST
♠ J 8 7 5
♡ A K 8 3
◇ 10 9 4 3 2
♣ - - -

SOUTH
♠ K 9 4 2
♡ Q J 5
◇ 7
♣ A K Q 9 6

WEST	NORTH	EAST	SOUTH
		Pass	1♣
Pass	1♠	Pass	3♠
Pass	4◇	Pass	5♣
Pass	5◇	Pass	5♠
Pass	Pass	Pass	

Bidding : Opening hand opposite opener who can jump-rebid = slam potential if a trump fit exists. North should recognise slam prospects upon hearing 3♠. With two suits unguarded, North should choose a cue sequence. 4◇ and 5♣ = primary cues and 5◇ = secondary cue. The focus is clearly on heart control. South's 5♣ bypassed 4♡ and so denied the ♡A and 5♠ denies second round control in hearts. Therefore North passes 5♠.

Lead : Ace of hearts. What could be easier?

Recommended play : East cashes two hearts and exits with a heart or a diamond. North should start at once on trumps by cashing the ace (or queen) first. When missing J-x-x-x, keep one top trump in each hand. When West shows out, play a spade to the 9, finessing against East's jack, and draw East's remaining trumps. After trumps are drawn, you have only winners left.

Notes : (1) Do not play diamonds or clubs before starting trumps. This may not cost but there is no benefit either. With nothing but winners outside trumps, draw trumps at once. Play a club early and East ruffs.
(2) Playing the king of spades on the first round of trumps is an error. As the cards lie, this gives East a trump trick and declarer will fail.

Hand 55 : Splinter with a void — Catering for a bad break

Dealer South : Both vulnerable

NORTH
♠ 9 7 4
♡ - - -
◇ K 8 7 4
♣ K 7 5 4 3 2

WEST
♠ A K Q 8 5
♡ A Q 8 6 2
◇ - - -
♣ J 9 6

EAST
♠ J 1 0 6 3 2
♡ K 9 5 4
◇ A Q J 3
♣ - - -

SOUTH
♠ - - -
♡ J 1 0 7 3
◇ 1 0 9 6 5 2
♣ A Q 1 0 8

WEST	NORTH	EAST	SOUTH
			Pass
1♠	Pass	4♣	Pass
4◇	Pass	5♣	Pass
5◇	Pass	5♡	Pass
7♠	Pass	Pass	Pass

Bidding : 4♣ = splinter, showing good spade support and a shortage in clubs. 4◇ is a primary cue, showing ace or void in diamonds. The cheaper first round control is shown first. 5♣ is a primary cue in the splinter suit and normally shows a void. Bypassing 4♡, it also denies the ♡A. 5◇ is a secondary cue, bid deliberately ahead of 5♡ to enable responder to show second round heart control. 5♡ = secondary cue, the ♡K.

Lead : 7 of spades. Choose a safe lead against a grand slam.

Recommended play : Draw trumps and then tackle the hearts, starting with ♡K. When North shows out, lead a low heart. If South plays low, finesse the ♡8. If South plays ♡10 or ♡J, take the ♡A, ruff a club in dummy and lead a heart, finessing the ♡8. Ruff a club in dummy and discard your other club loser on the ◇A.

Notes : (1) If East bid 5♠ over 5◇ to deny heart control, West would settle for 6♠. If East jumped to 6♠ over 5◇, this would promise second round heart control and West would bid 7♠.

(2) When missing J-10-x-x in a key suit, you need to retain two honors in the one hand to capture the two honors missing if the 4-0 break occurs. Therefore start the hearts by playing off the king first.

(3) After drawing trumps, you must not ruff a club, cash ◇A, ruff a diamond, ruff a club and then start on the hearts. You are now an entry short to capture South's hearts. When faced with the choice of taking ruffs or establishing a long suit, set up the long suit first.

Hand 56 : Primary and secondary cue bids — Double squeeze

Dealer West : Nil vulnerable

NORTH
♠ 8 4
♡ 1 0 9 8 5 4
◇ 1 0 6 2
♣ Q 1 0 5

WEST
♠ J 1 0 2
♡ K J 2
◇ A J 8 5
♣ K 3 2

EAST
♠ A K Q 7 5
♡ A Q 7 6 3
◇ 3
♣ A 6

SOUTH
♠ 9 6 3
♡ - - -
◇ K Q 9 7 4
♣ J 9 8 7 4

WEST	NORTH	EAST	SOUTH
1◇	Pass	1♠	Pass
1NT	Pass	3♡	Pass
3♠	Pass	4♣	Pass
4◇	Pass	4♡	Pass
5♣	Pass	5◇	Pass
5♡	Pass	7♠	All pass

Bidding : 3♠ = strong preference, justified because of the help in hearts. 4♣/4◇/4♡ = primary cues. 5♣/5◇/5♡ = secondary cues. Once East finds ◇A, ♣K and ♡K, East can bid seven.

3NT RKCB by East over 3♠ would also work if East follows up with Control Asks in clubs and hearts. 3NT should be RKCB here but with the delayed support for spades, it is arguable.

Lead : King of diamonds. Second choice, a trump.

Recommended play : The slam looks very easy with five spades, five hearts and three minor winners. Win the ◇A, draw trumps (North discards a diamond) and lead a heart. When South shows out, a hitch has occurred but do not give up. Win the heart, ruff a diamond, cross back to dummy with a heart and ruff a third diamond. On this third diamond, North has to let a club go (if a heart is discarded, all your hearts are good). Next, cash the ♡A and ♡Q, leaving yourself with ♡7 and ♣A-6. South has to make a discard from ◇Q and ♣J-9-8. If the ◇Q is thrown, dummy's ◇J is good and you discard a club from dummy. If South keeps the ◇Q and throws a club, you throw the ◇J from dummy. Now ♣A and a club to the king sees you make trick 13 with the ♣3! You have just executed a double squeeze. Well done!

Notes : (1) Were it not for West's 1◇ opening, South would be very keen to show the minor two-suiter.

(2) East might well choose to bid 7NT and the play would be similar. Instead of ruffing diamonds, declarer would cash five spades and discard the low diamonds on the fourth and fifth spade. The rest is the same.

(3) South has to keep the diamond guard (dummy's ◇J is the 'menace' against South) and North has to keep all the hearts (East's fifth heart is the 'menace' against North). If each keeps a red suit guarded, neither can keep a guard in the clubs.

CHAPTER 15
CUE BIDDING (2)

THIRD ROUND CUE BIDS

A tertiary cue shows third round control of the suit bid, either the queen or a doubleton. The rules and guidelines for tertiary cues are equivalent to the rules for secondary cues.

Hands which can locate third round controls are rare as the bidding is usually too high. Systems which can create a game-force and agree a trump suit at a low level have greater possibilities for third round cues. The main objective of cue bidding is to find specific first round and second round controls.

Third round control can also exist in short suit holdings such as voids or singletons :

Void = first, second and third round control
Singleton = second and third round control
Ace-singleton = first, second and third round control
Ace-doubleton = first and third round control
Ace-king-doubleton = first, second and third round control
A-K-x = first and second round control
A-Q-x = first and third round control
K-x = second and third round control
K-Q-x = second and third round control
x-x or Q-x-x = third round control

When a minor suit is trumps

In Chapter 13, it was suggested that key cards be shown after minor suit agreement at the four-level. If the partnership is not using that approach, then cue bidding will apply.

Situation A : Minor suit agreement at the four-level and responder returns to 4-of-opener's-major. This is intended as a natural bid, not a cue bid.

WEST	EAST	
1♠	2♣	4♠ is intended as a natural bid,
4♣	4♠ . . .	not forcing, not a primary cue. East has a limit spade raise.

WEST	W	E	EAST
♠ A K 9 8 5	1♠	2♦	♠ J 6 2
♡ A J	4♦	4♠	♡ K Q 2
◇ K Q 10 6	Pass		◇ A J 5 2
♣ J 8			♣ 7 3 2

Situation B : Minor suit agreement at the four-level. Three primary cue bids followed by a signoff in 5-minor.

Message : Only borderline slam interest. Bid on only if you have extra values.

WEST	EAST	
1♠	2♣	4◇ is a primary cue (3◇ would
3♣	4◇	be a stopper probe for 3NT). 4♡
4♡	4♠	and 4♠ are primary cues. The 5♣
5♣		signoff = 'I have no extra values, just a minimum opening.'

WEST	W	E	EAST
♠ J 4	1♡	2♣	♠ A K 6 2
♡ A K 9 7 2	4♣	4♠	♡ 6
◇ 3	6♣		◇ Q 5 2
♣ A K 6 5 3			♣ Q J 9 7 2

4♠ is a primary cue, showing slam interest and first round control in spades *and denying* first round control in diamonds, as 4◇ was bypassed. West bids 6♣ since there is no chance for a grand slam with the ◇A missing but West has sufficient values to make 6♣ a worthwhile chance.

Situation C : Minor suit agreement at the four-level. Two primary cue bids followed by a signoff in 5-minor.

Message : No control in the unbid suit. Pass if you also have no control, bid on if you have control.

WEST	EAST	
1♡	2♣	4◇ and 4♡ are primary cues. The 5♣ signoff says 'I have no
4♣	4◇	control in spades. Bid 6♣ if you
4♡	5♣ . . .	have spade control, else pass.'

WEST	W	E	EAST
♠ A K J 6 5	1♠	2◇	♠ 9
♡ 2	4◇	4♡	♡ A K 7
◇ A K 9 4 3	4♠	5◇	◇ Q J 8 7 5 2
♣ 9 5	Pass		♣ Q 4 2

4♡ and 4♠ are primary cues. The 5◇ signoff = no control in clubs. With no control in clubs either West passes.

This is the one drawback to cue bidding. It is too precise. When a cue bidding auction fails to reach slam it is often because the partnership lacks control in one suit. The cue bidding sequence reveals that. Regrettably, it also reveals it to the opponents and they invariably lead the danger suit. Had the auction been less informative, you may have received a more favorable lead, allowing one or more overtricks.

When to end a cue bidding sequence

Once cue bidding has begun, it continues until one partner or the other has sufficient knowledge to place the contract or until the sequence is broken by 4NT RKCB or by the 5NT Trump Ask (see later). If you know that six is a good chance but seven is out of the question, bid six. Do not continue with a cue bidding sequence which can help only the opponents.

If seven is still a chance, by all means keep on cue bidding. Persist with cue bidding if you need more information and cue bidding is able to provide what you need. You will often recognise that the information you need for seven (such as a key queen) cannot be found. Stop the cues and bid six.

Raising a major suit to the 5-level

If the bidding has reached 4♥/4♠ (the agreed major), raising to 5♥/5♠ says : 'Bid six if you have strong trumps.' What counts as strong trumps depends on what has been shown so far. Usually two of the top three trumps or A-J-10 in the major is enough to bid six. Since 4NT RKCB can usually find the top trump honors, the raise to 5-Major often occurs when a void is held. In that case the answer to RKCB may be ambiguous.

Cue bids at the 5-level and at the 6-level

A cue bid at the six-level is looking for a grand slam (since you are already committed to the six-level) and promises that no first-round controls are missing. The same applies to a cue bid at the five-level *above* the agreed trump suit. As this commits you to the six-level anyway, it must be looking for a grand slam and also promises that no first round controls are missing. You may sometimes be able to show a number of controls economically with a cue beyond five of the agreed trump suit. For example :

WEST	W	E	EAST
♠ A Q J 5 2	1♠	2♦	♠ - - -
♥ 7	3♦	4♥	♥ A 6 3 2
♦ J 8 7 4	5♥	7♦	♦ A K Q 6 5 2
♣ A 6 5	Pass		♣ K Q 9

East chooses 2♦ rather than 3♦ as it is not economical to jump-shift with a two-suiter. After 3♦, 4♥ is a primary cue showing slam interest. A bid of 3♥ would be a stopper probe for 3NT.

West's 5♥ is a secondary cue but because it is at the five-level *above* the agreed trump suit, it simultaneously promises first round control in all unbid suits. Thus it shows not only the second round heart control but also the ace of spades and the ace of clubs. That is enough to enable East to bid 7♦. Notice how much more efficient the 5♥ cue is than a primary cue of 4♠.

Blackwood or RKCB after cue bidding has begun

It is possible to revert to 4NT asking (or even 3NT asking) after one or more cue bids have been made. There are many possible reasons. Perhaps you need to check whether the key cards in trumps are held, perhaps you need to check whether a primary cue was a void or an ace, perhaps you had an unguarded suit and have now found partner has control in that suit. The answers to 4NT are the normal replies used by the partnership. If an ace has already been cue bid, it is still shown in reply to the 4NT ask.

WEST	EAST	4♣ and 4♦ are primary cues. 4NT
1♦	1♠	has its normal meaning, RKCB
3♠	4♣	or simple Blackwood, according
4♦	4NT	to partnership agreement.

Cue bidding by inference

A 1NT opener or a natural 2NT bidder can make a cue bid without raising the trump suit.

WEST	EAST	If East's 3♠ is natural, 3NT =
1NT	3♠	no support for spades. With
?		support for partner, raise to four-
2NT	3♠	level = weak support, new suit =
?		cue and a strong raise.

Assuming responder's bid is natural and RKCB support bids are not being used :

2NT : 3♥, 3♠ = heart support + the ace of spades
2NT : 3♥, 4♣ = heart support, ♣A but no ♠A
1NT : 3♠, 4♦ = spade support, ♦A but no ♣A

Where a change of suit is forcing, a jump-shift is often played as a splinter, particularly when the jump is to the four-level.

WEST	EAST	3♣ by West would have been
1♠	2♥	forcing. 4♣ by West is generally
4♣ . . .		played by experts as a splinter.

However, if splinters are not being used, the jump to 4♣ can be played as an inferential cue bid, showing good support for hearts, the values to raise to at least 4♥ plus the ace of clubs.

Cue bid after a splinter

If a player has made a splinter and later cue bids the splinter suit, that shows that the splinter was a void. It could logically be ace singleton, but many prefer not to splinter with ace singleton since partner's king or king-queen are less likely to be wasted values opposite the ace.

The 5NT Trump Ask

RKCB and splinters have taken away much of the need for cue bidding. 4NT can locate the top trumps and splinters can locate shortages. Still, there are many situations where cue bidding is valuable and may be the only way to solve the slam problems at hand. Once cue bidding has started, you can use 4NT to check on the top trumps but what if the cue bids have taken you beyond 4NT? In that case you need to use the 5NT Trump Ask to locate the top trump honors. A bid of 5NT without using 4NT first asks partner for the ace, king, queen of trumps (not the jack). The 5NT trump ask should be used only if there are no losers outside the trump suit and a grand slam is possible.

Replies to 5NT

6♣ = no top trump
6♦ = one top trump
6♥ = two top trumps
6♠ = three top trumps

Other schemes are possible, but 5NT comes up so rarely, it is better to have a simple set of replies which will not tax the memory and will be remembered easily when the situation arises. If you wish something more complex, see *Bridge Conventions, Defenses and Countermeasures*.

EXERCISES ON CUE BIDDING (2)

A. The bidding has started 1NT (15-18) : 3♠ (natural). What should opener rebid with these hands?

1. ♠ A Q 4 2	2. ♠ K 8 7	3. ♠ 9 8 6 2	4. ♠ A 4 3	5. ♠ A 8
♡ A 9 8 2	♡ K Q 6 2	♡ A K 6	♡ K Q 6 2	♡ Q J 2
◇ K 3	◇ A J 3	◇ A 3	◇ K Q 5 2	◇ K 8 5 2
♣ A 6 3	♣ Q 6 5	♣ A Q 7 3	♣ K J	♣ A K 9 8

B. Hearts are trumps. What would your reply be to the 5NT Trump Ask?

1. ♠ A 8 7	2. ♠ K Q 5	3. ♠ A J 4	4. ♠ A 4	5. ♠ 9
♡ K 6 2	♡ J 6 4 3	♡ A K 7 6 3 2	♡ A Q 7 6 4	♡ A K Q 5
◇ J 9 7 3 2	◇ 4	◇ - - -	◇ 4	◇ A Q J 9
♣ A K	♣ A K J 7 3	♣ J 9 6 4	♣ K Q 8 7 2	♣ A 10 4 2

PARTNERSHIP BIDDING : How should the following hands be bid? West is the dealer each time.

SET 29— WEST	SET 29 — EAST	SET 30 — WEST	SET 30 — EAST
1. ♠ J 9 7	1. ♠ A K 8 6 5 4 2	1. ♠ K Q 6 3	1. ♠ A J 8 7 5
♡ 8 6 3 2	♡ A	♡ Q 8 4	♡ A K 2
◇ A K Q	◇ 6 4 3 2	◇ - - -	◇ J 8 7
♣ 10 5 2	♣ A	♣ A K Q 9 4 2	♣ 6 3
2. ♠ A Q 9 7 3	2. ♠ K 8 6 5 4	2. ♠ K Q 6 3	2. ♠ J 8 7 5 4
♡ 3 2	♡ A K 6	♡ Q 8 4	♡ A K 2
◇ A J	◇ K 8 4 3	◇ - - -	◇ A J 8
♣ A 8 4 2	♣ 7	♣ A K Q 9 4 2	♣ 6 3
3. ♠ 10 8 7 5 4 2	3. ♠ K Q J 3	3. ♠ A Q J 6	3. ♠ K 2
♡ 6	♡ A K Q 2	♡ K 9 4 2	♡ A Q 8 7 5
◇ A 8	◇ K Q J 4 2	◇ A K 4 3	◇ Q J 5
♣ A 6 3 2	♣ - - -	♣ 7	♣ K 9 3
4. ♠ A 9 7 4 2	4. ♠ K Q J 3	4. ♠ K 2	4. ♠ A Q J 6
♡ 8 4	♡ A K Q 2	♡ A Q 8 7 5	♡ K 9 4 3 2
◇ A 8 3	◇ K Q J 4 2	◇ A 5 2	◇ K 4 3
♣ 7 5 2	♣ - - -	♣ A 9 3	♣ 7
5. ♠ A Q 10 6 3	5. ♠ K 9 7 2	5. ♠ Q J 8 7 2	5. ♠ A K 5 4 3
♡ A J 8 7	♡ 6 3	♡ A J 3	♡ K Q 7
◇ A 7 4	◇ K 6	◇ 4 3	◇ K Q 5 2
♣ 2	♣ A K Q J 4	♣ A 8 2	♣ 3
6. ♠ A 10 8 7 2	6. ♠ K 9 6 3	6. ♠ A K Q 7 5 2	6. ♠ 9 8 4 3
♡ 5 4	♡ A K 7 2	♡ Q 5	♡ K 6 2
◇ A K	◇ Q 7 5 2	◇ A K Q J	◇ 8 5
♣ A K 6 2	♣ 8	♣ A	♣ 7 4 3 2
7. ♠ A 10 8 7 2	7. ♠ K Q 6 3	7. ♠ A 5 3	7. ♠ 7 2
♡ 5 4	♡ A K 7 2	♡ K Q J 7 5	♡ A 9 6 4 3
◇ A K	◇ Q 7 5 2	◇ A 8 2	◇ Q
♣ A K 6 2	♣ 8	♣ 7 2	♣ A K Q 8 5
8. ♠ A 10 8 7 2	8. ♠ K Q 6 3	8. ♠ A 7	8. ♠ 10 9 5
♡ 5 4	♡ K Q 7 2	♡ A Q J 4 3	♡ K
◇ A K	◇ Q 7 5 2	◇ K Q J 6 2	◇ A 9 8 5 4
♣ A K 6 2	♣ 8	♣ 4	♣ A J 7 2

PLAY HANDS ON CUE BIDDING (2)

(These hands can be made up by using pages 160-167)

Hand 57 : Splinter — Trump Ask — Catering for a bad break

Dealer North : E-W vulnerable

NORTH
- ♠ A 9 8 7
- ♡ A 8 2
- ◊ - - -
- ♣ K Q 10 7 6 2

WEST
- ♠ 10
- ♡ J 6 4 3
- ◊ K Q 10 4
- ♣ J 8 4 3

EAST
- ♠ 4 3 2
- ♡ K 10 7 5
- ◊ A 9 6 5 3
- ♣ 5

SOUTH
- ♠ K Q J 6 5
- ♡ Q 9
- ◊ J 8 7 2
- ♣ A 9

WEST	NORTH	EAST	SOUTH
	1♣	Pass	1♠
Pass	4◊	Pass	5♣
Pass	5NT	Pass	6♡
Pass	7♠	All pass	

Bidding : 4◊ = splinter, strong spade raise and short in diamonds. 5♣ = primary cue. On hearing that, North figures the clubs should provide whatever discards South needs and the only problem remaining is the trump position. 5NT asks for South's top trumps and 6♡ = two of the top three honors. That is enough for North to bid the grand slam.

Lead : King of diamonds. The normal choice.

Recommended play : Ruff in dummy, cash ♠A and play a spade to the king, ruff another diamond, cross to the ace of clubs and draw the last trump, discarding a heart from dummy. Continue with a club to the king, cash the ♣Q and ruff a club. Dummy's clubs are now high. Cross to ♡A and run the clubs, discarding your remaining red suit losers.

Notes : (1) North could cue bid 5◊ over 5♣ but there is no need to do this. South would sign off in 5♠ (no heart control) and North could still continue with 5NT.
(2) Once South cue bids 5♣ North should figure there are no losers outside trumps.
(3) It is easy to go wrong. If declarer ruffs the diamond lead and draws three rounds of trumps, declarer is one trick short when the clubs do not break (it would be fatuous to finesse the ♣10). South should foresee the possibility of a 4-1 club break and ruff a second diamond just in case.

Hand 58 : Cue bid in support of a minor — Vienna Coup

Dealer East : Both vulnerable

NORTH
- ♠ 9 8 7 2
- ♡ Q J 10 6 3 2
- ◊ 6
- ♣ 4 2

WEST
- ♠ Q 4
- ♡ 4
- ◊ A K 10 9 8 7 3
- ♣ A 8 6

EAST
- ♠ A 10 6
- ♡ K 8 7
- ◊ Q J 5
- ♣ K Q 7 3

SOUTH
- ♠ K J 5 3
- ♡ A 9 5
- ◊ 4 2
- ♣ J 10 9 5

WEST	NORTH	EAST	SOUTH
		1NT	Pass
3◊	Pass	3♠	Pass
6◊	Pass	Pass	Pass

Bidding : 3♠ is a cue bid in support of diamonds. 1NT : 3◊ natural shows a strong single-suiter. Without support, opener would bid 3NT. With support, opener cue bids the cheapest ace. This is one of the few areas where one can cue bid at the three-level in support of a minor.

As 3♠ denied the ace of hearts, West knows there is no grand slam. As it happens 6NT is on, but East could just as easily have held Q-J-x or worse in hearts.

Lead : Queen of hearts. Choose the solid sequence.

Recommended play : Duck the first heart, ruff the ♡J continuation and draw trumps. It appears that a 3-3 break in clubs is necessary, but it does not cost to run all your trumps first. Errors in discarding are common. First, cash the ace of spades to isolate your ♠Q as a 'menace' against the player with the ♠K. This play of cashing an ace opposite a potential threat card is known as the Vienna Coup.

Then run all your trumps, keeping dummy's clubs intact. Be on the lookout for the ♠K. South is squeezed at trick 9. If the ♠K has not appeared, just play off your clubs. Dummy's fourth club will be a winner.

Notes : (1) West could also transfer to diamonds and follow up with 4◊ to start a cue bidding sequence.
(2) A spade lead does not defeat 6◊: win ♠A and play off seven rounds of diamonds, keeping ♡K and four clubs in dummy. At trick 8, South has to discard from ♠K ♡A ♣ J-10-9-5. This is a triple squeeze.
(3) The same triple squeeze would operate in 6NT on, say, a diamond (or ♣J) lead. Win the lead, cash ♠A and rattle off all the diamonds. South cannot hang on to ♠K, ♡A and all the clubs.

Hand 59 : Inferential cue bid — Trump endplay

Dealer South : Nil vulnerable

NORTH
♠ A K Q 10 5
♡ 9 8 2
♦ 10 2
♣ A Q 3

WEST
♠ - - -
♡ 7 6 5 4
♦ Q J 8 6 3
♣ 10 7 6 5

EAST
♠ J 8 7 3
♡ Q J 10
♦ 9 7 5
♣ 9 4 2

SOUTH
♠ 9 6 4 2
♡ A K 3
♦ A K 4
♣ K J 8

WEST	NORTH	EAST	SOUTH
			1NT
Pass	3♠	Pass	4◊
Pass	5♣	Pass	5♡
Pass	6♠	All pass	

Bidding : It is awkward to show the powerful one-suiter with a transfer. The sequence 1NT : 3-Major is used to cover this hand type. 4◊ is an inferential primary cue, showing spade support and a maximum 1NT. (Without spade support, South would rebid 3NT and with a weaker hand, South would raise to 4♠.) North cue bids 5♣ because of the worry of the unguarded hearts. When South cue bids 5♡, North bids the small slam. North does not have enough strength or distribution to look for a grand slam.

Lead : Queen of hearts. Simple when you have a sequence.

Recommended play : The hand looks like child's play until the first round of trumps is played. The bad break with J-x-x-x offside makes it appear that you have an inevitable spade loser as well as the certain heart loser. In cases like this, do not panic. If the other suits break normally you may yet survive the rotten split in trumps. The key to such hands is to reduce your trump length to the same length as the opponent with the trumps. If you can then force that opponent to lead trumps when all the other suits have been eliminated, you can succeed.

So, win the heart, play a spade to the ace, play off the diamonds and ruff a diamond (trump reduction). Next cash your club winners (stripping the clubs from the East hand) and your other heart winner. Finally, exit with your last heart. If West wins the third heart, you fail but if East wins it, East will have only spades left and will have to lead into your K-Q-10 tenace. The seemingly certain trump loser has vanished.

Notes : (1) 6NT is the best contract and makes 12 tricks almost all the time. On this layout, 6NT would fail.
(2) If East's hearts were say, Q-J-4, it would be vital for East to unblock the heart suit and keep only the 4, so that declarer cannot force East on lead. East would have to hope that the ♡10 was with West.

Hand 60 : Inferential cue — Jettison play— Ruffing finesse

Dealer West : N-S vulnerable

NORTH
♠ 10 9 2
♡ 8 7 6 5 4
♦ K J 10
♣ 5 2

WEST
♠ A 5 3
♡ A K
♦ Q 4 2
♣ Q J 10 9 8

EAST
♠ K Q J 7 6 4
♡ 3
♦ A 7 6 5 3
♣ A

SOUTH
♠ 8
♡ Q J 10 9 2
♦ 9 8
♣ K 7 6 4 3

WEST	NORTH	EAST	SOUTH
1NT	Pass	3♠	Pass
4♡	Pass	5♣	Pass
5♡	Pass	6♠	All pass

Bidding : With such strong spades opposite a 1NT opening, East intends to play in spades and not in diamonds. East therefore does not bother showing the diamonds at all. 4♡ = inferential cue, showing spade support, the ♡A and denying the minor suit aces. 5♣ = primary cue. 5♡ = secondary cue, showing the ♡K and denying the ◊K. With the ◊K missing, East settles for the small slam.

Lead : Queen of hearts. Lead the solid sequence.

Recommended play : Win ♡A and cash ♡K, discarding the ace of clubs. Then lead the ♣Q and discard a diamond when North plays low (ruffing finesse). If South takes the ♣K, win the return, draw trumps, ending in dummy and discard your diamond losers on the remaining club winners.

Notes : (1) A diamond lead would defeat the slam.
(2) Declarer might win the heart lead and decide to draw trumps and play ace and another diamond. This is a bit better than 50% but fails on the actual layout. The recommended line is superior.
(3) Jettisoning the ♣A is necessary on the actual deal since the West hand has so few entries.
(4) If South ducks the ♣Q and then ducks the ♣J next, North can ruff the third club with say, the ♠2. East can still succeed : overruff with the ♠6 (not the 4), cash ♠K and play ♠7 to the ace, lead ♣9 and discard a diamond. South wins but declarer can cross with ♠4 to ♠5 in order to reach the last club winner.

CHAPTER 16
TACTICS AT IMPS

Playing pairs, the challenge is to do better than all the other pairs on each board. At teams, your team of four players plays a match against one other team-of-four and your aim is to defeat just that team. A teams match may be short (perhaps just two boards) or long (20-board matches are common in the qualifying rounds of major tournaments). Most international tournaments are teams events.

Suppose Team A is playing Team B. At one table, one A pair sits North-South and one B pair sits East-West. Each board played at that table is moved to another table where the other A pair sits East-West and the other B pair sits North-South. The board is replayed and when scoring up, the difference in scores achieved at each table on each board is calculated. As only the scores involved in those two tables are taken into account, teams bridge is the fairest of all tournament bridge. The luck factor is virtually eliminated as your team has the same chance to do well on exactly the same boards as your opposing team.

Teams bridge is scored using IMPs (International Match Points) according to the following table :

Difference in scores	IMPs	Difference in scores	IMPs
0-10	0	750-890	13
20-40	1	900-1090	14
50-80	2	1100-1290	15
90-120	3	1300-1490	16
130-160	4	1500-1740	17
170-210	5	1750-1990	18
220-260	6	2000-2240	19
270-310	7	2250-2490	20
320-360	8	2500-2990	21
370-420	9	3000-3490	22
430-490	10	3500-3990	23
500-590	11	4000-up	24
600-740	12		

Suppose you score +400 in 3NT and on the same board, your teammates score +50. You add the two results together and so your team has scored +450. This equals +10 IMPs for your team, −10 for them.

Suppose you are −110 at your table and your teammates' score on the same board is +50. Add the scores together and your side is −60. This equates to −2 Imps for your side and +2 Imps for them.

The effect of the IMP-scale is to reduce the impact of large gains and losses. If your team loses 500 points on a board, that is −11 Imps. Lose 1000 and the score is −14 Imps. The second 500 points is only 3 additional Imps.

For each match, you tally up the Imps won by your side (+) and deduct the Imps scored by the opponents (−). The difference is the margin of your win or loss. This difference is often converted into Victory Points. This is a simple VP scale :

IMP Difference	VPs
0-1	5-5
2-4	6-4
5-8	7-3
9-13	8-2
14-19	9-1
20+	10-0

On this scale, each match is out of 10 Victory Points, the winner scoring the VPs on the left of the VP column and the loser scoring the VPs on the right. Victory Point scales also reduce the impact of large results. A win by 50 Imps is the same as a win by 20 Imps on the above scale. VP scales also eliminate minus-IMP scores from results sheets.

Scoring simply in + and − IMPs is fairer than using a conversion to Victory Points, but VP scales are widely used and many other Victory Point scales exist. The World Bridge Federation has produced a more complicated series of VP scales (varying according to the number of boards in the match) where a drawn match is 15-15, but the winners can score no more than 25 VPs while the losers can at worst be minus-5 VPs. The maximum result on the WBF scale is 25 to minus-5.

IMP Strategy

Just as pairs strategy is based on the method of scoring, so IMP strategy relates to the scoring approach. One of the most striking differences is in regard to overtricks. At pairs, because you are striving to beat so many pairs, you want to achieve the highest score reasonably possible. +400 in 3NT will score 0 matchpoints at pairs if all the others score +430. At teams the difference between +400 and +430 is only 1 IMP, while the difference between making 3NT for +400 and failing for −50 is 10 IMPs. The upshot is you do not jeopardise your contract at teams for the sake of a possible overtrick. Making your contract is the primary aim.

At pairs, safety plays which sacrifice a possible overtrick in order to ensure your contract by guarding against a bad break are shunned most of the time. At teams such safety plays are a vital ingredient of your declarer technique. Your aim as declarer is far clearer at teams : make your contract.

Defending at teams is also simpler : defeat their contract is your objective, not to restrict declarer to the minimum number of overtricks. If you can see the setting trick, grab it. Do not wait around hoping for more than one down unless you can see that it is perfectly safe to do so.

Strategy for partscores

At pairs, it is sensible to strive for the safe partscore but with 23-24 points, it is quite common to choose 1NT rather than a minor suit fit. At teams, you should always choose the safest contract. An 8-card or better trump fit will almost always be safer than 1NT or 2NT. Naturally you still strive for games but with only partscore values there is nothing wrong with a minor suit.

It is still vital to compete for partscores and the strategies covered in Chapters 17-18 are just as important for teams as for pairs. There is one slight difference : playing teams there is less emphasis on competing above them at the three-level. If they are in 3♦ and you might bid 3♠, at pairs you are quick to bid 3♠ if your side is known to have nine trumps. At teams, this approach is still relevant but you should have some prospects of making your contract (e.g., via an assessment by the losing trick count).

Very often, both sides will fail at the three-level. If they were making 3♦, —110, and you would be —100 in 3♠, the difference is 0 at teams but could be vital at pairs. If you were going to make +140 and collect +100 by defending against 3♦, your loss is only 1 IMP. However, if both sides would fail, it is foolish to be —100 when you could be +100. That is a difference of 5 IMPs and enough of those could cost you the match.

The non-vulnerable game

In deciding whether to try for a game when not vulnerable, you should be just a touch more optimistic than at pairs. At pairs, games are worth bidding if they are 50-50. At teams, if you bid say 4♠ and they stop in 3♠, then if ten tricks are made, you score +420 not vulnerable and they score +170. The difference is +6 IMPs. If only nine tricks are made, you are —50 while they are +140, a loss of 5 IMPS. Thus, bidding the game gains you little more than stopping in the partscore. If you are two down for —100, then the loss is 6 IMPs, the same as the gain for success. In general, if you have a borderline decision, prefer to bid the game when you are not vulnerable unless you can detect some risk of being doubled for penalties.

The vulnerable game

Here there is a significant difference in approach. At pairs, 50% is still the guideline but at teams, vulnerable games are worth bidding if the chance for success is around the 40% mark. Again, suppose you bid 4♠ and they stop in 3♠. If ten tricks are made, you score +620 vulnerable and they score +170. The difference of +450 translates into +10 IMPs. If only nine tricks are there, you are —100, they are +140, a loss of 6 IMPs for the 240 difference. Thus you gain 10 IMPs when you are right and lose only 6 IMPs when you are wrong.

Even if you are two down in 4♠, the loss is 340, 8 IMPs, still 2 IMPs less than the gain for bidding the game. If you are doubled and go two down, you lose 12 IMPs, just 2 IMPs more than your gain when your decision is right.

Recommended approach : Do stretch to bid your vulnerable games. Be bold but not reckless.

The practical advice is that you retain all your basic bidding structure but you should invite game with one point less than normal. While game on 25 points is about a 50% chance, you should be prepared to be in game on 24 points when vulnerable. Bid game if you can count 24 points or more, invite game if there might be 24 points between you. When replying to an invitation, make your normal decision. Partner has already fudged the extra point by inviting.

Minor suit games

At pairs, you avoid 5♣ and 5♦ like the plague. If you can make eleven tricks in a trump contract, you can make ten tricks in no-trumps most of the time. At pairs, the difference between 430/630 and 400/600 is likely to be critical. At teams it is of little consequence. In other words, at teams there is no reason to avoid game in a minor if you judge that this is likely to be safer than 3NT.

Small slams

To be worth bidding, a small slam should have a 50% or better chance for success. 33 points or more gives you the required edge. The losing trick count will help you gauge whether slam is likely to succeed with fewer than 33 points.

If your side has below 30 points, assume the other side will not bid the slam. With an ace and a king missing, be prepared to stay out of the slam. If you have plenty of points together, the other side is likely to be in the slam and so should you unless you can tell the slam is under 50%.

Grand slams

Bid these only if you can tell that they are virtually laydown. A grand slam that needs a 3-2 trump break is all right but only just. A grand slam that needs a finesse is poor odds. Be satisfied to have reached a good small slam. Often the opponents will have stopped in game.

Sacrifices

At pairs, if they bid 4♥ and can make it for 620, sacrificing in 4♠ doubled for only —500 is a triumph. At teams, you gain only 3 IMPs while if you are wrong and they were failing in 4♥, you are —500 when you could have +100, a gain of 12 IMPs. In other words, if you are right 4 times out of 5, you still only break even. Do not sacrifice at teams unless they are likely to make their contract and your sacrifice might make or go only one off. Two off is acceptable at favorable vulnerability.

EXERCISES ON TACTICS AT IMPS

A. Both sides are vulnerable. The bidding has started 1NT (15-18) from partner, Pass on your right. What action would you take with these hands : (a) at pairs?   (b) at teams?

1. ♠ K 8 7 4 2	2. ♠ K 8 7	3. ♠ 10 9 6	4. ♠ 8 4 3	5. ♠ 8
♡ 9 8 2	♡ K 6 2	♡ 9 7 6	♡ K Q 6 2	♡ Q 9 2
◊ Q 8 3	◊ 8 7 3	◊ 8 3	◊ K 10 9 2	◊ K J 5 2
♣ 6 3	♣ Q J 9 5	♣ A Q J 10 3	♣ 9 6	♣ A K 9 8 3

B. In each of the following situations, you are South with the hand given. What is your next action at teams? State whether vulnerability is relevant and whether your answer would be different at pairs.

1.

WEST	NORTH	EAST	SOUTH
			1◊
Pass	1NT	Pass	?

♠ K 3
♡ A J
◊ K J 10 9 7
♣ Q J 5 2

6.

WEST	NORTH	EAST	SOUTH
Pass	Pass	1♠	?

♠ K 3 2
♡ 8 4
◊ K Q 8 7 3
♣ A 5 2

2.

WEST	NORTH	EAST	SOUTH
			1NT
Pass	2♡	Pass	2♠
Pass	3♡	Pass	?

2♡ = transfer to spades; 3♡ = natural

♠ K 8 6 3
♡ A 8 5 4
◊ K Q 2
♣ A 9

7.

WEST	NORTH	EAST	SOUTH
		1♡	?

♠ 8
♡ 8 5
◊ K Q 7 4 3
♣ A 9 8 5 2

3.

WEST	NORTH	EAST	SOUTH
1◊	Pass	1♠	Pass
2♠	Pass	Pass	?

♠ K 7
♡ Q J 8 6 4
◊ 9 7
♣ A 10 5 2

8.

WEST	NORTH	EAST	SOUTH
	1♠	Pass	2♡
Pass	4♡	Pass	4NT
Pass	5♣	Pass	5◊
Pass	5♠	Pass	5NT
Pass	6◊	Pass	?

5♣ = 0 or 3 key cards; 5♠ = ♡Q; 6◊ = one king

♠ K Q 2
♡ A J 8 6 4 3
◊ A 7
♣ 5 2

4.

WEST	NORTH	EAST	SOUTH
	1◊	Pass	1♣
Pass	1NT	Pass	?

♠ K J 6 3
♡ 7 3
◊ K 10 4 2
♣ Q 9 2

9.

WEST	NORTH	EAST	SOUTH
	Pass	Pass	1♠
Pass	2♣*	Pass	?

*Drury, does not promise spade support

♠ K Q 10 6 3
♡ 7 6 3
◊ A K J
♣ 9 2

5.

WEST	NORTH	EAST	SOUTH
			1◊
Pass	1NT	Pass	?

♠ 8 3
♡ A J
◊ K Q 7 6 3
♣ A K 5 2

10.

WEST	NORTH	EAST	SOUTH
	1♠	Pass	1NT
Pass	2NT	Pass	?

♠ 8 3
♡ A J 2
◊ Q 7 6 3
♣ 10 6 5 2

PLAY HANDS ON IMP TACTICS
(These hands can be made up by using pages 160-167)

Hand 61 : 3NT v. 5♣ — Safety play at IMPs

Dealer North : Both vulnerable

	NORTH ♠ A Q 6 ♡ A K J ◊ Q 10 9 5 4 ♣ 8 3	
WEST ♠ J 10 9 4 2 ♡ Q 9 5 ◊ J ♣ J 10 6 5		**EAST** ♠ K 7 3 ♡ 10 8 7 4 3 ◊ A K 8 6 ♣ 9
	SOUTH ♠ 8 5 ♡ 6 2 ◊ 7 3 2 ♣ A K Q 7 4 2	

WEST	NORTH	EAST	SOUTH
	1NT	Pass	3NT
Pass	Pass	Pass	

Bidding : At pairs, South's 3NT reply is routine but even at teams you should be reluctant to try for 5-minor after partner has opened 1NT if you have only marginal game values and no singleton or void. It is true that North may have a weak holding in diamonds or one of the majors but this is not very likely as North has at most one point in clubs. In addition how would you find out where partner's weakness lies? Take a shot at 3NT on hands like this and take your medicine when it goes wrong.

Lead : 4 of hearts. Your aim is to defeat 3NT and the best chance is via your long suit as you have outside entries.

Recommended play : North captures West's queen and immediately ducks a club. If West returns a heart, North wins and cashes the rest of the clubs followed by the ♠A and top heart. Nine tricks.

Notes : (1) 5♣ would suffer a swift demise via two diamonds and a diamond ruff even if clubs were 3-2.
(2) If West shifts to the jack of spades after taking the club, North should rise with the ♠A. To finesse would risk failing if East began with ◊A-J-x and shifted to a low diamond after winning the ♠K.
(3) At pairs, North would not duck a club. The normal 3-2 club split (about 2/3 of the time) would bring in an overtrick most of the time. At pairs you play for the most tricks on the most common breaks. As the cards lie, 3NT would still succeed after playing ♣A, ♣K, ♣Q. East can discard a spade but what should East discard on the third club? Either red suit allows North to set up enough diamond tricks to make 3NT. At teams five club tricks are enough. Simply duck the club and make nine tricks without any headaches.

Hand 62 : Choosing the right slam — Safety play

Dealer East : Nil vulnerable

	NORTH ♠ 8 6 4 3 ♡ 4 ◊ 10 9 8 7 3 ♣ 8 3 2	
WEST ♠ A J ♡ A 9 6 5 ◊ A Q 6 ♣ A K 7 6		**EAST** ♠ Q 10 9 2 ♡ K J 7 3 ◊ K 4 2 ♣ Q 5
	SOUTH ♠ K 7 5 ♡ Q 10 8 2 ◊ J 5 ♣ J 10 9 4	

WEST	NORTH	EAST	SOUTH
		Pass	Pass
2NT	Pass	3♣	Pass
3♡	Pass	4NT	Pass
5◊	Pass	6♡	All pass

Bidding : At pairs, with most pairs bidding slam, East might take a shot at 6NT which fails on the actual layout. At teams, it is usually safer to play in the suit slam if the high card values are borderline for slam. 5◊ showed 1 or 4 key cards for hearts and East can tell it must be four. East can tell that West cannot have enough to make 7♡ a good bet and so settles for 6♡.

Lead : 10 of diamonds. Safest from an uninspiring collection.

Recommended play : Win with the ◊K and take the spade finesse at once. Continue with the ♡K and lead a low heart towards your A-9-6. If South plays low, insert the 9. When this holds, cash the ♡A, ♣Q, ♣K and ruff a club. Then take your diamond winners and black aces. You lose just one trump trick.

Notes : (1) If South inserts the ♡10 on the second round of hearts, take with ♡A. When North shows out, continue with ♣Q, ♣K, ruff your low club with ♡J and lead a heart towards ♡9-6.
(2) In 6NT you need four heart tricks. In 6♡, you can afford to lose a heart if the ♠K is onside.
(3) You have to take the spade finesse some time. By taking it early, you can gauge how best to play the hearts. If the spade finesse lost, you take the best line for four heart tricks : ♡A and then finesse ♡J. The safety play to make sure you do not lose two tricks in hearts is to cash the king and lead low towards A-9-6. If South follows, you should be safe. If South shows out, rise with ♡A, cash ♠A, cross to ♣Q and lead ♠Q. You may still need a little extra luck but that is your best line.

Hand 63 : Choosing the right slam — Strip and throw-in

Dealer South : N-S vulnerable

NORTH
♠ 9 4 3
♡ Q 8 5 2
♢ A 7 6
♣ A K 8

WEST
♠ K J 6
♡ 9 4
♢ J 8 4 2
♣ J 10 9 6

EAST
♠ 8 7 5 2
♡ 10 3
♢ Q 10 5 3
♣ 7 5 2

SOUTH
♠ A Q 10
♡ A K J 7 6
♢ K 9
♣ Q 4 3

WEST	NORTH	EAST	SOUTH
			1♡
Pass	2NT	Pass	3NT
Pass	4♡	Pass	4♠
Pass	5♣	Pass	6♡
Pass	Pass	Pass	

Bidding : After the Jacoby 2NT raise, South's 3NT shows 16+ HCP and no singleton or void. With an absolute minimum, North signs off but there is no stopping South. 4♠ is a cue bid, aimed at locating club control, and when North cue bids 5♣, South knows enough to bid 6♡. For 7♡, South needs North to hold ♠K, ♡Q, ♢A and ♣A-K. With so much, North would not have signed off over 3NT.

Lead : Jack of clubs. No contest.

Recommended play : South wins, draws trumps, cashes ♢K, ♢A and ruffs a diamond and plays off the clubs ending in dummy. Having stripped the minor suits, a spade is led from dummy and South inserts the 10 when East plays low. West wins with the jack but has to return a spade into South's A-Q or give declarer a ruff-and-discard.

Notes : (1) At pairs, it would be sensible to play in 6NT where declarer would take two finesses in spades. To reach 6NT, South would bid 4NT over 4♡ and bid 6NT after finding North with two key cards, the ♡Q and one king. 6NT would make 75% of the time but on this layout, 6NT would fail. In 6NT you do not have the strip-and-throw-in play available. If the opening lead is not ruffed, 6♡ is foolproof unless hearts are 4-0. At teams you play in the safer slam.
(2) In 6♡ it would be silly to take two spade finesses. Why settle for 75% when 100% is available?
(3) South should insert the ♠10 just in case East has K-J-x in spades. You may as well make all the tricks if both spade honors are onside.
(4) It makes no difference here but West should play back a spade when in with the ♠J. The ruff-and-discard is sure to cost. The spade return may work.

Hand 64 : Choosing the right slam at Imps — Setting up dummy's suit

Dealer West : E-W vulnerable

NORTH
♠ J 10 8 5
♡ 9
♢ 9 8 2
♣ 10 9 5 4 3

WEST
♠ A 9 6 4 3
♡ K Q 2
♢ K 6 4
♣ A 8

EAST
♠ K Q 2
♡ A J 8 6 4 3
♢ A 7
♣ J 2

SOUTH
♠ 7
♡ 10 7 5
♢ Q J 10 5 3
♣ K Q 7 6

WEST	NORTH	EAST	SOUTH
1♠	Pass	2♡	Pass
4♡	Pass	4NT	Pass
5♣	Pass	5♢	Pass
5♠	Pass	5NT	Pass
6♢	Pass	7♡	All pass

Bidding : The jump to 4♡ shows 15+ HCP and 3+ hearts. A 5♢ cue bid would be too awkward and so East chooses 4NT. The 5♣ reply shows 0 or 3 key cards, clearly three as West has shown a strong hand. 5♢ asked for the queen of trumps and 5♠ said, 'I have it'. East's 5NT asks for kings outside trumps and 6♢ shows one. East can count twelve tricks in top cards and hopes to set up an extra trick via dummy's spades.

Lead : King of clubs. Easy against a grand slam.

Recommended play : Win ♣A, draw trumps and continue with ♠K, ♠Q, ♠A and ruff a spade. Dummy's fifth spade is now a winner on which your club loser is discarded.

Notes : (1) At pairs, it would be reasonable to take a shot at 7NT. This would make if spades were 3-2 or if North started with singleton 10 or J. 7♡ makes despite a 4-1 break in spades and therefore 7♡ is the contract you should be in at teams.
(2) Playing in 7NT, East has 12 tricks. Win ♣A, and cash ♠K, ♠Q, ♠A. When spades do not break, declarer should play off all the hearts. North can afford to discard all the clubs after South's ♣K lead but if North lets go a seemingly innocuous diamond, South will be squeezed when the last heart is played.

CHAPTER 17
PARTSCORE COMPETITIVE BIDDING (1)

Your side has not entered the bidding early

When the opposition bidding dies out at a low level, should you pass it out and defend or should you back into the auction? In the following auctions, should South be inclined to sell out or come into the bidding?

(1) WEST	NORTH	EAST	SOUTH
1◇	Pass	1♠	Pass
2◇	Pass	Pass	?

(2) WEST	NORTH	EAST	SOUTH
1◇	Pass	1♠	Pass
2♠	Pass	Pass	?

There is a significant difference between the two auctions. In (1), there is no evidence of a trump fit for East-West. Indeed, East could be singleton or even void in diamonds. Where the bidding has not revealed a good trump fit, there is no urgency to compete. You should re-open only if you have something worthwhile to bid. That would be unusual given your silence on the previous round. A poor 6-card suit, too weak to overcall initially, would be justification. In auction (1), South might back in with 2♡ with something like :

♠ 7 3   ♡ 10 8 6 4 3 2   ◇ 4   ♣ A K 9 7

If their last bid was 1NT, you should bid only if you have a reasonably clearcut action. Otherwise you are risking a substantial penalty.

In (2), it is highly likely that East-West have at least eight spades together. If they have a definite trump fit, you should be eager to compete and should almost never sell out at the two-level.

The 3-over-2 rule

If the opponents bid and raise a suit and stop at the two-level, be quick to bid in the pass-out seat.

When they have a trump fit and about half the HCP between them, they can usually score eight tricks. If they have about half the HCP, then so does your side. If they have a trump fit, your side does too (almost always). Your job is to dislodge them from the safety of the two-level and push them to the jeopardy of the three-level.

You must be prepared to go the three-level yourself and possibly fail at the three-level. Even if you do not make your contract at the three-level, the cost will usually be less than what they would have scored if you had left them to play in two. Your bonus comes when they push on to the three-level. You have pushed them one higher than they wished to be and perhaps you can now defeat them. Having pushed them to the three-level, pass and defend. Do not push once more.

This advice about being prepared to compete applies only if there have been two passes to you. If you also pass, the bidding is over. The advice does not apply in the direct seat, when the last bid was on your right. In auction (2), North is in the direct seat over 1◇ and over 2♠. To bid in the direct seat, you need full values for your action. To bid in the pass-out seat needs courage more than points.

Suppose North did double 2♠. What would you expect North to hold?

As the action is in the direct seat, North should have about opening points or better with hearts and clubs, the unbid suits. North's failure to double 1◇ is sure to be due to inadequate support for spades.

Suppose in auction (2) South doubles 2♠. What can you expect from South?

South should hold at least four hearts and four clubs, but the point count is almost irrelevant. If they have 18-19-20-21-22 HCP their way, then your side has the balance of 22-21-20-19-18 HCP. So, suppose in auction 2, North-South have 20 HCP. Then if South has 12, partner will have 8, while if South has 7, partner will have 13. What South has does not matter, since the combined partnership total will be close to the 20-point mark.

Suppose you have decided to take action in the pass-out seat. What actions are available?

The Delayed Overcall

(3) WEST	NORTH	EAST	SOUTH
1♡	Pass	2♡	Pass
Pass	?		

North might bid 2♠, 3♣ or 3◇, a delayed overcall. If the suit overcall was available at the one-level, the failure to bid earlier is a lack of suit quality. Expectancy is a 5-card suit (a strong 4-card suit if nothing else appeals) but the suit does not require any suit quality. A 2♠ delayed overcall might be :

♠ J 8 7 4 2   ♡ A 2   ◇ K Q   ♣ 7 5 3 2

An important consequence is that partner need not be anxious later in the defense to lead your suit. The failure to overcall at once marks you with a poor suit. In (3) above, North might bid 3♣ with :

♠ A 5   ♡ K 2   ◇ K 9 3   ♣ J 8 6 5 3 2
(bad suit in a good hand), or with :

♠ 9 2   ♡ 8 7 4   ◇ 5 2   ♣ A K 8 6 3 2
(good suit in a poor hand)

After a delayed overcall by partner, never raise partner's suit if the opponents do not bid and almost never bid on if they have been pushed to the three-level. Do not be impressed if you hold 13-14 points. Partner has already taken your values into account when making the delayed overcall.

The Delayed Double

The delayed double is generally used when you are short in their suit and hold 3-4 cards in the unbid suits. If they have bid and raised a major, then the delayed double should include 4 cards in the other major and tolerance for the minors. If they have bid and raised a minor, the delayed double should be at least 4-3 in the majors.

(4)	WEST	NORTH	EAST	SOUTH
	1♠	Pass	2♠	Pass
	Pass	?		

To double, North should have at least 4 hearts and at least 4-3 in the minors. A shortage in clubs is permitted as long as North is prepared to remove a 3♣ reply to 3◊ (6 diamonds or a reasonable 5).

The reason for not doubling earlier is lack of strength. To double 1♠ North should have about the same strength as an opening hand. For a delayed double, the shape is important but the high card strength is largely irrelevant.

In reply to a delayed double, partner should choose the best suit at the cheapest level. Do not make a jump reply to a delayed double! Do not become excited because you seem to hold a good hand. The fact that the opponents have stopped at the two-level has marked you with some strength. Partner will have deducted the points in hand from 20 to make an estimate of your likely strength. If you feel you have a really good hand, you can be reasonably confident that the doubler will have a bad hand to compensate.

The aim is to push them to the three-level. Once that has been achieved, neither the doubler nor partner should push again. Push them once, not twice. 'Do not go to the well too often.' Bid again and a penalty double is imminent.

After you have pushed them to the three-level it is rarely right to make a penalty double after a delayed overcall or a delayed double. They have robbed you of nothing so that a penalty double is not needed. Defeating their contract will already gain a decent score for you. A penalty double at the three-level is warranted if the hand belongs to your side, if you have say 23 HCP or more and they have 17 or less. If that were the case, your side would have been in the bidding earlier.

The delayed 2NT overcall

(5)	WEST	NORTH	EAST	SOUTH
	1♠	Pass	2♠	Pass
	Pass	?		

What action should North take with :

♠ 9 5 3 2   ♡ 4   ◊ K Q 5 2   ♣ K J 3 2

Since they have bid and raised a suit and stopped at the two-level, it is right to take action, but North cannot afford to double. What if partner bids 3♡? You are then beyond anything that resembles sanity. An overcall or 3♣ or 3◊ lacks suit length and how can you tell which minor to bid?

The solution is to use a delayed 2NT overcall as a request to partner to bid but to choose only a minor suit. A delayed double says, 'Pick any suit' while a delayed 2NT says 'Pick one of the minors'.

The delayed 2NT cannot sensibly be a genuine no-trump hand. With a powerful balanced hand, you would have taken action on the previous round (1NT overcall or double). This use of 2NT follows the concept of the unusual 2NT overcall where an immediate overcall of 2NT shows at least 5-5 in the minors, about 6-11 HCP and a willingness to sacrifice should the opponents bid a major suit game. The delayed 2NT is usually 4-4 or 5-4 in the minors (with 5-5 you might have bid 2NT on the previous round). It might be 5-5 in the minors if the suit quality of the minors is poor.

The North hand after auction (5) above is ideal for the delayed 2NT. The 4-card holding in spades means that partner should be singleton or void in spades and therefore partner is very likely to have length in one of the minors.

Possible outcomes of the 3-over-2 rule

(a)	You let them play at the two-level	–110
(b)	You bid at the three-level and make	+110
(c)	You bid at the three-level and fail	–50/–100
(d)	They bid to the three-level and fail	+50/+100
(e)	They bid three and make it	–140
(f)	They double you at the three-level	–500

If you leave them unchallenged in a major suit at the two-level, you will be scoring –110 most of the time. If you take one of the foregoing delayed actions and commit yourself to the three-level, you will do better in three situations (b, c and d). If they push on to the three-level and make it, you are no worse off. Making three in 2♠ or making three in 3♠ is the same result.

Occasionally you will have a horror result, doubled and down some large number. If all of the above results were equally likely, the recommended strategy is still sensible. You come out in front 60% of the time (b, c and d), break even 20% of the time (e) and suffer 20% of the time (f). In fact, (f) is the least likely result. Most of the time you can make eight tricks in your trump fit and most of the time you will not be doubled. They have only about half the HCP and as they have a trump fit, a penalty double is not appealing. Experience indicates (b, c and d) occur about 70% of the time, (e) about 20% and (f) about 10% of the time. The important thing is not to focus on the bad times. When a calamity does occur, reflect on all the great results you have had.

Suppose the bidding has started :

(6)	WEST	NORTH	EAST	SOUTH
	1♡	Pass	2♡	Pass
	Pass	Dble	Pass	?

What action should South take with :

♠ 7 4   ♡ 8 6 3   ◊ Q J 5 2   ♣ A 9 6 4

It is not clear which minor to choose. Partner could be 4-3 in the minors, perhaps even 5-3. Why risk picking the wrong minor? Why not use the 2NT reply to a *delayed* double to ask partner to choose the minor? It would be rare to want to play in 2NT opposite a delayed double. The partnership can hardly have the strength to make 2NT viable. In reply to an immediate takeout double, 2NT is a natural, strong balanced hand (commonly 10-12 points). In reply to a delayed double, use 2NT for the minors.

When is it unwise to follow the 3-over-2 rule?
(a) When their trump fit may not exist
If the bidding does not reveal a good trump fit their way, usually after responder has given merely a preference, you need not compete as vigorously.

(7) WEST	NORTH	EAST	SOUTH
1♡	Pass	1NT	Pass
2◊	Pass	2♡	Pass
Pass	?		

They have stopped at the two-level but they have not bid and raised a suit. South's 2♡ preference need not be more than a doubleton and perhaps they are playing in a 7-card trump fit. Be wary of bidding here if you hold three cards in opener's suit as East is quite likely to score a defensive ruff in hearts if you buy the contract.

(b) Do not compete if they are playing in their third suit as trumps. For example :

(8) WEST	NORTH	EAST	SOUTH
1◊	Pass	1♡	Pass
1♠	Pass	2♣	Pass
Pass	?		

The only place left for you is clubs and they know so much about their hand patterns that a defensive cross-ruff is quite likely. When they finish in their third suit as trumps, declarer is quite likely to play the hand as a crossruff. Your best defense is to lead trumps at each opportunity.

(c) Do not compete against notorious underbidders.
You may know the regular underbidders in your club. If not, keep track of those pairs who are often scoring +170 when the field is in game. Once you have established who these chronic underbidders are, do not bother to compete against them in the partscore zone without full values. It is quite likely that they have missed a game and if you give them a second chance, they may bid on to game. Let sleeping dogs lie. The stronger your opponents, the safer it is to compete when they have stopped at the two-level. Strong players rarely miss game.

(d) If an opponent takes a long time before passing partner's two-level raise, do not back in.
The person who trances (thinks for a long time) and then passes is considering a game invitation. If you come in, they will frequently push on to game and make it. *Do not protect against a trancer.*

The 3-over-3 rule
When the opponents have competed to the three-level over your two-level bid, should you pass and defend or should you bid three over their three? Most of the time you will better off defending. Quite often neither side can make nine tricks, so why should you fail when they are about to fail? Do not assume that because they have bid to the three-level, they are bound to make nine tricks. The opponents are quite fallible.

One of the best guidelines in this area comes from counting the trumps held by your side :
At the three-level :
With eight trumps for your side : Pass and defend.
With nine trumps for your side : Bid 3-over-3.

Note that this guideline applies only when the bidding is already at the three-level. At the two-level, follow the 3-over-2 rule.

When both sides have a trump fit and one side has nine trumps, one side figures to make nine tricks. That is not necessarily the side that has the nine trumps, though. If nine tricks will be made, then if your side is the one making the nine tricks, it clearly makes sense to bid 3-over-3. If their side is going to make nine tricks, you should still bid 3-over-3, choosing to go one down (you should make eight tricks almost all of the time) rather than let them make their three-level partscore.

The partnership should be able to tell whether eight or nine trumps are held. If your side has bid and raised a suit, you should have eight trumps together. If either partner has an extra trump, then the partnership should hold nine trumps. If neither partner has an extra trump, then you have only eight trumps together. Playing 5-card majors, a raise of opener's major shows 3+ support. If responder actually has four trumps, responder knows the partnership has nine trumps and so responder is the one to take the push to 3-over-3.

This is a trouble area for those pairs who may raise partner's 4-card major with only 3-card support. It is much harder for such pairs to gauge whether the partnership has seven or eight or nine trumps.

If you are going to take the push to 3-over-3, it often pays to take the push at once. For example :

(9) WEST	NORTH	EAST	SOUTH
1♠	Pass	2♠	Pass
Pass	2NT	?	

If East intends to bid 3♠ later, East may as well bid 3♠ now. This shows no extra strength, just an extra trump. The advantage comes when South is unable to indicate the preferred minor and so North may have a tougher choice of lead.

The 4-over-3 rule
Do not bid a partscore hand to the four-level. If they outbid you at the three-level, pass and defend rather than push on to four. Most of the time you will fail in four. Why not hope they fail in three?

EXERCISES ON COMPETITIVE BIDDING (1)

A. The bidding has started :

WEST	NORTH	EAST	SOUTH
1♠	Pass	2♠	Pass
Pass	?		

What should North do now?

1. ♠ 5 3	2. ♠ J 7 3 2	3. ♠ 9 7 5	4. ♠ 4 3	5. ♠ 4 3
♡ A 9 8 2	♡ K Q 8 6 4 2	♡ 6 4	♡ K Q 6 2	♡ K Q 6 2
◊ K 7 4 3	◊ J 9	◊ A 9 7 3	◊ K 9 7 4 3 2	◊ 5
♣ Q 6 3	♣ 4	♣ A Q 7 3	♣ 5	♣ K 9 7 4 3 2

B. The bidding has started :

WEST	NORTH	EAST	SOUTH
1♡	Pass	2♡	Pass
Pass	Dble	Pass	?

What should South do now?

1. ♠ Q 7	2. ♠ K Q 5 4	3. ♠ A K 4 2	4. ♠ 8 5	5. ♠ 9
♡ K 6 2	♡ J 8 7 2	♡ 7 6 3	♡ Q 7 6 4	♡ K Q 5 2
◊ J 9 7 3 2	◊ 4	◊ Q 8	◊ 4 2	◊ Q J 7 3
♣ K 9 6	♣ J 10 6 3	♣ A 9 6 4	♣ K Q 8 7 2	♣ Q 10 6 2

COMPETITIVE BIDDING : How should the following hands be bid? West is the dealer each time and neither side is vulnerable.

SET 31— WEST	SET 31 — NORTH	SET 31 — EAST	SET 31 — SOUTH
1. ♠ 8 6	1. ♠ K Q 10	1. ♠ A 9 3	1. ♠ J 7 5 4 2
♡ K J 3 2	♡ 10 9 7	♡ Q 8 6 4	♡ A 5
◊ A J 7 4 2	◊ K 9 8	◊ 6 5 3	◊ Q 10
♣ K 7	♣ A 9 6 3	♣ Q 10 4	♣ J 8 5 2
2. ♠ A	2. ♠ K J 6 5 4	2. ♠ 9 8 3	2. ♠ Q 10 7 2
♡ J 10 8 3	♡ A K 6 4	♡ 9 2	♡ Q 7 5
◊ 9 7 6 5 4	◊ J	◊ K Q 8 2	◊ A 10 3
♣ J 10 2	♣ Q 8 7	♣ A K 5 3	♣ 9 6 4
3. ♠ K 5 2	3. ♠ Q 7 4	3. ♠ A J 8	3. ♠ 10 9 6 3
♡ 9 8	♡ A Q 7 3	♡ 6 4 2	♡ K J 10 5
◊ J 8 3	◊ Q 10 6 2	◊ K 5 4	◊ A 9 7
♣ A 9 6 3 2	♣ 10 8	♣ K Q 7 5	♣ J 4
4. ♠ 10 6 3	4. ♠ K 9 8 4	4. ♠ A 2	4. ♠ Q J 7 5
♡ 10 5 4	♡ K 6	♡ 9 8 3	♡ A Q J 7 2
◊ A 8 3 2	◊ 9 7 6	◊ Q J 10 4	◊ K 5
♣ A Q 2	♣ J 10 6 3	♣ K 9 8 4	♣ 7 5
5. ♠ A 6 3	5. ♠ K J 7 2	5. ♠ Q 8 5	5. ♠ 10 9 4
♡ A J 8 7 3	♡ Q 10 5	♡ K 6 4	♡ 9 2
◊ A 7	◊ K 9 6 5 2	◊ 10 4	◊ Q J 8 3
♣ J 8 2	♣ 4	♣ Q 9 7 5 3	♣ A K 10 6
6. ♠ A 6 2	6. ♠ J 9 8 4 3	6. ♠ K Q 7	6. ♠ 10 5
♡ K 8 3	♡ J 2	♡ Q 9 5	♡ A 10 7 6 4
◊ A Q 7 4 2	◊ 10 5	◊ J 9 8 3	◊ K 6
♣ 8 5	♣ A K J 3	♣ 10 7 4	♣ Q 9 8 2
7. ♠ 10 7 4	7. ♠ A K J 3	7. ♠ 8 5	7. ♠ Q 9 6 2
♡ A	♡ Q 10 4	♡ 8 7 6 5 3 2	♡ K J 9
◊ A 9 6 2	◊ J 8 3	◊ K Q 4	◊ 10 7 5
♣ J 9 8 7 3	♣ K 6 4	♣ A 10	♣ Q 5 2

PLAY HANDS ON COMPETITIVE BIDDING (1)
(These hands can be made up by using pages 160-167)

Hand 65 : Delayed overcall — 3-over-2 rule

Dealer North : Nil vulnerable

NORTH
- ♠ 865432
- ♥ A72
- ◇ 10
- ♣ K32

WEST
- ♠ 1097
- ♥ KJ94
- ◇ A92
- ♣ J109

EAST
- ♠ KJ
- ♥ Q1083
- ◇ K7543
- ♣ A8

SOUTH
- ♠ AQ
- ♥ 65
- ◇ QJ86
- ♣ Q7654

WEST	NORTH	EAST	SOUTH
	Pass	1◇	Pass
1♥	Pass	2♥	Pass
Pass	2♠	3♥	All pass

Bidding : With such a poor suit, North should not make a direct overcall of 1♠ and South should not bid 2♣ over 1◇. It would be premature for South to take action over 2♥. South is in the direct seat, not the pass-out seat. North must not sell out to 2♥ (3-over-2 rule). The delayed 2♠ overcall indicates length but not strength in spades. East-West should not sell out to 2♠. With a trump fit, be prepared to push to the three-level. As East has very good shape, East should take the push. Note the power of the spade suit in these partscore battles.

Lead : 10 of diamonds. With trump control, a singleton appeals.

Recommended play : 3♥ should be defeated. West wins the ◇10 lead and plays a trump. North rises with ♥A and switches to a spade. South wins, gives North a diamond ruff, wins the next spade and gives North another diamond ruff.

Notes : (1) Even on other leads, 3♥ should fail. On a club lead, the defense can take one club, two spades, one heart and one diamond and accurate defense will also come to five tricks on a spade or a heart lead.
(2) After ◇10 lead, North should rise with ♥A at once as North wants to obtain two ruffs.
(3) East-West are wise to bid to 3♥ as 2♠ can be made. Better to be minus-50 than minus-110.
(4) In 2♠, after the normal heart lead, North ducks, wins the next heart and ruffs a heart. After cashing ♠A, declarer exits with a diamond. Later declarer leads a second round of trumps. If declarer has to tackle clubs, play East for the ace. Lead a low club to the queen and duck the second round.

Hand 66 : Delayed double — 3-over-3 rule

Dealer East : N-S vulnerable

NORTH
- ♠ J98
- ♥ 873
- ◇ AK73
- ♣ K54

WEST
- ♠ Q762
- ♥ KQ
- ◇ 842
- ♣ J1063

EAST
- ♠ AK1043
- ♥ A962
- ◇ Q6
- ♣ 98

SOUTH
- ♠ 5
- ♥ J1054
- ◇ J1095
- ♣ AQ72

WEST	NORTH	EAST	SOUTH
		1♠	Pass
2♠	Pass	Pass	Dble
3♠	Pass	Pass	Pass

Bidding : With 7 losers, East should not try for game over 2♠. South should contest the partscore (3-over-2 rule). Short in spades and with support for the other suits, a delayed double is the best choice. If West were to pass, North would bid 3◇.

With nine trumps together, East-West should not pass out 3◇. Push on to 3♠ (3-over-3 rule). Playing 5-card majors, West is the one who knows the partnership has nine trumps. Rather than wait for 3◇ and then bid 3♠, West should bid 3♠ over the double ('take the push at once'). This will usually shut out North.

Lead : Jack of diamonds. Prefer the solid sequence.

Recommended play : North wins with ◇K and cashes ◇A. Whether North continues diamonds or switches, the defense can take only two diamonds and two clubs. When declarer comes in, three rounds of trumps are drawn, the ♥ K-Q are cashed and declarer later ruffs the heart loser in dummy.

Notes : (1) North-South gained nothing this time by competing over 2♠ but some East-West pairs might give up over 3◇ and some days 3♠ might fail.
(2) South should be prepared to make a delayed double despite the adverse vulnerability. 3◇ can be defeated but it is virtually impossible for East-West to find a penalty double. In 3◇, after ♠A and ♣9 switch, declarer wins with ♣K, ruffs a spade, comes to hand with a trump and ruffs the third spade. Declarer should lose one spade, one diamond and three hearts.
(3) If East unwisely switches to ♥A after cashing ♠A, 3◇ will succeed.

Hand 67 : Delayed 2NT — 3-over-3 rule

Dealer South : E-W vulnerable

```
              NORTH
              ♠ Q 8 6
              ♡ K Q 4 2
              ◇ 8 7
              ♣ A K 8 4
WEST                      EAST
♠ J 10                    ♠ A K 9 5
♡ 10 7                    ♡ 5 3
◇ A Q 10 3                ◇ K 9 5 4
♣ Q 10 9 5 3              ♣ 7 6 2
              SOUTH
              ♠ 7 4 3 2
              ♡ A J 9 8 6
              ◇ J 6 2
              ♣ J
```

WEST	NORTH	EAST	SOUTH
			Pass
Pass	1♣	Pass	1♡
Pass	2♡	Pass	Pass
2NT	Pass	3◇	3♡
Pass	Pass	Pass	

Bidding : East should not bid over 1♣ or over 2♡ (direct seat). When 2♡ comes back to West (3-over-2 rule), the adverse vulnerability should not prevent West competing. The delayed 2NT is a takeout bid for the minors. Even though North opened 1♣, East-West may have a better fit in clubs than diamonds. With an extra trump, South takes the push to 3♡ (3-over-3 rule) but East-West do not compete further (4-over-3 rule).

Lead : Jack of spades. J-x is a poor lead, J-10 is a good start.

Recommended play : If declarer covers with the queen, East cashes three spades (king, ace, 9) and shifts to a diamond, giving the defense the first three tricks. If declarer ducks the lead, so does East. West continues with the ♠10 and East should overtake with the ♠K, cash the ♠A and then switch to a diamond.

Notes : (1) If West led a low club, declarer could succeed by risking to duck in dummy.
(2) Even though South followed the 3-over-3 rule, 3♡ fails. That is the West's reward for not selling out to 2♡ which would have succeeded.
(3) 3◇ would have also failed (two hearts, two clubs and a club ruff). It is quite common for both to fail at the three-level. It is important to realise that the 3-over-2, 3-over-3 and 4-over-3 guidelines are not infallible. Their success rate is better than 80% which is excellent but there will still be occasions when following the rules will lead to a loss. Since this will be rare, it is sensible to abide by the rules.

Hand 68 : Delayed 2NT — Taking the push at once

Dealer West : Both vulnerable

```
              NORTH
              ♠ K Q 10
              ♡ K J 8 6 4
              ◇ A 10
              ♣ 6 3 2
WEST                      EAST
♠ A 7 3 2                 ♠ 8 5
♡ 9                       ♡ 10 5 3
◇ Q 9 8 4 3               ◇ K J 6 2
♣ K 8 5                   ♣ A Q 7 4
              SOUTH
              ♠ J 9 6 4
              ♡ A Q 7 2
              ◇ 7 5
              ♣ J 10 9
```

WEST	NORTH	EAST	SOUTH
Pass	1♡	Pass	2♡
Pass	Pass	2NT	3♡
Pass	Pass	Pass	

Bidding : Neither East nor West is worth early action. When 2♡ comes back to East, 3-over-2 applies. 2NT shows at least 4-4 in the minors and no interest in the unbid major. Playing 5-card majors, South knows that the partnership has 9+ hearts together and so takes the push at once to 3♡ (3-over-3 rule). West does not compete to 4◇ because of the 4-over-3 rule.

If South passes 2NT, West would bid 3◇ and playing 4-card majors, North should push on 3♡. East-West should then pass.

Lead : If South bid 3♡ over 2NT, East might well lead the 8 of spades. If West did bid 3◇, the ◇2 would be East's choice.

Notes : (1) On ♠8 lead to West's ace, North should play the king (partly to unblock, partly to try to fool West in case East's lead was a singleton). If West returns a spade, North wins with ♠Q, draws trumps and overtakes ♠10 with ♠J, followed by a discard on the ♠9. Making 3♡ is South's reward for 3♡ over 2NT.
(2) If West wins ♠A and shifts to a diamond, it is too late. Declarer wins, draws trumps and continues with ♠Q, followed by ♠10 overtaken by the jack.
(3) If West ducks the first spade, North wins with ♠K, draws trumps with ♡K, ♡J, ♡Q, followed by ♠Q.
(4) If West has had the chance to bid 3◇, East would start with the ◇2. West's queen knocks out North's ace and now the defense can come to five tricks. North draws trumps and shifts to the ♠K. West wins and leads a low club (as only one diamond can be cashed, club tricks are needed). East wins, cashes ◇K and a second club. West wins the third club for one down. If West did return a diamond after winning ♠A, East would have to shift to clubs next.
(5) East-West can actually make 4◇, but this is the exception rather than the rule. Abide by the 4-over-3 rule and you will make the right decision more than 80% of the time.

CHAPTER 18
PARTSCORE COMPETITIVE BIDDING (2)

Your side has entered the bidding
(a) You bid but partner did not reply

The decision whether to bid a second time will be influenced by three factors :

(1) Are you stronger than your original action promised?

(2) Have the opponents bid and raised a suit to the two-level?

(3) Are you short in the opposition suit?

If the answer to (1) is YES, you should try to find a second action if the bidding has not gone beyond the two-level.

If the answer to the first question is NO, but the answer to (2) is YES, you should strive to bid again (3-over-2 rule). If the answer to (3) is YES, you should bid again if the bidding is not beyond the two-level. If the answer to all three questions is YES, you should definitely bid on. If the answer to all three questions is NO, you should pass.

Competing on the second round

If your first action was an opening bid, do not repeat the suit if you have no extra length in that suit. If your original bid was an overcall, do not rebid your suit if it is only a 5-card suit. Overcalling and repeating the suit should be a 6-card suit. With a 5-3-3-2 or 5-4-3-1 short in their suit, choose a takeout double. If desperate to bid again but unsuitable for a double and no worthwhile second suit, you may repeat a 5-card suit if the suit quality is 8 for a two-level rebid, 9 for a three-level rebid.

(1)	WEST	NORTH	EAST	SOUTH
	1♣	1♥	2♣	Pass
	Pass	?		

North should generally bid again. The aim of competing in such situations is similar to competing when you have not been in the bidding at all on the first round : *Push them to the three-level and then defend at the three-level (3-over-2).*

If your initial action was a takeout double and the situation indicates you should compete further :

Double again is still for takeout, as partner has not bid yet, and is usually the best second action.

Doubling first and bidding a new suit next shows a good 5+ suit, a strong hand and a one-suiter.

(2)	WEST	NORTH	EAST	SOUTH
	1♣	Dble	2♣	Pass
	Pass	?		

With a normal takeout double, North should double again. If North bids 2◊, 2♥ or 2♠, this would show a good 5+ suit in a one-suiter of 16 points or more.

If you opened 1NT and LHO overcalls, passed back to you :

(3)	WEST	NORTH	EAST	SOUTH
	1NT	2♥	Pass	Pass
	?			

In standard methods, double by a 1NT opener is for penalties. It makes more sense to play these re-opening doubles for takeout since partner has passed. If you do, make sure you have agreed on this with your partner. To double for takeout as a 1NT opener you should have a doubleton in their suit.

If you opened 1NT, partner passes and RHO makes an overcall :

(4)	WEST	NORTH	EAST	SOUTH
	1NT	Pass	Pass	2♥
	?			

Again, standard style is to treat double here as penalties. It is unlikely that you will have enough in your own hand to be confident of taking six tricks in defense. A sound approach for low-level penalty action is to expect a two-trick defeat. Then, if your A-K suit takes only one trick instead of the expected two, you should still beat their contract. On the score of frequency, it is better to play double in this auction as takeout, with a doubleton in their suit. Again, this requires partnership agreement.

(b) You have bid and partner has replied

In all normal situations you should not sell out at the two-level unless you sense a misfit.

If they have bid and raised a suit to the two-level, keep on bidding (3-over-2).

If your side has bid and raised a suit to the two-level, keep on bidding if they bid above you at the two-level (3-over-2).

(5)	WEST	NORTH	EAST	SOUTH
	1◊	1♠	2◊	2♠
	Pass	Pass	?	

OR

(6)	WEST	NORTH	EAST	SOUTH
	1♣	1♥	1♠	2♥
	2♠	Pass	Pass	?

In both of these auctions, it is unsound for the bidding to be passed out at 2♠. You do *not* require any extra strength to push on to the three-level when you are in the pass-out seat. You simply have to recognise that the situation demands that you compete further. As long as the partnership appreciates this strategy, then bidding in the direct seat to the three-level would show extras. If West in (5) or North in (6) bid over 2♠, this would show better than a minimum opening/overcall.

The Law of Total Tricks

Discovered in the 1950s by Frenchman Jean-René Vernes and popularised in the 1990s by Larry Cohen's book, *To Bid Or Not To Bid*, the Law of Total Tricks is a useful tool in competitive auctions. The law states that on any deal the total number of trumps is usually equal to the total number of tricks. Total trumps = North-South's longest trump fit + East-West's longest trump fit. Total tricks = tricks taken by North-South in their trump fit + tricks taken by East-West in their trump fit. The Law is the basis of the 3-over-2, 3-over-3 and 4-over-3 rules. If both sides have an 8-card fit, total trumps = 16. If the points are roughly equal, then each side is likely to win eight tricks. Therefore, do not sell out to them at the two-level, since they figure to make their contract. Better to bid to three and go one down than to have them make their partscore : the 3-over-2 rule.

One side has an 8-card fit, the other side has a 9-card fit. Total trumps = 17, so total tricks = 17. If the points are about equal, one side figures to make nine tricks and the other side eight tricks. Therefore, if the bidding has reached the three-level it is sensible to bid above them at the three-level. If your side is making nine tricks, you will make your contract and if their side is the one making nine tricks, you are better off going one down than letting them make their partscore : 3-over-3 rule.

Example Deal :

```
                 NORTH
                 ♠ K Q 10
                 ♡ 10 9 7
                 ◇ K 9 8
                 ♣ A 9 6 3
 WEST                          EAST
 ♠ 8 6                         ♠ A 9 3
 ♡ K J 3 2                     ♡ Q 8 6 4
 ◇ A J 7 4 2                   ◇ 6 5 3
 ♣ K 7                         ♣ Q 10 4
                 SOUTH
                 ♠ J 7 5 4 2
                 ♡ A 5
                 ◇ Q 10
                 ♣ J 8 5 2
```

This exercise deal from the previous chapter is a good illustration of the Law. North-South have eight spades and East-West have eight hearts. Total trumps = 16. As each side has 20 HCP, each side figures to take eight tricks. Playing in spades, North-South should lose 1 spade, 1 heart, 1 diamond and 2 clubs : eight tricks. Playing in hearts, East-West should lose 1 spade, 1 heart, 2 diamonds and 1 club : eight tricks. Total tricks = 16, so total trumps = total tricks.

You need not know the underlying theory but you do need to know the principles and guidelines for competing which flow from the Law of Total Tricks.

While it is not hard to estimate how many trumps your side has, it is hard to be certain of their combined trump length. If you know your side has nine trumps and they have a trump fit, you can count on 17 total trumps and so 17 total tricks. With the points shared, neither side is likely to make ten tricks. Therefore, compete above them at the three-level but do not push to four : 4-over-3 rule.

Many players push too hard here and are unwilling to sell out to the three-level. Experience shows that with only partscore points, the four-level is usually too high. You need 25-26 points to make 4♡ or 4♠ and you need the same to have a decent play for 4♣ or 4◇. Follow the 4-over-3 rule and you will come out in front most of the time. Also, at the four-level, they are much keener to double.

Doubling the opponents for penalties

If you have a trump fit, it is unsound to look for penalties at the one-level or two-level. Prefer to support your partner. The best penalties at a low level come when you are strong in the enemy suit and short in partner's suit, no more than a doubleton, and at least 20 HCP for your side.

If you have a trump fit and the bidding has reached the three-level, you will bid above them at the three-level if your side has nine trumps (3-over-3). However, what if they have bid to the three-level and your side has only eight trumps?

If the points are roughly equal, 20-20, 21-19, 22-18, do not double when your side has a trump fit. Where the points are so shared, consider it **nobody's hand** and if you do not have the nine trumps needed to bid 3-over-3, simply pass and defend. However, if you have a clear superiority in points, 23-17 or 24-16, it is **your hand**. If unable to bid 3-over-3, double for penalties.

The same applies when they have bid 3-over-your-3. If it is nobody's hand, pass and defend. If it is your hand, double. Do not bid 4-over-3.

Competing after they have opened 1NT and responder removes to a suit at the two-level

(7) WEST	NORTH	EAST	SOUTH
1NT	Pass	2♡	Pass
Pass	?		

Be reluctant to sell out in this type of auction. It is true that they may have a 5-2 fit but most of the time it is a 5-3 or 6-2 fit. With three cards in their suit, you need sound values to bid but if short in their suit a takeout double is often the best action.

(8) WEST	NORTH	EAST	SOUTH
1NT	Pass	2◇	Pass
2♡	Pass	Pass	?

Where responder's action is a transfer, do not take action in the direct seat (North above should pass 2♡) as responder could still have a strong hand. After two passes, be prepared to compete, using double for takeout and 2NT for the minors.

EXERCISES ON COMPETITIVE BIDDING (2)

A. The bidding has started :

WEST	NORTH	EAST	SOUTH
1♣	1♡	2♣	Pass
Pass	?		What should North do now?

1. ♠ J432	2. ♠ KJ4	3. ♠ QJ98	4. ♠ 43	5. ♠ Q43
♡ AQ643	♡ AK762	♡ KQJ93	♡ KQ962	♡ AQ962
◊ K98	◊ QJ6	◊ 42	◊ AK73	◊ 5
♣ 7	♣ 42	♣ J9	♣ 52	♣ AJ103

B. The bidding has started :

WEST	NORTH	EAST	SOUTH
1NT	Pass	2♡*	Pass
*Transfer	2♠	Pass	Pass	?	What should South do now?

1. ♠ 7	2. ♠ K962	3. ♠ K2	4. ♠ 85	5. ♠ 96
♡ K962	♡ J8	♡ 76	♡ AQ64	♡ 82
◊ J973	◊ AJ	◊ QJ84	◊ KJ2	◊ AJ3
♣ AQ96	♣ J10632	♣ A10643	♣ K852	♣ AKJ863

COMPETITIVE BIDDING : How should the following hands be bid? West is the dealer each time and neither side is vulnerable.

SET 32— WEST	SET 32 — NORTH	SET 32 — EAST	SET 32 — SOUTH
1. ♠ 864	1. ♠ KQ1052	1. ♠ 97	1. ♠ AJ3
♡ KJ73	♡ 1065	♡ Q82	♡ A94
◊ AJ74	◊ K9	◊ Q653	◊ 1082
♣ K10	♣ A73	♣ Q842	♣ J965
2. ♠ Q107	2. ♠ KJ654	2. ♠ 983	2. ♠ A2
♡ 109853	♡ AK64	♡ J2	♡ Q7
◊ 9765	◊ J	◊ AKQ82	◊ 1043
♣ K	♣ Q87	♣ A103	♣ J96542
3. ♠ K54	3. ♠ Q7	3. ♠ AJ8	3. ♠ 109632
♡ QJ1073	♡ 98	♡ K64	♡ A52
◊ 83	◊ Q10762	◊ K54	◊ AJ9
♣ 632	♣ AJ108	♣ KQ75	♣ 94
4. ♠ 1062	4. ♠ K984	4. ♠ A3	4. ♠ QJ75
♡ AJ1054	♡ 63	♡ 9872	♡ KQ
◊ AJ82	◊ K97	◊ Q1043	◊ 65
♣ 8	♣ J1063	♣ A94	♣ KQ752
5. ♠ A63	5. ♠ K874	5. ♠ J10952	5. ♠ Q
♡ AQ8	♡ 973	♡ K64	♡ J1052
◊ A72	◊ J853	◊ 104	◊ KQ96
♣ K862	♣ A3	♣ 975	♣ QJ104
6. ♠ Q864	6. ♠ 92	6. ♠ AKJ73	6. ♠ 105
♡ J87	♡ K1052	♡ 93	♡ AQ64
◊ QJ10	◊ A952	◊ 874	◊ K63
♣ J63	♣ AQ10	♣ K75	♣ 9842
7. ♠ Q104	7. ♠ J986	7. ♠ AK753	7. ♠ 2
♡ A653	♡ Q102	♡ 87	♡ KJ94
◊ J84	◊ 93	◊ KQ62	◊ A1075
♣ J108	♣ Q964	♣ 53	♣ AK72

PLAY HANDS ON COMPETITIVE BIDDING (2)
(These hands can be made up by using pages 160-167)

Hand 69 : Re-opening double — 3-over-3 rule

Dealer North : N-S vulnerable

	NORTH		
	♠ Q J 5 2		
	♡ K 8		
	◇ A Q 8 6 3		
	♣ Q 8		

WEST		**EAST**
♠ 10 9 4		♠ K 7 6
♡ 9 3		♡ A Q J 6 2
◇ J 10 9		◇ 7
♣ A J 6 3 2		♣ K 7 5 4

	SOUTH
	♠ A 8 3
	♡ 10 7 5 4
	◇ K 5 4 2
	♣ 10 9

WEST	NORTH	EAST	SOUTH
	1◇	1♡	2◇
Pass	Pass	Dble	Pass
3♣	3◇	All pass	

Bidding : With 5-3 in the majors, overcalling 1♡ is preferable to double when under 16 HCP. East has every reason not to sell out to 2◇ : extra values, they have bid and raised their suit to the two-level and East is short in their suit. Double is the best re-opening action. If 1◇ was a 4+ suit, South has no reason to push to 3◇. When West bids 3♣, North is in 3-over-3 territory and with an extra trump, North should compete with 3◇. Following 4-over-3, neither East nor West push to 4♣.

Lead : 4 of clubs. East has no attractive lead. As West bid clubs, a club becomes the preferred choice.

Recommended play : West wins with the ♣A and should switch to the ♡9. East wins and cashes the ♣K and a second heart. East should exit safely via a low heart or a trump. North draws trumps but loses a spade trick later as long as East covers the ♠Q or ♠J. One down.

Notes : (1) Had East passed 2◇, North-South would score +90.

(2) After winning ♣A, West notes that there is at most one more trick in clubs for the defense. East would have led a heart from A-K-x-x-x and so East is likely to have A-Q-x-x-x or similar. Therefore West should switch to a heart. On the actual deal, the heart switch is not essential.

(3) East-West have done well not to sell out to 2◇ and North-South have done well not to give up at 3♣ which would make ten tricks along normal lines.

(4) East-West have 9 clubs, North-South 9 diamonds. Total trumps 18. East-West make ten tricks in clubs, North-South eight tricks in diamonds. Total tricks 18. Swap over North's ♡K and South's ♠A and both sides make nine tricks. When a finesse works for one side, it loses for the other.

Hand 70 : Delayed double — 3-over-3 rule

Dealer East : E-W vulnerable

	NORTH
	♠ 8 6
	♡ A 9 7
	◇ K 10 9 4 3 2
	♣ 8 2

WEST		**EAST**
♠ A Q J 4 2		♠ K 10 7 5
♡ 6 4 3		♡ Q 8
◇ J 8 7		◇ A Q
♣ J 10		♣ K 9 6 5 3

	SOUTH
	♠ 9 3
	♡ K J 10 5 2
	◇ 6 5
	♣ A Q 7 4

WEST	NORTH	EAST	SOUTH
		1♣	1♡
1♠	2♡	2♠	Pass
Pass	3◇	Pass	3♡
Pass	Pass	3♠	All pass

Bidding : North is good enough for 2♡ over 1♠ but not strong enough for 2◇ which would indicate 10+ points. South in the direct seat passes 2♠ to indicate a minimum overcall. North does not sell out to 2♠ (3-over-2). North could bid 3♡ but 3◇ is used to suggest an alternative contract. 3◇ indicates good diamonds and minimum heart support. With four hearts, North would choose 3♡. East-West push on to 3♠ (3-over-3).

Lead : Ace of hearts. It is not attractive to lead an ace in a trump contract but opposite an overcall it is safer than usual.

Recommended play : South should discourage the hearts as South wants a club switch. Staring at the ◇K, North can tell the shift should be to clubs. North plays the ♣8, low, queen, jack. South cashes ♡K and ♣A, followed by a third club. West ruffs high, draws trumps and takes the diamond finesse. Nine tricks.

Notes : (1) If West's 1♠ showed 4+ spades, West should take the push to 3♠, but if East-West use the double of 1♡ to show four spades and 1♠ shows five, then East takes the push to 3♠ over 3◇.

(2) After North suggests diamonds, South is quick to revert to hearts.

(3) If left in 3♡, South is likely to succeed, either by setting up the diamonds or by ruffing two clubs in dummy. The trump position is favorable for South with the queen doubleton with East.

Hand 71 : Re-opening action — When to compete, when to sell out

Dealer South : Both vulnerable

WEST	NORTH	EAST	SOUTH
			Pass
1♠	2◇	Pass	Pass
Dble	Pass	3♣	Pass
Pass	Pass		

NORTH
- ♠ K J 6 4
- ♡ J 10 6
- ◇ A K Q 10 2
- ♣ J

WEST
- ♠ A Q 9 8 3
- ♡ A Q 7
- ◇ 7
- ♣ A 10 6 5

EAST
- ♠ 2
- ♡ 9 5 2
- ◇ J 5 4 3
- ♣ K 9 4 3 2

SOUTH
- ♠ 10 7 5
- ♡ K 8 4 3
- ◇ 9 8 6
- ♣ Q 8 7

Bidding : When 2◇ comes back to West, a re-opening double is the most flexible action. West has extra strength and is short in the enemy suit, two of the key signs for keeping the bidding open. North should take no further action after 3♣ as East-West are already at the three-level and there is no evidence that North-South have 9+ trumps.

Lead : 8 of diamonds. You need a very strong reason to choose something other than partner's suit.

Recommended play : North wins with the ◇Q and should shift to the ♣J. North should diagnose that the hand is likely to play as a cross-ruff with dummy short in diamonds and East probably short in spades. The best defense against a cross-ruff is leading trumps at every opportunity. Declarer can win with the ♣A, play ♠A and ruff a spade, take the heart finesse, ruff a third spade, cross to the ♡A and play the fourth spade. When North follows, East can throw the heart loser. This line yields ten tricks.

Notes : (1) Declarer should play the hand on ruffing lines rather than draw trumps. Declarer could ruff diamonds in dummy and spades in hand and this should also lead to ten tricks.

(2) If North unwisely competes further with 3◇, East-West can exact a heavy penalty. East leads ♠2 to the ace and ruffs the ♠9 return (high card = high suit entry). East shifts to a heart, won by West, and ruffs another spade. A heart to the ace is followed by a fourth spade, ruffed by East with the ◇J. A club to the ace gives the defense seven tricks and +300. Better to sell out to 3♣.

Hand 72 : 3-over-2 rule — 3-over-3 rule

Dealer West : Nil vulnerable

WEST	NORTH	EAST	SOUTH
1♣	Dble	Pass	1♠
Pass	2♠	Pass	Pass
Dble	Pass	3♣	3♠
Pass	Pass	Pass	

NORTH
- ♠ A K 9 8
- ♡ K Q 7 5 3
- ◇ A J
- ♣ J 4

WEST
- ♠ Q
- ♡ A J 10
- ◇ Q 7 6 3
- ♣ K Q 10 3 2

EAST
- ♠ J 10 3
- ♡ 9 6 4
- ◇ K 10 5
- ♣ 9 8 6 5

SOUTH
- ♠ 7 6 5 4 2
- ♡ 8 2
- ◇ 9 8 4 2
- ♣ A 7

Bidding : North is too strong for an overcall and with both majors, double would be preferable anyway. West is not strong enough to take action over 1♠. North's 2♠ shows 4-card support and about 16-18 points, 5 losers. When South passes, West is in 3-over-2 territory. Double for takeout is the most flexible and East can do little else but 3♣. South knows the partnership has nine trumps and so pushes on to 3♠ (3-over-3 rule).

Lead : King of clubs. Better to lead from a K-Q combination than from split honors or from a suit with just one honor.

Recommended play : Win with the ♣A and lead a heart. West should play low and the king wins. Cash ♠A and lead a low heart from dummy. West wins with the ♡J, cashes the ♣Q and shifts to a low diamond. On the actual layout, it works to win the ◇A, cash ♠K and ruff a heart, but playing the ◇J gives declarer easier access to dummy later. East wins and returns, say, a diamond. The ◇A wins, the ♠K is cashed and a heart is ruffed. South makes nine tricks, losing one trick in each suit. If West had started with four hearts, declarer could make nine tricks via a crossruff on the recommended line.

Notes : (1) A bid by West (in the direct seat) over 1♠ would indicate a strong hand after partner was unable to bid at the one-level.

(2) West's later double of 2♠ should be played as competitive for takeout. It is a sensible principle at duplicate that a double after the opponents bid and raise a suit to the two-level is for takeout.

(3) It is not so tough for South to bid 3♠. North went 2♠ opposite possibly no values at all. South has one sure trick with the ace of clubs and an extra trump as well.

CHAPTER 19
DOUBLES

Negative Doubles

You will find all the basic material on negative doubles in the *Guide To Better Bridge*. There are three areas worth discussing in your regular partnerships.

1. Negative double after a 1♡ overcall

WEST	NORTH	EAST	SOUTH
1♣	1♡	Dble	

versus

WEST	NORTH	EAST	SOUTH
1♣	1♡	1♠	

Many partnerships use the double to show exactly four spades and the 1♠ bid to show 5+ spades. In each case the strength is 6+ points.

Other partnerships prefer to use the 1♠ bid to show 4+ spades and the double to deny four spades. The theory is that we can handle 1♣ : (Pass) : 1♠ as a 4-card suit well enough and 1♣ : (1◇) : 1♠ shows 4+ spades and we can manage that as well, so why do we need 1♣ : (1♡) : 1♠ to show five spades? Why not use the 1♠ bid for 4+ spades as usual and harness the double to deal with the problem hands, the 6-9 point hands with the unbid minor and which cannot bid 1NT because of the lack of a stopper in hearts?

After 1♣ : (1♡) : ? what would you call with these?

♠ 6 3	♠ 6 3 2	♠ 5 4 2
♡ 9 6 2	♡ 9 6 2	♡ 6 3 2
◇ K Q 3 2	◇ K Q 7 3	◇ K 10 8 5 3
♣ K 8 6 3	♣ Q 7 5	♣ A 2

If 1♣ can be a 3-card suit, then raising to 2♣ with only 4-card support is not attractive although it is rarely fatal. On the second and third hands, it would be normal to pass 1♡. Using the double to show 6-9 points without 4 spades would allow you to double on each of the above. It would be reasonable to play this negative double as promising 4+ cards in the unbid minor. This would certainly help competitive action later if fourth player raises to 2♡.

2. Rebids by the opener when fourth player raises the suit overcalled

WEST	NORTH	EAST	SOUTH
1♣	1♠	Dble	2♠
?			

What action should West take with these hands?

(1)	(2)	(3)
♠ 6 4	♠ K 3 2	♠ 4 2
♡ 9 3	♡ 9 6 4 2	♡ Q J 3 2
◇ K Q 3	◇ K Q	◇ K Q
♣ A K 8 6 3 2	♣ A Q 4 2	♣ A K J 9 2

As responder need have no more than 6 points for the double, opener needs about 19 points to bid game. If opener is going to bid at the three-level with 12 points or with 17-18, how can responder ever tell when to push on to game and when to leave it at three? If opener bids 3♣ with (1), what would opener do with the ♡A instead of the ♡9?

If opener bids 3♡ on (2) with a 7-loser, 14-point hand, how can opener describe the superior 6-loser hand (3)?

The recommended solution is that opener should pass 2♠ with a minimum opening without four hearts. On (1) opener should pass. If 2♠ reverts to responder, the 3-over-2 rule (see Chapters 17-18) will ensure that the bidding does not end there. Responder can now support opener's minor with four, bid the other minor with five or double again with other patterns.

A bid by opener should show the 16-18 point 5-6 loser hand (bid 3♡ on hand 3) while double by opener shows four hearts in a minimum hand. This is important so that your side is not cut out of a heart contract by a further spade raise.

3. The negative double as an invitational raise

WEST	NORTH	EAST	SOUTH
1♡	2◇	?	

In standard style, 2♡ is a modest raise and many play that the jump to 3♡ is a limit raise (10-12). The game raise of 4♡ is still used as a pre-emptive raise while bidding the enemy suit covers hands of 13+ points including those with support for opener.

Those who use pre-emptive jump raises or the Jacoby 2NT do not relish the loss of these bids. However, 2NT is needed here as a natural bid, 10-12 points, their suit stopped, no primary support for opener's major and no 4+ cards in the other major.

To cover the gamut of raises one can play :

2♡ = normal single raise
3♡ and 4♡ = pre-emptive raises
3-their-suit = game-force raise (like the Jacoby 2NT)
Double and support opener at 3-level = limit raise
2NT = natural, 10-12
Double and bid their suit next time = game force without primary support for opener

Once they have bid, the usefulness of a pre-emptive raise to the three-level is doubtful. One could use 2♡ as 6-9 points and 3-card support, 3♡ as 6-9 points with 4-card support and the rest as above. The jump to the three-level will have some pre-emptive effect but the hand will include some defense. In addition, jumping to the three-level with 4-card support follows the principles from the Law of Total Tricks.

Responsive doubles

(1) At the two-level

WEST	NORTH	EAST	SOUTH
1◊	Dble	2◊	?

With 6+ points, South is expected to bid and a bid of 2♡ or 2♠ would show 6-9 points and a 4+ suit. What should South do with two 4-card majors?

♠ K 7 5 4	South could bid 2♡ or 2♠ but it
♡ K 5 3 2	is silly to pick one of the majors
◊ 10 5 3	and find you are in a 4-3 fit with
♣ J 8	a 4-4 fit in the other major.

The solution is to use double here for takeout. This is sensible since a penalty double has little value when they have bid and raised a suit to the two-level. South's double here after partner has made a takeout double and third player has raised opener's suit is called a 'responsive double'. It usually shows two 4- or 5-card suits of the same rank. At the two-level, 6+ points is the expected strength.

If the suit opened is a major, (1♡) : Double : (2♡) for example, the responsive double shows both minors. The responsive double is valuable in eliminating the guess when the suits are of equal value and you have four or five cards in each..

The responsive double can also be used with stronger hands :

♠ K 7 5 4	After the same start as above,
♡ K 5 3 2	South would double and raise
◊ 10 5 3	partner's major to the three-level
♣ A 8	as a game invitation.

If West pushes on to 3◊, passed back to South, South would pass with 6-9 points (3-over-3 rule) but with 10-12 points, South should double again.

With 13+ points and both majors, South could start with a double and raise partner's major to game. If West raises to 3◊, South could insist on game and partner choosing the major by bidding 4◊.

The responsive double applies only if third player raises opener's suit. If responder changes suit, double is best played as penalties.

WEST	NORTH	EAST	SOUTH
1◊	Dble	1♠	Dble

South's double is a penalty double. It shows 6+ points and 4+ spades. Exposing a probable psyche is an important use for the double in this context. South may have been planning to bid 1♠ or 2♠ or more. East's spades may be genuine but there are enough larcenous players in the bridge jungle to require a survival kit of penalty doubles here.

(2) At the three-level

WEST	NORTH	EAST	SOUTH
1◊	Dble	3◊	?

South is expected to be a bit stronger to bid a major here and double would still be responsive with equal length in the majors. Expectancy would be an 8-loser hand or just a touch under. Likewise, a bid of 3♡ or 3♠ has game-inviting overtones.

WEST	NORTH	EAST	SOUTH
1♠	Dble	3♠	?

Double by South would show both minors and game-invitational values. Expectancy is at least 4-4 in the minors and about a 7-loser hand.

WEST	NORTH	EAST	SOUTH
1♡	Dble	3♡	?

It is worth discussing this particular sequence in your partnerships. You can treat the double here in the same way as above, a responsive double showing both minors and inviting game.

There is a case for treating this auction differently and using 3♠ as purely competing for the partscore with a 5+ spade suit (3-over-3 rule) and to use the double as a game invitation in spades. The 3♠ bid could then be quite weak, as low as 6 points as long as advancer (the partner of the doubler or overcaller) had more than four spades.

My preference is to use the double as responsive with both minors and to bid 3♠ with respectable values, allowing partner to raise to game with better than a minimum double. However, there is merit in the other approach.

(3) At the four-level

WEST	NORTH	EAST	SOUTH
1◊	Dble	4◊	?

If responder has a semblance of sanity, you will have little need for a penalty double. South's double should show both majors and game-inviting values or better. You can hardly be precise here as you have lost so much bidding space.

Where the opposition suit is a major, responder's support may be no more than four trumps. Double as responsive for the minors is still recommended but if partner does not have a great holding in the minors, partner can leave the double in. Advancer should have 10+ HCP for the double. If advancer wants to insist on partner choosing a minor, bid 4NT.

Doubling no-trumps for takeout

WEST	NORTH	EAST	SOUTH
1♠	Pass	1NT	?

Traditionally the double of 1NT is for penalties but there is little value doubling a 1NT response for penalties. The opponents have about 20 points together and most of the strength sits over the doubler. For quite some time, double by South in auctions like the above have been played as a takeout double of the suit opened.

WEST	NORTH	EAST	SOUTH
1♡	Dble	2NT	?

Most play East's 2NT over the double as a good raise of the suit opened. Double by South in this context is best used as a responsive double, showing both minors (and sacrifice possibilities) after a major suit opening and both majors after a minor suit opening. The double should show only competitive values. Bid their suit with game invitational values.

Competitive doubles

The competitive double is a double (intended for takeout) which occurs later in the auction than a straightforward takeout double or a negative double. Bridge terminology could improve in this area. So many doubles these days are meant for takeout that their description would improve if prefaced by the player making the double. Thus, the traditional takeout double after an opening bid could be a 'defender's double', the negative double would be 'responder's double' and a second round double by opener would naturally be 'opener's double'.

A competitive double occurs generally on the second round of bidding or is a double for takeout by the advancer.

WEST	NORTH	EAST	SOUTH
1♥	2♦	2♥	Dble

This double by advancer is akin to the negative double. It would indicate spades and tolerance for clubs or diamonds as well.

WEST	NORTH	EAST	SOUTH
1♥	1♠	2♦	Dble

It is strange to have a double for takeout when there is only one suit left. However, it is silly to use double for penalties when the suit doubled is forcing. South's double here shows a club suit plus tolerance for spades.

Competitive doubles are common when following the rule of 3-over-2 :

WEST	NORTH	EAST	SOUTH
1♦	1♠	Dble	2♠
Pass	Pass	Dble	

East's first double is negative, a responder's double. East's second double is competing for the partscore. East is not prepared to sell out to 2♠.

Competitive doubles by opener occur when responder has bid. After a major suit response, the double by opener is used to show 3 card support and so the double is known as a 'support double' :

WEST	NORTH	EAST	SOUTH
1♦	Pass	1♠	2♣
Dble			

Opener's double shows 3-card spade support. The strength might be a minimum opening but it might also be a strong hand. After hearing responder's reply to the double, opener might be intending to bid on to game.

One of the great benefits of the competitive double occurs when the double is not used.

WEST	NORTH	EAST	SOUTH
1♦	Pass	1♠	2♣
?			

Given that the double shows 3-card support, what would it mean if West bid 2♠? This should show the 4-card raise. The ability to distinguish between 3-card support and 4-card support is essential if the partnership is to compete sensibly when the bidding has reached the three-level.

A rebid by opener of 2♦ would show long diamonds but would also deny three spades (failure to double). A rebid of 2♥ by opener would be a reverse, strong hand with 4 hearts and 5+ diamonds but it would deny three spades (failure to double). One consequent benefit is that since opener has denied 3-card support, responder's rebid of the same suit should be a 6+ suit (or an extremely strong 5-card suit).

Opener needs no extra strength to double to show the 3-card support. Pass by opener would show a minimum opening with no attractive descriptive rebid available. The implication is less than 3-card support for partner although opener is allowed to pass with poor 3-card support if the enemy bidding has caused opener to revalue the hand to a sub-minimum opening.

The primary concern of any competitive double is the major suits. Thus, the competitive double focuses first on 3-card support for responder's major and second on any unbid major.

WEST	NORTH	EAST	SOUTH
1♣	Pass	1♦	1♠
Dble			

Opener's double here would show four hearts, just as a regular negative double or takeout double of 1♠ would imply four hearts. This in turn allows responder to bid 1♦ freely over 1♣ with 4 diamonds and 4 hearts. There is no risk that a 4-4 heart fit will be missed since opener has the double available to show the hearts.

Many duplicate players follow the general principle that *all doubles of a suit at the one- or two-level are for takeout regardless of the preceding auction.* Some add a few restrictions (such as doubles after a redouble are for penalties, doubles after a takeout double has been passed for penalties are also for penalties) but it is quite workable to play all suit doubles at low level are for takeout. This would include doubles of an overcall after partner's 1NT opening.

Playing for penalties

The best low level penalties arise when you are short in partner's suit and strong in the enemy suit. If a double is stipulated as takeout, then to obtain penalties you pass. Partner is very likely to re-open the bidding with a takeout double of some kind and again you pass this for penalties.

How high should competitive doubles be played?

The more you play competitive doubles, the more you appreciate their value. Most play competitive doubles only at the one- or two-level. Negative doubles are often played to the four-level and responsive doubles to the 4♦ level. Doubles of pre-emptive action are usually played for takeout in the same way that doubles of pre-emptive openings are played for takeout. You are more likely to have a hand short in the pre-empt suit than long in that suit.

EXERCISES ON DOUBLES

A. The bidding has started :

WEST	NORTH	EAST	SOUTH
1◇	1♠	Dble	2♠
?			

What should West do now?

1. ♠ 74	2. ♠ 962	3. ♠ 74	4. ♠ 85	5. ♠ 63
♡ K6	♡ K8	♡ K962	♡ AJ64	♡ Q2
◇ AJ843	◇ AJ8632	◇ Q973	◇ KJ973	◇ KQJ953
♣ AQ64	♣ KJ	♣ AK9	♣ AK	♣ AKJ

B. The bidding has started :

WEST	NORTH	EAST	SOUTH
1♡	Dble	2♡	?

What should South do now?

1. ♠ J432	2. ♠ J4	3. ♠ J98	4. ♠ 94	5. ♠ 32
♡ Q6	♡ Q632	♡ 974	♡ J98	♡ A2
◇ K9873	◇ K9873	◇ AK42	◇ AJ74	◇ 86543
♣ 97	♣ 42	♣ 1095	♣ K952	♣ A1083

C. The bidding has started :

WEST	NORTH	EAST	SOUTH
1◇	Pass	1♠	2♣
?			

What should West do now?

1. ♠ J432	2. ♠ KJ4	3. ♠ J98	4. ♠ 9	5. ♠ 3
♡ AQ6	♡ AK7	♡ 9	♡ J98	♡ A2
◇ K9873	◇ QJ652	◇ AKJ742	◇ AKJ742	◇ KQ865
♣ K	♣ 42	♣ K95	♣ K95	♣ A10832

COMPETITIVE BIDDING : How should the following hands be bid? West is the dealer each time and neither side is vulnerable.

SET 33— WEST	SET 33 — NORTH	SET 33 — EAST	SET 33 — SOUTH
1. ♠ 864	1. ♠ KQ1052	1. ♠ 97	1. ♠ AJ3
♡ KJ73	♡ 1065	♡ AQ82	♡ 94
◇ AJ74	◇ K9	◇ 1065	◇ Q832
♣ K10	♣ A73	♣ Q842	♣ J965
2. ♠ 1054	2. ♠ KJ6	2. ♠ AQ983	2. ♠ 72
♡ 985	♡ AK63	♡ 102	♡ QJ74
◇ AQ765	◇ J	◇ K982	◇ 1043
♣ 54	♣ KQ762	♣ 103	♣ AJ98
3. ♠ 754	3. ♠ KQJ62	3. ♠ A983	3. ♠ 10
♡ QJ107	♡ 85	♡ A643	♡ K92
◇ AJ83	◇ K1076	◇ 4	◇ Q952
♣ 63	♣ 108	♣ AKJ5	♣ Q9742
4. ♠ A1065	4. ♠ K984	4. ♠ 32	4. ♠ QJ7
♡ J	♡ 1075	♡ 982	♡ AKQ643
◇ A8742	◇ K9	◇ QJ103	◇ 65
♣ Q87	♣ J1062	♣ A943	♣ K5
5. ♠ 10	5. ♠ K864	5. ♠ AJ752	5. ♠ Q93
♡ AQ874	♡ J53	♡ 92	♡ K106
◇ A72	◇ 108643	◇ KJ95	◇ Q
♣ KJ62	♣ 4	♣ 75	♣ AQ10983
6. ♠ K92	6. ♠ 86	6. ♠ AQ1054	6. ♠ J73
♡ 2	♡ Q107	♡ 8654	♡ AKJ93
◇ AK95	◇ 10842	◇ 63	◇ QJ7
♣ AQ1032	♣ 9654	♣ J8	♣ K7

PLAY HANDS ON COMPETITIVE DOUBLES

(These hands can be made up by using pages 160-167)

Hand 73 : Competitive double — Trump technique

Dealer North : E-W vulnerable

NORTH
- ♠ 7 5 4
- ♡ K J 10 6
- ◇ A 9 8 3
- ♣ 6 3

WEST	NORTH	EAST	SOUTH
	Pass	Pass	1♣
Pass	1◇	1♠	Dble
Pass	2♡	Pass	4♡
Pass	Pass	Pass	

WEST
- ♠ 10
- ♡ Q 7 2
- ◇ Q J 5 2
- ♣ Q 9 7 4 2

EAST
- ♠ K Q J 6 2
- ♡ 9 5
- ◇ K 10 7 6
- ♣ 10 8

SOUTH
- ♠ A 9 8 3
- ♡ A 8 4 3
- ◇ 4
- ♣ A K J 5

Bidding : After a 1♣ opening, when you have 4 diamonds and a 4-card major, it is usually best to respond 1◇. East is just strong enough to come in with 1♠ at this vulnerability. After East's 1♠ overcall, South's double shows 4 hearts. There is no additional message in this auction and no promise of 3-card diamond support. The missing major takes priority. When North can bid 2♡, South's hand is worth 19 points, enough to bid game.

Lead : King of spades. The obvious choice.

Recommended play : Take ♠A and start a cross-ruff : ◇A, diamond ruff, ♣A, ♣K, club ruff with the ♡J. If East had the ♡Q, East would almost certainly overruff. When the ♡J holds, ruff another diamond and lead another club, ruffing with the ♡10. When the fourth diamond is ruffed in dummy, declarer is home (even if East discarded a diamond on the third club and ruffs in with ♡9, forcing out the ♡A).

Notes : (1) If declarer starts with ♠A, ♡K and runs the ♡J (playing East for the ♡Q), West wins and a third trump leaves declarer at least one trick short.

(2) Cashing the top hearts first could be risky if trumps are 4-1. Leaving the trumps alone and starting on a cross-ruff gives declarer a chance to overruff either opponent.

(3) It would be reasonable for declarer to play a spade at trick 2, since a spade trick can be set up. If East cashes two spades and leads a fourth spade, North can overruff West.

Hand 74 : Support double — Trump technique

Dealer East : Both vulnerable

NORTH
- ♠ J 7 3
- ♡ A K Q 9 3
- ◇ Q J 7
- ♣ K 7

WEST	NORTH	EAST	SOUTH
		1♣	Pass
1♠	2♡	Dble	Pass
2♠	Pass	4♠	All pass

WEST
- ♠ A Q 10 5 4
- ♡ 8 6 5 4
- ◇ 6 3
- ♣ J 8

EAST
- ♠ K 9 2
- ♡ 2
- ◇ A K 9 5
- ♣ A Q 10 3 2

SOUTH
- ♠ 8 6
- ♡ J 10 7
- ◇ 10 8 4 2
- ♣ 9 6 5 4

Bidding : It is risky to come into the bidding when both opponents are bidding, but North has enough. East's double shows 3-card support for spades (2♠ would thus show 4-card support). West is content with two spades but with 16 HCP and a singleton in North's suit, East has enough to bid the game.

Lead : Ace of hearts. Clearcut.

Recommended play : South should signal with the ♡J. This will discourage a heart continuation if North does not have the queen (the ♡J denies the ♡Q) and will tell North it is safe to continue the hearts if North does have the queen. If North shifts to a low diamond, declarer can win, cash ♠K and ♠A, then lead the ♣J to take the club finesse while dummy still has a trump. North covers, and the ace wins. West can draw the last trump and set up an extra club trick to make eleven tricks.

Notes : (1) If North continues with a heart at trick 2, declarer ruffs in dummy. Declarer cannot afford to draw trumps for if the club finesse loses, West could lose a club and three hearts.

(2) On a heart continuation ruffed at trick 2, declarer should play a low club to the jack. North wins but dummy's clubs are set up. If North plays a third heart, dummy ruffs with the 9, the ♠K is cashed followed by ◇A, ◇K, diamond ruff and trumps are drawn. Making eleven tricks.

Hand 75 : Penalty pass — Competitive double — Defensive technique

Dealer South : Nil vulnerable

WEST	NORTH	EAST	SOUTH
			1♡
Pass	1♠	2♣	Pass
Pass	Dble	Pass	Pass
Pass			

NORTH
♠ A J 6 5 2
♡ 9 2
◊ K J 9 5
♣ 7 5

WEST
♠ K 8 7 4
♡ J 5 3
◊ 10 8 6 4 3
♣ 4

EAST
♠ Q 9 3
♡ K 10 6
◊ Q
♣ A Q 10 9 8 3

SOUTH
♠ 10
♡ A Q 8 7 4
◊ A 7 2
♣ K J 6 2

Bidding : Even though both opponents have bid, East's suit is good enough to justify 2♣. With good trumps and short in partner's suit, South has the right hand type for penalties. South passes and when North re-opens with a competitive double, South passes for penalties. No action by North is as attractive as a double which leaves 2♠, 2♡, 2NT, 3◊ or a penalty pass open. The double gives you the most options and is usually the best action when you have enough to bid but no clearcut choice.

Lead : 10 of spades. Nothing else suggests itself.

Recommended play : North wins with the ♠A and could give South a spade ruff. North however should switch to the ♡9. If South had ♡A-K, South might have led a heart, and so South's hearts might well be headed by A-Q or K-Q. In either case, South will welcome a heart switch. East ducks and South wins with the ♡Q, cashes the ♡A and leads the ♡8 to give North a ruff. North recognises the ♡8 as a suit preference signal for spades and returns the ♠2, low card for the low suit, diamonds. After South ruffs the spade, South is in no need of any more ruffs and so South continues with ◊A and another diamond. South comes to two more trump tricks and declarer is held to five tricks. Three down, +500 to North-South.

Notes : (1) North-South can make 3NT or 4♡, but it is unlikely that they will reach game.

(2) If North returns a spade at trick 2, it is unlikely that North will come to a heart ruff and declarer might escape for two down.

Hand 76 : Bidding after negative double — Hold-up play — Defensive technique — Card combination

Dealer West : N-S vulnerable

WEST	NORTH	EAST	SOUTH
Pass	1◊	1♠	Dble
2♠	3♣	Pass	3NT
Pass	Pass	Pass	

NORTH
♠ 8 6
♡ K J
◊ A J 8 4 3
♣ A K 7 4

WEST
♠ J 7 4
♡ Q 10 8 3
◊ Q 9 7 6
♣ J 8

EAST
♠ A Q 10 9 5
♡ 6 5 2
◊ 5
♣ Q 10 9 2

SOUTH
♠ K 3 2
♡ A 9 7 4
◊ K 10 2
♣ 6 5 3

Bidding : East has enough to overcall but West's raise is a bit skimpy. If challenged, West would claim the vulnerability made him do it. North's 3♣ denies four hearts and shows about 16-18 points. That is enough to encourage South to take a shot at 3NT. Note South's problem if 3♣ could be a minimum opening or could be 16-18. That is why opener should bid at the three-level in these auctions only with the 16-18 hand (all right, all right, an excellent 15 will do).

Lead : 4 of spades. Any other lead could lead to a divorce.

Recommended play : If East wins with the ace of spades and returns a spade, South should hold off with the king. South wins the third spade and should then lead a club to the ace, followed by a low diamond to the 10. West wins but has no more spades. South comes to nine tricks easily.

Notes : (1) East should not play ♠A at trick 1. The bidding marks South with the ♠K and East can afford to put in the 9. This will discover whether South started with K-J-x (and West perhaps with 7-4-2). It is very hard for South to duck the 9 (East may have Q-J-10-9-x in spades and West A-7-4 and then South would make no spade tricks. If South does duck, East can continue with the ♠Q and if South ducks again to try to block the suit, East will have scored a spectacular triumph.

(2) After South takes the first or second spade, South needs to bring in the diamond suit. The bidding gives no clearcut indication who has the ◊Q. As dummy's diamond tenace has the 8 as well, it is best to start with ◊K, followed by ◊10. This caters for West holding Q-9-x-x. You cannot deal with Q-9-x-x with East.

(3) If South starts with ◊K and then ◊2 to the jack, West playing low each time, West scores a diamond trick. Because of the ◊8 in dummy, it is vital to lead the ◊10 after the ◊K.

CHAPTER 20
MICHAELS CUE BIDS

The unusual 2NT overcall showing a weak two-suiter with at least 5-5 in the minors has been around for a long time. It is a useful tool to find a good sacrifice against their major suit games. Used properly, the unusual 2NT fulfils an important role in your duplicate armoury. (For more about the Unusual 2NT, see the *Guide To Better Bridge*.)

It was not long before the question was asked, 'Why do we have a bid only for both minors? Why can't we show other two-suiters too?' Michaels Cue Bids were devised to answer that question. This is how they work :

(1♠) : 2♠ = 5+ hearts and a 5+ minor
(1♡) : 2♡ = 5+ spades and a 5+ minor
(1♢) : 2♢ = at least 5-5 in the majors
(1♣) : 2♣ = at least 5-5 in the majors

The normal strength is less than an opening hand.

Bidding the enemy suit at once was traditionally used to show a huge hand, one that would have been opened with a game-forcing bid. These bids were used to insist on game whereas a double followed by a new suit or a jump rebid were not forcing on advancer. Such powerhouse hands are rare and just as weak twos are preferred over strong twos, so the Michaels Two-Suiters have taken over from the game force cue bids.

After a minor suit opening, the Michaels Cue shows at least 5-5 in the majors. After their 1♢ opening, you would bid 2♢ with these :

♠ J 10 9 6 2	♠ K Q J 3 2	♠ Q J 7 6 3 2
♡ A K 10 7 3	♡ J 10 9 7 4 2	♡ J 9 8 6 4 2
♢ 8	♢ 3	♢ 5
♣ 6 4	♣ 9	♣ - - -

After a major suit opening, Michaels shows 5+ cards in the other major and a 5+ minor. These would be suitable for 2♡ Michaels over their 1♡ opening :

♠ Q J 8 6 3	♠ J 10 6 3 2	♠ A J 7 5 4 2
♡ 9	♡ 9	♡ 6 3
♢ K Q 9 3 2	♢ 3	♢ K 10 8 5 2
♣ 6 4	♣ K Q 7 5 4 2	♣ - - -

For a 5-5, the expected strength is 7-11 HCP. For a 6-5 the strength can drop by two points or so, and for a 7-5, 6-6 or freakier, the point count is hardly relevant because of the great playing strength. For a 5-5, you should have at least four honor cards in the two long suits. For a 6-5, three honors will do. The expected playing strength is 6-7 losers for a minimum and 5-6 losers for a maximum.

The aim is not just to find a good sacrifice but also to find your own good major suit games. With a strong fit (4+ cards) in partner's major, advancer needs only three useful tricks to bid game.

Advancer's action opposite major suit Michaels

(a) With a weak hand

With no ambitions for game, advancer should support partner's major if possible. Bid it at the cheapest level or make a jump bid as a pre-empt. With no fit for the major, advancer can bid 3♣. Partner corrects to 3♢ with diamonds.

| WEST | NORTH | EAST | SOUTH |
| 1♡ | 2♡ | Pass | ? |

If weak, South can bid 2♠ or pre-empt with 3♠. The jump to 4♠ might be pre-emptive but might also be based on game-going values. With a doubleton in spades and a doubleton or worse in one of the minors, it would be prudent to bid 2♠. It is highly likely that partner's minor is opposite your minor suit shortage.

With no fit for spades, South bids 3♣ and North will correct to 3♢ with diamonds.

Some play that 3♣ and 3♢ are genuine suits and advancer should use 2NT to ask for partner's minor. This is playable but it is superior to use 2NT as a strong bid to find out more about partner's shape and strength.

(b) With a strong hand

You may bid game in partner's suit or 3NT, bid the enemy suit to ask for a stopper for 3NT or use the 2NT enquiry with sufficient values to invite game or insist on game.

Replies to 2NT after a major suit Michaels

Easiest is to play 3♣ or 3♢ shows the minor and bid the known major with a 6-card suit :

3♣ = second suit is clubs
3♢ = second suit is diamonds
3-other major = 6 cards in the major

Over 3♣ or 3♢, advancer's bid of 3-of-partner's major or a raise of the minor invites game, while a bid of the enemy suit shows a strong hand but unsure of the best game.

A more complex set of replies to 2NT is possible : see 'Expert methods' on the next page.

Advancer's action opposite minor suit Michaels

With a weak hand, support the major where you hold more cards. With equal length, choose the stronger holding. Jumps to 3-major are pre-emptive.

With a strong hand, bid game or bid the other minor (natural and forcing), bid their suit to ask for a stopper for 3NT or use the 2NT strong enquiry to which opener replies 3♣ (5-5, minimum), 3♢ (5-5, maximum), 3♡ (6 hearts) or 3♠ (6 spades).

Michaels only in the majors

Some play that bidding their major is Michaels but bidding their minor is natural. Given the frequency of artificial club openings and fake diamonds, this is a sensible approach. However, on the basis of frequency and usefulness, you will be better off playing Michaels in all suits. The hands suitable for a natural overcall of their minor can be bid by (1♣) : 3♣ or (1◊) : 3◊ as an intermediate jump or by passing and bidding the minor later if you judge the hand is not worth a three-level jump.

Michaels with strong hands

The basic Michaels two-suiter is a weak hand, below 12 HCP. With similar shape and opening points, you can start with an overcall or a double, depending on the suits held and the suit strengths. If you double, you must be strong enough to remove an unwelcome reply to a good 5+ major.

Many pairs play that Michaels can be the usual weak holding or a very strong hand, about 3-4 losers. The strong variety must be good enough that you intend to bid again if third player jumps to game. For example :

WEST	NORTH	EAST	SOUTH
1♥	2♥	4♥	Pass
Pass	?		

With the strong variety, North should double with five spades and bid 4♠ with six spades. South can remove to 5♣ ('pass-or-correct' : pass with clubs, bid 5◊ with diamonds) with no tolerance for the spades.

WEST	NORTH	EAST	SOUTH
1♠	2♠	4♠	Pass
Pass	?		

With the strong hand, North can double or bid 5♣/5◊ with 6-minor or 4NT with six hearts.

How to bid your powerhouse if you play Michaels

To show a strong hand after they open, start with a double. After partner's minimum suit reply :
Bid new suit or raise partner = 16-18, 5 losers
Jump new suit or jump-raise partner = 19+, 4 losers
Bid the enemy suit = very powerful, usually 3 losers or better. Even these powerhouse hands need to be bid conservatively if no trump fit exists and you do not have a self-sufficient suit (Suit Quality 10).

WEST	S	W	N	E	EAST
♠ A K 3	1◊	Dbl	No	1♠	♠ 10 7 5 2
♥ K Q J 8	No	2◊	No	?	♥ 6 3
◊ 6					◊ 8 7 5 4 2
♣ A K Q 3 2					♣ 9 6

After the doubler bids the enemy suit, a sound idea is to have advancer repeat the first suit bid with a hopeless hand (even without 5+ cards in that suit). The doubler is allowed to pass that bid. On the hand above East would bid 2♠ and West can pass this. With reasonable values making game likely, the advancer rebids anything other than the original suit reply. The bidding will then continue to game.

Expert methods

For a more complex scheme of rebids after advancer's 2NT, you could use :
3♣ = minimum, second suit is clubs
3◊ = minimum, second suit is diamonds
3♥ = maximum, second suit is clubs
3♠ = maximum, second suit is diamonds
3NT = 6-5 with 6-Major and 5+ clubs
4♣ = 6-5 with 5-Major and 6+ clubs
4◊ = 6-5 with 5-Major and 6+ diamonds
4♥ = 6-5 with 6-Major and 5+ diamonds

Advancer should be able to place the contract after this information. The replies for a 6-5 spill into the four-level as it is unlikely that advancer will want to end in 3NT opposite such freak shape.

Bidding after their Michaels Cue Bid in a major

Suppose the bidding has gone 1♠ : (2♠). Responder has a choice of these actions :
3♠ = sound raise to the two-level
3♣/3◊ = new suit, natural, forcing
3♥ (their suit) = limit raise of opener's suit or better (10+ points). Opener bids 3♠ if minimum.
Double = looking for penalties, the same sort of hand which would redouble after 1♠ : (Double).
2NT = natural, 10-12 points, inviting 3NT. Should have their major stopped and stoppers in both minors.
3NT = Natural, to play, stoppers in the unbid suits.
4♣/4◊/4♥ = splinter, as usual over 1♠

If third player doubles partner's Michaels Cue, all bids retain their usual meaning. Redouble says, 'Please make the cheapest possible bid, then pass my rebid.' This allows advancer to escape into a long, strong suit.

If third player bids, advancer passes with a weak hand unless a sacrifice is attractive. Be reluctant to sacrifice with a balanced hand and do not sacrifice with only 3-card support for partner. With a good hand, support partner's major (3-major invites game), double for penalties, bid game or bid 4NT to ask for partner's minor.

Bidding after their Michaels Cue Bid in a minor

Suppose the bidding hast started 1◊ : (2◊) showing both majors.
3◊ = sound raise to 2◊
4◊ or 5◊ = pre-emptive
3♣ = 6-9 points, long clubs, not forcing
2♥ = 10+ points, game try or stronger in clubs. May have diamond support as well.
2♠ = 10+ points, game try or better in diamonds

This approach is similar to bidding over their unusual 2NT where 3♣ = game try or better in hearts and 3◊ = game try or better in spades.
3♥/3♠/4♣ = splinter raise, game force
Double = Looking for penalties, 10+ points
2NT = Natural and limited, both majors stopped
3NT = Natural with stoppers in both majors

The structure follows analogous paths when the bidding has started 1♣ : (2♣).

EXERCISES ON MICHAELS CUE BIDS

A. Right hand opponent has opened 1♡. What action would you take, playing Michaels, with these hands?

1. ♠ A J 4 3 2	2. ♠ K J 10 5 2	3. ♠ J 9 8 6 4 3	4. ♠ A K 4 3 2	5. ♠ K 6 4 3 2
♡ A Q	♡ 2	♡ ---	♡ 2	♡ 2
◇ K 9 8 6	◇ Q J 10 6 3	◇ 4	◇ K Q J 9 8 4 3	◇ Q 4
♣ 7 2	♣ 4 2	♣ Q 9 7 6 4 2	♣ ---	♣ K 8 5 3 2

B. The bidding has started (1♡) : 2♡ : (Pass) : to you. What would you do with these hands?

1. ♠ 7	2. ♠ K 9 6 2	3. ♠ K 9 7 5 4	4. ♠ Q 5	5. ♠ 9 6
♡ K 9 6 2	♡ J 8 4 2	♡ 7 6 2	♡ A Q 6 4	♡ 8 7 5 4 2
◇ J 9 7 3 2	◇ A J	◇ Q J 8 4	◇ A K 4	◇ A K 3 2
♣ A 9 6	♣ A 7 2	♣ 3	♣ Q 8 5 2	♣ 6 3

C. The bidding has started :

WEST	NORTH	EAST	SOUTH
1♠	2♠	Pass	2NT
Pass	?		What should North rebid with these hands?

1. ♠ 7	2. ♠ 2	3. ♠ 9 7	4. ♠ ---	5. ♠ 9
♡ K 10 9 6 2	♡ K J 8 7 4 2	♡ K Q J 6 2	♡ A Q 6 4 2	♡ K 7 5 4 2
◇ J 9	◇ 7	◇ A J 10 8 4	◇ A 4 3	◇ K Q 9 7 4 3 2
♣ Q J 10 6 4	♣ A J 10 9 2	♣ 3	♣ J 10 9 8 5	♣ ---

COMPETITIVE BIDDING : How should the following hands be bid? West is the dealer each time and neither side is vulnerable.

SET 34 — WEST	SET 34 — NORTH	SET 34 — EAST	SET 34 — SOUTH
1. ♠ 8 6	1. ♠ K Q 10 5 2	1. ♠ 9 7	1. ♠ A J 4 3
♡ K J 7 3 2	♡ 10 6 5	♡ Q 8	♡ A 9 4
◇ A K 9	◇ ---	◇ Q J 6 5 3	◇ 10 8 7 4 2
♣ K 10 2	♣ A 9 8 7 3	♣ Q J 6 4	♣ 5
2. ♠ A 7	2. ♠ Q 6 4 2	2. ♠ K J 9 8 3	2. ♠ 10 5
♡ A 8 7 5	♡ 3	♡ K Q 9 4 2	♡ J 10 6
◇ J 9 6	◇ A K 3	◇ 8 2	◇ Q 10 7 5 4
♣ 9 8 7 4	♣ Q J 6 5 2	♣ 10	♣ A K 3
3. ♠ Q	3. ♠ J 8 7 5 4	3. ♠ A K	3. ♠ 10 9 6 3 2
♡ Q J 10 7	♡ A 8 3	♡ K 9 6 5 4	♡ 2
◇ K 8 4	◇ 2	◇ J 10 6	◇ A Q 9 7 5 3
♣ A K 6 3 2	♣ 10 8 7 4	♣ Q J 5	♣ 9
4. ♠ A K 10 5 4	4. ♠ 7 3	4. ♠ Q 8	4. ♠ J 9 6 2
♡ K 3	♡ A J 10 6 4 2	♡ 8 7 5	♡ Q 9
◇ J 5	◇ ---	◇ Q 10 8 7 4 2	◇ A K 9 6 3
♣ Q 6 4 2	♣ K 10 9 5 3	♣ 8 7	♣ A J
5. ♠ A 6 3	5. ♠ Q J 7 4 2	5. ♠ K 10 9 5	5. ♠ 8
♡ A K J 10 7	♡ 9 3	♡ 2	♡ Q 8 6 5 4
◇ 2	◇ K Q J 6 5	◇ A 10 9 7	◇ 8 4 3
♣ K J 6 2	♣ 3	♣ A 7 5 4	♣ Q 10 9 8
6. ♠ 10 9 7 5 4 2	6. ♠ Q	6. ♠ K J 8 3	6. ♠ A 6
♡ K Q 8 7 2	♡ J 10 9 5	♡ 3	♡ A 6 4
◇ 6	◇ J 10 9 4	◇ A 8 5 3 2	◇ K Q 7
♣ 3	♣ K 9 8 6	♣ J 7 5	♣ A Q 10 4 2

PLAY HANDS ON MICHAELS CUE BIDS
(These hands can be made up by using pages 160-167)

Hand 77 : Michaels — Sacrifice — Defensive technique

Dealer North : Both vulnerable

NORTH
♠ Q J 5 2
♡ 9 8
◇ A J 8 6 3
♣ 5 2

WEST
♠ 9
♡ K 10 7
◇ K Q 10 9 5
♣ A 8 6 4

EAST
♠ K 6 3
♡ A Q J 6 5 2
◇ 7 2
♣ K 7

SOUTH
♠ A 10 8 7 4
♡ 4 3
◇ 4
♣ Q J 10 9 3

WEST	NORTH	EAST	SOUTH
	Pass	1♡	2♡
2NT	4♠	Dble	All pass

Bidding : Over South's 2♡, 2NT = 10+ HCP with support for opener. A jump to 4♡ by West would be a shape raise, 2NT is a raise based on strength. This enables your side to gauge whose hand it is. After a shape raise, you may wish to sacrifice, after a strength raise you tend to defend. With only one defensive trick, North should bid 4♠. Opposite seven losers, North brings two tricks and so 4♠ should be no more than two down. With values in spades, East doubles to indicate a desire to defend. West may overrule this with great shape or considerably extra strength.

Lead : 3 of spades or ace of hearts. A trump lead is often best when the opponents are sacrificing.

Recommended play : On a trump lead, North ducks this to the queen, repeats the spade finesse and draws the last trump. The clubs are set up and the defense takes two hearts and two clubs. One down.

Notes : (1) East-West can take 4♠ two down if East can ruff the third club with the ♠K. The defense might achieve this via ♡A lead, encouraged by West. East continues with the 2 of hearts, a suit preference signal for clubs. If West switches to a low club to the king and a club comes back, East-West can collect 300.
(2) East-West can always make 4♡ but if East-West push on to 5♡, North-South will have a stunning victory if South leads the ♠A and switches to the singleton diamond. North wins and can give South a diamond ruff for one down.
(3) If North-South do not play Michaels and South merely overcalls 1♠, it would be tougher to find 4♠.

Hand 78 : Michaels with a strong hand — Shape raise — Sacrifice decision

Dealer East : Nil vulnerable

NORTH
♠ Q J 10 6 4
♡ 10 9 6 5
◇ A
♣ J 10 2

WEST
♠ 3
♡ A Q J 7 2
◇ K Q 10 9 7 2
♣ A

EAST
♠ 8 2
♡ 8 4
◇ J 8 5
♣ K 8 7 5 4 3

SOUTH
♠ A K 9 7 5
♡ K 3
◇ 6 4 3
♣ Q 9 6

WEST	NORTH	EAST	SOUTH
		Pass	1♠
2♠	4♠	Pass	Pass
5◇	Pass	Pass	Pass

Bidding : West has only three losers. You can use Michaels with this strength as long as you do not pass out 4-Major if they bid it. North has a shape raise and 4♠ shows 4+ trumps, decent shape but fewer than 10 HCP. West is not going to sell out to 4♠ and 5◇ shows 6+ diamonds and 5 hearts. East has no trouble passing but South has a tough problem deciding whether to pass, double or push on to 5♠. The balanced hand suggests not sacrificing and South has no significant defensive tricks against 5◇. Many would pass on the South cards.

Lead : Queen of spades or ace of diamonds.

Recommended play : On the ♠Q lead, South may well overtake and switch to a trump. North wins and may shift to a club or continue spades. West wins, crosses to dummy with a trump and takes the heart finesse. The ♡A is cashed, felling the king, followed by a low heart ruffed in dummy. A club taken by West allows the last trump to be drawn and the hearts are set up. Eleven tricks opposite next to nothing.

Notes : (1) On ◇A lead followed by a spade shift won by South and a second trump, the play follows similar lines. The second trump is won in dummy and then comes heart finesse, ♡A and a heart ruff.
(2) Double by West over 4♠ shows better defensive values while 4NT is used to show 6+ hearts. Then, if not interested in hearts, advancer bids 5♣ and partner will correct to diamonds if necessary.
(3) Given South has no defensive values against 5◇ (perhaps one spade trick but the ♡K looks badly placed), South could choose to sacrifice in 5♠. North's shortage on the bidding is likely to be in diamonds. West would double 5♠ but the defenders can collect four tricks (two hearts and two clubs) for +300 after the ♣A lead, while the ◇K lead would give South the chance to escape for one down..

Hand 79 : Michaels over a minor — Sacrifice — Competitive judgement

Dealer South : N-S vulnerable

```
            NORTH
            ♠ Q
            ♡ J 10 9 5
            ◊ J 10 9 4
            ♣ K 9 8 6
WEST                        EAST
♠ 10 9 7 6 4 2              ♠ K J 8 3
♡ K Q 8 7 2                 ♡ 3
◊ 6                         ◊ A 8 5 3 2
♣ 3                         ♣ J 7 5
            SOUTH
            ♠ A 5
            ♡ A 6 4
            ◊ K Q 7
            ♣ A Q 10 4 2
```

WEST	NORTH	EAST	SOUTH
			1♣
2♣	Pass/3♣	4♠	Dble
Pass	Pass	Pass	

Bidding : West's 2♣ shows at least 5-5 in the majors. You need little strength with a 6-5 pattern. North has a tough problem. Opposite genuine clubs, 3♣ is reasonable. If the 1♣ opening might be short, Pass is more prudent. East has the ideal hand to take a shot at game : 4+ support for one of the majors, short in the other major and an outside ace. East bids 4♠ hoping to make and expecting not to be worse than one down. It is hard for South with three aces and 19 points to avoid the double.

Lead : Ace of spades followed by a second spade. A trump lead is often best when your side has the majority of high cards.

Recommended play : East wins the second trump and leads a heart. South grabs the ace of hearts and can take the ace of clubs but that is all for the defense. There is no way to beat 4♠ as the cards lie.

Notes : (1) If South ducks the heart, dummy wins, a low heart is ruffed followed by ◊A, diamond ruff and another low heart ruffed. This sets up dummy's hearts and declarer makes eleven tricks.
(2) If South grabs the ace of hearts and fails to cash the ♣A, East can discard two clubs on the top hearts and set up the fifth heart to discard the third club. This again gives declarer eleven tricks.
(3) Note the effectiveness of the Michaels 2♣ bid. Without that, how would East-West manage to find 4♠? You would not want to overcall 1♠ on the West cards. Left alone, North-South would reach 3NT and if West leads a heart, 3NT would be easy.
(4) The winning move for North-South is to sacrifice in 5♣, one down if West collects the diamond ruff but making on a non-diamond lead. It is no easy task for North-South to find 5♣.

Hand 80 : Michaels — Penalties — S.O.S. rescue

Dealer West : E-W vulnerable

```
            NORTH
            ♠ Q J 10 6 3
            ♡ K 3
            ◊ K Q 10 9 5
            ♣ 9
WEST                        EAST
♠ 5 4                       ♠ A K 9 8 7
♡ A Q 9 8 5 4               ♡ 10 7
◊ A 2                       ◊ J 8 7 6
♣ K 5 4                     ♣ Q 3
            SOUTH
            ♠ 2
            ♡ J 6 2
            ◊ 4 3
            ♣ A J 10 8 7 6 2
```

WEST	NORTH	EAST	SOUTH
1♡	2♡	Dble	Rdble
Pass	2♠	Dble	3♣
Dble	Pass	Pass	Pass

Bidding : North has a very sound Michaels Cue at favorable vulnerability. East's double is for penalties, showing strength in North's suit(s) and shortage in partner's. It is not hard for South to deduce North's suits. South wants to play in 3♣ but if South bids 3♣, North will correct to diamonds. To play in your own long suit, start with a redouble. This asks partner to make the cheapest possible bid (2♠ here) and then pass your next bid. West does not have a great double of 3♣ but knowing East has 10+ points and a shortage in hearts, the double is reasonable.

Lead : Ace of hearts. Hoping for East to have a singleton heart.

Recommended play : After ♡A and a second heart taken by dummy, declarer leads ♠Q won by East who might switch to a diamond. West takes ◊A and plays the ♡Q, ruffed in dummy and overruffed by East. Declarer loses 1 spade, 1 heart, 1 overruff, 1 diamond and 1 club. One down.

Notes : (1) If East shifts to a trump at trick 4, South plays low and West wins. South now loses one spade, two hearts, one diamond and one club. One down.
(2) One down in 3♣ doubled is as good as South can do. 2♠ doubled or 3◊ doubled would be no better.
(3) East-West can make 3NT as the cards lie but it is very hard to reach that spot.
(4) If East-West end up in some number of hearts, declarer is going to struggle after the lead of the queen of spades. If declarer elects to finesse the queen of hearts, not a farfetched play by any means, declarer could easily suffer a spade ruff and a club ruff.

CHAPTER 21
INTERFERENCE OVER YOUR 1NT
THE LEBENSOHL CONVENTION

There are dozens of conventions for bidding after they have opened 1NT. No doubt you have your favorite. For more information about some of the better methods after they open 1NT, see *Bridge Conventions, Defenses and Countermeasures*. Here we are concerned with covering as many problems as possible if they interfere over your 1NT opening.

WEST	NORTH	EAST	SOUTH
1NT	2♡	?	

How does your partnership cope in the East seat? The standard treatment here is to play double for penalties, suit bids at the cheapest level not forcing and bid of the enemy suit to replace Stayman.

At duplicate most top pairs prefer to play more sophisticated methods :

(1) Double for takeout

Penalty doubles are great when they come along but most sensible opponents have a strong suit and do not go for large numbers when they come in over your 1NT. Is responder more likely to have length and strength in their suit or a shortage in their suit? On the score of frequency, the takeout double is more valuable.

One of the problems with the standard approach is that there is no game invitational bid to show a missing major. You can bid their suit as Stayman but this is forcing to game. What if responder has:

♠ Q 9 7 2	To bid 2♠ is silly and 2NT can
♡ 9 4	lose the spades. How much easier
♢ K Q 9 3	if responder can double 2♡ for
♣ J 6 4	takeout to show this hand type.

(2) Lebensohl 2NT

This is the preferred approach among most top pairs. A suit bid at the two-level merely competes for the partscore. It is not even invitational (double covers the invitational hands). A change of suit at the three-level is natural and forcing.

The 2NT response is *Lebensohl* and requires the 1NT opener to bid 3♣. Responder may be intending to pass 3♣ with a weak competitive hand with long clubs. After opener's forced 3♣, a new suit lower ranking than the enemy suit is to play, merely competing for the partscore.

WEST	NORTH	EAST	SOUTH
1NT	2♠	3♡...	

East's 3♡, a new suit at the three-level, is forcing.

WEST	NORTH	EAST	SOUTH
1NT	2♠	2NT	Pass
3♣	Pass	3♡...	

East's 3♡, preceded by the Lebensohl 2NT, is not forcing and not even encouraging.

There are four strong actions for responder :

Immediate 3NT response = game points but no stopper in their suit and no 4-card major

Immediate bid of their suit = game points, at least one unbid major (4 cards) but no stopper in their suit

2NT Lebensohl followed by a 3NT rebid after the forced 3♣ puppet = game points, no 4-card major but at least one stopper in their suit

2NT Lebensohl followed by a bid of their suit after the forced 3♣ puppet = game points, at least one 4-card major plus a stopper in their suit

The memory guide here is that the more often you bid no-trumps, the happier you are with no-trumps. Thus, using 2NT Lebensohl and following up with a strong action shows the stopper. Showing a strong hand without 2NT denies the stopper.

Thus, the Lebensohl 2NT allows responder to play in a partscore at the three-level in a suit lower-ranking than their suit and also allows responder to describe various game-going hand types with or without a major and with or without at least one stopper in their suit. If responder shows no stopper and opener has no stopper either, it would be prudent to play somewhere other than in 3NT.

WEST	NORTH	EAST	SOUTH
1NT	2♡	2NT	Pass
3♣	Pass	3♠...	

What is the distinction between this sequence and responder's bidding 3♠ at once over 2♡? Both sequences must be strong since with a weak hand, East could bid just 2♠. Following the above memory guide, travelling via 2NT shows a stopper in their suit and 5+ spades while the direct 3♠ bid shows 5+ spades but denies a stopper in their suit.

The same would apply to hearts in this auction :

WEST	NORTH	EAST	SOUTH
1NT	2♢	3♡...	

versus

WEST	NORTH	EAST	SOUTH
1NT	2♢	2NT	Pass
3♣	Pass	3♡...	

2♡ was available as a weak action merely to compete for the partscore so that both these sequences are strong. In the first, East is showing 5+ hearts but no stopper in the diamonds. In the second, East shows 5+ hearts and at least one stopper in diamonds. Knowing whether responder does or does not have a stopper in the enemy suit must help opener make a sensible decision.

What if their interference is artificial

Many conventions show a suit other than the suit bid, such as 2♣ showing hearts and another or 2◊ showing spades and a minor. In this case, the enemy suit is the suit shown, not the suit bid. One consequence is that you have three bids of the enemy suit available, one at the two-level, one at the three-level immediately and one at the three-level after Lebensohl 2NT. The three-level bids have their usual meanings and the two-level bids can be used for takeout with a singleton or void in that suit.

WEST	NORTH	EAST	SOUTH
1NT	2♡*		?

*Showing 5+ spades

(1)	(2)	(3)
♠ 8 6 3	♠ K 3 2	♠ ---
♡ K 10 8 7	♡ K 10 8 7	♡ J 9 8 6
◊ A 9	◊ A 9	◊ K Q 5 3
♣ K J 4 2	♣ Q 7 5 3	♣ K 8 6 3 2

(1) Bid 3♠ (four hearts but no stopper in spades).
(2) Bid 2NT and over the puppet 3♣, rebid 3♠ (four hearts plus a stopper in spades).
(3) Bid 2♠, game-force with a spade singleton or void.

If their bid shows two suits

WEST	NORTH	EAST	SOUTH
1NT	2◊		?

If 2◊ is used to show both majors, East-West will not be looking to play in a major. Bid 2♡ if short in hearts or 2♠ if short in spades. The jump to 3♡ asks for a stopper in hearts and may have a spade stopper. Opener can bid 3♠ to ask for help there. Responder's 3♠ asks for a spade stopper and shows a heart stopper.

If East bids 2NT and follows up with 3♡ or 3♠, this asks for a stopper in the suit bid and shows a stopper in the other major.

More on the takeout double

WEST	NORTH	EAST	SOUTH
1NT	2♡	Dble	

Where the overcall is 2♡ natural, the takeout double need not have four spades. The double should be based on game-inviting values. With enough for game, three-level action with or without Lebensohl is available.

Opener can bid 2♠ if minimum with four spades (over which responder can bid 2NT or 3-minor without four spades), 2NT if minimum without four spades or 3♠/3NT if maximum.

WEST	NORTH	EAST	SOUTH
1NT	2◊	Dble	

Where the overcall is 2◊ natural, the double shows inviting values but need not have a major. Opener can bid at the two-level if minimum and 3-Major or 3NT if maximum. If opener's rebid is unsuitable, responder rebids naturally.

WEST	NORTH	EAST	SOUTH
1NT	2♠	Dble	

Over 2♠, double should include four hearts. If minimum, opener needs to know whether 3♡ is safe.

Expert methods

When they interfere over your 1NT, one problem is that your partnership loses transfers. Lebensohl recaptures Stayman on game-going hands and the takeout double does the work of Stayman on game-inviting hands. Would it not be attractive to have transfers as well?

Transfer Lebensohl

It is possible to have transfers by using 2NT or higher bids as Lebensohl combined with transfers.

WEST	NORTH	EAST	SOUTH
1NT	2♠		?

2NT = Lebensohl requiring opener to bid 3♣. As usual, responder is allowed to pass this. If responder continues, 3♠ and 3NT have the usual Lebensohl meanings, while 3◊ or 3♡ shows that 2NT was a transfer : 3◊ = 5+ clubs, 4 diamonds and enough for game and 3♡ = 5+ clubs, 4 hearts and enough for game.

3♣ = Transfer to diamonds. Opener may super-accept by bidding 3NT or with 3♠ to ask for a spade stopper.

3◊ = Transfer to hearts. Opener may super-accept via 4♡ or 3♠ to ask for a spade stopper.

3♡ = Both minors and slam potential. If responder is 5-4 in the minors, it will be 5 diamonds - 4 clubs. With the minors the other way around, responder would bid 2NT and rebid 3◊ over 3♣ (see above).

WEST	NORTH	EAST	SOUTH
1NT	2♡		?

2♠ = Natural, 5+ spades, not forcing

2NT = Lebensohl requiring opener to bid 3♣, as above. If responder continues, 3♡ and 3NT have the usual Lebensohl meanings, while 3◊ or 3♠ shows that 2NT was a transfer : 3◊ = 5+ clubs, 4 diamonds and enough for game and 3♠ = 5+ clubs, 4 spades and enough for game.

3♣ = Transfer to diamonds. Super-accepts are allowed as above.

3◊ = Transfer to *spades*. This is necessary as 3♡ is the Lebensohl bid, showing four spades and no stopper in hearts.

3♠ = Both minors and slam potential. If responder is 5-4 in the minors, it will be 5 diamonds - 4 clubs (see above).

The principles are :

2NT requires 3♣ as usual. If responder continues with their suit or 3NT, then 2NT was Lebensohl. If responder continues with a new suit, then 2NT was a transfer, showing 5+ clubs and the new suit.

3♣ is always a transfer to diamonds.

3◊ is always a transfer to the other major.

3-other-major = both minors and slam prospects.

Where a major suit has not been bid, then 3◊ can be used as a transfer to hearts and 3♡ as a transfer to spades, 3♠ as the hand with both minors and slam potential. This method may be needed if their bid has not promised an anchor suit.

EXERCISES ON LEBENSOHL

A. Partner 1NT, right hand opponent 2♡ natural. What action would you take, playing standard Lebensohl?

1. ♠ AJ43	2. ♠ AJ52	3. ♠ J43	4. ♠ J43	5. ♠ K6432
♡ AQ	♡ 752	♡ 85	♡ A8	♡ A8
◊ 8643	◊ 8643	◊ AK62	◊ QJ53	◊ Q4
♣ 752	♣ AQ	♣ QJ53	♣ K842	♣ J852

B. The bidding has started 1NT : (2◊ overcall, showing spades and a minor) to you. What do you do now?

1. ♠ 75	2. ♠ 2	3. ♠ 54	4. ♠ 54	5. ♠ 96
♡ K962	♡ K962	♡ QJ762	♡ QJ762	♡ J2
◊ 932	◊ AJ3	◊ QJ74	◊ AKJ4	◊ 932
♣ AQJ6	♣ A8742	♣ 32	♣ 32	♣ KJ9843

C. WEST : 1NT, NORTH : 2♠ (natural). What should East do with these hands if playing Transfer Lebensohl?

1. ♠ 7	2. ♠ 2	3. ♠ 9	4. ♠ 7	5. ♠ 9
♡ K10962	♡ KQ8742	♡ KJ6	♡ KJ6	♡ 542
◊ AQ93	◊ 73	◊ AJ108	◊ AJ1083	◊ KJ97432
♣ J106	♣ A962	♣ KQ853	♣ KQ85	♣ 62

PARTNERSHIP : How should the following hands be bid, playing standard Lebensohl? West is the dealer each time and there is no opposition action other than the bidding shown.

SET 35— WEST	SET 35 — EAST	SET 36 — WEST	SET 36 — EAST
1. **North bids 2♡**	1. **North bids 2♡**	1. **North bids 2♡**	1. **North bids 2♡**
♠ A962	♠ K1054	♠ A96	♠ Q852
♡ Q3	♡ 1065	♡ AQ3	♡ 82
◊ KQ9	◊ A8	◊ KQ9	◊ A732
♣ KQ104	♣ J732	♣ J1043	♣ KQ6
2. **North bids 2♡**	2. **North bids 2♡**	2. **North bids 2♡**	2. **North bids 2♡**
♠ Q3	♠ K1052	♠ AK3	♠ Q852
♡ A962	♡ 1065	♡ J43	♡ 82
◊ KQ9	◊ A8	◊ KQ8	◊ A732
♣ KQ104	♣ J732	♣ A742	♣ KQ6
3. **South bids 2♡**	3. **South bids 2♡**	3. **South bids 2♠**	3. **South bids 2♠**
♠ A3	♠ K105	♠ 75	♠ AK3
♡ 42	♡ A65	♡ J108743	♡ 962
◊ Q97642	◊ J83	◊ 954	◊ KQ8
♣ 643	♣ AKJ7	♣ K5	♣ A742
4. **South bids 2♡**	4. **South bids 2♡**	4. **South bids 2♠**	4. **South bids 2♠**
♠ A3	♠ KQJ5	♠ 75	♠ 983
♡ 42	♡ A65	♡ J108743	♡ AK62
◊ 642	◊ J83	◊ 954	◊ KQ
♣ Q97642	♣ AJ3	♣ K5	♣ AJ102
5. **North bids 2♠**	5. **North bids 2♠**	5. **North bids 2♠**	5. **North bids 2♠**
♠ J5	♠ 93	♠ 75	♠ J42
♡ KQ63	♡ A2	♡ AJ3	♡ KQ
◊ Q83	◊ AK9764	◊ K54	◊ QJ83
♣ AKJ7	♣ 643	♣ AK652	♣ QJ43

PLAY HANDS ON LEBENSOHL OVER 1NT
(These hands can be made up by using pages 160-167)

Hand 81 : Lebensohl sequence to replace Stayman — Deceptive defense

Dealer North : Nil vulnerable

NORTH
- ♠ A K 7 4
- ♡ 8 4
- ◊ Q 10 6 2
- ♣ Q 3 2

WEST
- ♠ 3
- ♡ K Q J 10 9
- ◊ J 7
- ♣ 10 8 6 5 4

EAST
- ♠ 10 9 8 5
- ♡ A 7 6
- ◊ 9 8 5 4 3
- ♣ J

SOUTH
- ♠ Q J 6 2
- ♡ 5 3 2
- ◊ A K
- ♣ A K 9 7

WEST	NORTH	EAST	SOUTH
	Pass	Pass	1NT
2♡	3♡	Pass	4♠
Pass	Pass	Pass	

Bidding : If East-West have a method to show a heart-club two-suiter, then West might use it, but the hearts are so good and the clubs so weak, that 2♡ is eminently reasonable. North's 3♡ replaces Stayman and, playing Lebensohl, shows 4 spades and no stopper in hearts. Facing a passed hand, South has an easy 4♠ rebid. If North were an unpassed hand, South would bid 3♠ to show four spades and a maximum 1NT in case North had ambitions for slam.

Lead : King of hearts. Automatic.

Recommended play : East can see that the defense will take at most two hearts and perhaps a minor suit king with West. East decides to try a little subterfuge in case West has led from a 5-card suit. East overtakes the ♡K with the ace and returns the ♡6. West wins and West and South both think East started with a doubleton heart. When West plays the third heart, almost every declarer would ruff high in dummy. That creates a trump trick for East and holds declarer to ten tricks.

Notes : (1) There is a slight risk that South started with two hearts and the third heart will give South a ruff and discard, but the risk is worth taking. If your ruse works, what a story to tell for weeks afterwards.
(2) Holding South to ten tricks should give East-West a top board.
(3) The alternative line is to take the second heart and switch to the ♣J, hoping West has the ♣K.

Hand 82 : Competing over their overcall — Creating an extra trump trick

Dealer East : N-S vulnerable

NORTH
- ♠ A 3
- ♡ J 3
- ◊ 7 3 2
- ♣ 9 8 6 5 4 3

WEST
- ♠ Q 4
- ♡ 9 8 7 6 4
- ◊ Q 9 6 4
- ♣ A Q

EAST
- ♠ 9 8
- ♡ K Q 5 2
- ◊ A K J
- ♣ K J 10 2

SOUTH
- ♠ K J 10 7 6 5 2
- ♡ A 10
- ◊ 10 8 5
- ♣ 7

WEST	NORTH	EAST	SOUTH
		1NT	2♠
3♡	Pass	4♡	All pass

Bidding : At unfavorable vulnerability, you need six sure tricks for a two-level overcall and some hope of seven tricks. South has just enough. West's 3♡ shows five hearts and is forcing when playing Lebensohl.

If East-West were playing transfer Lebensohl, West would bid 3◊, East 3♡, West 3♠ to ask for a stopper and East 4♡. South would lead the singleton club. Judging the lead to be very likely a singleton, North should signal with the ♣9, suit preference for spades if South gains the lead in trumps. South would take the ♡A on the first round, lead a spade and receive a club ruff.

Lead : Ace of spades. It is normal to lead partner's suit.

Recommended play : South encourages and wins the second spade. It should be clear to South that if West has 9-10 HCP that North cannot hold the ♣A. South therefore leads a third spade, North ruffs with the jack of hearts (uppercut) and South has two trump tricks.

Notes : (1) A club lead would also work but how could North tell? Unless there are clear indications, you should stick to partner's bid suit.
(2) Although the third spade gives declarer a ruff-and-discard, declarer has no useful loser to discard. With no tricks available outside trumps, try for a trump promotion.

Hand 83 : Lebensohl sequence to replace Stayman — Defensive technique

Dealer South : E-W vulnerable

NORTH
♠ A J 7
♡ A K
◇ K 8 6
♣ J 9 8 3 2

WEST
♠ Q 10 9 6 4
♡ 9 4
◇ 7 5 2
♣ K 6 4

EAST
♠ 3
♡ Q J 10 7 6 5
◇ Q 10 9 3
♣ A 7

SOUTH
♠ K 8 5 2
♡ 8 3 2
◇ A J 4
♣ Q 10 5

WEST	NORTH	EAST	SOUTH
			Pass
Pass	1NT	2♡	3♡
Pass	3NT	All pass	

Bidding : A sound overcall over 1NT should have about six playing tricks. The point count is not as important as the playing tricks. South's 3♡ replaces Stayman : it shows four spades and denies a stopper in hearts. North has no problem in rebidding 3NT.

Lead : Queen of hearts. What else?

Recommended play : Declarer has six top tricks and should tackle the clubs. Even if both finesses worked in spades and diamonds, that would come to only eight tricks. The best chance for success is to cross to the king of spades and lead a low club from dummy. West should rise with the ♣K and send back a heart. North wins and if a second club is played, declarer is two down. If instead declarer tried the diamond finesse and the spade finesse that would hold the losses to one down. Although both finesses work this time, the more common result of this line would be three down. It is better for North to hope that West started with only two hearts and both club honors.

Notes : (1) West should reason that if North has ♣ A-J-x-x or longer, the ♣K is doomed anyway. West goes up with the ♣K to preserve partner's hoped for entry to the hearts later. There is almost no risk of colliding with East's ♣A singleton. That would give North six clubs.
(2) If West ducks with the ♣K, North plays the ♣9. It does not help East to duck this, for North plays a second club. Now East's entry is eliminated before the hearts are set up.
(3) Note North's technique in crossing to dummy and leading the first club from there. If North leads the first club from hand, the defense can hardly get it wrong.

Hand 84 : Showing a stopper in their suit — Unblocking technique

Dealer West : Both vulnerable

NORTH
♠ K 9 7 4 3 2
♡ - - -
◇ 9 8 7 2
♣ J 10 8

WEST
♠ J 6
♡ A 8 5 2
◇ 6 3
♣ A 6 5 4 3

EAST
♠ A 10 5
♡ 7 6 3
◇ A K 4
♣ K Q 9 7

SOUTH
♠ Q 8
♡ K Q J 10 9 4
◇ Q J 10 5
♣ 2

WEST	NORTH	EAST	SOUTH
Pass	Pass	1NT	2♡
2NT	Pass	3♣	Pass
3NT	Pass	Pass	Pass

Bidding : North is too weak and has the wrong shape for a weak two opening. West's 2NT forces 3♣ and the 3NT rebid denies four spades and promises at least one stopper in hearts.

Lead : King of hearts. No reason to prefer the ◇Q.

Recommended play : If clubs are 3-1, the club suit is blocked. Declarer should duck the first heart, duck the second heart and duck the third heart. Once East is void in hearts, declarer can discard the blocking club on the ♡A and take 1 spade, 1 heart, 2 diamonds and 5 clubs.

Notes : (1) If East wins the ♡A on the first, second or third round, there are only eight tricks. There is no way to reach the fifth club in dummy.
(2) If South switches to ◇Q after the first or second heart, the ♡A is the entry to dummy later.
(3) If South switches to ◇Q after three rounds of hearts, East wins, cashes ♣K, ♣Q and plays a club to the ace. East's last club is discarded on dummy's ♡A and dummy's remaining club winners can now be cashed.

CHAPTER 22

DEFENSE TO WEAK TWOS

Against their natural weak two

For defenses against multi-twos, see Chapters 23-24.

Over their weak actions your primary aim is to cope with your strong hands. This is quite a task as you have lost the one-level and most of the two-level. Showing weak hands over their weak two has little value, and so jump overcalls are strong while 2NT shows a strong balanced hand and not the unusual 2NT for the minors. The basic strategy is to play partner to provide at least two tricks. Thus, an overcall at the three-level shows a 6-loser hand while (2♠) : 4♥ should be a 5-loser hand. If partner provides the expected two tricks, these levels should be safe enough. The recommended approach :

2NT = 16-18 balanced with at least one stopper in their suit. 15 HCP will do with a double stopper.

3NT = 21-22 balanced, at least one stopper in their suit. With 19-20 balanced or 23+, start with a double.

Double = for takeout. Same values as for a double at the one-level. If minimum, the hand must be short in their suit with 4+ cards in the other major.

Suit bid = natural, strong 5+ suit. 2♠ over (2♥) might be a 6-loser or 7-loser hand but a three-level overcall should be 5-6 losers. With 4 losers, the hand is too strong for an overcall. Start with a double. The jump to 3♠ over (2♥) should be a 5-loser hand. If better than this, start by doubling.

Bidding their suit asks partner to bid 3NT with a stopper in their suit. The usual hand is a long, running minor suit and at least seven winners on top. With a game-force powerhouse, start with a double and bid their suit on the next round to force to game.

4♣ or 4♦ = 5+ cards in the minor suit bid *and 5+ cards in the other major*, a 5-loser hand or better. With a strong minor single-suiter, start with a double.

4NT = the 'unusual', with both minors, at least 5-5. The hand should be no worse than a 4-loser hand.

After (2♥/2♠) : Pass : (Pass) to you, reduce the requirements for 2NT, double and suit bids by 3 points.

After (2♥) : 2NT or (2♠) : 2NT

Advancer may choose from :

3♣ = Stayman

3♦ = Transfer to the other major

Their suit = singleton or void in their suit, forcing to game, typically a 4-4-4-1 or 5-4-3-1 with a 5-card minor

3-other-major = at least 5-4 in the minors, forcing to game, slam interest

This approach is very similar to Transfer Lebensohl (see page 119).

4♣/4♦ = natural, game force, slam interest

After (2♥) : Double or (2♠) : Double

The standard approach is to bid at the cheapest level with a poor hand and give a jump response with about 10 points or more. The problem here is that you have lost so much bidding space. While it is all right to jump to 3♣/3♦ after (1♥/1♠) : Double, you do not want to jump to 4♣ or 4♦ and so bypass 3NT. Even without that, a three-level reply to the double has a very wide range. After (2♠) : Double : (Pass) : 3♥, how is the doubler expected to judge what to do next if the advancer could be 0, 1, or 2 points or could be a reasonable 7-9 points?

The preferred solution is to harness the Lebensohl concept for this area. In reply to the double :

2NT = Lebensohl, requesting the doubler to bid 3♣. Advancer may be intending to pass 3♣ or bid a suit at the 3-level to show a hand in the 0-6 point range. With a weak hand, advancer will have at best 2 cover cards.

3-level suit bid = around 7-10 HCP or 8 losers, encouraging but not forcing.

(2♥) : Double : (Pass) : 3♠ = 8 losers, 5+ spades.

Bidding 2NT first and then bidding 3♠ over the forced 3♣ shows 8 losers and only four spades.

3NT = Single stopper in their suit

2NT-followed-by-3NT-over-3♣ = Double stopper

Bid their suit = game force with a singleton or void in their suit

2NT-and-later-bid-their-suit = game force, stopper probe but 2+ cards in their suit

If the doubler is very strong, 4 losers or better, decline the 3♣ puppet. Advancer should then bid on with one trick or better. If the doubler bids the enemy suit over 2NT Lebensohl, this shows a 3-loser or better hand. With 19-20 balanced, the doubler should accept the 3♣ puppet. 19-20 balanced has a lot of losers.

Other Lebensohl situations

Because the Lebensohl principle is so valuable, it has been harnessed to other auctions analogous to the reply to a double of a weak two.

WEST	NORTH	EAST	SOUTH
1♠	Pass	2♠	Double
Pass	?		

Use 2NT Lebensohl with a weak hand and bid at the three-level with 7-10 points, 8 losers.

After (1♠) : Double : (2♠), however, Lebensohl does not apply as advancer is not obliged to bid at all.

WEST	NORTH	EAST	SOUTH
2♦	Pass	2♥	Double
Pass	?		

After a multi-2♦, South's double of the 2♥ reply = a double of a weak 2♥. North's 2NT = Lebensohl.

EXERCISES FOR DEFENDING AGAINST WEAK TWOS

A. The bidding has started with (2♠) on your right. What action would you take with these hands?

1. ♠ K 7 3	2. ♠ K 7 3	3. ♠ 3	4. ♠ 8	5. ♠ 8
♡ A 2	♡ A J	♡ 6	♡ K Q 10 5 2	♡ A K 8 3 2
◇ A K 5 3 2	◇ A K 8 4	◇ K Q J 9 3	◇ A K J 4 3	◇ A K Q
♣ Q 9 3	♣ A J 4 2	♣ A Q J 7 4 3	♣ 9 2	♣ A Q J 5

B. The bidding started (2♡) : Double : (Pass) to you. What is your reply to the double with these hands?

1. ♠ A Q 8 7 4	2. ♠ A Q 7 4	3. ♠ 7 2	4. ♠ 7 2	5. ♠ K 4
♡ 6 3	♡ 6 4 3	♡ 7 5 3 2	♡ 7 5 3 2	♡ A Q 4
◇ J 8 7 2	◇ J 8 7 5 2	◇ Q J 6 4	◇ Q J 6 4	◇ A J 9 3
♣ 9 5	♣ 2	♣ 7 4 2	♣ A J 2	♣ J 10 3 2

C. The bidding has started (2♠) : Double : (Pass) : 2NT, (Pass) back to you, the doubler. What action should you take with these hands, given that 2NT is Lebensohl, requesting 3♣ from you?

1. ♠ 4 3	2. ♠ 7 2	3. ♠ A 4 2	4. ♠ 2	5. ♠ 3
♡ K Q 7 6	♡ A Q J 3 2	♡ Q 6 4	♡ A K 6 4	♡ A Q 3
◇ A K 4 2	◇ A K	◇ A K J 5	◇ K Q J 10	◇ A K J
♣ K 5 2	♣ K Q 9 3	♣ A Q 2	♣ A K Q 2	♣ K Q J 7 4 3

PARTNERSHIP BIDDING : How should the following hands be bid? West is the dealer each time.

SET 37 — WEST	SET 37 — EAST	SET 38 — WEST	SET 38 — EAST
1. North opens 2♡	1. North opens 2♡	1. North opens 2♠	1. North opens 2♠
♠ A Q 7 2	♠ 6 3	♠ 8 7 4 2	♠ 3
♡ 6 4 2	♡ A Q 3	♡ K 2	♡ A Q 3
◇ Q 9 8	◇ A K 6 2	◇ 8 6 5	◇ A K J
♣ 9 8 4	♣ A Q J 3	♣ 10 9 5 2	♣ K Q J 7 4 3
2. South opens 2♠	2. South opens 2♠	2. South opens 2♡	2. South opens 2♡
♠ 6 3	♠ 7 5 4	♠ A Q 6 3	♠ 7 2
♡ A Q 3	♡ K 7 6 4 2	♡ 8 5	♡ Q J 4
◇ A K 6 2	◇ 9 7 3	◇ A 6 4	◇ K Q 9 7 3
♣ A Q J 3	♣ 8 5	♣ K J 3 2	♣ 9 8 7
3. North opens 2♠	3. North opens 2♠	3. North opens 2♡	3. North opens 2♡
♠ J 7 2	♠ 6 3	♠ 7 2	♠ A Q 6 3
♡ J 10 8 6 4 2	♡ A K	♡ Q J 4	♡ 8 5
◇ 7 4	◇ A K Q 8	◇ K Q 9 7 3	◇ A 6 4
♣ 7 6	♣ A Q J 3 2	♣ 9 8 7	♣ A K 6 2
4. South opens 2♠	4. South opens 2♠	4. North opens 2♡	4. North opens 2♡
♠ A Q 8	♠ 7 5 4	♠ 9 6 5	♠ K Q J 7 3
♡ J 9	♡ K 10 7 4 3	♡ J 7 5	♡ 8
◇ A K 6 2	◇ 9 7	◇ 9 3 2	◇ A K J 6 4
♣ Q J 3 2	♣ A K 5	♣ A Q 4 3	♣ 8 2
5. South opens 2♡	5. South opens 2♡	5. South opens 2♠	5. South opens 2♠
♠ K 3	♠ Q J 8 7 5 2	♠ 7	♠ A K 3 2
♡ A 10 3	♡ 6	♡ A Q 7 5 3	♡ J 6
◇ K 6 4	◇ A Q J	◇ A K 4	◇ Q 9 6 2
♣ K Q J 3 2	♣ 9 7 4	♣ A K J 2	♣ Q 8 5

PLAY HANDS ON DEFENDING AGAINST WEAK TWOS
(These hands can be made up by using pages 160-167)

Hand 85: Game force after their weak two — Trump reduction — Defensive countermeasure

Dealer North : N-S vulnerable

NORTH
- ♠ A K Q 9 8 5
- ♡ 5
- ◇ 10 6 2
- ♣ 9 7 4

WEST	NORTH	EAST	SOUTH
	2♠	Dble	Pass
2NT	Pass	3♠	Pass
4♡	Pass	Pass	Pass

WEST
- ♠ 7 6 2
- ♡ J 10 8 6 4 2
- ◇ 7 4
- ♣ Q 8

EAST
- ♠ J 3
- ♡ A K
- ◇ A K Q 8
- ♣ A K J 3 2

SOUTH
- ♠ 10 4
- ♡ Q 9 7 3
- ◇ J 9 5 3
- ♣ 10 6 5

Bidding : With 25 HCP and better than 3 losers, East has enough to insist on game. With 3♠ as Michaels, huge hands are shown by double first, bid their suit later. West uses Lebensohl 2NT, planning to sign off in 3♡. Over East's 3♠, West has an easy 4♡. East does not know how many hearts West has but there is nothing to suggest that 5♣ or 5◇ will be better. As it happens, 5♣ is easier than 4♡ but for all East knows, West could have a singleton or void in clubs. 5♣ could be hopeless with 4♡ comfortable. After much soul-searching, East passes 4♡.

Lead : Ace of spades. What else?

Recommended play : South plays high-low on the first two spades and North continues with a third spade, ruffed with the king of hearts. South discards a club. The ♡A is cashed, followed by a club to the queen and the jack of hearts, revealing the bad break. South wins and returns a diamond, taken in dummy. West should now fail. West can tempt South by playing ♣A, ♣K but as long as South does not ruff, South will come to an extra trump trick. West can ruff a club and ruff a diamond but is in hand at trick 12.

Notes : (1) If South ducks the ♡J, West can succeed via trump reduction technique : a club to the ace, club ruff, diamond to the ace and club ruff. A diamond to dummy at trick 11 holds South to one trump trick.
(2) The same technique is available if South captures ♡J and exits with a club. Recognising that a trump reduction is West's only hope, South must play a diamond to attack dummy's later entry. This leaves West one entry short. West can reduce the trumps to the same length as South's but dummy has no entry at trick 11.
(3) If North fails to lead a third spade, West has no problem drawing South's trumps.

Hand 86 : 2NT over weak two — Transfer by advancer

Dealer East : E-W vulnerable

NORTH
- ♠ Q J 8 7 5 2
- ♡ 6
- ◇ A J 9
- ♣ 9 7 4

WEST	NORTH	EAST	SOUTH
		2♡	2NT
Pass	3◇	Pass	3♠
Pass	4♠	All pass	

WEST
- ♠ A 6
- ♡ 8 4 2
- ◇ 7 6 5 2
- ♣ A 10 8 6

EAST
- ♠ 10 9 4
- ♡ K Q J 10 9 5
- ◇ Q 8 4
- ♣ 2

SOUTH
- ♠ K 3
- ♡ A 7 3
- ◇ K 10 3
- ♣ K Q J 5 3

Bidding : With a 5-3-3-2 and a 5-card minor, it is more attractive to bid no-trumps than the minor provided the hand fits the requirements for the no-trump overcall. North has enough to jump to 4♠ but unless you have a strong reason to be declarer, you should use a transfer sequence. In these auctions, 3◇ is a transfer to the other major. With enough for game and only five spades, North would rebid 3NT over 3♠ but with six spades, North should bid the spade game.

Lead : 4 of hearts. West has no reason to choose another lead.

Recommended play : Win ♡A and lead the king of spades, taken by West. If West exits with a trump or a heart, trumps are drawn and South starts on the clubs. West should hold off with the ace until the third round and then play a heart, ruffed in dummy. Declarer should finesse East for the ◇Q. 11 tricks.

Notes : (1) If West takes the ♣A on the first or second round of clubs, declarer can set up the fifth club and avoid the need to pick the diamond position. Given East has opened with a weak two at unfavorable vulnerability and West has turned up with both black aces, East figures to have the ◇Q.
(2) If West gives East a club ruff after winning ♠A, declarer is held to ten tricks. If West switches to a diamond after taking the ♠A, South has an easy path to 11 tricks.
(3) If North bids 4♠ over 2NT, East might lead the singleton club which would defeat 4♠. West wins, gives East a club ruff and gives East a second club ruff after taking ♠A. With South declarer, why would West lead a club?

Hand 87 : Rejecting the Lebensohl puppet — Counting and card reading

Dealer South : Both vulnerable

NORTH
- ♠ 9 5
- ♡ 10 8 6 2
- ◊ 8 7 5
- ♣ 10 9 4 3

WEST
- ♠ 7
- ♡ A Q 7 5 3
- ◊ A K 4
- ♣ A K J 2

EAST
- ♠ A K 3 2
- ♡ J 4
- ◊ Q 9 6 2
- ♣ Q 8 5

SOUTH
- ♠ Q J 10 8 6 4
- ♡ K 9
- ◊ J 10 3
- ♣ 7 6

WEST	NORTH	EAST	SOUTH
			2♠
Dble	Pass	2NT	Pass
3♡	Pass	4NT	Pass
5♣	Pass	6NT	All pass

Bidding : East was planning to reach 3NT and show two stoppers in spades by using 2NT followed by 3NT next. West is expected to bid 3♣ but West is strong enough to reject the puppet. 3♡ shows 5+ hearts, 19+ points and 4 losers. That spurs East into slam mode. East cannot be sure that slam will be a good bet but it would be timid to play this in just game. 4NT is RKCB setting hearts as trumps and 5♣ shows 0 or 3 key cards, clearly three. With no obvious trump fit, East opts for 6NT.

Lead : Queen of spades. The obvious start.

Recommended play : East wins and leads a low heart, in case South has the king of hearts singleton. The queen wins and a low heart is conceded in order to cater for a 3-3 split. South wins and continues with the jack of spades, taken by East who continues with a club to the ace and the ♡A, with East and South both pitching spades. The clubs are cashed, South discarding spades, followed by the ◊A and ◊K, South dropping the ◊J under the king. East has to decide whether to play for diamonds 3-3 or whether to finesse the 9 of diamonds. After a moment's reflection, East confidently plays a diamond to the queen. 12 tricks.

Notes : (1) If East leads the jack of hearts early, South should cover with the king. If East leads a low heart, South should play low. There is no benefit in rising with king-doubleton in front of dummy's A-Q.
(2) At trick 12, when North follows to the 4 of diamonds, declarer knows that North's last card is the 10 of hearts and therefore the remaining diamond must be with South.

Hand 88 : Responding to the takeout double — Card reading and trump management

Dealer West : Nil vulnerable

NORTH
- ♠ K J 9 6 2
- ♡ J 9 6 5
- ◊ J
- ♣ K 6 5

WEST
- ♠ Q 8 7
- ♡ A
- ◊ 9 8 6 5 4
- ♣ 10 7 3 2

EAST
- ♠ 5
- ♡ K Q 10 7 4 3
- ◊ A 10 2
- ♣ 9 8 4

SOUTH
- ♠ A 10 4 3
- ♡ 8 2
- ◊ K Q 7 3
- ♣ A Q J

WEST	NORTH	EAST	SOUTH
Pass	Pass	2♡	Dble
Pass	3♠	Pass	4♠
Pass	Pass	Pass	

Bidding : South has an obvious double and North's 3♠ shows 5+ spades and around 7-10 points. With only four spades and the same strength, use 2NT Lebensohl and rebid 3♠ over the 3♣ puppet. With 16 HCP and six losers, South is worth a shot at 4♠.

Lead : King of hearts. Nothing else is attractive.

Recommended play : West takes the ♡A perforce and returns a diamond (not a club, obviously). East wins and continues with ♡Q and a third heart. North ruffs with dummy's ace of spades and follows with the 10 of spades, letting it run if West plays low. If necessary, the spade finesse is repeated. 10 tricks.

Notes : (1) If North fails to ruff the third heart or ruffs low, West scores a trump trick. One down.
(2) Given East started with a weak two, the ♠Q is more likely to be with West. It is usually right to play the partner of the pre-emptor for length in the other suits and thus key queens or jacks in those outside suits. After East turns up with 9 HCP (♡ K-Q and ◊A), it is even more likely that West has the ♠Q. Therefore, ruff the third heart high and then finesse against West.

CHAPTER 23

THE MULTI-2◇ OPENING

The multi-2◇ opening is the most popular of the multi-openings. In the quest for greater efficiency, players have tried to compress more and more meanings into fewer bids. Why use two opening bids for the weak twos in the majors when you can get by with just one? This approach enables your system to cover many more hand types and one measure of a system's value is the number of hands with which it can cope. Most who play a multi-2◇ use it to cover :
(a) a weak two in hearts, *OR*
(b) a weak two in spades, *OR*
(c) a number of strong hand types.

Some do use it differently but the above is the most common structure. A typical multi-2◇ :

Weak two in hearts *OR*
Weak two in spades *OR*
21-22 points balanced *OR*
9½-10 playing tricks in clubs *OR*
9½-10 playing tricks in diamonds.

This frees the 2♡/2♠/2NT openings for other purposes. Some use only the weak options for the multi-2◇ (but not all countries permit this use) and there are countless varieties for the strong possibilities.

RESPONDING TO 2◇

2♡ = 'Pass or correct' : Pass with hearts. If not, opener bids 2♠ (weak two in spades), 2NT (the strong balanced option) or bids at the three-level to show other strong options (e.g., 3♣ = 9½-10 playing tricks in clubs, 3◇ = the same in diamonds).

If opener removes to 2♠, the bidding proceeds as after a weak 2♠ opening (see Chapter 9). If opener removes to 2NT, bidding proceeds as though the opening bid was 2NT (see Chapter 4). Bidding, if any, after other strong options is natural.

2♠ = 'Pass or correct' : To play if opener has the weak two in spades. 2♠ is used when responder has an excellent fit for hearts (good shape and 3+ support) but is not so good in spades. 2♠ operates as a game invitation in hearts. Opener passes with the weak two in spades. With the weak two in hearts, opener bids 3♡ if minimum and 4♡ if maximum. Other rebids (e.g., 2NT, 3♣, 3◇) show the strong options.

3♡/3♠/4♡ = pre-emptive in the major suit bid. Opener passes if holding that major. If not, bid the other major or make a natural, strong rebid. Responder will be prepared for the strong rebid.

3♣/3◇ = Natural, strong responses. Opener rebids naturally (jump to 4-Major with a SQ of 10).

2NT = Strong enquiry. This is used for hands which are worth game or a game invitation opposite a weak two. 2NT is normally based on a strong opening hand (13+ points) and more than three quick tricks.

If opener has a strong option opposite the 2NT reply, there should be sufficient values for a slam. The replies at the three-level are used for the weak two types :

3NT = A-K-Q-x-x-x in the major suit. Responder will usually be able to tell which major is held. If not, bid 4♡ and opener will bid 4♠ with spades.

3♠ = Spades, minimum points, only one top honor
3♡ = Hearts, minimum points, only one top honor
3◇ = Spades, better than the 3♠ reply, so either minimum with two top honors *or* maximum points
3♣ = Hearts, better than the 3♡ reply, so either minimum with two top honors *or* maximum points
4♡/4♠ = Maximum weak twos with a SQ of 10
4NT = The strong balanced option. You can use 5♣ Stayman and transfers but there is little room to explore. Most of the time, responder will bid either 6NT or 7NT.
4♣/4◇ = Other strong options. A new suit by responder is best played as a cue bid with opener's suit as trumps.

Over 3♠ or 3♡, responder should be able to place the contract. Over 3♣ or 3◇, responder can 'relay', that is, enquire further by making the cheapest bid (3◇ over 3♣ or 3♡ over 3◇). Opener then rebids :

1st step = minimum points, two top honors. This is opener's major and so responder can pass opposite the minimum.
2nd step = maximum points, two top honors
3rd step = maximum points, one top honor

The memory guide for opener's rebid is :

Min - max - max, 2 - 2 - 1 honors

This scheme gives responder as much information as can be obtained by the Ogust 2NT enquiry in response to a natural weak two. The Multi-2◇ thus will not lag behind a natural weak two.

If responder is contemplating 3NT and one top honor in opener's suit is enough, responder will know that with opener's first reply. If responder needs two honors, responder uses the 'relay'.

If responder does not use the 'relay', bidding opener's major is a sign-off (even at the three-level) and so are other game bids. Bidding the other major below game is natural and forcing (responder had no chance earlier to bid the other major without risking a pass), while a minor suit rebid is best used as a cue bid with opener's major as trumps.

What if they double partner's 2◊ opening?

Any bid by responder has its usual meaning.

Pass = 5+ diamonds. Opener passes, bids the major or shows the relevant strong option.

Redouble = 'Bid 2♡ and then pass my next bid.' This allows responder to escape into a long, strong suit. Opener will bid 2♡ with either weak two, show the strong option (leave the redouble in with a strong hand in diamonds!), or bid 2♠ with a weak two in spades *and* a suit quality of 10.

What if they bid over partner's 2◊ opening?

If they bid 2♡ or 2♠, double is for takeout. Partner will be pleased to leave it in with six in their suit. 2NT and suit bids have their normal meaning.

If they bid 2NT, double is penalties; bidding a major invites game; minor suit bids are natural, forcing.

If they bid at the three-level or higher, double is for takeout and 'Pass or correct' applies to a major suit bid.

Defending against the multi-2◊

It is tough defending against any multi opening if the opening does not promise a specific suit (no 'anchor suit'). This is because both partners lack a cue bid of the enemy suit to show a strong hand.

The 'no anchor suit' feature also makes multi-twos unpopular with administrators. You may find that you are not permitted to use multi-twos at your local club and perhaps not even in events below national championship level. This is unfortunate since it is attractive to be able to show so many weak hand types. Often you can make a game with less than half the high card strength and you may also be able to locate a profitable sacrifice.

This is the recommended defense to a multi-2◊ :

Double = 16+ points, any shape except for the 2NT and 3NT bids

2NT = 19-21 balanced

3NT = 22-24 balanced

Suit bids = natural, good suit but below 16 HCP, a strong 5-card major and a good opening at the two-level, a strong suit and 6-losers at the three-level.

Jump to 3-Major = 6+ suit and a 5-loser hand.

Otherwise pass and wait for responder to bid. If responder makes a weak bid in a major, double is best used for takeout. In fourth seat, treat the action by RHO as though that is their opening.

WEST	NORTH	EAST	SOUTH
2◊	Pass	2♡	?

South should treat the position as though there has been a weak 2♡ opening on the right. It would be wrong to pass with a strong hand (unless you are very strong in hearts). The bidding could end at 2♡.

In reply to the double of 2◊ :

2♡ = artificial negative, 0-7 points. Further bidding is natural. Jump rebids by opener are very strong but are not forcing. **All others** = 8+ points and forcing to game, with 3NT showing any 4-3-3-3 with 12-14 points.

How to use your 2♣ opening if you are using the other twos as multis

The strong options in the multi-2◊ opening should be very closely defined. As a result, most of your very strong hands will still start with a 2♣ opening. Benjamin Twos work well because they provide two strong opening bids to distinguish the game force hands from those just below that strength. It is possible to retain much of this benefit even if opening 2♣ on all or almost all the strong hands.

Use the 2♣ opening to show a game-going hand (either 23+ HCP or 10+ tricks) or a hand of 8½-9 playing tricks with a 6+ suit, usually a one-suiter hand with 19+ points. You will need to dovetail the content of the 2♣ opening with the strong options for the multi-2◊. There is no point in having an overlap. For example, if the multi-2◊ includes a long strong minor with 9-10 playing tricks, then 2♣ might include the minor one-suiters just below this strength, perhaps 8-8½ playing tricks, 19+ points or the equivalent.

Responses to 2♣

2◊ = Artificial negative, 0-7 points.

Others = natural, game forcing, 8+ points. Suit responses are 5+ suits in principle.

2NT = natural positive reply, balanced hand.

7 points is borderline. With 7 HCP made up of an ace and a king, give a positive reply. Do the same with 7 HCP including a suit headed by the A-Q. These are 1½ quick tricks which make slam a fair bet opposite a game force.

After a positive reply, if opener bids game sooner or later, this shows the 8½-9 trick hand and slam bidding is responder's responsibility.

After 2♣ : 2◊, opener's rebids are :

2♡ = *artificial*, 23+ HCP or 10+ playing tricks

2♠ = Natural game force, 5+ spades

2NT = 21-22, balanced. Continue as though the opening bid had been a 21-22 2NT.

3♣ / 3◊ / 3♡ / 3♠ = 8½-9 playing tricks

4♣ / 4◊ / 4♡ / 4♠ = 9½-10 playing tricks

3NT = Long, solid minor, 9 playing tricks, stoppers in at least two other suits

Thus opener's two-level suit rebids are stronger than the three-level and four-level one-suiter rebids.

After 2♣ : 2◊, 2♡

2♠ = artificial, second negative, 0-4 points

Other replies are natural with 5-7 points.

After 2♣ : 2◊, 2♡ : 2♠, opener's rebids are:

2NT = 23-24 balanced. Not forcing. Continue as though the opening had been a 23-24 2NT.

3NT = 25-28 points, balanced

4NT = 29-30 points, balanced

5NT = 31-32 points, balanced

Suit bids = natural and forcing to game. Open 2♣ + rebid 2♡ + suit rebid = game force.

EXERCISES FOR THE MULTI 2◇ (weak two in either major, 23-24 balanced or 9-10 tricks in a minor)

A. Partner has opened 2◇. What is your response with each of these hands?

1. ♠ A 7 3	2. ♠ K Q 7 6 2	3. ♠ 3	4. ♠ A J 7	5. ♠ 8
♡ 8 2	♡ - - -	♡ Q 9 3	♡ 9 2	♡ 7 2
◇ K Q 7 5 3 2	◇ K Q	◇ A K 9 4 3	◇ A Q J 4	◇ Q J 9 8 5 3 2
♣ 7 6	♣ A K J 8 4 2	♣ K Q 4 2	♣ K Q 9 2	♣ J 9 4

B. The bidding has started 2◇ : 2NT. What is opener's rebid with these hands?

1. ♠ 4 3	2. ♠ 6 2	3. ♠ A K 8 7 4 2	4. ♠ A K Q 8 7 2	5. ♠ K Q J 10 4 2
♡ K Q 10 7 6 3	♡ K J 10 4 3 2	♡ 9 6 4	♡ 6 4	♡ 7
◇ J 6 4	◇ 8 4	◇ 8	◇ 9 2	◇ K 5 3
♣ 6 2	♣ K 8 4	♣ Q J 2	♣ 7 4 2	♣ 7 4 2

C. RHO has opened 2◇, multi. What action would you take with these hands?

1. ♠ A Q 8 3	2. ♠ J 8 5	3. ♠ A 6	4. ♠ A 5	5. ♠ K 3 2
♡ K 9	♡ K Q 2	♡ K Q J 9 7	♡ K Q J 7 4 3	♡ 8
◇ Q J 8	◇ A K 7	◇ 7 4	◇ A K	◇ Q J 9 8 6 3
♣ A J 4 2	♣ A K 3 2	♣ K 10 4 3	♣ 8 4 2	♣ A Q 7

COMPETITIVE BIDDING : How should the following hands be bid? West is the dealer each time and neither side is vulnerable.

SET 39— WEST	SET 39 — NORTH	SET 39 — EAST	SET 39 — SOUTH
1. ♠ J 8	1. ♠ A K 10 7 5 2	1. ♠ 9 4	1. ♠ Q 6 3
♡ J 7 5 3	♡ 10 6	♡ K Q 8 2	♡ A 9 4
◇ K J 10	◇ 9 4	◇ Q 7 6 5	◇ A 8 3 2
♣ K J 3 2	♣ 8 7 6	♣ Q 10 4	♣ A 9 5
2. ♠ K 7	2. ♠ A J 6 5 4	2. ♠ 9 8	2. ♠ Q 10 3 2
♡ A 10 9 8 5 3	♡ 6 4	♡ K Q J 2	♡ 7
◇ Q 7 6 5	◇ J 10	◇ 2	◇ A K 9 8 4 3
♣ 2	♣ Q 9 8 6	♣ A 10 7 5 4 3	♣ K J
3. ♠ 5 2	3. ♠ Q 7 6 4 3	3. ♠ A 8	3. ♠ K J 10 9
♡ Q J 10 7 3 2	♡ A 8 5	♡ K 6 4	♡ 9
◇ 8 3	◇ Q 10 6	◇ 9 7 5 4	◇ A K J 2
♣ A 3 2	♣ Q 9	♣ J 8 7 4	♣ K 10 6 5
4. ♠ A Q 10 7 6 2	4. ♠ 9 8	4. ♠ K 5 3	4. ♠ J 4
♡ 10 6 5	♡ A 9 8 7 4 3	♡ J	♡ K Q 2
◇ K 2	◇ J 9	◇ A Q 10 5 4	◇ 8 7 6 3
♣ 8 3	♣ J 10 6	♣ K 9 4 2	♣ A Q 7 5
5. ♠ A Q 6 3 2	5. ♠ 4	5. ♠ K 8 5	5. ♠ J 10 9 7
♡ 7 2	♡ K Q J 9 8 3	♡ A 6 4	♡ 10 5
◇ 7 2	◇ J 8 5 3	◇ A K 10 4	◇ Q 9 6
♣ K 8 6 2	♣ 9 3	♣ Q J 7	♣ A 10 5 4
6. ♠ 8 6 4	6. ♠ 9 2	6. ♠ K J 7 3	6. ♠ A Q 10 5
♡ A J 8 7 6 3	♡ K Q 10 5 2	♡ 9	♡ 4
◇ Q J 10	◇ A 9 5	◇ 8 7 4	◇ K 6 3 2
♣ 3	♣ 10 7 4	♣ K 8 6 5 2	♣ A Q J 9

PLAY HANDS ON THE MULTI-2◇ OPENING
(These hands can be made up by using pages 160-167)

Hand 89: Responding to a multi-2◇ — Action by fourth player — Playing for penalties

Dealer North : E-W vulnerable

NORTH
♠ 8 6 4
♡ A J 8 7 6 3
◇ Q J 10
♣ 3

WEST	NORTH	EAST	SOUTH
	2◇	Pass	2♡
Dble	Pass	Pass	Pass

WEST
♠ A Q 10 5
♡ 4
◇ K 6 3 2
♣ A Q J 9

EAST
♠ 9 2
♡ K Q 10 5 2
◇ A 9 5
♣ 10 7 4

SOUTH
♠ K J 7 3
♡ 9
◇ 8 7 4
♣ K 8 6 5 2

Bidding : South bids 2♡ ('pass-or-correct') and West doubles for takeout. (If West's majors were reversed, West would pass. With a weak two in spades, North would correct 2♡ to 2♠ and West could double that for takeout.) North's pass confirms the weak two in hearts and East's pass confirms that North-South are in deep trouble. Leave the double in when you are strong in trumps, particularly sitting over the long suit, and your side has at least half the HCP. It is true that passing could miss a game (here East-West make 3NT easily) but game may not be on and perhaps you can do even better by defending.

Lead : 2 of diamonds. Second choice, the 4 of hearts.

Recommended play : East wins with the ace and shifts to the 9 of spades, jack from South and queen from West who shifts to the 4 of hearts. If declarer ducks this, East wins with the 10 and returns the 2 of spades, low from dummy, 10 from West who cashes the ace of spades on which East discards the 9 of diamonds (top from a remaining doubleton). Next comes the king of diamonds and the ◇3, ruffed by East who switches to clubs. The defense takes three spades, two diamonds and a diamond ruff, three hearts and one club. That leaves North five down, +1100 to East-West, adequate compensation for the missed 3NT.

Notes : (1) South is better off to rise on the ♡A and lead a second diamond. Now East has no convenient entry to lead a second spade. West wins and exits with a diamond but now North-South escape for 'only' –800.
(2) South would like to run from 2♡ doubled but there is nowhere to go. If South does attempt a rescue, East-West double everything thereafter for penalties.
(3) On an initial trump lead, ducked in dummy, East wins, shifts to a spade and the play proceeds as before.

Hand 90 : Competing against the multi — Card-reading to avoid a fatal mistake

Dealer East : Both vulnerable

NORTH
♠ 9 3
♡ A K Q J 9 8
◇ A 3
♣ A 8 2

WEST	NORTH	EAST	SOUTH
		2◇	Pass
2♡	4♡	All pass	

WEST
♠ ---
♡ 6 5 2
◇ Q J 9 8 5 2
♣ K J 9 7

EAST
♠ K Q J 10 6 4
♡ 3
◇ 7 6 4
♣ Q 10 4

SOUTH
♠ A 8 7 5 2
♡ 10 7 4
◇ K 10
♣ 6 5 3

Bidding : West fears the worst upon hearing 2◇. If someone doubles after East corrects to spades., it is not easy to judge whether to play there or run. With a good 5-5, you might start an S.O.S. redouble sequence. As it happens, 3◇ plays better than 2♠ but this need not be so. North knows that East's suit is spades. Rather than waste time and give the opponents more space, North hopes for two tricks from partner and jumps straight to 4♡. As East is likely to have the weak two in spades and West has given a weak reply, it is not too much to expect partner to produce two tricks. Any decent partner would.

Lead : King of spades. All your leads should be this easy.

Recommended play : What a good fellow South is. There are the two tricks needed. Careful, do not squander one of those tricks. Declarer should play low in dummy and low again on the next spade. The third spade is ruffed by North who draws trumps, crosses to the ◇K and discards a loser on the ♠A.

Notes : (1) It is not easy to avoid the instinctive play of the ♠A at trick 1. You need to be conscious that East has a weak two in spades and therefore six spades. Add the five in dummy and your two and that leaves West with a void. If you play the ♠A, West ruffs and your ten easy tricks have been telescoped into nine. If you fell for this trap, they may soon be calling you 'the magician' : you make tricks disappear.
(2) It is not easy for North-South to find the highest scoring spot of 3NT.
(3) If declarer does play the ♠A at trick 1 and West ruffs, West should return a trump or the ◇Q. A club switch works but on other layouts, it might help declarer take an extra finesse with dummy very short of entries.

Hand 91 : Inviting game — High level takeout double — Opening lead   Defensive technique

Dealer South : Nil vulnerable

WEST	NORTH	EAST	SOUTH
			2◊
Pass	2♠	Pass	4♡
Pass	Pass	Dble	Pass
4♠	Pass	Pass	Pass

```
                NORTH
                ♠ 9 8
                ♡ K Q J 2
                ◊ 2
                ♣ A 10 7 5 4 3
WEST                        EAST
♠ A J 6 5 4                 ♠ Q 10 3 2
♡ 6 4                       ♡ 7
◊ Q 10                      ◊ A K 9 8 4 3
♣ Q 9 8 6                   ♣ K 2
                SOUTH
                ♠ K 7
                ♡ A 10 9 8 5 3
                ◊ J 7 6 5
                ♣ J
```

Bidding : North's 2♠ is to play opposite a weak two in spades and invites game opposite a weak two in hearts. South has a maximum weak 2♡ and so bids 4♡ (3♡ would be a minimum). East is awkwardly placed over 2♠. Double would be takeout of spades and East is happy to defend a spade contract. East's double of 4♡ is logically for takeout since South has shown six hearts and North's 2♠ = a strong fit for hearts. With no attractive suit, West may leave the double in. Here 4♠ is sensible.

Lead : Ace of clubs.

Recommended play : North continues with the *ten* of clubs at trick 2 and South ruffs. Recognising the 10 as a suit preference for hearts, South leads a low heart (the 9 is a good card, saying you do not want hearts returned). North overtakes with the jack and leads a third club. Dummy ruffs high, but South overruffs. One down after an exceptionally fine defense.

Notes : (1) Even if East-West fail, they have done well as 4♡ is unbeatable. The defense can take one diamond and two spades but South can comfortably set up the club suit, using dummy's trumps as entries.
(2) If North does not find the winning lead, North would be better off sacrificing in 5♡. Say North leads the king of hearts. The best South can do is overtake and switch to the ♣J. North takes the ace and gives South a club ruff but that is the end of the North-South defense. On the ◊2 lead, West should win in hand and play as safely as possible for ten tricks via ♠A and another spade. West should recognise that 4♠ is an excellent contract for East-West and making an overtrick is less important than ensuring the contract.
(3) The ♣A lead is not far-fetched if North elects to defend. South is unlikely to have more than one defensive trick. Therefore, ruffs are needed to defeat the contract. After leading the ♣A North can decide whether to continue clubs or try for a diamond ruff.

Hand 92 : Delayed competitive action — Playing for penalties

Dealer West : N-S vulnerable

WEST	NORTH	EAST	SOUTH
Pass	2◊	Pass	2♡
Pass	Pass	Dble	Pass
2NT	Pass	3♣	Dble
Pass	Pass	Pass	

```
                NORTH
                ♠ 7 5 3
                ♡ A K Q 9 5 3
                ◊ 9 8 4
                ♣ 2
WEST                        EAST
♠ Q 4                       ♠ K 9 8 6
♡ J 8 4 2                   ♡ 7 6
◊ 7 6 5                     ◊ K Q J
♣ K 8 5 3                   ♣ A 9 7 4
                SOUTH
                ♠ A J 10 2
                ♡ 10
                ◊ A 10 3 2
                ♣ Q J 10 6
```

Bidding : East is too weak to take action at once over 2◊ and South is too weak to do more than 2♡. After North passes to confirm a weak two in hearts, most tournament players would compete with a takeout double. This shows modest values because of East's failure to double 2◊ (to show 16+ points). South waits in ambush and West bids 2NT Lebensohl. 3♣ at once by West would show a maximum passed hand as East can have up to 15 HCP. When East bids 3♣ as required, South lowers the boom.

Lead : 10 of hearts. Try not to smile as you see dummy.

Recommended play : North should overtake and cash a second heart. The defense will come to one spade, two hearts, one diamond and two clubs for two down, +300.

Notes : (1) Note how Lebensohl can be used even in these belated auctions. Lebensohl has a fringe benefit when advancer intends to pass 3♣. It follows the principle 'If you are in deep trouble, let partner be declarer!'
(2) East should not be deflected from competing in future in auctions such as these just because of an occasional rotten result. To be a successful pairs player, you have to compete, you have to be pushy. With that kind of approach, you are bound to stumble and hurt yourself from time to time.

CHAPTER 24

OTHER MULTI-TWO OPENINGS

2♥/2♠/2NT openings when using a Multi-2◇

If the multi-2◇ includes the weak twos in the majors, the question arises 'What do the 2♥ and 2♠ openings now mean?', and if 2◇ also includes the balanced 21-22 hand, what does 2NT now mean?

Some use 2♥ and 2♠ to show strong natural openings just short of game-force values. Most prefer to use the freed bids to show weak two-suiter hand types. This is a common approach :

2♥ = Hearts and a minor suit
2♠ = Spades and another suit
2NT = Both minors

The pattern should be 5-5 at least and the strength should be about 6-10 HCP, below opening values. The above combination covers all two-suiters.

Over 2♥ or 2♠, responder may pass or raise the major pre-emptively. With no tolerance for the major, bid 3♣ with a weak hand. Opener passes with clubs or bids the second suit held. A suit bid other than 3♣ is strong and forcing. With other strong hands, you can use the 2NT relay. Opener then bids the second suit. With a maximum 6-5, opener shows the 6-card suit (rebid the major or bid the second suit at the four-level).

The RCO 2♥, 2♠ and 2NT openings

These show weak 2-suiters, 6-10 HCP and at least a 5-5 pattern. RCO stands for Rank-Colour-Odd.

2♥ = Rank. Same rank. Major suits or minors. For example, open 2♥ with :

♠ K Q 10 4 2	_or_	♠ 8 3
♥ Q J 9 6 4		♥ 3
◇ 9 2		◇ K 10 8 7 4
♣ 5		♣ A J 10 6 3

2♠ = Colour. Same colour. Red suits or blacks. For example, open 2♠ with :

♠ A Q J 7 5	_or_	♠ 8 3
♥ 6		♥ Q 9 7 4 3 2
◇ 9 4		◇ K J 7 6 3
♣ J 10 7 5 2		♣ - - -

2NT = Odd. Two suits of different colour and different rank, so spades + diamonds _or_ hearts + clubs. Memory guide : NT = Non-Touching. For example, open 2NT with :

♠ A 10 7 6 2	_or_	♠ 8
♥ 5		♥ Q J 10 7 4
◇ K J 10 7 4		◇ 4
♣ 6 3		♣ K J 10 9 7 2

A useful memory guide for the RCO order is **Responder Can Operate**. At adverse vulnerability, it is prudent to be maximum or have a 6-5.

The CRASH Convention

CRASH is similar to RCO Twos except that 2♥ is colour (C), 2♠ is rank (RA) and the SH for opening 2NT is the abbreviation for _shape_, referring to the pointed suits, spades-diamonds, or the rounded suits, hearts-clubs. There is little difference between the methods. RCOs have a slight advantage in opening 2♥ with both majors, while with CRASH, the opening bid with both majors is 2♠. Holding both majors gives you a competitive edge. Silly to give this advantage away, isn't it? Using RCO, you can often stop at the two-level after a 2♥ opening. Playing CRASH, you usually have to reach the three-level to locate your major suit fit. This tilts the scale in favor of RCO Twos.

Responding to RCO 2♥ or 2♠ with a weak hand

Pass = you know which suits partner has and prefer the suit partner has bid. If you have five cards in one possible combination and eight in the other, the odds are strong that partner has the two-suiter where you hold five cards. If you are 4-9 in the combinations, it is very, very likely that partner has the combination opposite your 4.

Otherwise bid a suit where you have 3+ cards. Usually choose your cheapest option. Any suit bid is P/C, 'pass-or-correct'.

With a 4+ fit with a suit in each combination, you may wish to pre-empt. Jump replies to 3♠, 4♣ or 4◇ are pre-emptive and are P/C, 'pass-or-correct'. Any jump to game in a suit is also P/C. To play in your own suit, use the 2NT enquiry and bid game in your suit after opener's reply.

Responding to 2♥ or 2♠ with a strong hand

With enough to invite game or force to game, bid 2NT, asking for opener's suits and strength. Opener bids the cheaper suit if minimum and the higher suit if maximum. A maximum creates a game-force.

After 2♥ : 2NT relay, opener rebids :
3♣ = minors and minimum
3◇ = minors and maximum
3♥ = majors and minimum
3♠ = majors and maximum

After 2♠ : 2NT relay, opener rebids :
3♣ = black suits and minimum
3◇ = red suits and minimum
3♥ = red suits and maximum
3♠ = black suits and maximum

Replies at the 4-level show a maximum with 6+ cards in the suit bid.

Responding to 2NT with a weak hand

Did a suit, pass-or-correct, but 3♣ is not available as that is the strong relay. If you figure partner has hearts and clubs and you prefer clubs, you cannot escape below 4♣ if you bid. With a very weak hand, it may be better to pass 2NT and if they double 2NT, you can later escape to 3♣. Pass 2NT also if weak with very long diamonds and you figure opener has hearts and clubs. Maybe you can escape into your diamonds later.

Responding to 2NT with a strong hand

Over 2NT the strong relay is 3♣, again asking for opener's suits and range. Opener rebids :

3♦ = diamonds + spades and minimum
3♥ = hearts + clubs and minimum
3♠ = diamonds + spades and maximum
3NT = hearts + clubs and maximum

Replies at the four-level show a 6-5 pattern with six cards in the suit bid and a maximum.

Responder's action after opener's reply to the relay (2NT over 2♥/2♠ or 3♣ over 2NT)

After a minimum reply, responder can pass or bid opener's other suit as a signoff. Other bids below game are forcing. Game bids are to play.

After a maximum reply, game bids are to play and suit bids below game are all forcing.

Responder often wants to set a trump suit early in order to use RKCB. This can be achieved by responder bidding 4♣ or 4♦ after opener's reply to the relay. 4♣ or 4♦ sets the minor suit bid if that is one of opener's suits. If not, 4♣/4♦ sets opener's major suit. In the case of both majors with opener, 4♣ sets hearts and 4♦ sets spades. For example :

WEST	EAST	Over 3♣/3♦, 4♣/4♦ sets the
2♥	2NT	minor suit bid. Over 3♥/3♠, 4♣
?		sets hearts and 4♦ sets spades.

If responder wants to sign off over 3♣, responder can pass or convert to 3♦.

WEST	EAST	Over 3♣/3♠, 4♣ sets clubs and
2♠	2NT	4♦ sets spades. Over 3♦/3♥, 4♣
?		sets hearts, 4♦ sets diamonds.

If responder wants to sign off after a minimum reply, responder can do so at the three-level.

WEST	EAST	Over 3♦/3♠, 4♣ sets spades
2NT	3♣	and 4♦ sets diamonds. Over 3♥,
?		4♦ sets hearts, 4NT sets clubs.

4♣ is needed as a signoff over 3♥ and so 4NT is necessary to set clubs. Over 3NT (maximum with hearts and clubs), 4♣ sets clubs, 4♦ sets hearts.

Action if they bid over your RCO opening

1. They double 2♥ or 2♠

Pass = pass-or-correct : 'If this is one of your suits, this is where I wish to play.'
Suit bids = pass-or-correct.
2NT = Strong relay as usual.

Redouble = 'Please make the cheapest bid and pass my next bid.' This allows responder to escape into a long suit with no fit for either of opener's suits.

If the double is passed back to opener, pass if holding the suit doubled. If not, opener can show extra shape : Redouble = extra length in the distant suit. Bidding the cheaper suit shows equal length or longer in the cheaper suit. Other bids show the fragment with a 5-5-3-0. For example :

W	N	E	S	
				Rdble = longer diamonds
2♥	Dble	No	No	2♠ = 3-0-5-5 pattern
?				3♣ = equal or clubs longer

2. They double your 2NT opening

Suit bids are still pass-or-correct except for 3♣ which is still the strong relay. Responder's pass of 2NT doubled = a preference for clubs over hearts. 3♣ is not available as a rescue since 3♣ is the artificial relay. Responder's redouble asks opener to bid 3♣ and pass responder's next bid.

If the double is passed back to opener, opener redoubles to show extra length in the distant suit and bids the cheaper suit with equal suits or with greater length in the cheaper suit.

3. They bid a suit over your RCO opening

Double = takeout at the two-level or three-level and shows game-inviting values or better. It is possible to play the double for penalties but experience has shown that using the double for takeout is more effective. Opener can of course leave the double in with 5+ cards in the suit bid. Doubles at the four-level or higher are penalties.

Suit bids = pass-or-correct, but showing decent strength. Suits bids below game show game-inviting values and if maximum, opener should bid game.

Bidding the enemy suit = force to game and asks opener to bid the cheaper suit held. If opener has their suit, bid the other suit held or 3NT.

Defending against RCO Twos

Use the same basic defensive approach as against the multi-2♦ (see Chapter 23) :

Double = 16+ points, any shape except for the 2NT and 3NT bids
2NT = 19-21 balanced
3NT = 22-24 balanced
Suit bids = natural, good suit but below 16 HCP

The negative reply to a double of 2♠ or 2NT is 3♣. If strong in the suit doubled, you may leave the double in. If you have no clearcut action, it is often best to pass and wait for the suits to be clarified before entering the fray. It is no fun to come into the bidding and land in one of opener's 5-card suits.

Pass and later double at the two-level or three-level is takeout but less than 16 HCP.

In fourth position treat any weak action by RHO as their opening bid. If the bidding starts, multi on your left : Pass : Pass to you, double = 12+ HCP.

EXERCISES FOR RCO TWOS

A. Partner has opened 2♠, RCO. What action should you take as responder with neither side vulnerable?

1. ♠ 9 7	2. ♠ K 7 6 4 2	3. ♠ J 9 8 4 2	4. ♠ J 9 7 2	5. ♠ 8 6 2
♡ A 8 2	♡ 6	♡ K 9 6 3	♡ 2	♡ A 9 8 2
◊ Q 7 5 3	◊ A 8 4 3	◊ A 4 3	◊ Q J 4 3 2	◊ K Q 8 5 2
♣ K 7 6 3	♣ 9 8 4	♣ 2	♣ K Q 2	♣ 4

B. You opened 2NT (RCO) and partner has responded 3♣, relay. What is your rebid with these hands?

1. ♠ A J 9 8 4	2. ♠ K J 10 7 4	3. ♠ 2	4. ♠ 4	5. ♠ 3
♡ 6	♡ 7 2	♡ K Q J 4 2	♡ A Q J 7 3	♡ A K 7 3 2
◊ Q J 7 5 2	◊ K Q J 8 3	◊ 9 5	◊ 10 8	◊ 5
♣ 9 3	♣ 9	♣ J 10 8 7 4	♣ Q J 10 9 2	♣ Q J 10 7 4 2

C. RHO has opened 2♡ RCO (majors or minors). What action would you take with neither side vulnerable?

1. ♠ A J 4 3 2	2. ♠ 7 5	3. ♠ K J 4 2	4. ♠ A 9 2	5. ♠ A K 8 3
♡ K 3	♡ 6	♡ Q J 6 4	♡ 6	♡ Q 7 4 3
◊ K 6 4 2	◊ A 9 8 4	◊ A J 8	◊ A K Q 2	◊ 8
♣ 6 2	♣ A K J 8 4 2	♣ A K	♣ A J 7 4 2	♣ A J 3 2

COMPETITIVE BIDDING : How should the following hands be bid? West is the dealer each time and neither side is vulnerable. Both sides are playing R.C.O. two-suited openings.

SET 40 — WEST	SET 40 — NORTH	SET 40 — EAST	SET 40 — SOUTH
1. ♠ A J 8	1. ♠ K 10 7 5 3	1. ♠ 4	1. ♠ Q 9 6 2
♡ J 7 5 3	♡ 10 6 4 2	♡ Q 8	♡ A K 9
◊ K 10	◊ 9 4	◊ Q J 7 6 5	◊ A 8 3 2
♣ J 9 3 2	♣ A 5	♣ K Q 10 8 4	♣ 7 6
2. ♠ Q 7	2. ♠ K J 6 5 4	2. ♠ A 9 8	2. ♠ 10 3 2
♡ A 10 9 8	♡ 6 3	♡ K Q J 2	♡ 7 5 4
◊ K 7 6 5	◊ 10	◊ Q J 9 4	◊ A 8 3 2
♣ 7 4 2	♣ K Q 10 8 6	♣ A J	♣ 9 5 3
3. ♠ 6	3. ♠ K 9 5 4 3	3. ♠ A Q 8 7 2	3. ♠ J 10
♡ 7	♡ A Q 10	♡ J 4	♡ K 9 8 6 5 3 2
◊ A Q 10 9 5	◊ 6 2	◊ J 8 7 4 3	◊ K
♣ Q 10 9 6 4 2	♣ A 7 3	♣ J	♣ K 8 5
4. ♠ 9 7 2	4. ♠ ---	4. ♠ A K 4	4. ♠ Q J 10 8 6 5 3
♡ J 10 9 6 5	♡ 4 3	♡ A 7	♡ K Q 8 2
◊ K 2	◊ Q 10 9 5 3	◊ A 8 6 4	◊ J 7
♣ A 8 3	♣ K J 7 6 5 2	♣ Q 10 9 4	♣ ---
5. ♠ A J 10 9 5	5. ♠ K Q	5. ♠ 8 3	5. ♠ 7 6 4 2
♡ 7	♡ Q 9 8 5 3	♡ K J	♡ A 10 6 4 2
◊ Q J 9 8 3 2	◊ 7 6	◊ K 10 5 4	◊ A
♣ 6	♣ A Q J 8	♣ K 10 9 5 4	♣ 7 3 2
6. ♠ 7 2	6. ♠ Q J 10 6 5	6. ♠ A K 8	6. ♠ 9 4 3
♡ K 8 3 2	♡ 9	♡ A Q J 5 4	♡ 10 7 6
◊ K 9 6 5	◊ Q J 10 8 4 3	◊ 7	◊ A 2
♣ A 9 4	♣ 5	♣ K Q 8 3	♣ J 10 7 6 2

PLAY HANDS ON RCO TWOS

(These hands can be made up by using pages 160-167)

Hand 93 : Competitive bidding — Card reading

Dealer North : Both vulnerable

NORTH
- ♠ A J 8
- ♡ J 7 5 3
- ◇ K 7
- ♣ J 8 3 2

WEST
- ♠ Q 9 6 2
- ♡ A K 9
- ◇ A 8 3 2
- ♣ 7 6

EAST
- ♠ K 10 7 5 3
- ♡ 10 6 4 2
- ◇ 9 4
- ♣ A 5

SOUTH
- ♠ 4
- ♡ Q 8
- ◇ Q J 10 6 5
- ♣ K Q 10 9 4

WEST	NORTH	EAST	SOUTH
	Pass	Pass	2♡
Pass	3♣	Pass	Pass
Dble	Pass	3♠	All pass

Bidding : South's 2♡ = majors or minors. RCOs are not for the fainthearted. West is too weak for immediate action. North bids 3♣, the desired contract opposite the minors and prepared to reach 3♡ opposite the majors. If weaker, North might bid 2♠, false preference. South's pass confirms the minors and West should compete even though vulnerable. Treat the position as though the bidding had started 3♣ : Pass : Pass. If you would re-open then, you should re-open now. East is content with 3♠ since West's pass over 2♡ showed 15 points or less.

Lead : King of clubs.

Recommended play : East wins with the ace of clubs and leads a spade to the queen. North wins and returns a club, won by South who shifts to a diamond. Declarer takes the ace and leads a spade to the 10. The last trump is drawn and declarer loses one trick in each suit.

Notes : (1) Note that North-South would make 3♣ if left there. You will not always be right to compete on the West cards but passing is likely to be the losing action more often than not. North is a passed hand and South has made a weak opening. As partner is bound to have some values, West's double is not so heroic.
(2) If South leads the ◇Q, the defense must shift to clubs urgently lest declarer set up the ♡10 for a club pitch
(3) As South is 5-5 in the minors, spades are likely to be 3-1 with South having the singleton. There is slight extra confirmation from the opening lead. If South had two spades and one heart, South might have led the singleton heart. The failure to lead a heart carries a suggestion that South has one spade, two hearts.

Hand 94 : Pre-emptive response — Competitive decisions

Dealer East : Nil vulnerable

NORTH
- ♠ J 10
- ♡ K 9 8 6 5 3 2
- ◇ K
- ♣ K 8 5

WEST
- ♠ A Q 8 7 2
- ♡ J 4
- ◇ J 10 7 4 3
- ♣ J

EAST
- ♠ 6
- ♡ 7
- ◇ A Q 10 9 5
- ♣ Q 10 9 6 4 2

SOUTH
- ♠ K 9 5 4 3
- ♡ A Q 10
- ◇ 6 2
- ♣ A 7 3

WEST	NORTH	EAST	SOUTH
		2♡	Pass
4♠	Pass	5♣	Pass
5◇	Pass	Pass	Pass

Bidding : East's 2♡ = majors or minors. It is dangerous for South to bid in the direct position on these modest values. West can tell there is a ten-card fit in spades or diamonds and so jumps to 4♠ pre-emptively. On a good day 4♠ may make and if East-West have the majors, North-South have a mighty club fit. East's 5♣ says, 'I have the minors' and West corrects to 5◇. West expects 5◇ to fail but knows it should be a good sacrifice against their heart contract.

Lead : 6 of hearts. East has both minors and West has shown good spades. That leaves only hearts.

Recommended play : South takes the ace and might switch to a spade (in case West has the ♡K and North the ♠A). West wins and leads the jack of clubs. North should allow this to go to South, otherwise South will be exposed to a ruffing finesse later. West later ruffs a club, leads a diamond (North's singleton king is a delight), draws trumps and ruffs out the clubs. Making 11 tricks.

Notes : (1) North-South do very well in hearts but how should they enter the auction? To bid at once over 2♡ on the South hand is very risky. Over 4♠, 5♡ by North could be one of the great debacles of all time if East does have the majors. South might well double 5♣ and now North can bid 5♡ because East has the minors, West's 4♠ implies weak hearts and South's double shows some values.
(2) 4♡ is unbeatable and the defense has to be careful defending 5♡. If East leads the spade singleton and West cashes two spades, a third spade will allow 5♡ to make. East should signal violently for a diamond shift (in case North has K-x in diamonds) or, at teams, ruff the second spade and cash the ◇A.

Hand 95 : Competitive bidding — Slam play technique

Dealer South : N-S vulnerable

NORTH
- ♠ A K 8
- ♡ A Q J 10 5
- ♢ 7
- ♣ K Q 8 3

WEST
- ♠ Q J 10 6 5
- ♡ 9
- ♢ A J 10 8 4 3
- ♣ 5

EAST
- ♠ 9 4 3
- ♡ 7 6 4
- ♢ Q 2
- ♣ J 10 7 6 2

SOUTH
- ♠ 7 2
- ♡ K 8 3 2
- ♢ K 9 6 5
- ♣ A 9 4

WEST	NORTH	EAST	SOUTH
			Pass
2NT	Dble	Pass	Pass
3♢	Dble	3♠	4♡
Pass	4NT	Pass	5♡
Pass	6♡	All pass	

Bidding : West's 2NT = spades-diamonds *OR* hearts-clubs. North's double shows a very strong hand. There is no urgency for East to bid here and the same applies to South. West's 3♢ = spades-diamonds with diamonds longer or equal length. (With spades longer, use redouble to show extra length in the further suit. East bids 3♣ and West's 3♢ then = 6+ spades and 5 diamonds.) North's double of 3♢ = takeout and East corrects to 3♠. South ventures 4♡ and that spurs North on to slam. As South should have at most two spades, North needs only two other losers covered.

Lead : Queen of spades. Leading the singleton club or the ♢A are both reasonable gambles.

Recommended play : Win with the ♠A and draw two rounds of trumps with ♡A, ♡Q. When West shows out, leave the last trump out and lead dummy's singleton diamond. When East plays low, West is sure to have the ace, so duck the diamond to West. Win West's exit, cash ♠K and ruff the spade loser in hand. Continue with ♣A, ♣K, ♣Q (East who has the last trump is known to have club length) and ruff dummy's fourth club. Ruff a diamond high and draw the last trump.

Notes : (1) It would be easy enough for North-South not to reach this good slam.
(2) If declarer draws three rounds of trumps early, declarer will not be able to ruff both a spade and a club.
(3) At the vulnerability, North-South should bid game or slam rather than take the penalties in 3♠ doubled.
(4) East-West should not sacrifice over 6♡ since they do not have a great trump fit, perhaps 6♡ will fail and minus-800 will be a bad board anyway, as many pairs will not reach this slam.

Hand 96 : Competitive bidding — Opening lead inferences from the auction

Dealer West : E-W vulnerable

NORTH
- ♠ Q 7
- ♡ A 10 9 8
- ♢ K 7 6
- ♣ 7 4 3 2

WEST
- ♠ K J 10 6 5
- ♡ 6 4 3
- ♢ - - -
- ♣ K Q 10 8 6

EAST
- ♠ 8 4 2
- ♡ 7 5
- ♢ 10 8 5 4 3 2
- ♣ A 5

SOUTH
- ♠ A 9 3
- ♡ K Q J 2
- ♢ A Q J 9
- ♣ J 9

WEST	NORTH	EAST	SOUTH
2♠	Pass	Pass!	Dble
Pass	2NT	Pass	3♣
Pass	3♡	Pass	4♡
Pass	Pass	Pass	

Bidding : 2♠ = red suits *OR* black suits. It takes some courage to pass on the East cards but with eight red cards and five black cards, the odds are strong that West has the black suits. With a weak hand, East does not want to be at the three-level with such skimpy support. Playing RCOs can be a test of courage.

South doubles and West's pass confirms the black suits. North's 2NT shows values (the negative reply to a double of 2♠ or 2NT is 3♣). South bids 3♣ Stayman, planning to end in 3NT or 4♡.

Lead : 2 of diamonds. The reasons follow later.

Recommended play : West ruffs the lead, plays a low club to East's ace and receives another diamond ruff. The ♣K is cashed and declarer is one down.

Notes : (1) As North-South have used a Stayman sequence it is very likely that they have a 4-4 fit in hearts. If so, West must have three hearts and therefore West's shape will be 5-3-0-5. Expecting West to ruff the first diamond, East leads the *two* of diamonds as a suit preference signal for a club return in case that is not obvious after dummy appears.
(2) 2♠ East-West would make comfortably, but 3♠ is touch and go.
(3) If East leads a spade, declarer should place West with the ♠K and go up with the ♠A, draw trumps and make 10 tricks. The risk of a diamond ruff is low but the chances are tiny that East is leading from the ♠K.
(4) If East leads the ♣A, West needs to signal that a diamond switch is needed. On a discouraging signal, East might simply switch to a spade. The ♣Q on the ace might be enough to jolt East into the right action.

APPENDIX
DEFENDING AGAINST THEIR SYSTEMS

It is not the province of this book to cover every convention or everything that you may encounter in your tournaments. For more details on conventions, how to defend against them and how to counter their defenses, it is worth consulting *Bridge Conventions, Defenses and Countermeasures*.

There are a number of systems and conventions which you are likely to meet quite often. It is important that you are ready and prepared to deal with them.

DEFENSE AGAINST STRONG 1♣ OPENINGS

The most common of these is Precision which enjoyed considerable popularity during the '70s but is now somewhat on the wane. The basic Precision approach is :

1♣ = 16+ points, any shape
1♡/1♠ = 11-15 points, 5+ major
2♣ = 11-15 points, 5+ clubs
1NT = 13-15 balanced
1◊ = 11-15, all opening hands not covered by the above opening bids.

There are many strong 1♣ systems. One modern version is Moscito which resembles Precision but the common openings show 10-14 points rather than 11-15 and 4-card major suit openings are permitted. The Moscito net-work :

1♣ = 15+ points, any shape
1♡/1♠ = 10-14 points, 4+ major. The bid of one major denies the other major.
1NT = 10-14, both majors
2♣ = 10-14 points, 5+ clubs
1◊ = 10-14, no 4-card major

The Achilles heel of the strong 1♣ systems is the 1♣ opening. As this merely advertises strength and reveals no suits yet, this is the moment of greatest danger for them. When they open 1♣, your side is unlikely to have game and so your aim should be to damage their auction as far as possible. The following approach works well :

Bid with bad hands, pass with good hands.

It is safe to pass with a decent hand since the 1♣ opening is forcing and you will have an opportunity to bid on the next round if you wish. Therefore, pass on all hands with 13+ HCP and good 12s. If you take action on the next round, partner will know you have 13 points or more.

If the responder to 1♣ bids the 1◊ negative, treat opener's rebid as their opening bid and take action accordingly. In other words, if opener rebids 1NT, use your normal defense to a 1NT opening. If opener rebids 1♡ or 1♠, bid as though they had opened 1♡ or 1♠.

If responder to 1♣ gives a positive response, this is usually forcing to game in their methods. Now you would do well to keep out of the auction. If they have game values and you have 13+ HCP, partner must have very little. You are wise to stay quiet and let them bid to their destination. You ought to be defending and with your strength sitting over the strong opener, your prospects in defense figure to be favorable. In addition, by not bidding, you will have given declarer no inkling of the location of the missing high card strength.

Action with weak hands

Jump bids = pre-empts at the three-level, weak jump overcall single-suiters at the two-level. Suit Quality of 9 at the three-level and 8 at the two-level is advisable.

2NT = a freak two-suiter, any 6-5 or wilder shape. Lesser shapes are shown with a double or via an overcall at a lower level (see below). Over 2NT, advancer should bid the cheapest tolerable suit. Partner may pass or raise or remove to the cheapest suit held. All bidding is natural.

Suit bids = the suit bid and the next suit along :
(1♣) : 1◊ = diamonds + hearts
(1♣) : 1♡ = hearts + spades
(1♣) : 1♠ = spades + clubs
(1♣) : 2♣ = clubs + diamonds

Double = the suit doubled and its non-touching mate :
(1♣) : **Double** = clubs + hearts

No-trumps = the other pair of non-touching suits :
(1♣) : 1NT = diamonds + spades

5-5 or 5-4 patterns are sensible but at favorable vulnerability or after partner has passed, two 4-card suits are acceptable, particularly with a 4-4-4-1. With a 4-4-4-1, show the two stronger suits or if your hand is quite weak, choose the cheapest bid to show your suits. Suppose North opens (1♣) strong. What should East do, nil vulnerable, with :

```
(1)  ♠ A Q 7 2    (2)  ♠ Q 8 6 3   (3)  ♠ 8 7 6 3
     ♡ 9 6 4 2         ♡ J 9 6 4        ♡ Q 9 6 4
     ◊ K Q 9 7         ◊ K J 7 2        ◊ K 9 7 4 2
     ♣ 9               ♣ 8              ♣ - - -
```

With (1), bid 1NT to show spades and diamonds, your good suits. This is likely to work better than 1◊ (diamonds + hearts) or 1♡ (hearts + spades). With (2), if you wish to come in, bid 1◊. It would be all right to bid 1♡ but not 1NT which commits you to the two-level while either of the others lets you out at the one-level. With (3), you want to show your longest suit, the diamonds, and 1◊ is better than 1NT, again because it lets you out at a cheaper level if partner does not have decent support for you.

Advancer's job is to push the bidding as high as discretion allows. Raise to the two-level with 4-card support and jump to the three-level with 5-card support. Bidding a suit other than partner's shown suits is natural and not forcing, and also very risky if the suit is not strong.

With some ambitions for game, advancer bids 1NT after a one-level bid and 2NT after a two-level bid. In reply, partner bids clubs with a minimum hand while any other bid is natural and shows the upper range, around 9-11 points.

It is particularly important to interfere quickly if the opponents are playing relay methods. A simple overcall will usually not disrupt their relays. A jump overcall will. If partner shows a two-suiter at the one-level, this will not hamper them but if you can raise the bidding to the two-level or three-level, you will have jammed their relays and they will have to start a natural auction at a high level.

These disruptive methods are so effective that you should adopt them also against strong 2♣ and 2◇ openings. Over 2♣, your actions are the same as over 1♣ except that everything is one level higher. Naturally, you will need more shape to come in at this higher level and it is vital to keep an eye on the vulnerability, too.

Over 2◇, jumps to 3♡ or higher are pre-empts, bids at the two-level show the suit bid and the next suit along, while 3♣ = clubs + diamonds and 3◇ = diamonds + hearts. Double of 2◇ = diamonds + spades (the suit bid and the non-touching suit), while 2NT = clubs + hearts (the other non-touchers).

Once you are used to this approach, you will want to use this interference also against pairs that use game-force relay responses. For example, suppose they bid (1♡ natural) : (1♠ artificial game force reply). As they have shown the values for game, your aim is to disrupt, disrupt, disrupt. No matter what game force relay they use, you adopt the same structure : Jump bids are weak one-suiters, a suit overcall shows the suit bid and the next suit along, double = the suit bid + the non-touching suit and no-trumps shows the other non-touching suits. Thus, after their (1♡ : 1♠ game force relay), for example :

2♣ = clubs + diamonds
2◇ = diamonds + hearts
2♡ = hearts + spades
2♠ = spades + clubs
Double = spades + diamonds
1NT = hearts + clubs, the other non-touching suits.

Jumps to 3♣ or higher are weak one-suiters and 2NT is the 6-5 or freakier hand.

If you can push the bidding up by more than three steps you will usually be able to wipe out their relay methods or make them far less effective as the bidding drags them too high. You will find that this approach provides a lot of action. It is not only fun but also highly effective.

DEFENSE AGAINST THE UNUSUAL 2NT

After 1♡ : (2NT) or 1♠ : (2NT), a simple defense would be :

Double is looking for penalties, 3-partner's-major is a sound raise but not forcing, 3-other-major is natural and forcing, while bidding 3-minor asks for a stopper in the suit bid in a quest for 3NT.

You will no doubt be interested in something more sophisticated and also more effective :

Double = Looking for penalties. Responder needs about 10 HCP or more, a strong 4+ holding in at least one of their minors and a shortage in opener's major. If advancer removes to 3-minor, opener should double if strong in that minor. Otherwise, opener should pass in case responder is able to double this minor for penalties. (The double of 2NT is similar to responder's redouble in :

WEST	NORTH	EAST	SOUTH
1♠	Dble	Rdble...	

East's redouble seeking penalties should have 10+ HCP, a shortage in opener's suit and strong holdings in at least two of the unbid suits.)

3-opener's-major = natural, weaker than a normal limit raise but respectable, 8-9 HCP or a good 6-7.

4-opener's-major = natural, pre-emptive, exactly the same as 1♡ : 4♡ or 1♠ : 4♠. Not a strong bid. This will help opener decide whether to double or whether to bid on if they sacrifice in 5-minor.

3-other-major = strong 6+ suit, 6-9 HCP, denies support for opener's major, not forcing.

3♣ = 10+ HCP, game invitation or better in hearts. If the opening bid was 1♠, the 3♣ response may yet have spade support.

3◇ = 10+ HCP, game invitation or better in spades. If the opening bid was 1♡, the 3◇ response denies heart support. With heart support and spades as well, start with the 3♣ response.

After 3♣ or 3◇, if opener bids 3-Major as an intended signoff, responder passes only with the 10-11 point minimum. With more, responder should bid on to game or higher. If responder has shown support for opener's major, a bid of 4-minor by either partner is a cue bid while 3NT is best used as RKCB based on opener's major.

Over the 3♣ reply, 3◇ by opener is a waiting bid. Responder can then bid 3♡, non-forcing, or 3♠ non-forcing if the opening bid was 1♠, but any other bid by responder is forcing to game. Again 4-minor would be a cue bid and 3NT RKCB.

4♣ or 4◇ over 2NT = standard splinter raise of opener's major. For further bidding, see Chapter 6 on splinters.

4NT = RKCB with opener's major as trumps. It would be cheaper, of course, to bid 3♣ or 3◇ and perhaps use 3NT as RKCB later but the opponents are not always so co-operative. Responder may well be concerned about a pre-emptive leap of 5♣ or 5◇ shutting out the key card asking mechanism.

Coping with interference to RKCB 3NT or 4NT

If they bid over your RKCB enquiry, you can play DOPI. In the basic version Double = 0, Pass = 1, but playing RKCB, we can do better. For example :

WEST	NORTH	EAST	SOUTH
1♠	2NT	4NT	5◊
?			

Pass = 0 or 3 key cards
Double = 1 key card
5♡ = 2 key cards, no trump queen
5♠ = 2 key cards plus the trump queen
5NT = 4 key cards, no trump queen
6♣ = 4 key cards plus the trump queen. If four key cards are not enough for the slam, partner's reason for bidding 4NT should make interesting listening.

Over the pass, double by partner says, 'Pass if you have 0 key cards, bid on with 3.' This allows the partnership to collect penalties when the lack of key cards may make even the five-level dangerous. When bidding on, Step 1 = no trump queen and Step 2 shows the trump queen.

After the double, showing one key card, partner can pass if that makes slam unappealing and the five-level risky. A bid by partner here, or after the pass showing 0 or 3 key cards, will have its usual meaning (trump queen ask, king ask, etc.).

Slam Sacrifice Doubles

With the proliferation of weak two-suited openings and two-suited overcalls (such as the Michaels Cue Bid), you will often find that your side has an excellent trump fit. What if the opponents bid to a slam? It may be clear to you that a sacrifice will cost relatively little because of your good trump fit, but it would still be silly to sacrifice if their slam is likely to fail. It is no great triumph to be down only 300 if you could have been +100.

If their slam is very likely to make, be prepared to sacrifice if you have a great trump fit and your hands are not balanced. Sacrifices on balanced hands are usually too expensive. If you have a good chance to beat their slam, do not take a sacrifice.

The problem is, how can you tell? When your side is clearly the sacrificing side, you have established an excellent trump fit and the opponents have bid to six or seven, slam sacrifice doubles work like this :

Against a small slam :
The player in the direct seat should—
Double with 2 defensive tricks. That ends the bidding.
Pass = 0 or 1 defensive trick.
When the pass reverts to partner :
Pass with 2 defensive tricks.
Sacrifice with no defensive trick as partner has at most one defensive trick.
Double = 1 defensive trick. After this double, partner will pass if also holding 1 defensive trick (each partner has one trick) and will sacrifice if holding no defensive trick.

Against a grand slam :
Double in the direct seat with one trick. Partner must pass if you double. With no defense or merely potential for a trick, pass. After the pass, partner should pass with one reasonably certain trick or better, double with potential for one trick and sacrifice with no hope for a trick. If partner has doubled in the passout seat, you should leave the double in if you also have potential for a trick and sacrifice with no vestige of a trick in defense. If you have potential for a trick and partner's double indicates potential for a trick, there is sufficient chance of defeating the grand slam to reject the sacrifice. If only one of you has potential for a trick, the odds favor sacrificing.

The tough aspect is recognising what is likely to be a defensive trick or what has potential for a trick. You will not always be right but having some method to avoid silly sacrifices is better than having no method at all.

The 3NT, 4♣ and 4◊ Openings

In standard methods, the 4♣ and 4◊ openings are pre-empts based on one playing trick better than a 3♣ or 3◊ opening. The 3NT opening is often played as the Gambling 3NT : a solid 7+ minor and little else. The Gambling 3NT is out of favor with top players because defending against it is relatively simple (lead an ace).

There are other useful approaches for these opening pre-empts. One is the Namyats Convention :
4♣ = a strong 4♡ pre-empt
4◊ = a strong 4♠ pre-empt
The hand should contain exactly eight playing tricks. The major suit should be solid, or a one-loser suit (SQ 10) with an ace outside as compensation. It follows that an opening bid of 4♡ or 4♠ will not be as strong, either in playing tricks or in suit strength.

The 3NT Pre-empt

If playing Namyats or something similar, the 3NT is commonly used as a multi : a pre-empt of 4♣ or 4◊. Opener's suit need not be solid.

Defending against Namyats
Against 4♣ or 4◊ :
Bid their suit = strong takeout with 0-1 cards in their suit.
Double = takeout but weaker than bidding their suit.
4NT = strong two-suiter in the minors
Against their 3NT opening
Double = strong hand. Suggests doubling them for penalties if they run to 4-minor.
4♣ = takeout for the majors with no preference or preference for hearts
4◊ = also takeout for the majors, but with definite preference for spades
4♡ or 4♠ = natural, to play.
Pass and double their run to 4♣ or 4◊ = takeout double but weaker than immediate action

ANSWERS TO EXERCISES AND QUIZZES

Page   **Answers and Comments**

12 **A.** 1. No   2. 2♣   3. 2♣. Not strong enough to transfer to hearts and then bid spades.
4. 6NT. With 33 points or more together and a grand slam unlikely, play in 6NT rather than 6-Major.
5. 2♣. If partner is minimum choose 3NT (even if partner has 4 hearts). Opposite a maximum, bid 6NT.
B. 1. 2♥   2. 3♠   3. 3◇ (maximum, both majors)   4. 3♣ (maximum, no major)   5. 2◇
C. 1. 2♠. Not worth game opposite a minimum.   2. Bid 4♥ (or use the 4♣ transfer to 4♥).
3. Bid 4♠ (or use the 4◇ transfer to 4♠).   4. 2NT. Not enough for game opposite a minimum. When
1NT : 2NT is used as a transfer (see Chapter 2) and so is not available for the invitational raise, use 2♣ and
sign off in 2NT if opener is minimum.   5. 4♥. The kings and the club tenace justify not using a transfer.

Bidding Set 1											
1. W	**E**	**2. W**	**E**	**3. W**	**E**	**4. W**	**E**	**5. W**	**E**	**6. W**	**E**
1NT	2♣*	No	1NT	1NT	2♣	No	1NT	1NT	2♣	No	1NT
2NT	3♣	2♣	2◇	2♥	2♠	2♣	3◇	2♥	3NT	2♣	2◇
No		2♠	No	2NT	3◇	4♥*	No	No		4♠*	No
*Prepared to be				No							
in game opposite						**Or transfer to*		*3NT = c. 80%*		**Or transfer to*	
a maximum.						*4♥ via 4♣.*		*4♥/4♠ = 36%*		*4♠ via 4◇.*	

#5 : 3NT is not certain but is a far better chance than 4♥ or 4♠. If a diamond is not led, you are home and
have chances for an overtrick. If a diamond is led, all is well if diamonds are 4-3. If diamonds are 5-2 or
worse, you are in trouble only if the player with the diamond length is on lead. It would be most unlikely
that the opening leader would choose a doubleton diamond.

Bidding Set 2											
1. W	**E**	**2. W**	**E**	**3. W**	**E**	**4. W**	**E**	**5. W**	**E**	**6. W**	**E**
1NT	2♣	1NT	2♣	No	1NT	No	1NT	1NT	2♣	1NT	2♣
3♣	3NT	3♥	3NT	2♣	3♥	2♣	3◇	3◇	4♠*	2◇	4NT
No		No		3NT	No	4♠*	No	No		5♠	5NT
						*Or transfer to		**Two outside Ks*		6◇	7NT
						4♠ via 4◇.		*= no transfer*		No	

#1 and #2 : East uses 2♣ purely to find opener's point range.
#6 : Note how East, knowing that West is 4-4 in the majors, can count to thirteen tricks and bid 7NT.

19 **A.** 1. 2◇, transfer to hearts   2. 2♥, transfer to 2♠. You cannot afford to use Extended Stayman to
check both majors as a 3-level reply from opener would push you too high.   3. 2♠, transfer to clubs.
4. 2♣. Too good for a transfer and signoff in diamonds. You plan to bid 3NT opposite a maximum and 3◇
opposite a minimum.   5. 2♣. Stayman. Bid game opposite a maximum, partscore opposite a minimum.
B. 1. 2♥   2. 2♥   3. 2♥. No super-accept with a 4-3-3-3.   4. 3♥ (or 3♣), super-accept.   5. 3♥
C. 1. 3NT. You are maximum but with only two hearts, choose no-trumps.   2. 3♥. The hearts are good
but the hand is a bare minimum.   3. 4♥. You are maximum with three trumps. The trumps need not be
strong.   4. Pass. You are minimum and have only two hearts.   5. 4♥. You have only 16 HCP but give
yourself one more for the doubleton and upgrade the hand for the 4-card support and you are worth 4♥.

Bidding Set 3											
1. W	**E**	**2. W**	**E**	**3. W**	**E**	**4. W**	**E**	**5. W**	**E**	**6. W**	**E**
1NT	2◇	1NT	2♥	No	1NT	No	1NT	1NT	2♥	No	1NT
2♥	No	2♠	2NT	2◇	2♥	2♥	3♠*	3♠	4♠	2◇	2♥
		3♠	No	2NT	4♥	No**		No		2NT	4♥
		Although 4-3-3-3,		No		**3◇ as a super-*		*East would have*		No	
		West should				*accept trial bid*		*passed 2♠ by*			
		choose spades.				*is a sound choice.*		*West.*			

**You can hardly blame West in #4 for passing 3♠, but swap West's red suits and 4♠ is a really great spot.
Tough game, bridge.

Bidding Set 4											
1. W	**E**	**2. W**	**E**	**3. W**	**E**	**4. W**	**E**	**5. W**	**E**	**6. W**	**E**
1NT	2♠	No	1NT	1NT	2NT	No	1NT	No	1NT	1NT	2♡
3♣	No	2NT	3◇*	3♣*	3NT	2♣*	2◇	2◇	2♡	2♠	3♠*
		No		No		2NT	No	3♡*	4♡	4♠	No
		*No super-accept		*3♣ = super-		*Not suitable		*shows 6-7		*shows 6-7	
		without 3+ ◇s.		accept		for a transfer		HCP and 6 ♡s		HCP and 6 ♠s	

#4 : There is no transfer sequence for an invitational hand with no major suit. For such hands, use 2♣.

#5 : Note that 3NT makes the same number of tricks as a heart contract. Despite the 9-card fit, 4♡ should fail.

26   **A.**   1. 2♠, transfer to clubs, planning to show the hearts next. This hand is strong enough to show the minor suit.   2. 2♣, Stayman. As this is too weak to look for a slam, do not show the minor suit. If a fit in hearts comes to light, bid 4♡. Otherwise rebid 3NT.   3. 3NT. To win at pairs you need courage. The hand is not strong enough to transfer to clubs and then show the diamonds.
4. 3♡. The single-suiter with slam potential.   5. 4♡. You could transfer to hearts and then bid 4♡, but with the two outside kings it is worth having the lead come up to your hand.
B.   1. 4♡. Not enough to justify a 4◇ cue bid. Choose the 4-4 fit rather than the 5-3.   2. 4◇. Shows heart support, a maximum 1NT, the ◇A and no ♣A.   3. 4♠. Support for spades but a poor hand (minimum values and no doubleton).   4. 3NT. You have no fit with either major.   5. 3♠. Your hand is minimum but you have two good features : 4-card support plus a doubleton in partner's second suit.
C.   1. 4♣. Only 16 points but excellent support for a possible club slam.   2. 4♡. Great support but poor shape and only minimum values.   3. 3NT. No support for either suit.   4. 3♠. This shows support for hearts, a maximum 1NT and the ♠A. You have all three good features.   5. 3NT. Despite the support for clubs, all your values are concentrated in the suits in which partner is short. In such cases, choose 3NT.

Bidding Set 5											
1. W	**E**	**2. W**	**E**	**3. W**	**E**	**4. W**	**E**	**5. W**	**E**	**6. W**	**E**
No	1NT	1NT	2◇*	1NT	2NT	No	1NT	1NT	2◇	No	1NT
2♡	2♠	2♡	4♡	3◇	3♠	3NT	No	2♡	3NT	2♡	2♠
3NT	4♠	No		3NT	No	*Do not transfer*		No		3♡	4♠
No		*Not 4♣ which*				*with length in the*				No	
		might be doubled				*minors and no*					
		for the lead.				*slam chances.*					

#6 : West's 3♡, a new suit after a transfer, committed the partnership to game and showed 5+ spades and 4+ hearts. East should support the spades but give weak preference despite the good hearts. East has minimum point count and no ruffing values. Bid 3♠, strong preference, with better shape or maximum points.

Bidding Set 6											
1. W	**E**	**2. W**	**E**	**3. W**	**E**	**4. W**	**E**	**5. W**	**E**	**6. W**	**E**
1NT	2◇	1NT	3NT	1NT	2♡	No	1NT	1NT	2♡	1NT	2♡
2♡	2♠	No		2♠	3◇	2◇	2♡	2♠	3♣	2♠	3♣
3♣*	4♠	*No slam, no*		3♠	4◇*	3♣*	4♡	4♠	No	3◇*	3♡*
No		*minor.*		4♡*	4♠	*A passed hand*				3♠*	4NT
Cue for spades				5♣*	6♠	*can afford to*				5♡	7♣
				Cue bids		*show a minor.*				*Cue bids*	

#1 : East has shown 5 hearts and 4 spades but West should choose the 4-4 fit at pairs. After responder bids a second suit, a new suit by opener shows support for responder's *second* suit and the ace in the suit bid.

#4 : It is not recommended to introduce a minor suit into a transfer sequence if there are only enough values for game. A passed hand can do so since opener knows the limited nature of responder's hand. Although the aim is for 3NT, you may occasionally find a minor suit game when 3NT is judged hopeless.

#6 : West's 3◇ is a cue bid agreeing clubs as trumps. Over 3♡, West can afford to cue bid 3♠ even though holding the king and not the ace. When partner has shown length in a suit, it is safe enough to make a first round cue with the king in partner's suit. If partner has the ace, partner will recognise that you are showing the king. If partner is missing both the ace and the king, partner will still expect the suit to have a loser.

31 **A.** 1. 3♣, Stayman   2. 3♦, transfer to hearts   3. 3♦   4. 3♠ if using the 3♠ response to show precisely five spades and four hearts, otherwise 3♣ Stayman.   5. 3♥, transfer, intending to pass 3♠.
B. 1. 4♥.   2. 4♥. No value in looking for a spade fit.   3. 3NT. Promises 4 spades.
4. 3♠. Shows 4 spades and slam potential.   5. 4NT. If you find 3 aces and 2 kings, bid 7♥ or 7NT.
C. 1. 3NT. No fit for either major. Responder has 5 hearts and 4 spades.   2. 4♥
3. 4♣. Choose the 4-4 rather than the 5-4. 4♣ = cue, supporting spades.   4. 4♠. Not worth a 4♦ cue.
5. 4♦. Shows support for spades, a maximum 2NT, ruffing potential, the ♦A and no ♣A.

Bidding Set 7		**2. W**	**E**	**3. W**	**E**	**4. W**	**E**	**5. W**	**E**	**6. W**	**E**
1. W	**E**	2NT	3♦	2NT	3♦	No	2NT	No	2NT	2NT	3♥
No	2NT	3♥	No	4♥	No	3♥	3♠	3♦	3♥	3♠	3NT
3♥	3♠			*East would pass*		4♠*	No	3NT	No	4♠	No
4♠	No			*3♥. Note how*		**Too good*				*With 3-card*	
Note how badly				*good 4♥ is.*		*to pass 3♠.*				*support, choose*	
3NT plays.										*the major game.*	

#1 and #4 : It would be timid to pass 3♠.
#3 : After a transfer over 2NT, opener should super-accept with 4-card support and an outside doubleton.

Bidding Set 8		**2. W**	**E**	**3. W**	**E**	**4. W**	**E**	**5. W**	**E**	**6. W**	**E**
1. W	**E**	2NT	3♣	No	2NT	No	2NT	2NT	3♠	No	2NT
2NT	3♣	3♥	3NT	3♦	3♥	3♦	3♥	4♥	No	3♥	3♠
3♠	4♠	4♠	No	3♠	3NT	3♠	4♥	*or*		4♥*	4♠
No				No		4NT	5♥	2NT	3♣	No	
						No		3♥	4♥	**Shows 5-5 in*	
								No		*the majors.*	

#4 : West is definitely worth a slam try once opener supports one of the majors.
#5 : Bid 2NT : 3♠ if using that response to show precisely 5 spades and 4 hearts. If not, travel via 3♣.
#6 : Responder could not afford to bid 4♥ with only a 4-card suit. There might not be an 8-card fit in either major. Bidding game in a new suit is taken as showing at least a 5-card suit.

36 **A.** 1. 2♥, asking to play in 2♥ or 2♠. Denies the values to invite game and is looking for the best partscore.   2. 2♣, checkback   3. 2♠, signoff   4. 2♣, checkback   5. 3NT
B. 1. 2♦, minimum   2. 2♥, better than hand 1 (better clubs, better hearts)   3. 2♥   4. 3NT. Shows 14 points and denies 3 hearts. The clubs are too poor to show.   5. 3♣, maximum with 5 clubs
C. 1. 3NT.   2. 4♦, heart support, maximum values and the ♦A   3. 4♥, weaker than the cue bid raise
4. 3♠, stronger than 4♠   5. 4♠, weak with spade support

Bidding Set 9		**2. W**	**E**	**3. W**	**E**	**4. W**	**E**	**5. W**	**E**	**6. W**	**E**
1. W	**E**	1♦	1♠	No	1♦	No	1♣	1♣	1♠	No	1♦
1♣	1♠	1NT	2♣	1♥	1NT	1♠	1NT	1NT	2♣	1♠	1NT
1NT	2♥	2♦	No	2NT	3♣	2♦	2♠	3♠	4♠	2♣	2♦
No				No		No		No		2♥	No
2♥ = 6-9 points				*2NT requires 3♣*		*2♦ = 6-9 points*		*3♠ = 14 points*			

#2 : If the values indicate only a partscore, you are usually better off in a trump fit than in 2NT. On the East-West cards, 2NT is highly likely to fail and 2♦ has good chances for an overtrick.
#3 : Since 2♣ is used as Checkback, you need a way to sign off in clubs. As 2NT is not needed for the invitational hands (travel through 2♣), 2NT requires opener to bid 3♣. This allows responder to pass with the weak hand and long clubs (or with club support if the opening bid was 1♣). If responder bids on after opener has taken the 3♣ 'puppet', the auction becomes game-forcing. If responder rebids his first suit after 3♣, that shows a 6+ suit and if responder bids a new suit, this shows a 5-5 pattern at least.
#4 : Spades first, diamonds next after a 1♣ opening shows 5+ spades and 4+ diamonds, otherwise respond 1♦.
#6 : It is quite a triumph to be able to stay low on these combined hands.

Bidding Set 10											
1. W	**E**	**2. W**	**E**	**3. W**	**E**	**4. W**	**E**	**5. W**	**E**	**6. W**	**E**
1♣	1♥	1♣	1♥	1♣	1♠	1♣	1♦	1♣	1♠	1♣	1♠
1NT	2♣	1NT	3♥	1NT	2NT	1NT	2♣	1NT	4♥	1NT	3♣
3♥	4♥	3NT	No	3♣	No	2♦	No	4♠	No	3♠	3NT
No										No	
		3♥ = game force with 5+ hearts		*2NT requires West to bid 3♣.*				*4♥ = 6-5. Prefer the 6-2 fit lest 4♥ is forced off.*			

#1 : West's 3♥ shows 14 points and three hearts. West's 1NT denied four spades.

#3 : East judges that 3♣ will play better than 1NT.

#4 : The diamond fit is not certain but is very likely.

#5 : When faced with the choice of playing a 6-2 fit or a 5-3 fit, prefer the 6-2. If there is a 4-1 trump break, the 5-3 fit may collapse if the 5-card holding is forced to ruff too often. The 6-2 fit is more likely to survive a bad break.

#6 : East's 3♣ rebid is forcing to game and shows 4+ spades with 4+ clubs. When East rebids 3NT after West shows the delayed 3-card spade support, East is showing exactly 4 spades. If East wanted to sign off in 3♣, East would use the 2NT puppet to 3♣.

42   **A.**   1. 4♥. Too weak for a splinter.   2. 4♣. Splinter raise, short in clubs   3. 3♠. Splinter
     4. 2♣. Do not make an immediate splinter with only 3-card support.   5. 4♦. Splinter.
     B.   1. 4♠. Minimum hand and now the ♣Q is wasted.   2. 4NT. Even though the clubs are wasted, you are very strong elsewhere. Opposite 3 key cards, slam should be a good bet.   3. 4♦. Cue bid to show slam interest.   4. 4♠. The club holding is terrible opposite a singleton or void.   5. 4♠. The club shortage is wasted. Singleton opposite a singleton means no ruffing values there in either hand.
     C.   1. 3♣. Natural and forcing.   2. 4♥. Not strong enough to continue with a 4♣ delayed splinter.
     3. 3♠. Delayed splinter, short in spades and 3-card heart support.   4. 3♠. Delayed splinter. Great slam prospects opposite just three aces or ♥A-Q-x-x-x-x and ♣A.   5. 4♥. Too weak to splinter.

Bidding Set 11											
1. W	**E**	**2. W**	**E**	**3. W**	**E**	**4. W**	**E**	**5. W**	**E**	**6. W**	**E**
1♠	4♣	1♠	4♣	1♦	1♥	1♦	1♥	1♣	1♠	1♣	1♠
4NT	5♥	4♠	No	4♣	4NT	4♣	4♥	2NT	3NT	4♠	4NT
6♠	No			5♥	6♥	No		4♠	No	5♥	6♠
West's clubs are ideal for slam.		*West's clubs are awful opposite a singleton.*		No		*East has terrible clubs.*		*2NT = 19-20 game force*		No	
				4♣ = splinter						*4♠ = 4-2-2-5*	

#1 : Although opener has just a minimum opening, the club holding is perfect. Opposite a singleton or a void, West has no club losers and only five losers outside. As East's splinter shows the high card values for a game raise, opener can expect 4+ cover cards from responder. That reduces West's losers from 5 to 1. Basic cover card expectancy is 7-9 points = 2 cover cards, 10-12 points = 3, 13-15 points = 4 and so on.

#3 : Even though East has only minimum high card values, the club holding is ideal. East has five losers outside the clubs and West's strong rebid makes it very likely that West will be able to cover those five losers. Slam should be a good bet as long as two aces are not missing.

#4 : This East hand is much worse than the East in #3. The ♣K is probably useless and having only four trumps is a drawback. Slam on a 4-4 fit usually requires 30+ HCP.

#5 : With the 19-20 HCP balanced hand, opener can rebid with a jump to 2NT here to force to game and show the strength and shape of the hand. When responder bids 3NT or a new suit, opener can then show the spade support. If opener regularly follows this path with the 19-20 flat hands, then the jump to 4-Major as in #6 should be a 5-4-2-2 pattern : not 4-4-3-2 or 4-3-3-3 (rebid with a jump to 2NT) and no singleton or void because of the failure to splinter. A different but sensible approach is to play that opener's jump raise to game in responder's major is a weak, distributional hand (sort of a gambling game raise by opener). With a full value raise to game, use the 2NT jump rebid for the flattish hands including the 5-4-2-2s (and revert to responder's major next round) or give a splinter raise with a shapely hand and 4-card support.

Bidding Set 12					
1. W **E** 1♥ 4♥ No *East is too weak for a splinter which should be 10 or more HCP.*	**2. W** **E** 1♣ 1♠ 2♣ 3♥ 4♦ 4NT 5♦ 6♣ *3♥ = splinter* *4♦ = cue bid*	**3. W** **E** 1♣ 1♠ 2♣ 2♥ 4♦ 4NT 5♦ 6♥ No *4♦ = splinter*	**4. W** **E** 1♠ 2♥ 4♣ 4♦ 5NT 6♦ 7♥ No *4♣ = splinter* *4♦ = cue bid* *5NT = trump ask*	**5. W** **E** 1♠ 2♥ 4♣ 5♣ 5♥ No *4♣ = splinter* *5♣ = cue bid* *5♥ = sign-off*	**6. W** **E** 2♣ 2♦ 2♠ 4♣ 7♠ No *2♣ = game force* *2♦ = negative* *4♣ = splinter*

#2 : As 2♥ by East would be forcing, it is sensible to harness the jump to 3♥ as a splinter raise of clubs.

#3 : Even though West has a minimum opening, it costs nothing to show the splinter support for hearts. With spades and diamonds reversed, West would jump to 4♥ over 2♥.

#4 : Once East can cue bid 4♦, West figures that the spades should dispose of any extra diamond losers in the East hand. The remaining problem is whether East has the ace of hearts. 4NT would not solve that question, since a 5♥ reply to show two aces leaves West wondering which other ace East holds. The 5NT trump ask is covered in Chapter 15. 6♦ shows one of the top three honors in trumps.

#5 : East's cue bid of 5♣ does not encourage West at all since with a void opposite, the ace is of little value. West's signoff also focuses on diamond control as the problem and as East has no control in diamonds either, a poor slam is avoided.

#6 : Once East has shown the weakness of the hand with the negative reply, East can freely splinter next round.

47 A. 1. 2♣ in standard, 3♥ if playing limit raises, or 3♦ Bergen raise   2. 2NT Jacoby
3. 4♥ in any approach   4. 3♠, splinter   5. 4NT. All you need to know is how many aces partner has. You will sign off in 5♥ opposite one, bid 6♥ opposite two and bid 7♥ if partner has three.
B. 1. 3♦. Shows the singleton diamond.   2. 3♦. Singleton diamond. May be weak or strong.
3. 4♦. Shows strong suit, K-Q-x-x-x or better.   4. 4♠. Weak 5-3-3-2/5-4-2-2.   5. 3NT. 16+ HCP.
C. 1. 4♥. The doubleton K-Q of diamonds is a dreadful holding opposite partner's shortage.
2. 3♠ or 3NT. Your diamond holding is excellent facing a singleton or void. You can cue bid with 3♠ or ask for aces with 3NT.   3. 3♥. This shows slam interest but denies the ♠A (failure to cue bid 3♠).
4. 3NT. Asking for aces since hearts have been set as trumps.   5. 3♥. Your diamond holding is poor but you have extra points and so should show some slam interest.

Bidding Set 13					
1. W **E** 1♠ 2NT 3♣ 3NT 4♦ 6♠ No *3♣ = short suit* *4♦ = one ace*	**2. W** **E** 1♠ 2NT 3♣ 4♠ No *East is minimum and the club holding is poor.*	**3. W** **E** 1♠ 2NT 3NT 4♠ 4NT 5♥ 6♠ No *3NT = 16+* *4♠ = signoff*	**4. W** **E** 1♥ 2NT 4♣ 7♥ No *4♣ = 5+ clubs,* *at least two top* *honors*	**5. W** **E** 1♥ 2NT 4♣ 4NT 5♦ 5NT 6♥ 7NT *East can count* *thirteen tricks.*	**6. W** **E** 1♠ 2NT 4♠ No *4♠ = minimum* *and no short* *suit*

#1 : Jacoby is for opener what a splinter raise is for responder. Just as it is valuable for responder to reveal a short suit, so locating a short suit with opener can be vital in appraising slam chances. East could not be happier after finding opener has a singleton or void in clubs. With only four losers outside clubs, even a minimum opening should supply enough winners to cover four losers.

#2 : Opposite a singleton, a doubleton can only eliminate one extra loser. You then need extra high card values to bid on to slam.

#3 : East has a minimum 2NT and signs off despite opener's strong rebid. Opener is allowed to bid on despite the signoff and here West has ample to try for slam. Facing 13+ points, opener can expect responder to provide four cover cards and West has just five losers.

#4 : As East is staring at the ♣Q, East knows that West's 4♣ must be no worse than A-K-x-x-x. West's clubs should provide whatever discards East needs. Unable to locate the ♣J, East should not attempt 7NT.

#5 : This time East has ♣Q-J-x opposite the promised ♣A-K-x-x-x. That should bring in five club tricks. Counting five tricks in hearts and the outside aces gives East twelve tricks. When 5NT locates an extra king with opener, East can take a sensible shot at 7NT. Playing teams, East would settle for 7♥ which is a touch safer.

#6 : West's 4♠ shows a minimum opening with no short suit. The pattern will be 5-3-3-2, 6-3-2-2 or 5-4-2-2. While it is a triumph to reach good slams, it is just as much a triumph to avoid silly slams.

Bidding Set 14		2. W	E	3. W	E	4. W	E	5. W	E	6. W	E
1. W	E	1◊	2NT	1◊	2NT	1♣	2NT	1♣	2♣	1◊	2NT
1◊	2NT	3♥	4♣	3♥	3NT	3♣	3◊	2♥	3◊	3◊	4♣
3NT	No	4NT	5♥	No		3♥	5♣	3NT	No	4◊	4♥
		6◊	No	*In minor suit*		Pass		2♣ = *inverted*		4NT	5♠
3NT = *minimum*		3♥ = *short suit*		*Jacoby, 3NT is to*		3♣ *denies a void*		*minor raise*		5NT	6◊
balanced hand		4♣ = *cue bid*		*play, not asking*		*or a singleton*		2♥ *and 3◊ are*		7NT	No
				for aces				*stopper bids*			

#4 : After West's 3♣ denying a shortage and also denying a minimum balanced hand, 3◊ and 3♥ show stoppers. As West's 3♥ denies a spade stopper, East knows that 3NT and 6♣ are both poor spots.

#5 : While you might use 2NT with one unguarded suit (as in #4 where it might have been necessary to protect the ♥K), it is better to use a forcing minor raise with two weak suits. If playing 1♣ : 3♣ as the forcing raise, West would bid 3♥ (stopper-showing and denying a diamond stopper) and East would bid 3♠ (promising a diamond stopper and *asking* for a spade stopper), over which West would bid 3NT.

#6 : As West's 3◊ showed a good hand (it denied a minimum balanced hand as well as denying a shortage), East was too strong to sign off in 3NT. 4♣ and 4♥ were cue bids and West did the rest.

53   **A.**   1. Pass. No worthwhile suit.   2. 1♥. Strong suit.   3. 2♠. A weak two in third seat is all right with a strong 5-card suit.   4. 1◊. Otherwise pass.   5. 1♠. The only lead you really want.
     B.   1. 1♣. Length + spades = 16, therefore open.   2. Pass. Length + spades = 13.   3. 2♥. 4th seat weak two = 8-12 points   4. 3♣. Otherwise pass.   5. 4♠. To avoid a competitive auction.
     C.   1. 3♥. Limit hand with 6 respectable hearts.   2. 4♥. Suit Quality 10.   3. 3NT.
     4. 2♠. Fourth suit in case partner has 3-card heart support.   5. 2♠. Too strong for 3♥ (not forcing) but the hearts are not good enough for 4♥. Bid 2♠ fourth suit and rebid 3♥ forcing.

Bidding Set 15		2. W	E	3. W	E	4. W	E	5. W	E	6. W	E
1. W	E	1♥	1♠	1♣	1◊	1♣	1◊	1♣	1◊	1◊	1♥
1◊	1♥	2♣	2◊	1♥	1♠	1♥	2♠	1♥	2♠	1♠	1NT
2♣	2♠	2NT	3♠	2♠	No	2NT	3NT	3◊	5◊	2♣	2◊
3♥	4♥	4◊	4NT	1♠ = *natural*		No		No		No	
No		5♥	6♠	*and forcing*		2♠ = *4th suit*		2♠ = *4th suit*		*East should not*	
2♠ = *4th suit*		2◊ = *4th suit*				*forcing, denies*				*pass 1♠.*	
		4◊ = *cue bid*				*four spades*					

#1 : It would be premature and misguided to rebid 3NT over 2♣.

#2 : After fourth suit, East's 3♠ is forcing to game. Without spade support, West would rebid 3NT. Having denied 3-card spade support by bidding 2NT over 2◊, West's 4◊ shows maximum values, within the context of the auction, and a doubleton spade. West upgrades the hand because of the queen of spades. With a rag doubleton in spades, West would simply raise to four spades.

#3 and #4 : After 1♣ : 1◊, 1♥ responder's 1♠ is natural, 4+ spades and forcing. 2♠ is used as fourth suit.

#5 : West's 3◊ shows 3-card diamond support and denies a spade stopper. West's 3◊ is not forcing and opposite minimum values, East is not worth a slam try.

#6 : Having responded to 1◊, it is no more difficult to rebid after 1♠. The 1NT rebid shows only 6-9 points.

Bidding Set 16		2. W	E	3. W	E	4. W	E	5. W	E	6. W	E
1. W	E	No	1♥	No	1♥	No	1♠	No	1♠	No	1◊
No	1♠	2♣	2◊	4♥	No	2♣	2◊	2♥	No	1♠	No
2♣	2◊	2♥	No	*If worth 4♥, bid*		3♥	4♥			*East's 1◊ gives*	
2♥	No	2♣ = *Drury*		*it even after 3rd*		No				*West the best*	
2♣ = *Drury but*				*seat opener.*		2♣ = *Drury*				*lead.*	
not promising						2♥ = *natural +*					
spade support						*game-force*					

#1 : East's 2◊ denies game interest. West's sequence shows four hearts only (failure to respond 2♥ at once).

#2 : You are doing well to be able to stop in 2♥ with 3♥ having no reasonable chance for success.

#3 : East might feel morose on hearing West leap to 4♥ but all will be forgiven when dummy appears.

#4 : Note how Drury leads you to the superior 4-4 heart fit while Pass : 1♠, 3♠ would land you in 4♠.

#6 : North-South obviously will be bidding on but this as high as East-West should go.

58 **A.** 1. 2♡. Maximum weak two. 2. 1♠. Too strong for a weak two. 3. Pass. Hearts too weak for 2♡.
4. Pass. Do not open a weak two with four cards in the other major. 5. 2♠.

B. 1. 4♡. With four trumps and a singleton, you should bid game opposite a weak two regardless of
strength, either to make or as a sacrifice. 2. Pass. You need better than three winners to try for
game, but you could try a pre-emptive raise to 3♡. 3. Pass. With a misfit, pass below 16 HCP. 4.
2NT. You have more than three winners. Bid game opposite a maximum and sign off in 3♡ opposite
a minimum. 5. 2NT. Bid 3NT opposite a maximum and 3♡ opposite a minimum. Opener will bid
4♡ with a Suit Quality of 10.

C. 1. 3◇. Minimum with two top spade honors.   2. 3NT. A-K-Q-x-x-x.
3. 3♡. Maximum points but only one top spade.   4. 3♣. Minimum and only one top honor in spades.
5. 3♠. Maximum and two top honors in spades.

Bidding Set 17											
1. W	**E**	**2. W**	**E**	**3. W**	**E**	**4. W**	**E**	**5. W**	**E**	**6. W**	**E**
2♡	2NT	No	2♡	2♠	4♠	2♠	4♠	No	2♠	2♡	2NT
3♠	4♡	No		No		No		4♠	No	3♣	3♡
No				*With 4 trumps*		*East might*		*2♠ is OK in*		No	
Treat 8 HCP and				*and a singleton,*		*consider a*		*third seat on a*		*3♣ = minimum*	
three cover cards				*bid game.*		*4NT or 3♡*		*strong 5-card*		*and bad suit. 3♡*	
as maximum.						*psyche.*		*suit.*		*may be too high.*	

#4 : East can tell that the opponents have at least 25 HCP (East has 5 and West has at most 10) and that the
opponents have at least eight hearts (West should not have four hearts with a 2♠ opening) and eight
diamonds (as West should not have five diamonds as well as six spades). The missing spades will be 1-1 or
2-0 and so East can tell that the opponents can make a game for sure and possibly slam. This is no time to
be timid. 4♠ is the very least that East should do, at any vulnerability. As the opponents have game on,
East-West will lose little in a spade sacrifice, East could well try some bluff manoeuvre. Bidding 3♡
(natural and forcing) may steal their suit. If doubled, you can always run back to spades. 4NT asking for
aces is a pretense of slam values. Partner is bound to have insufficient aces and so you will sign off in 5♠.
Only at adverse vulnerability would it be likely to cost you to reach 5♠ doubled. Against less gullible
opponents, a 2NT reply showing game invitational values or better is a more subtle psyche. You need to
judge what your opponents will swallow.

Bidding Set 18											
1. W	**E**	**2. W**	**E**	**3. W**	**E**	**4. W**	**E**	**5. W**	**E**	**6. W**	**E**
2♡	No	2♡	3NT	2♡	3NT	2♠	2NT	2♠	2NT	2♠	2NT
East hopes N-S		No		4♡	No	3♠	4♠	3◇	3NT	3NT	4♠
will bid and East		*West would bid*		*With worse*		*With 3½+*		*East can count*		*Prefer the major*	
can double for		*4♡ with a Suit*		*hearts, West*		*tricks, try*		*nine tricks but*		*if you need to set*	
penalties.		*Quality of 10.*		*would pass 3NT.*		*for game.*		*not ten.*		*up tricks.*	

#4 : Opposite a minimum, East would sign off in 3♠. Remove West's ♣K and 3♠ is perhaps too high.
#5 : One of the great boons of the 2NT Ogust structure is to be able to locate the top honors in opener's
major and thus judge when 3NT is the best contract despite the good major suit fit.
#6 : When you need to take a finesse, or you need to establish winners by knocking out an ace, and thus
losing the lead, it is preferable to play in the major suit game and not 3NT. If East-West play in 3NT on #6,
a heart lead or a club lead may not defeat the contract but may well hold declarer to nine tricks. That would
result in a very poor board as ten tricks in spades are virtually certain.

63 **A.** 1. 1♡. Rebid 3♡. With 5-6 losers, you can afford a 1-opening. You need two tricks from partner
for game and with that, partner will respond to your 1-opening. 2. 2♣. 9 playing tricks and 16 HCP.
3. 1♡. Longest suit is too weak for 2♣.   4. 2♣. Too many HCP for 1♠.   5. 2♣, and rebid 3♣.

B. 1. 2◇, but you will certainly bid on the next round. 2. 2♠. 8+ points and 5+ spades.
3. 2NT. 8+ points and no 5+ suit.   4. 3◇.   5. 2♠. The least of evils.

C. 1. 3♡. Shows 6+ hearts and nine playing tricks exactly. 3NT would be an acceptable gamble.
2. 3NT. Nine playing tricks and a solid 6+ minor. You should be prepared to risk the heart position.
3. 3♣.   4. 2NT. Shows 23-24 points balanced, not forcing.
5. 2♠. The spades are not good enough or long enough for a jump to 3♠.

Bidding Set 19											
1. W	**E**	**2. W**	**E**	**3. W**	**E**	**4. W**	**E**	**5. W**	**E**	**6. W**	**E**
2♣	2♦	2♣	2♦	No	2♣	No	2♣	No	2♣	2♣	2♦
3♥	No	3♥	4♥	2♦	3♠	2♦	3♠	2♦	3NT	2♥	4♣
3♥ = 9 playing		No		No		4♠	No	No		4♦	4♠
tricks.		*East has potential*		*3♠ = 9 playing*		*West has one*		*3NT is a sensible*		6♥	No
		for one trick.		*tricks.*		*sure trick.*		*gamble.*		*4♣ = splinter*	

#1 and #2 : One of the great advantages of the Benjamin 2♣ opening is how it allows opener to describe the playing strength so accurately (9 tricks here) and as a consequence, responder is able to bid game on the slightest values, as in #2.

#6 : Note again how the weak hand splinter enables the partnership to bid a slam on low HCP total.

Bidding Set 20											
1. W	**E**	**2. W**	**E**	**3. W**	**E**	**4. W**	**E**	**5. W**	**E**	**6. W**	**E**
2♣	2♠	No	2♣	2♣	2♥	No	2♣	2♣	3♣	No	2♣
3♣	3♠	2♥	2♠	2♠	4♠	2♠	3♦	3♥	4NT	2♦	2NT
4♠	4NT	2NT	3NT	No		4♦	4NT	5♥	5NT	3♣	3♠
5♥	5♠	No		*4♠ is weaker*		5♥	6♦	6♥	6NT	4NT	5♠
No				*than 3♠ here.*				*Worth the risk.*		6♠	No

#1 : Although 5♠ may fail, it would be conservative for East not to try for a slam. Give West the ♠A instead of the ♦K-Q and 6♠ is a great contract. Even ♥A instead of ♦K-Q gives 6♠ very good chances.

#2 : When there is no trump fit, slam needs the full high card values.

#3 : The responsibility for slam bidding after a 2♣ opening usually falls on responder's shoulder. 3♠ here by East would be a stronger raise and suggest hopes for slam.

#4 : East should have about nine playing tricks and as West has two aces and ruffing potential in hearts and clubs, it is not hard for West to envisage slam possibilities. That is why West raises to 4♦.

#5 : Although it is not appealing to ask for aces with no control in two unbid suits, East has no better choice over 3♥. In addition, as West has a strong hand and at most five points in hearts, it is very likely that West will have the controls needed in spades and diamonds. Note the use of 5NT for kings, even though an ace is missing, to investigate the prospects of 6NT. This occurs quite often at pairs.

#6 : After 2♣ : 2♦, 2NT, the most practical use for 3♣ is Stayman. West should see slam prospects opposite 23-24 points balanced when East shows four spades and denies four hearts.

67 **A.** 1. 2♥. Artificial negative, 0-7 points, any shape. 2. 2♥. Nice hand but still a negative.

    3. 3♦. Natural positive reply. 4. 2NT. 8+ points, no 5-card suit. 5. 3♣. Least of evils.

    B. 1. 2♠. Natural, and game-forcing. 2. 4♥. Suit Quality 10 and only just under three losers.

    3. 3♠. Sets spades as trumps and asks partner to cue bid any ace.

    4. 2NT. 25-27 balanced, game-force.   5. 3NT. Balanced hand, 28-30 points.

    C. 1. 3♥. 5+ hearts, 0-7 points. 2♥ was artificial. 2. 3♠. Stronger than 4♠. Promises an ace or a king (or a singleton or void if only three trumps are held). 3. 4♦. Splinter. Shows 4+ trumps and a singleton or void in diamonds. 4. 4♠. Spade support but poor hand. 5. 2NT. No spade support, no 5+ suit.

Bidding Set 21											
1. W	**E**	**2. W**	**E**	**3. W**	**E**	**4. W**	**E**	**5. W**	**E**	**6. W**	**E**
2♦	2♥	No	2♦	2♦	2♥	No	2♦	No	2♦	2♦	2♥
2NT	3♣	2♥	2♠	4♠	No	2♥	2♠	2♥	2NT	2♠	3♥
3♠	4♠	2NT	3♥	*West has three*		4♣	4NT	3♣	3♥	5♥	No
3♣ = Stayman		4♥	No	*losers, East less*		5♦	7♠	4♥	No	*5♥ asks for*	
				than 1½ tricks.		*4♣ = splinter*		*3♣ = Stayman*		*good trumps.*	

#1 : 4♠ is a much better spot than 3NT. What kills no-trumps is not the lack of stoppers but short suits. Here the doubleton heart opposite the doubleton heart spells probable doom for 3NT.

#3 : While slam is possible, it is usually poor odds where the 2♦ opener has three clearcut losers and partner gave a negative response, denying 1½ quick tricks. Such slams are generally 50% at best.

#4 : This is an impressive grand slam to reach. Aren't splinters marvellous when they crop up?

#6 : Even opposite these miserable trumps 6♥ could make. Opposite ♥K-x-x-x-x-x, 6♥ would be excellent.

Bidding Set 22

1. W	E	2. W	E	3. W	E	4. W	E	5. W	E	6. W	E
No	2♦	2♦	3♣	2♦	2NT	No	2♦	2♦	2♥	No	2♦
2NT	3NT	3♥	4♥	3♣	3♥	2♥	2♠	3NT	6NT	3♥	3♠
6NT	No	4NT	5♥	3NT	7NT	2NT	3♥	No		3NT	6NT
3NT = balanced		5NT	6♦	*3NT = 25-27*		4♥	4NT	*The 3NT rebid*		*Opposite a*	
25-27, no major		7NT	No	*balanced with*		5♦	7♥	*shows 28-30,*		*positive, East*	
				four spades				*balanced.*		*has enough for*	
										6NT.	

#1 : Where opener has 25+ balanced and responder shows 8+, opener should pass the decision to responder when opener is minimum. Opener's strategy is to show the 25-27 balanced by bidding 3NT and leaving the decision for a small slam or a grand slam to responder.

#2 : Note the vital pairs strategy of checking for kings to determine whether 7NT is there rather than just 7♥.

#3 West's 3♣ Stayman followed by 3NT shows 25-27 points. East knows the partnership has 37+ points.

#4 : East has a one-loser hand and needs to find only the ♥A to bid the grand slam after the heart fit is found. East must not try 7NT here as the spade suit may not produce five tricks in no-trumps.

#5 : A 2NT rebid by West would show 25-27 HCP and a balanced hand. The 3NT rebid shows 28-30 points balanced and leaves further action to responder. Here East has an easy 6NT rebid. Note that even with West's great strength, 3NT could fail opposite a Yarborough.

#6 : East can tell from the points West has shown that 6NT should be a reasonable prospect.

72   **A.** 1. 5♥. 2 key cards, no ♥Q.   2. 5♠. 2 key cards plus the ♥Q.   3. 5♣. 0 or 3 key cards.
4. 5♣. 0 or 3 key cards. Says nothing about the trump queen.   5. 6♣. 5 key cards + the trump queen.
   B. 1. Pass. Two aces are missing.   2. Pass. You are missing two aces or one ace + the ♦K.
3. 6♦. You are missing one ace.   4. 5♥, asking for the trump queen. If partner has 3+ diamond support and shows the trump queen , bid 7NT.   5. 7NT. Partner has the ♦K. What more do you need?

Bid Set 23

(1)		(2)		(3)		(4)		(5)		(6)		(7)		(8)	
W	E	W	E	W	E	W	E	W	E	W	E	W	E	W	E
2♦	2♥	2♦	2♥	No	2♦	No	2♦	1♥	2NT	1♥	2NT	1♣	1♠	1♣	1♠
2♠	3♠	2♠	3♠	3♣	3♠	3♣	3♠	3♣	4♥	3♣	4♥	3♠	4NT	3♠	4NT
4NT	5♣	4NT	5♦	4♠	4NT	4♠	4NT	4NT	5♥	4NT	5♣	5♣	6♠	5♦	7♠
5♠	No	6♠	No	5♦	6♠	5♥	7NT	No		6♥	No	5♣ = 0 or 3		5♦ = 1 or 4	
								2NT=Jacoby		2NT=Jacoby		*key cards*		*key cards*	

Note in each case how RKCB helps you solve the slam problems while simple Blackwood would not.

#1and #2 : East has the same shape, the same points, the same high cards, but in #1, slam is a poor bet while in #2, the king in the right place makes slam virtually laydown.

#3 and #4 : This time West has the same shape, same points, same high cards. In #3, the wrong black king keeps East-West down to the small slam while in #4, the right black king means 7NT is secure.

#5 and #6 : Again the right king gives you the slam, the wrong king makes slam a terrible prospect.

#7 and #8 : Locating the trump king means a grand slam on #8 but just a small slam on #7.

Bid Set 24

(1)		(2)		(3)		(4)		(5)		(6)		(7)		(8)	
W	E	W	E	W	E	W	E	W	E	W	E	W	E	W	E
1♣	1♥	1♣	1♥	1♠	2♦	1♠	2♦	1♦	1♠	1♦	1♠	2♦	2♥	2♦	2♥
2♥	4NT	2♥	4NT	2♥	4♠	2♥	4♠	3♠	4NT	3♠	4NT	3♥	4♥	3♥	4♥
5♥	6♥	5♠	7♥	4NT	5♦	4NT	5♦	5♣	5♦	5♣	5♦	4NT	5♦	4NT	5♦
5♥ = 2 key		*5♠ = 2 key*		5♥	5♠	5♥	5NT	5♥	6♠	5♠	7♠	5♥	5♠	5♥	5NT
cards, no ♥Q		*cards + ♥Q*		No		6♠	No	*5♥ = no ♠Q*		*5♠ shows ♠Q*		6♥	No	7♥	No

Note in each case how locating the trump queen or finding it is missing solves your slam decisions.

#3 and #4 : East's sequence implies just 3-card spade support. After finding East with one ace, West gives up on slam when the ♠Q is missing and bids slam when East has the ♠Q on #4.

78   **A.**   1. 6◊. West's 6♣ asks for the club holding, excluding the ace of clubs. 6◊ says, 'No ♣K, no ♣Q'. 2. 6♠. Shows ♣K but no ♣Q.   3. 6◊. No ♣K, no ♣Q   4. 6♡. ♣Q but no ♣K.   5. 6NT. ♣K + ♣Q.

     B.   (a) 1. 5NT. With 3 key cards, keep bidding and show or deny the trump queen next. 5NT shows 3 key cards and the trump queen.   2. Pass. After a signoff, bid on only with the higher number of key cards.   3. 5♠. Shows 3 key cards but no trump queen.   4. 5♠.   5. 5NT. 3 key cards plus the trump queen. If showing kings simultaneously, bid 6♣ (see page 83).

     (b) 1. 6♣. No outside king.   2. 6♡. Two kings.   3. 6♣.   4. 6◊. One outside king.   5. 6◊

Bid Set 25															
(1)		(2)		(3)		(4)		(5)		(6)		(7)		(8)	
W	**E**	**W**	**E**	**W**	**E**	**W**	**E**	**W**	**E**	**W**	**E**	**W**	**E**	**W**	**E**
1♠	4◊	1♠	4◊	1♡	4♣	1♡	4♣	1♣	1♡	1♣	1♡	1♣	1◊	1♠	2♣
4NT	5♡	4NT	5♠	4NT	5♣	4NT	5♣	3♡	3NT	3♡	3NT	3♣	4♣	4♣	4♠
5♠	No	6♠	No	5♡	5♠	5♡	5NT	4◊	4♡	4◊	4♡	4♡	7NT	5♣	No
		With 10		6♡	No	7♡	No	No		4♠	6♡	4♣ *set clubs*		4♠ = *1 or 4*	
		trumps show		*5♠ = no ♡Q*				*3NT=RKCB*		*4♠ = no ♡Q*		4◊ = *0 or 3*		*key cards*	
		the trump Q										*key cards*			

#1 and #2 : With nine trumps missing queen and jack, the chance of no loser is around 40%. With ten trumps, the odds improve to almost 80%. Therefore if you know that the partnership holds ten trumps you can show the trump queen in your RKCB answer structure.

#3 and #4 : West signs off in 5♡ in case East has 0 key cards. In #3, East bids 5♠ to show 3 key cards but no ♡Q. In #4, 5NT shows 3 key cards plus the ♡Q.

#5 : Using 3NT as RKCB saves you being possibly too high in 5♡.

#6 : East signs off in 4♡ in case West has 1 key card. 4♠ = 4 key cards but no trump queen.

#7 and #8 : Raising the minor to the four-level is used as setting the trump suit and invoking RKCB at the same time. Partner is allowed to ask for key cards or show the key cards held. Over 4♣, 4◊ = RKCB ask and 4♡/4♠/4NT/5♣ are the standard RKCB replies.

Bid Set 26															
(1)		(2)		(3)		(4)		(5)		(6)		(7)		(8)	
W	**E**	**W**	**E**	**W**	**E**	**W**	**E**	**W**	**E**	**W**	**E**	**W**	**E**	**W**	**E**
No	2◊	1♠	4NT	No	2◊	1♠	2NT	1♠	2NT	1◊	1♠	1◊	1♡	2◊	3♣
2NT	3♠	5♠	5NT	2♡	2♠	3♣	3NT	3♣	3NT	3♠	3NT	3♠	3NT	4♣	4♠
4♠	4NT	6◊	7NT	3♠	3NT	4♣	4♡	4♣	4◊	4♠	4NT	4♠	4NT	4NT	5◊
5◊	5♡	No		4♣	4NT	5♣	7♠	4♠	5♡	5◊	6♣	5♡	7♡	5♡	6♣
5NT	6♡	*6◊ = 1 king*		5♡	6NT	No		6♣	7♠	6♡	7NT	No		7NT	No
6NT	7NT			No										4♠ = *1 or 4*	
						2NT = Jacoby		*3NT=RKCB*		*5◊ = 1 king*		*3♠ = splinter*		*key cards*	
6NT = ♡Q				*5♡ =*		*3NT = RKCB*		*4♠ = ♠Q*		*6♡ = ♣Q*		*5♡ = 2 kings*		*5◊ = ♣Q*	
				2 kings		*5♣ = ♡K*		*6♣ = ♡K*						*6♣ = ♡K*	

#1 : West's 4♠ shows spade support but no ace (failure to cue bid). East locates the ♠K and ♠Q and follows up with an ask for the ♡Q. When West admits to this as well, East can count thirteen tricks.

#2 : After 5♠, East can count twelve top tricks. 7♠ is safe but East checks on kings and can bid 7NT when West shows one king.

#3 : East knows an ace is missing but when West shows two kings, 6NT must be as safe as 6♠.

#4 : After opener's reply to the Jacoby 2NT, either partner can use 3NT as RKCB. 4♣ showed 0 or 3 key cards, clearly three since West is known to have a singleton club. 4♡ was a Control Ask in hearts and when West showed the ♡K, East could see the grand slam.

#5 : Similar to #4 but East also has to find the trump queen. 4◊ asked for the ♠Q and 4♠ said 'Yes, I have it.'

#6 : East asks with 3NT and finds two key cards plus the trump queen. 4NT asks for kings and West shows one. Then 6♣ is a Control Ask in clubs and when West shows the ♣Q, East can count thirteen top tricks.

#7 : After a minor suit opening and a splinter, it is sensible to retain 3NT as natural but after a 3♠ splinter agreeing hearts, 3NT is better employed as RKCB. As West is likely to have diamond length for this sequence, East would make a Control Ask in 6◊ if West had shown only one king and bid seven only if West had ◊K.

#8 : After the minor suit raise to the four-level, East gives RKCB answers (but 4◊ would still be RKCB ask), 4NT asks for the trump queen and 5♡ is a Control Ask in hearts. West can count thirteen tricks.

83 **A.** 1. 3♠. You have the values for slam but need to find club control.   2. 4♣. Spade control needed. 3. 3NT RKCB. You have no void and you do have first or second round control in every suit. That makes it attractive to ask rather than to cue bid.   4. 3NT. RKCB.   5. 4♦. You need to locate control in both black suits.

B. 1. 5♥. No ace to cue.   2. 5♦. Shows the ace of diamonds. If partner then bids 5♥, pass. Spade control is missing.   3. 5♦, and follow with 5♠ over 5♥.   4. 5♦. You need a strong reason not to cue bid when a cue bid below the trump suit is available and partner has started cue bidding. West could have: ♠3 ♥AK953 ♦K5 ♣AK632.   5. 6♥. You have ♦A and second round spade control.

Bid Set 27															
(1)		**(2)**		**(3)**		**(4)**		**(5)**		**(6)**		**(7)**		**(8)**	
W	**E**	**W**	**E**	**W**	**E**	**W**	**E**	**W**	**E**	**W**	**E**	**W**	**E**	**W**	**E**
2♦	2♥	2♦	2♥	2♦	2♥	No	2♦	No	2♦	No	2♦	1♦	1♠	1♣	1♠
2♠	3♠	2♠	3♠	2♠	3♠	2♥	2♠	2♥	2♠	3♥	3♠	1NT	3♣	3♠	4♦*
4♣*	4♦*	4♣*	4♥*	4♣*	4♠	4♣**	4♥*	3♠	4♣*	4♠	5♣*	3♠	4♣*	5♣*	5♦*
7♠	No	6♠	No	6♠	No	5♦*	7♠	4♦*	4♥*	5♦*	5♥*	4♦*	4NT	5♠	No
*Cue bids						No		4♠	6♠	6♣*	7♠	5♦	6♠		
						**Splinter		No		No		No			

#1, #2 and #3 : West's challenge is to find out whether East has an ace and whether it is the ♦A. If East has it, West can bid seven; if not, six will have to do.

#4, #5 and #6 : Here East needs to find controls in two suits : the ace of diamonds and second round club control with West. If West has both, East can bid the grand slam.

#7 : After locating diamond control, responder can sensibly switch over to RKCB.

#8 : West's 5♣ denied first round heart control and 5♠ denied second round heart control, so East passes.

Bid Set 28															
(1)		**(2)**		**(3)**		**(4)**		**(5)**		**(6)**		**(7)**		**(8)**	
W	**E**	**W**	**E**	**W**	**E**	**W**	**E**	**W**	**E**	**W**	**E**	**W**	**E**	**W**	**E**
1♦	1♠	1♠	4♦**	1♠	4♣**	1♠	4♣**	1♠	4♣**	1♠	2♥	1♠	2♥	1♠	2♥
1NT	3♥	4♥*	4♠	4NT	5♠	4♦*	4♥*	4♦*	5♣*	3♥	4♦*	3♥	4♦*	3♥	4♦*
3♠	4♣*	No		6♠	No	4NT	5♦	7♠	No	4♥	No	5♣*	5♦*	4♠*	4NT
4♦*	4♥*	4♠ = no ace				6♠	No			4♥ = no		5♥	No	5♣	5NT
5♣*	5♦*	to cue, no								ace to cue				6♣	6♥
5♥*	7♠	void in ♦s												No	
*Cue bids		**Splinter													

#1 : It is very tough to find the key major suit jacks which make 7NT a good bet.

#2 : East's 4♠ tells West that the partner is missing the ♣A and has a diamond loser as well. It is risky to reach the five-level with these cards.

#3 : Opener's hand is much better suited to asking with 4NT than cue bidding.

#5 : When East cue bids the club void and simultaneously denies the ♥A, East must have virtually all the cards held to justify the 4♣ splinter.

#7 : West's 5♣ denies first round spade control and 5♥ indicates that the problem is in spades. You might make 6♥ (if they do not lead a spade) by taking the club finesse, but you should take no pride in it.

#8 : After locating control in spades, East can switch to 4NT RKCB.

88 **A.** 1. 4♣. Cue bid showing spade support and a maximum 1NT.   2. 4♠. Spade support but weak. 3. 4♣.   4. 4♠. No ace to cue bid. You must not go beyond 4♠ in standard methods, but if 3♠ shows a slam-going one-suiter, you should bid 4NT with this hand.   5. 3NT. Denies spade support.

B. 1. 6♦. One top honor.   2. 6♣. No top trump.   3. 6♥. Two top honors.   4. 6♥. 5. 6♠. Three top honors . . . or you could simply bid the grand slam.

Bid Set 29 (1)		(2)		(3)		(4)		(5)		(6)		(7)		(8)	
W	E	W	E	W	E	W	E	W	E	W	E	W	E	W	E
No	2♣	1♠	4♣**	No	2♦	No	2♦	1♠	2NT	1♠	4♣**	1♠	4♣**	1♠	4♣**
2NT	3♠	4♦*	4♥*	2♠	3♠	2♠	3♠	3♣	4♣*	4♦*	4♥*	4♦*	4♥*	4♦*	4♠
4♦*	4♥*	4NT	5♠	4♣*	4NT	4♦	4NT	4♦*	5♣*	4NT	5♥	4NT	5♠	5♣*	5♥*
5♦*	6♣*	5NT	6♥	5♥	6♠	5♥	7♠	5♥*	5NT	6♣	No	5NT	6♦	6♠	No
6♦*	7♠	7♠	No	No		No		6♥	7♠	♠Q missing		7♠	No		
No		**Splinter						6♥ = two							
*Cue bids								top trumps							

#1 : 4♦ shows spade support and the ♦A. As East should have about nine winners, West is worth the cue bid with three winners. The hand is a rare example of being able to show third round control (6♦). Usually cue bidding is concerned only with first and second round controls (because you run out of bidding space).

#2 : West knows from East's 5♠ bid that East has 5+ trumps (as 5♠ showed, in theory, the trump queen). Therefore West knows East will have enough trumps to take care of all the club losers.

#3 : After West's 4♣ cue and 5♥ two key cards, East can tell that either the ♦A or the ♠A is missing.

#4 : East can tell that West has the ♦A and the ♠A as 4♦ denied the ace of clubs.

#5 : The bidding could also go 1♠ : 3♣, 3♥ : 3♠, 4♦ cue : 5♣ cue, 5♥ cue : 5NT, 6♥ : 7♠.

#6 : West starts a cue bidding sequence to locate control in hearts. When East shows the ace of hearts, West reverts to 4NT RKCB. On finding that the queen of trumps is missing, West settles for the small slam.

#7 : If East had bid 6♣ in reply to 5NT to show no king outside spades, West could still ask for the ♦Q with 6♦ over 6♣ and bid the grand slam if East has the ♦Q.

#8 : 4♠ said 'no ace to cue' and now West should be worried about the hearts. When East bids 5♥ to show second round control in hearts, West is prepared to take a shot at six. At the very worst the slam will be on a finesse, given East should have around 12 HCP or more for the splinter.

Bid Set 30 (1)		(2)		(3)		(4)		(5)		(6)		(7)		(8)	
W	E	W	E	W	E	W	E	W	E	W	E	W	E	W	E
1♣	1♠	1♣	1♠	1♦	1♥	1♥	4♣**	1♠	4NT	2♦	2♥	1♥	4♦**	1♥	2♦
4♦**	4♥*	4♦*	4♥*	4♣**	4NT	4♦*	4NT	5♠	6♠	2♠	3♠	4♠*	4NT	4♣**	5♣*
5NT	6♦	5NT	6♣	5♣	6♠	5♣	5♠	No		4♣*	4♠	5♣	7♥	5♥*	5NT
7♠	No	6♠	No	No		6♦	7♥			5♦*	5♥*	No		6♥	7♦
*Cue bids		6♣ = no				No				6♠	No			No	
**Splinter		top spade				6♦ = ♠K									

#1 : After East cue bids ♥A, West figures that East's heart losers can be discarded on the clubs once they are established. 5NT asks for trump honors and 6♦ = 1. 4NT would not help as East could have the ♦A and the ♥A for the 5♥ reply.

#2 : When East denies the ♠A by bidding 6♣, West has to be content with the small slam.

#3 : East has no cue bid but is too strong to give up in game. In such a case take your chances on the unguarded suit and make the RKCB ask.

#4 : East has a good hand with which to ask after West encourages slam with the 4♦ cue. As West has cue bid an ace already, the 5♣ reply must be three key cards. 5♠ was a Control Ask in spades.

#5 : East could splinter but the hand is so strong that East may as well ask, planning to bid 7♠ if West can produce three aces.

#6 : 3♠ shows support plus at least one control somewhere. 4♠ = no ace and 5♥ = second round control. Whether the second round heart control is the king (probably, because of the failure to splinter) or a singleton, West has found out that the small slam is a good contract and that a heart lead does not pose a threat.

#7 : Once East hears spade control, East can take charge of the auction.

#8 : East cannot cue bid 4♥ over 4♣. That would be taken as an offer to play in 4♥. West's 5♥ is a cue beyond five of the trump suit and so promises first round control in spades as well. With second round spade control, West would have jumped to 6♦ over 5♣. With the ♥K to help establish West's hearts, East figures a grand slam should be a good bet if no top trump is missing.

93 **A. (a)** 1. 2♠ via a transfer is reasonable but you might choose to pass. 2. Invite 3NT. 3. Invite 3NT. 4. Use a Stayman sequence and invite game. 5. Bid 3NT and take your chances. **(b)** 1. Transfer to 2♠. This will be safer than 1NT most of the time. 2. Bid 3NT. 3. Bid 3NT. The vulnerable game can be bid on the slimmest values. 4. Use a Stayman sequence and bid game. 5. Transfer to 3♣ and then bid 3♢, forcing to game. You do not mind reaching 5-minor at teams.
B. 1. Bid 2♣ at teams. At pairs you can gamble on the pass. 2. At teams, support spades with 3♠, the safer game. At pairs, support hearts (4♣ cue), which may score an extra trick some of the time. 3. Double at teams and pairs. Do not sell out if they bid and raise a suit to the two-level (see Chapter 17). 4. At teams you should bid 2♢, the safer partscore. At pairs, you might well pass 1NT. If you bid 2♢, the opponents are very likely to compete in hearts. They are less likely to compete at teams. 5. At teams you might bid 2♣ not vulnerable but if vulnerable, bid 3♣ and insist on game. At pairs, prefer 2NT despite the weakness in spades. At pairs you live by the sword . . . 6. At teams you should pass at any vulnerability. Game is unlikely, partner is a passed hand and your diamonds are not so great. At pairs you should risk the overcall. 7. At teams overcall 2♢ or pass. At pairs, use the unusual 2NT if not vulnerable. If vulnerable, a 2♢ overcall will do. 8. At teams bid 7♡. Partner figures to have something like ♠ A x x x x ♡ K Q x x ♢ K x ♣ A x. Even if spades are 4-1, you will be able to set up the fifth spade for your thirteenth trick. At pairs, try 7NT. Partner might have the ♠J and the spades will be 3-2 most of the time. 9. At pairs, and at teams not vulnerable, bid 2♢, minimum. At teams vulnerable, show a non-minimum and reach game somewhere. 10. Pass at teams and at pairs and at any vulnerability. At teams vulnerable, partner has already fudged the extra point with the invitation. The inviter bids with one point less, not the accepter.

99 **A.** 1. Double 2. 3♡. Partner should have one spade at most and so is likely to have some hearts. 3. 2NT. Shows 4-4 in the minors, denies 4 hearts. 4. Double. If partner bids 3♣, you have an easy removal to 3♢. 5. Bid 3♣. You would like to double but you cannot afford 4♣ over 3♢.
B. 1. 3♢ 2. 2♠ 3. 2♠. Do not give a jump response to a delayed double. If you do, partner will soon stop competing. 4. 3♣ 5. 2NT. Shows both minors in reply to a delayed double. Do not consider passing the double, even for a second.

Bidding Set 31

1.	WEST	NORTH	EAST	SOUTH
	1♢	Pass	1♡	Pass
	2♡	Pass	Pass	2♠
	3♡	Pass	Pass	Pass

2.	WEST	NORTH	EAST	SOUTH
	Pass	1♠	Pass	2♠
	Pass	Pass	2NT	3♠*
	Pass	Pass	Pass	

**If playing five-card majors*

#1 : South is far too weak to come in on the first round but the delayed overcall is mandatory.
#2 : If playing 4-card majors, South should pass 2NT and West who has the extra trump would bid 3♠. This sequence has the drawback that West will have the chance to reply to 2NT while if South can bid 3♠ at once, West will almost certainly be kept out.

3.	WEST	NORTH	EAST	SOUTH
	Pass	Pass	1♣	Pass
	2♣	Pass	Pass	Dble
	Pass	2♡	3♣	All pass

4.	WEST	NORTH	EAST	SOUTH
	Pass	Pass	Pass	1♡
	Pass	1♠	Pass	2♠
	Pass	Pass	2NT	Pass
	3♢	Pass	Pass	Pass

#3 : There is a strong case for West bidding 3♣ at once over the double. If West does not, East must. You cannot afford to sell out at the two-level when your side has a trump fit or when their side has a trump fit.
#4 : East's 2NT shows both minors. As North-South have only eight spades, they allow the opponents to play at the three-level.

5.	WEST	NORTH	EAST	SOUTH
	1♡	Pass	2♡	Pass
	Pass	Dble	Pass	2NT
	Pass	3♢	All pass	

6.	WEST	NORTH	EAST	SOUTH
	1♢	Pass	2♢	Pass
	Pass	Dble	Pass	2♡
	3♢	Pass	Pass	Pass

North would have removed 2♡ to 2♠ and South would then have corrected this to 3♣.

#5 : South's 2NT in reply to the delayed double shows both minors.

7.	WEST	NORTH	EAST	SOUTH
	Pass	1♣	Pass	1♠
	Pass	2♠	Pass	Pass
	2NT	Pass	3◊	All pass

104 A. 1. Double   2. Double   3. Double. If partner bids 2◊, remove this to 2♡ to offer partner the choice between hearts and spades.   4. 2◊. You do not want to double and hear 2♠.
5. Pass. With length and strength in the enemy suit, pass and defend. Pity partner did not double 2♣ for takeout. You would have left the double in.
B. 1. Double   2. Pass. Length and strength in their suit.   3. 2NT. Takeout for the minors.
4. Double. The meek shall inherit the earth, but they lose at pairs.
5. 3♣. You were happy to pass and defend no-trumps. You have far less defense against spades.

Bidding Set 32					2.	WEST	NORTH	EAST	SOUTH
1.	WEST	NORTH	EAST	SOUTH		Pass	1♠	2◊	Pass
	1◊	1♠	2◊	2♠		Pass	Dble	Pass	3♣
	Pass	Pass	3◊	All pass		3◊	Pass	Pass	Pass

#1 : As North-South have only eight spades, they let the opponents have the three-level. Both 3◊ and 3♠ should fail by one trick.
#2 : West has already shown a poor hand by passing East's overcall. The 3◊ bid shows the diamond length. Top defense can take 3◊ two down.

3.	WEST	NORTH	EAST	SOUTH	4.	WEST	NORTH	EAST	SOUTH
	Pass	Pass	1NT	Pass		Pass	Pass	Pass	1♣
	2◊	Pass	2♡	Pass		1♡	Dble	2♡	2♠
	Pass	2NT	Pass	3◊		Pass	Pass	3♡	All pass
	Dble	Pass	3♡ (pass?)	All pass					
West's double of 3◊ just shows high card values									

#3 : Courage is needed to compete after a strong 1NT opening. West should make a show of strength at some point since the transfer could have been no points at all. At pairs, East might leave the double in but at teams, removing the double to 3♡ is by far the safer action.

5.	WEST	NORTH	EAST	SOUTH	6.	WEST	NORTH	EAST	SOUTH
	1NT	Pass	2♡	Pass		Pass	1◊	1♠	Dble
	2♠	Pass	Pass	Dble		Pass*	2♡	Pass	Pass
	Pass	3◊	All pass			2♠	Pass	Pass	3♡
						Pass	Pass	Pass	
					*With such poor shape and no obvious trick in defense,				
					West should pass rather than raise to 2♠ at once.*				

7.	WEST	NORTH	EAST	SOUTH
	Pass	Pass	1♠	Dble
	2♠	Pass	Pass	Dble
	Pass	3♣	All pass	

110 A. 1. Pass. Too weak to bid at the three-level.   2. Pass. Too weak for 3◊.   3. Double. In this auction, the double shows four hearts in a minimum hand.   4. 3♡. Four hearts and 16-18 points.
5. 3◊. Expectancy is six diamonds and 16-18 points (like 1◊ : 1♡, 3◊).
B. 1. 2♠. Too good to pass.   2. 3◊   3. 3◊. The only lead you want.   4. Double. Shows 4-4 in the minors and 6+ points.   5. Double. 3◊ would be reasonable but double can hardly land you in the wrong minor suit, while 3◊ might be the inferior spot.
C. 1. 2♠. Shows a minimum opening and four spades.   2. Double. Shows three spades, strength undisclosed.   3. Double   4. 2◊. Denies three spades.   5. Pass. Hoping partner will be able to re-open with a competitive (takeout) double which you will pass in order to play for penalties.

Bidding Set 33

1.	WEST	NORTH	EAST	SOUTH
	1♦	1♠	Dble	2♠
	Dble	Pass	3♥	All pass

2.	WEST	NORTH	EAST	SOUTH
	Pass	1♣	1♠	Dble
	2♠	3♥	Pass	4♥
	Pass	Pass	Pass	

#1 : West's double shows four hearts but only a minimum opening.
#2 : West's 3♥ shows four hearts but a hand in the 16-18 range.

3.	WEST	NORTH	EAST	SOUTH
	Pass	Pass	1♣	Pass
	1♦	1♠	Dble	Pass
	2♥	Pass	4♥	All pass

East's double shows 4 hearts. South should spot the misfit and stay out of the bidding.

4.	WEST	NORTH	EAST	SOUTH
	Pass	Pass	Pass	1♥
	Dble	2♥	Dble	2♠
	Pass	3♥	All pass	

East's double is responsive, both minors. 2♠ by South is a long suit game try.

5.	WEST	NORTH	EAST	SOUTH
	1♥	Pass	1♠	2♣
	Pass	Pass	Dble	Pass
	Pass	Pass		

West passes 2♣ for penalties and wishes can come true, as East re-opens with a double.

6.	WEST	NORTH	EAST	SOUTH
	1♣	Pass	1♠	2♥
	Dble	Pass	2♠	Pass
	4♠	Pass	Pass	Pass

*West's double showed 3 spades exactly.

115 **A.** 1. Bid 1♠.   2. 2♥. Michaels.   3. 2♥. With extreme shape, the point count is irrelevant.
    4. Bid 2♦, and bid 4♠ over their 4♥. You could use Michaels 2♥ but if they bid 4♥ passed back to
    you, are you going to bid 5♦ or 4♠? Better to bid 2♦ now than guess later. It is wildly unlikely that
    2♦ will be passed out.   5. Bid 2♥ at favorable vulnerability. Otherwise, pass. The suits are too poor.
B. 1. 3♣. Partner will bid 3♦ with diamonds.   2. 4♠, likely to make.   3. 4♠, a sacrifice but might
even make on a very lucky day.   4. 2NT. Game is likely, probably in 3NT, but partner might have
six spades.   5. Bid 2♠. Partner is highly likely to have spades and clubs.
C. 1. 3♣. Second suit is clubs.   2. 3♥. Shows six hearts.   3. 3♦. Second suit is diamonds.
    4. 3♣.   5. 4♦. 6+ diamonds and 5 hearts.

Bidding Set 34

1.	WEST	NORTH	EAST	SOUTH
	1♥	2♥	Pass	4♠
	Pass	Pass	Pass	

2.	WEST	NORTH	EAST	SOUTH
	Pass	1♣	2♣	2♠
	4♥	Pass	Pass	Pass

2♠ = 10+ points with 5+ diamonds. North would do well to bid 5♦ which is only one off.

3.	WEST	NORTH	EAST	SOUTH
	1♣	Pass	1♥	2♥
	3♥	4♠	Dble	All pass

*Michaels can also be used over the response.
4♥ cannot be defeated and neither can 4♠. It is hard
for East-West with 29 HCP not to double 4♠.*

4.	WEST	NORTH	EAST	SOUTH
	1♠	2♠	Pass	2NT
	Pass	3♥	Pass	4♥
	Pass	Pass	Pass	

*3♥ showed six hearts. Over a 3♣ reply, East could
continue with 3♠, forcing, or 3♥ invitational.*

5.	WEST	NORTH	EAST	SOUTH
	1♥	2♥	Dble	3♣
	Dble	3♦	Dble	All pass

*East's double of 2♥ tells opener that penalties are
the order of the day.*

6.	WEST	NORTH	EAST	SOUTH
	Pass	Pass	Pass	1♣
	2♣	Pass (3♣?)	4♠	Dble
	Pass	Pass	Pass	

*You have to feel sorry for South, opening with 19
HCP and East-West reach an unbeatable game.*

120 **A.** 1. 2NT and follow up with 3♥ to show 4 spades and hearts stopped.   2. Bid 3♥ at once, to show four spades and no stopper in hearts.   3. 3NT. Enough points for game but no 4 spades and no stopper in hearts.   4. 2NT and follow up with 3NT to promise a stopper in hearts.
5. 2NT and follow up with 3♠ to show five spades and a stopper in hearts.
B. 1. 3♣. Shows four hearts and no spade stopper.   2. 2♠. Game values with a singleton or a void in spades.   3. 2♥. Merely competing for the partscore.   4. 3♥. Natural and forcing. If playing transfer Lebensohl, bid 3♦.   5. 2NT and pass the forced 3♣ ('puppet').
C. 1. 3♦. Transfer to hearts. Follow up with 3♠ over 3♥ to express concern about the spades.
2. 3♦ and follow up with 4♥.   3. Bid 2NT and continue with 3♦ over 3♣. This shows the values for game with 5+ clubs and 4 diamonds. If partner bids 3♥, you should raise to 4♥ to complete the picture of your hand.   4. 3♥. This is artificial and shows both minors with at least 5 diamonds and interest in slam. With 5+ hearts, responder would use the 3♦ transfer (see #1 and #2).
5. 3♣, transfer to diamonds. Competing for the partscore.

Bidding Set 35									
(1)		**(2)**		**(3)**		**(4)**		**(5)**	
WEST	**EAST**	**WEST**	**EAST**	**WEST**	**EAST**	**WEST**	**EAST**	**WEST**	**EAST**
1NT	(2♥) Dble	1NT	(2♥) Dble	No	1NT (2♥)	No	1NT (2♥)	1NT (2♠)	3NT
2♠	Pass	2NT	Pass	2NT	3♣	2NT	3♣	4♣	5♦
East's double is for		*East's double is for*		3♦	Pass	Pass		*3NT = no spade*	
takeout.		*takeout.*						*stopper*	

#1 : East's double is for takeout but does not guarantee four spades. West's 2♠ shows four spades and minimum points. Without spade support, East would rebid 2NT or 3-minor. If West had maximum points, West could bid 3♠, 3NT or 3♥.

#3 : 2NT Lebensohl forced East to bid 3♣. West's 3♦ then showed long diamonds but no interest in game. With game invitational values, West would double and remove a minimum bid from East to 3♦. The sequence chosen shows enough to compete for the partscore but not enough to invite game.

#5 : If East has no spade stopper, then West sees little value in staying in 3NT. Note how the opposition interference helps East-West. Had North kept quiet, East would have responded 3NT none the wiser about the flaw in the spade department. West's 4♣ is not forcing and East takes a sensible shot at 5♦. If West has no stopper in spades, West's high cards should be useful in hearts, diamonds and clubs.

Bidding Set 36									
(1)		**(2)**		**(3)**		**(4)**		**(5)**	
WEST	**EAST**	**WEST**	**EAST**	**WEST**	**EAST**	**WEST**	**EAST**	**WEST**	**EAST**
1NT	(2♥) 3♥	1NT	(2♥) 3♥	No	1NT (2♠)	No	1NT (2♠)	1NT (2♠)	3NT
3NT	Pass	4♠	Pass	2NT	3♣	2NT	3♣	4♣	Pass
		4♠ is a practical		3♥	Pass	3♥	4♥		
		shot at game.							

#1 : East's 3♥ shows four spades and denies a stopper in spades. West has no rebid problem.

#2 : With no stopper in hearts either, West shuns 3NT. A 4-3 major suit game is no thing of joy but is the most practical move here. If East had the jack of spades as well, 4♠ would be an excellent game. On the actual cards, it will need a fair slice of luck. 3♥ is forcing to game so there is no chance of stopping in 3♠ (which would in fact show four spades and maximum values, suitable for slam if responder is interested).

#3 : West does not have much but it is silly to sell out to 2♠. The sequence chosen indicates merely a desire to compete for the partscore. It denies the values to invite game. Such strength is shown by a double. Add a king to the West hand and West would start with a double and remove a minimum bid to 3♥ and a maximum bid to 4♥.

#4 : Even though West's action is merely competing for the partscore, opener should raise to game with all three ingredients required for a super-accept : 3+ support, maximum points and an outside doubleton.

#5 : East's 3NT shows the values for game with no stopper in spades and no four hearts. With no spade stopper opposite, West does not fancy 3NT and bids 4♣, not forcing. With no aces and only one king, East is wise to let the bidding stop in 4♣. With maximum values, West could jump to 5♣ over 3NT or bid 4♠ to show 4-4 in the minors and a maximum.

124 A. 1. 2NT. Much better than 3◊.   2. Double. Too strong for 2NT. If partner bids 2NT Lebensohl, bid 3♣ but over any other action you have enough for 3NT.   3. 4NT. This shows both minors, at least 5-5 and a 4-loser hand or better. While 4NT does entail some risk, other actions could easily see you missing game or not finding your best trump fit.   4. 4◊. You are showing 5+ diamonds and 5+ hearts in a 5-loser hand or better. After a pre-empt, play partner to provide two tricks for you, and therefore deduct two losers from your own loser count to estimate the playing potential of the partnership hands. On the other side of the table, partner should not be impressed until holding more than two tricks for you.   5. Double. If partner bids 2NT Lebensohl, bid 3♠ to force to game. If partner bids 3♣ or 3♡, you have slam potential. Over 3◊ from partner, you can bid 3♡, which is forcing after partner has shown some values.

B. 1. 3♠. Shows five spades and around eight losers, not forcing.   2. 2NT and follow up with 3♠ to show the same values as in #1 but with only four spades. If you have 9 or 10 losers, 2♠ is enough.
3. 2NT and follow up with 3◊ over 3♣ to show a rotten hand with 4+ diamonds.
4. 3◊. By not using the 2NT route to 3◊ you are showing 4+ diamonds and about 7-10 HCP.
5. 2NT followed by 3NT over the 3♣ puppet. This sequence shows the values for 3NT with a double stopper in hearts. With similar values and only one stopper, bid 3NT at once.

C. 1. 3♣, as requested. No justification for any other action. If partner continues with 3◊ or 3♡, pass. If partner continues with 3♠ asking for a spade stopper, rebid 4◊.   2. 3♡. With a 4-loser hand, you are strong enough to reject the 3♣ puppet. 3♡ shows 5+ hearts and a 4-loser hand, asking partner to try for game with one trick or better. Opposite ♡K-x-x and ♣J-x-x-x you would be happy enough to reach 4♡ but if you bid 3♣, that is where you might play.   3. Bid 3♣. Although you have a very strong hand, you do have six losers. Opposite a very weak hand, game is not likely.   4. 3♠. This shows game values in a 3-loser hand or better.   5. 4♣. Shows excellent clubs in a 3-4 loser hand.

Bidding Set 37									
(1)		(2)		(3)		(4)		(5)	
WEST	EAST	WEST	EAST	WEST	EAST	WEST	EAST	WEST	EAST
	(2♡) Dble	(2♠) Dble	2NT		(2♠) Dble	(2♠) 2NT	3◊	(2♡) 2NT	3◊
2♠	2NT	3♣	3♡	2NT	3♠	3♡	3NT	3♠	4♠
3NT	Pass	Pass		4♡	Pass	Pass		Pass	

#1 : Although West has eight points, West has too many losers to push the bidding to 3♠ (via 2NT Lebensohl). 2♠ will be quite enough if partner cannot bid any higher. East's 2NT rebid shows 19-20 points, balanced. With 16-18, East would have bid 2NT at once.

#2 : You may miss game occasionally by passing it out in 3♡ but most of the time 3♡ will be quite high enough. On the actual cards 4♡ is a terrible spot (as three rounds of spades will create a trump trick for the defense) and yet East has five hearts (might have only four) and has a useful king (the hearts could be jack high or even worse). If West had the same values and four hearts, it would not be a terrible thing to take a gamble (perhaps a gambol?) at 4♡. If that goes wrong, be quick to apologise and ward off any post mortem.

#3 : No one promised you that your decisions will always be easy. East will not enjoy the 4♡ development but what else should East do over 2NT? With 23 HCP and only three losers. East must make the strongest move to reach game. East will be fearful about passing 4♡ (on a bad day West might have only four hearts) but to remove it to 5♣ is a sheer guess. 5♣ could be hopeless with 4♡ laydown. If you are going to guess, you may as well pass 4♡. Choose the guess that will give you the highest scoring result.

#4 : West's 2NT shows a balanced 16-18 and spades stopped. 3◊ is a transfer to hearts, the unbid major, and 3NT offers West the choice between 3NT and 4♡.

#5 : East's 3◊ is a transfer to *spades*. It makes no sense to transfer to hearts, opener's 6-card major, so after (weak two) : 2NT, advancer's 3◊ bid is always the transfer to the other major. As you can transfer to the other major, you do not need a bid of 3♠ here as a natural bid. Use it as a slam try with both minors. After a transfer, partner should jump to game in advancer's major with the three super-accept ingredients : 3+ trumps, maximum values and an outside doubleton. Here West has a simple accept and East has enough to bid 4♠ with six spades and ten points.

Bidding Set 38									
(1)		(2)		(3)		(4)		(5)	
WEST	EAST	WEST	EAST	WEST	EAST	WEST	EAST	WEST	EAST
(1♠)	Dble	(2♥)	Dble 3♦	(2♥)	Dble	(2♥)	4♦	(2♠)	Dble 2NT
2NT	4♣	Pass		3♦	3♥	4♠	Pass	3♥	4NT
5♣	Pass			3NT	Pass			5♣	6NT
								Pass	

#1 : With a four loser hand, East is too strong to overcall just 3♣. Start with a double and follow up with 3♣ over partner's 3♦ or 3♥ bid (which shows some values). Over 2NT, East should jump to 4♣ to show the excellent clubs and the 4-loser hand. It is true that you may miss 3NT some days but you cannot cater for everything. To rebid 3♠ over 2NT shows a better hand than this. 4♣ can be dropped, while 3♠ commits you to game. With four losers and a long minor that is not warranted. West makes a sensible decision to take a shot at 5♣ as the West hand is better than it might be. West has four clubs and need not have any. West has a probable winner with the king of hearts and potential for a ruff because of the doubleton. On the actual East-West cards, 5♣ is an excellent game.

#2 : East's 3♦ shows respectable values, about 7-10 points, but it is not forcing, of course. West has no reason to push higher.

#3 : The bidding starts as in #2 but this time East has enough points to make a game try. One consequence of playing Lebensohl is that you lose the natural 2NT reply to the double. That is a flaw but it is a tradeoff against the benefits that flow from advancer being able to express hand strengths more accurately. Most top pairs are prepared to forego the natural 2NT reply in exchange for the Lebensohl benefits. East's 3♥ asks for a stopper in hearts and with a stopper, West bids 3NT. With no stopper in hearts, West would continue with 3♠ (3-card suit, Q-x-x or better, as 3♦ already denied four spades), 4♣ with 4+ clubs or 4♦ with extra length there and no other suit to bid. Over 3♥, if West is at the top of the range, West could jump to game or bid 4♥ to ask partner to pick a game.

#4 : 4♦ showed 5+ diamonds and 5+ spades, with a 5-loser hand or better. With weaker suits, East might bid just 2♠. Over 4♦, with equal length in diamonds and spades, West naturally gives preference to spades.

#5 : With 4 losers, West is too strong for 3♥. Start with a double and bid the hearts next time. East bids 2NT en route to 3NT to show two stoppers in spades. West naturally thinks East has a poor hand, looking to sign off after the 3♣ puppet. With 4 losers, West is strong enough to reject the puppet and 3♥ shows 5+ hearts and a 4-loser hand. Opposite that sort of strength, East is worth a move towards slam. If West has only four losers, East should be able to cover most of them. The jack of hearts may also be helpful in setting up extra tricks there. 4NT is RKCB setting hearts as trumps but East is intending to end in 6NT unless two key cards are missing (if so, bail out in 5♥).

129 **A.** 1. 2♥. Catering for a weak two in hearts.   2. 3♣. Forcing. Over partner's likely 3♥, bid 3♠, still forcing and follow up with 4♠ over 3NT or 4♣. If partner jumps to 4♥ over 3♣ to show Suit Quality 10, you should pass.   3. 2♠. To play opposite the probable weak two in spades. However, if partner has a weak two in hearts, you want to be in game.   4. 2NT. If partner bids 3♥, weak suit and minimum hand you should pass. If partner bids 3♣, relay with 3♦ and pass if opener bids 3♥ to show a minimum. After any other reply, you are worth game.   5. Pass. A calculated gamble but even if partner has a strong hand, game may not be on.

B. 1. 3♣. Weak two in hearts. Although minimum, you have two top honors in hearts. 3♥ would show a minimum weak 2♥ with only one top honor in hearts.   2. 3♥. Speak of the devil.

3. 3♦. Showing a weak 2♠ which is maximum or which has two top honors in spades.

4. 3NT. This shows A-K-Q-x-x-x in either major. If responder is not sure which major, responder bids 4♥ and opener corrects to 4♠ with spades.   5. 4♠. Shows a maximum weak 2♠ with a suit quality of 10. Such a suit is playable opposite a singleton or a void.

C. 1. Double. Over a natural weak two, you would bid 2NT to show 16-18. Over a multi-two, where their suit is unknown, it works better to use 2NT for 19-21 balanced and double with the 16-18 balanced. If partner bids 2♥, the negative reply, you will hunt for the best partscore (here bid 2♠ over 2♥, even with just a 4-card suit). Without four spades you would rebid 2NT, if balanced, over 2♥.

2. 2NT, 19-21 balanced.   3. 2♥. Shows a sound overcall but below 16 HCP (failure to double).

4. Jump to 3♥ to show a strong 6+ suit (Suit Quality of 9+) and a 5-loser hand.

5. 3♦. An overcall at the three-level should show a decent suit and about a 6-loser hand.

Bidding Set 39

1.	WEST	NORTH	EAST	SOUTH		2.	WEST	NORTH	EAST	SOUTH
	Pass	2◊	Pass	2NT			2◊	Pass	2♠	Pass
	Pass	3◊	Pass	3♡			4♡	Pass	Pass	Pass
	Pass	3♠	Pass	3NT						
	Pass	Pass	Pass							

#1 : With better than three winners, South is worth a try for game. Opposite a minimum weak 2♡, South would stop in 3♡. North's 3◊ shows spades and not the worst possible hand. 3♡ asks for further information and 3♠ shows minimum points with two top honors in spades. South knows North must have ♠A-K-x-x-x-x and virtually nothing else (since North has 6-8 HCP only). South can see nine tricks in spades and also nine tricks in 3NT. Guess what South should choose.

#2 : East must not bid 2♡ which could be passed out. With game prospects opposite a weak two in hearts but not opposite a weak two in spades, bid 2♠. Partner will pass with spades, bid 3♡ with a weak 2♡ minimum and 4♡ with a weak 2♡ maximum. North-South have a good spade fit but how should North-South enter the bidding? South could bid 3◊ but West will still bid 4♡. What then for North-South?

3.	WEST	NORTH	EAST	SOUTH		4.	WEST	NORTH	EAST	SOUTH
	2◊	Pass	2♡	Dble			2◊	Pass	2♡	Pass
	Pass	3♠	Pass	4♠			2♠	Pass	2NT	Pass
	Pass	Pass	Pass				3♠	Pass	4♠	All pass

#3 : Treat the reply to a multi-2◊ as their opening. South therefore treats East's 2♡ as a weak 2♡ opening and doubles. You do not need 16+ points here, just what you would need to double a regular weak 2♡ opening (since responder has revealed a relatively weak hand). West's pass confirms a weak two in hearts. North replies to the double as though replying to a double of a 2♡ opening (see Chapter 22). 3♠ shows five spades and game-inviting values. 2NT in reply to the double would be Lebensohl here.

#4 : East bids 2♡, expecting West to have a weak two in hearts. When West shows a weak two in spades, East has definite game prospects. 2NT over 2♠ is now regular Ogust (see Chapter 9) and 3♠ shows a maximum with two top honors in spades. Neither North nor South is worth any bid.

5.	WEST	NORTH	EAST	SOUTH		6.	WEST	NORTH	EAST	SOUTH
	Pass	2◊	Dble	2♡			2◊	Pass	2♡	Dble
	2♠	Pass	2NT	Pass			Pass	Pass	Pass	
	3♠	Pass	4♠	All pass						

#5 : East's double shows 16+ points, any shape. South usually takes the same action over the double as over a pass by East. Pass by South would show 5+ diamonds and allow North to leave it in 2◊ with support. Redouble by South would say, 'Make the cheapest bid and pass my next bid. My suit is better than yours.' With a weak hand, West would pass 2♡ and leave further action to South. 2♠ = 4+ spades, 8+ HCP *and is forcing to game*. 2NT and 3♠ are natural rebids.

#6 : East makes the normal 2♡ pass-or-correct reply and South doubles 2♡ for takeout. West passes to show a weak two in hearts and North passes for pleasure. You can imagine East's thoughts : 'Partner opens a lousy weak two and I have to suffer as declarer in this hopeless mess.' 2♡ doubled should be a massacre. It would have been unfortunate timing for North to make a frisky 2♡ overcall.

134 A. 1. 3♣. To play opposite the black two-suiter. With the red suits, partner will bid 3◊. At teams you should definitely pass 3◊. At pairs, passing 3◊ is also a good move although bidding 3♡ is attractive. The problem is that the opponents have an excellent spade fit and you do not want them to find it. If you bid 3♡, you give them one extra chance to enter the auction. Pass 3◊ and only one opponent has the opportunity to back in. If left in 3◊, you should score very well, whether you make it or not.

2. 3◊. To play opposite the red two-suiter. You would be delighted if partner revealed the black suits.

3. 4♡. Prepared to play in 4♡ opposite the red two-suiter and even happier to hear partner correct to 4♠ with a black two-suiter.   4. 4◊. Prepared to play 4◊ opposite the reds and good enough black suit values to welcome a correction to 4♠.   5. Pass. It's dollars to doughnuts that partner has the black suits, so stop at the lowest level with this semi-misfit. No need to drag yourself into the three-level. If it turns out that partner actually has the red suits, everyone will have a hearty laugh, the opponents as they wipe partner out and your side as you chalk up a top because they have missed 4♠. Even if partner were to go eight down, you are in front if they can make 4♠.

134 B. 1. 3◇. Minimum with spades-diamonds.   2. 3♠. Maximum with spades-diamonds
     3. 3♡. Minimum with hearts-clubs.   4. 3NT, Maximum with hearts-clubs.
     5. 4♣. Maximum with six clubs

    C. 1. Pass. To bid 2♠ here is fraught with danger. Opener could easily have 5 spades and 5 hearts.
     2. 3♣. Now it is overwhelmingly likely that opener has the majors.
     3. 2NT. Shows 19-21 balanced. With 16-18 balanced, start with a double.
     4. Double. Showing 16+ HCP and any shape other than those suitable for a 2NT or 3NT bid.
     5. Pass. If opener reveals the minors, you can then double for takeout.

Bidding Set 40

1.	WEST	NORTH	EAST	SOUTH		2.	WEST	NORTH	EAST	SOUTH
	Pass	Pass	2♡	Pass			Pass	2♠	2NT	Pass
	3♣	Pass	Pass	Dble			3♣	Pass	3♡	Pass
	Pass	3♠	All pass				4♡	Pass	Pass	Pass

#1 : 2♡ = majors or minors. West bids 3♣, pass-or-correct, intending to play in 3♡ if East has the majors. East's pass confirms the minors. It is asking a lot to expect South to bid with a balanced hand opposite a passed partner but in these auctions, it is vital to compete if short in their suit. South should treat this position as though LHO had opened 3♣ : Pass : Pass. If you would bid in that auction, you should bid here as well. Therefore South should double 3♣ for takeout (much more efficient than penalty doubles in these auctions). One plus is that partner knows you have below 16 HCP (failure to double 2◇). That is why North will not get too excited and will not look to bid more than 3♠.

#2 : 2♠ = red suits or black suits. 2NT = 19-21 balanced and 3♣ = Stayman.

3.	WEST	NORTH	EAST	SOUTH		4.	WEST	NORTH	EAST	SOUTH
	2♡	Pass	4♠	Pass			Pass	2♡	Dble	Rdble
	5♣	Pass	5◇	All pass			Pass	2♠	Pass	Pass
							Dble	Pass	2NT	Pass
							3NT	Pass	Pass	Pass

#3 : 2♡ = majors or minors. With a 5-card fit for each of opener's possible combinations, responder should pre-empt to the four-level. East's 4♠ = 'Pass with the majors, bid on with the minors.' West corrects to 5♣ and East converts to 5◇. East expects 5◇ to fail (on a lucky day it might make) but it should be a good sacrifice against the probable heart game for North-South. On the actual cards, North-South can make 4♡ but how should they enter the bidding? For further discussion, see Deal 94.

#4 : 2♡ = majors or minors. Double = 16+, any shape. South has little doubt about the rank of opener's suits ('very rank' would be South's thoughts). South wants to play in 2♠ but if South bids 2♠, North will naturally correct to the minors. That would push South up to 3♠, not a rosy prospect on the known misfit. That is the function of the redouble, to allow responder to escape into his own long suit. Redouble says, 'Make the cheapest bid possible and then pass my next bid.' West is happy to pass for the moment and North dutifully bids 2♠ despite the void. It is important for partner to have faith. Hope and charity are also useful attributes. East has said it all with the 16+ double and the bidding reverts to West who tries a competitive double. This is not ideal but what else can West do? West can hardly pass with 8 HCP opposite partner's 16+. North must still have faith and not run or redouble for rescue. East could leave the double in and 2♠ would be beaten. If East bids 2NT, West should raise to 3NT. With three spades and modest hearts it would not be wise to suggest a heart contract in the face of the obvious North-South misfit.

5.	WEST	NORTH	EAST	SOUTH		6.	WEST	NORTH	EAST	SOUTH
	2NT	Pass	3◇	Pass			Pass	2NT	Dble	Pass
	Pass	Dble	Pass	4♡			Pass	3◇	Dble	3♠
	Pass	Pass	Pass				4♡	Pass	4NT	Pass
							5♡	Pass	6♡	All pass

#5 : 2NT = non-touching suits. 3◇ = Pass-or-correct. West's pass confirms diamonds-spades. North has enough for a takeout double showing the other two suits and South is worth 4♡. East might consider a sacrifice (5◇ is only two down) but with secondary values in clubs and hearts, pass is recommended. Perhaps 4♡ will fail.

#6 : 2NT = odd suits. Dble = 16+. There is no urgency for South or West to bid yet. 3◇ = diamonds-spades and East's double = takeout of diamonds. South corrects to 3♠ and West is worth 4♡. That is enough to galvanise East into slam mode. 4NT = RKCB with hearts set as trumps.

PLAY HANDS FOR NORTH

(After each hand, the dealer is given, followed by the vulnerability, e.g., S/E-W means Dealer South, East-West vulnerable.)

1 N/Nil	2 E/N-S	3 S/E-W	4 W/Both	5 N/N-S	6 E/E-W
♠ K J 7 5	♠ 9 6 2	♠ 8 4	♠ Q J 7 3	♠ A 9	♠ 9 8 4
♥ A Q	♥ Q 5	♥ A K Q 10	♥ K Q J	♥ Q 10 2	♥ A K 10 9 7
♦ A Q 10 6	♦ K 10 9	♦ Q 6 5	♦ 10 5 2	♦ J 7 6 4 3 2	♦ 10 9 3 2
♣ 9 8 3	♣ Q 9 7 5 4	♣ A K 7 6	♣ 8 6 4	♣ J 10	♣ 5

7 S/Both	8 W/Nil	9 N/E-W	10 E/Both	11 S/Nil	12 W/N-S
♠ J 10 9	♠ A Q 7	♠ A K 7 6	♠ A 9	♠ K 7 6 4	♠ J 9 2
♥ 10 8 7 4	♥ A 6 5 4	♥ K 8 6 2	♥ K 8 5 4	♥ 10 9 5	♥ A K Q 3
♦ K 10 8	♦ K 8 4	♦ Q 7 2	♦ J 10 9 6	♦ A 7 2	♦ Q 9 5
♣ A Q 5	♣ A J 8	♣ A 6	♣ J 6 3	♣ 10 7 4	♣ A 9 3

13 N/Both	14 E/Nil	15 S/N-S	16 W/E-W	17 N/Nil	18 E/N-S
♠ A 2	♠ 9 6 4	♠ K 10 9 6 3	♠ J 10 8 4 3	♠ A K 3	♠ J 10 8 4
♥ A 7 5 4	♥ 10 5	♥ Q 8 7 2	♥ - - -	♥ 10 3	♥ A 9 5 4
♦ A 8 4 3	♦ Q J 10 8 7	♦ 9 5	♦ 10 7 6 4	♦ A K 8 6 2	♦ J 9 2
♣ A K Q	♣ Q 5 4	♣ 7 4	♣ Q 7 5 2	♣ 7 5 4	♣ J 3

19 S/E-W	20 W/Both	21 N/N-S	22 E/E-W	23 S/Both	24 W/Nil
♠ A K J 9 6	♠ K 7	♠ 9 7 6 4	♠ K Q 7 3	♠ A 10 9 6	♠ A K Q J 8 2
♥ 8 6 2	♥ 9 7 5 3	♥ - - -	♥ K 7 3	♥ - - -	♥ K Q 3
♦ 5	♦ K 8 3	♦ A 9 8 7 3	♦ A 8 6 4 2	♦ 10 7 6 4 3	♦ - - -
♣ K J 3 2	♣ 8 7 4 3	♣ A 10 9 5	♣ 3	♣ J 7 5 4	♣ A Q 7 2

25 N/E-W	26 E/Both	27 S/Nil	28 W/N-S	29 N/Both	30 E/Nil
♠ 10 8	♠ A 6	♠ A 2	♠ 10 9 7 2	♠ K 7 6 4	♠ A J 10 7 5
♥ Q J 8 5 4	♥ 6 5 3 2	♥ A Q 7 4	♥ 8 4	♥ A Q	♥ A 10 2
♦ A 10 6	♦ A 9 7 5 3	♦ K 7 2	♦ 9 8 4	♦ 10 7 5	♦ 10 8 3
♣ A J 10	♣ Q 2	♣ 9 7 6 2	♣ K J 9 5	♣ Q 10 8 3	♣ A J

31 S/N-S	32 W/E-W	33 N/Nil	34 E/N-S	35 S/E-W	36 W/Both
♠ A K J 9	♠ K J 4 2	♠ 6	♠ 5 3	♠ 7 4	♠ J 10 8
♥ 6 5	♥ 9 5 3	♥ A K J 9 8 3	♥ 6 5 4 2	♥ J 10 9 8	♥ A 9 8
♦ 8 7 3	♦ A 9 6	♦ J 10	♦ K Q 10	♦ K Q 9	♦ A Q 10
♣ Q 8 4 3	♣ J 8 6	♣ 7 4 3 2	♣ J 9 6 5	♣ K J 6 5	♣ 10 7 5 4

37 N/N-S	38 E/E-W	39 S/Both	40 W/Nil	41 N/E-W	42 E/Both
♠ K Q 9 8	♠ 10 6 5 4	♠ J 5 4	♠ 8 7 6 5	♠ 2	♠ Q 10 7 5
♥ 10	♥ 8 6 3	♥ K Q J 6 4 2	♥ K 3	♥ K Q	♥ 10 9
♦ Q 9 3 2	♦ 5 3	♦ Q 3	♦ K Q 10 9	♦ A Q J 9 8 6	♦ 10 9 8 6 5 3
♣ K 7 6 4	♣ J 8 6 4	♣ J 2	♣ 8 7 3	♣ A K Q J	♣ 5

43 S/Nil	44 W/N-S	45 N/Both	46 E/Nil	47 S/N-S	48 W/E-W
♠ Q 10 5 3	♠ J 9 5 4 3	♠ K Q 10 6 3	♠ J 8 7 5	♠ 10 8 5 2	♠ A K Q 9 5 4
♥ J 9 8 6 4	♥ - - -	♥ A J 8 7	♥ - - -	♥ 10 9 7 2	♥ A J 9 5
♦ 6 2	♦ 10 9 8 5 4	♦ K 6 4	♦ K Q 5 3	♦ Q 10 3	♦ A 4
♣ 10 8	♣ K J 9	♣ 8	♣ J 7 6 4 2	♣ J 8	♣ 2

PLAY HANDS FOR NORTH

(After each hand the dealer is given, followed by the vulnerability, e.g., W/Both means Dealer West, both sides vulnerable.)

49 N/Nil	50 E/N-S	51 S/E-W	52 W/Both	53 N/N-S	54 E/E-W
♠ K 7 5 4 2	♠ 8 7 2	♠ A 7 6 4	♠ Q 9 5 4 3	♠ J 5 3	♠ A Q 10 6 3
♥ A K 5 2	♥ 10 9 8 7	♥ 4	♥ 9 8 5 3 2	♥ K 8 4	♥ 7 6 2
◊ A K Q	◊ K J 9 6	◊ K Q 8	◊ K Q 8	◊ A K Q 8	◊ A K Q
♣ A	♣ 10 2	♣ A 8 6 3 2	♣ - - -	♣ 5 4 3	♣ J 8

55 S/Both	56 W/Nil	57 N/E-W	58 E/Both	59 S/Nil	60 W/N-S
♠ 9 7 4	♠ 8 4	♠ A 9 8 7	♠ 9 8 7 2	♠ A K Q 10 5	♠ 10 9 2
♥ - - -	♥ 10 9 8 5 4	♥ A 8 2	♥ Q J 10 6 3 2	♥ 9 8 2	♥ 8 7 6 5 4
◊ K 8 7 4	◊ 10 6 2	◊ - - -	◊ 6	◊ 10 2	◊ K J 10
♣ K 7 5 4 3 2	♣ Q 10 5	♣ K Q 10 7 6 2	♣ 4 2	♣ A Q 3	♣ 5 2

61 N/Both	62 E/Nil	63 S/N-S	64 W/E-W	65 N/Nil	66 E/N-S
♠ A Q 6	♠ 8 6 4 3	♠ 9 4 3	♠ J 10 8 5	♠ 8 6 5 4 3 2	♠ J 9 8
♥ A K J	♥ 4	♥ Q 8 5 2	♥ 9	♥ A 7 2	♥ 8 7 3
◊ Q 10 9 5 4	◊ 10 9 8 7 3	◊ A 7 6	◊ 9 8 2	◊ 10	◊ A K 7 3
♣ 8 3	♣ 8 3 2	♣ A K 8	♣ 10 9 5 4 3	♣ K 3 2	♣ K 5 4

67 S/E-W	68 W/Both	69 N/N-S	70 E/E-W	71 S/Both	72 W/Nil
♠ Q 8 6	♠ K Q 10	♠ Q J 5 2	♠ 8 6	♠ K J 6 4	♠ A K 9 8
♥ K Q 4 2	♥ K J 8 6 4	♥ K 8	♥ A 9 7	♥ J 10 6	♥ K Q 7 5 3
◊ 8 7	◊ A 10	◊ A Q 8 6 3	◊ K 10 9 4 3 2	◊ A K Q 10 2	◊ A J
♣ A K 8 4	♣ 6 3 2	♣ Q 8	♣ 8 2	♣ J	♣ J 4

73 N/E-W	74 E/Both	75 S/Nil	76 W/N-S	77 N/Both	78 E/Nil
♠ 7 5 4	♠ J 7 3	♠ A J 6 5 2	♠ 8 6	♠ Q J 5 2	♠ Q J 10 6 4
♥ K J 10 6	♥ A K Q 9 3	♥ 9 2	♥ K J	♥ 9 8	♥ 10 9 6 5
◊ A 9 8 3	◊ Q J 7	◊ K J 9 5	◊ A J 8 4 3	◊ A J 8 6 3	◊ A
♣ 6 3	♣ K 7	♣ 7 5	♣ A K 7 4	♣ 5 2	♣ J 10 2

79 S/N-S	80 W/E-W	81 N/Nil	82 E/N-S	83 S/E-W	84 W/Both
♠ Q	♠ Q J 10 6 3	♠ A K 7 4	♠ A 3	♠ A J 7	♠ K 9 7 4 3 2
♥ J 10 9 5	♥ K 3	♥ 8 4	♥ J 3	♥ A K	♥ - - -
◊ J 10 9 4	◊ K Q 10 9 5	◊ Q 10 6 2	◊ 7 3 2	◊ K 8 6	◊ 9 8 7 2
♣ K 9 8 6	♣ 9	♣ Q 3 2	♣ 9 8 6 5 4 3	♣ J 9 8 3 2	♣ J 10 8

85 N/N-S	86 E/E-W	87 S/Both	88 W/Nil	89 N/E-W	90 E/Both
♠ A K Q 9 8 5	♠ Q J 8 7 5 2	♠ 9 5	♠ K J 9 6 2	♠ 8 6 4	♠ 9 3
♥ 5	♥ 6	♥ 10 8 6 2	♥ J 9 6 5	♥ A J 8 7 6 3	♥ A K Q J 9 8
◊ 10 6 2	◊ A J 9	◊ 8 7 5	◊ J	◊ Q J 10	◊ A 3
♣ 9 7 4	♣ 9 7 4	♣ 10 9 4 3	♣ K 6 5	♣ 3	♣ A 8 2

91 S/Nil	92 W/N-S	93 N/Both	94 E/Nil	95 S/N-S	96 W/E-W
♠ 9 8	♠ 7 5 3	♠ A J 8	♠ J 10	♠ A K 8	♠ Q 7
♥ K Q J 2	♥ A K Q 9 5 3	♥ J 7 5 3	♥ K 9 8 6 5 3 2	♥ A Q J 10 5	♥ A 10 9 8
◊ 2	◊ 9 8 4	◊ K 7	◊ K	◊ 7	◊ K 7 6
♣ A 10 7 5 4 3	♣ 2	♣ J 8 3 2	♣ K 8 5	♣ K Q 8 3	♣ 7 4 3 2

PLAY HANDS FOR EAST

(After each hand, the dealer is given, followed by the vulnerability, e.g., S/E-W means Dealer South, East-West vulnerable.)

1 N/Nil	2 E/N-S	3 S/E-W	4 W/Both	5 N/N-S	6 E/E-W
♠ Q 10 4	♠ 10 7 5 3	♠ 10 6 5	♠ A 8 4 2	♠ Q 3	♠ J 7 6
♥ J 7 3	♥ A 9 6 3 2	♥ 6 4	♥ A 7 5 3	♥ J 9 6 4	♥ 6 3 2
◇ K 9 4 3	◇ 7 6	◇ 8 4 2	◇ 6 3	◇ A K Q 8	◇ K J 5
♣ K Q 7	♣ K 3	♣ 10 8 4 3 2	♣ A K 10	♣ A 7 6	♣ 10 7 3 2

7 S/Both	8 W/Nil	9 N/E-W	10 E/Both	11 S/Nil	12 W/N-S
♠ A 5 3 2	♠ K 10 8 3 2	♠ 10 3	♠ Q 8 7 4	♠ A Q J 10 9 8	♠ 8 7
♥ K Q J 6	♥ K 9 3 2	♥ 9 7	♥ A Q 6	♥ K	♥ 10 9 5 4
◇ A 2	◇ 7	◇ A J 10 6 3	◇ 7 4 2	◇ 9 6 4	◇ A 8 2
♣ K 6 4	♣ Q 6 2	♣ J 4 3 2	♣ A K Q	♣ J 6 5	♣ Q J 10 2

13 N/Both	14 E/Nil	15 S/N-S	16 W/E-W	17 N/Nil	18 E/N-S
♠ Q 9	♠ K 8 3 2	♠ J 8 5	♠ 9 7 6	♠ J 10 6 5 2	♠ 6 5
♥ K Q 9 8	♥ K 7 6 4 2	♥ J 10 9 6 4	♥ J 10 9 5 4 3	♥ Q	♥ J 8 2
◇ Q 9 6 5 2	◇ 3 2	◇ K 2	◇ 8 2	◇ 10 7 5	◇ A K Q 4
♣ J 5	♣ 8 3	♣ 10 9 5	♣ 10 6	♣ K 10 6 3	♣ A 9 8 6

19 S/E-W	20 W/Both	21 N/N-S	22 E/E-W	23 S/Both	24 W/Nil
♠ Q 8 5	♠ J 9 6 2	♠ K 5 2	♠ 5 2	♠ 5	♠ 9 7 6
♥ K Q J 7	♥ A K 10	♥ A J 7 6 4	♥ J 9 8 4	♥ Q 8 3	♥ - - -
◇ J 9 3	◇ A 7 2	◇ Q J 4 2	◇ J 10	◇ K Q 5 2	◇ Q J 10 7 4 2
♣ 9 6 4	♣ 9 6 2	♣ Q	♣ A K 10 5 4	♣ A K 9 3 2	♣ K J 10 5

25 N/E-W	26 E/Both	27 S/Nil	28 W/N-S	29 N/Both	30 E/Nil
♠ A K J 5 2	♠ K Q 10 9 7	♠ 8 6 5 4	♠ A 4	♠ 8	♠ 6 2
♥ 10 6 2	♥ A Q	♥ 8 6 5	♥ A J 7 2	♥ 10 8 6 4	♥ K J 8 5 4
◇ 8 4	◇ 6 4	◇ Q 9	◇ A K 10 7	◇ Q 9 2	◇ J 7 6 2
♣ Q 9 6	♣ A 7 5 4	♣ K J 8 3	♣ 8 7 4	♣ A K J 9 4	♣ 9 2

31 S/N-S	32 W/E-W	33 N/Nil	34 E/N-S	35 S/E-W	36 W/Both
♠ 6 5 4	♠ 10 8 7	♠ K J 9 7	♠ A Q J 10 6 4	♠ 9 8 2	♠ Q 9 6 4
♥ A K 10 9 7	♥ A Q 8	♥ 7 5 2	♥ Q 9	♥ Q 5 3	♥ K
◇ A 9 2	◇ 8 5 3	◇ K Q 9 2	◇ 7 5 4	◇ A 6 4	◇ 8 7 5 4
♣ K 9	♣ A 9 7 2	♣ J 6	♣ 3 2	♣ A Q 7 4	♣ Q J 9 8

37 N/N-S	38 E/E-W	39 S/Both	40 W/Nil	41 N/E-W	42 E/Both
♠ A 4 2	♠ A 9	♠ K 10 9	♠ J	♠ K Q 9	♠ 8
♥ A K Q 9 8 7 3	♥ Q J 10 7 5	♥ A 10 9	♥ 9 5 4 2	♥ J 10 9 8 3	♥ A K Q J 2
◇ A 4	◇ 10 6	◇ J 10 9 5 2	◇ 7 6 3	◇ 7	◇ A Q J
♣ Q	♣ Q 10 9 2	♣ 6 5	♣ A K Q J 5	♣ 8 7 4 2	♣ K Q J 2

43 S/Nil	44 W/N-S	45 N/Both	46 E/Nil	47 S/N-S	48 W/E-W
♠ 7 4	♠ 2	♠ J 8 7 5	♠ A K Q 6 4 2	♠ A J 9 6 4	♠ J 10 7 3
♥ 10 3	♥ J 7 6 5 4	♥ 9 4 3 2	♥ A 9 5 4 3	♥ 4	♥ - - -
◇ A K J	◇ A 7 3	◇ Q J 10	◇ A	◇ K 5	◇ 9 8 6 5 2
♣ 9 7 6 5 4 2	♣ 8 7 6 2	♣ J 3	♣ 8	♣ A K Q 5 2	♣ Q 7 6 5

PLAY HANDS FOR EAST

(After each hand, the dealer is given, followed by the vulnerability, e.g., W/Both means Dealer West, both sides vulnerable.)

49 N/Nil
♠ 6
♥ Q 9 8 6
♦ J 10 9 2
♣ Q 10 5 3

50 E/N-S
♠ A 4 3
♥ A K Q 6 2
♦ 2
♣ Q 8 6 3

51 S/E-W
♠ 3
♥ 10 8 7 5
♦ 10 9 5 4
♣ J 10 7 5

52 W/Both
♠ A J 7
♥ J 10
♦ A J
♣ K Q 10 9 5 2

53 N/N-S
♠ 10 9 8
♥ 10 9 7 6 5 2
♦ 9 5
♣ 7 2

54 E/E-W
♠ J 8 7 5
♥ A K 8 3
♦ 10 9 4 3 2
♣ - - -

55 S/Both
♠ J 10 6 3 2
♥ K 9 5 4
♦ A Q J 3
♣ - - -

56 W/Nil
♠ A K Q 7 5
♥ A Q 7 6 3
♦ 3
♣ A 6

57 N/E-W
♠ 4 3 2
♥ K 10 7 5
♦ A 9 6 5 3
♣ 5

58 E/Both
♠ A 10 6
♥ K 8 7
♦ Q J 5
♣ K Q 7 3

59 S/Nil
♠ J 8 7 3
♥ Q J 10
♦ 9 7 5
♣ 9 4 2

60 W/N-S
♠ K Q J 7 6 4
♥ 3
♦ A 7 6 5 3
♣ A

61 N/Both
♠ K 7 3
♥ 10 8 7 4 3
♦ A K 8 6
♣ 9

62 E/Nil
♠ Q 10 9 2
♥ K J 7 3
♦ K 4 2
♣ Q 5

63 S/N-S
♠ 8 7 5 2
♥ 10 3
♦ Q 10 5 3
♣ 7 5 2

64 W/E-W
♠ K Q 2
♥ A J 8 6 4 3
♦ A 7
♣ J 2

65 N/Nil
♠ K J
♥ Q 10 8 3
♦ K 7 5 4 3
♣ A 8

66 E/N-S
♠ A K 10 4 3
♥ A 9 6 2
♦ Q 6
♣ 9 8

67 S/E-W
♠ A K 9 5
♥ 5 3
♦ K 9 5 4
♣ 7 6 2

68 W/Both
♠ 8 5
♥ 10 5 3
♦ K J 6 2
♣ A Q 7 4

69 N/N-S
♠ K 7 6
♥ A Q J 6 2
♦ 7
♣ K 7 5 4

70 E/E-W
♠ K 10 7 5
♥ Q 8
♦ A Q
♣ K 9 6 5 3

71 S/Both
♠ 2
♥ 9 5 2
♦ J 5 4 3
♣ K 9 4 3 2

72 W/Nil
♠ J 10 3
♥ 9 6 4
♦ K 10 5
♣ 9 8 6 5

73 N/E-W
♠ K Q J 6 2
♥ 9 5
♦ K 10 7 6
♣ 10 8

74 E/Both
♠ K 9 2
♥ 2
♦ A K 9 5
♣ A Q 10 3 2

75 S/Nil
♠ Q 9 3
♥ K 10 6
♦ Q
♣ A Q 10 9 8 3

76 W/N-S
♠ A Q 10 9 5
♥ 6 5 2
♦ 5
♣ Q 10 9 2

77 N/Both
♠ K 6 3
♥ A Q J 6 5 2
♦ 7 2
♣ K 7

78 E/Nil
♠ 8 2
♥ 8 4
♦ J 8 5
♣ K 8 7 5 4 3

79 S/N-S
♠ K J 8 3
♥ 3
♦ A 8 5 3 2
♣ J 7 5

80 W/E-W
♠ A K 9 8 7
♥ 10 7
♦ J 8 7 6
♣ Q 3

81 N/Nil
♠ 10 9 8 5
♥ A 7 6
♦ 9 8 5 4 3
♣ J

82 E/N-S
♠ 9 8
♥ K Q 5 2
♦ A K J
♣ K J 10 2

83 S/E-W
♠ 3
♥ Q J 10 7 6 5
♦ Q 10 9 3
♣ A 7

84 W/Both
♠ A 10 5
♥ 7 6 3
♦ A K 4
♣ K Q 9 7

85 N/N-S
♠ J 3
♥ A K
♦ A K Q 8
♣ A K J 3 2

86 E/E-W
♠ 10 9 4
♥ K Q J 10 9 5
♦ Q 8 4
♣ 2

87 S/Both
♠ A K 3 2
♥ J 4
♦ Q 9 6 2
♣ Q 8 5

88 W/Nil
♠ 5
♥ K Q 10 7 4 3
♦ A 10 2
♣ 9 8 4

89 N/E-W
♠ 9 2
♥ K Q 10 5 2
♦ A 9 5
♣ 10 7 4

90 E/Both
♠ K Q J 10 6 4
♥ 3
♦ 7 6 4
♣ Q 10 4

91 S/Nil
♠ Q 10 3 2
♥ 7
♦ A K 9 8 4 3
♣ K 2

92 W/N-S
♠ K 9 8 6
♥ 7 6
♦ K Q J
♣ A 9 7 4

93 N/Both
♠ K 10 7 5 3
♥ 10 6 4 2
♦ 9 4
♣ A 5

94 E/Nil
♠ 6
♥ 7
♦ A Q 10 9 5
♣ Q 10 9 6 4 2

95 S/N-S
♠ 9 4 3
♥ 7 6 4
♦ Q 2
♣ J 10 7 6 2

96 W/E-W
♠ 8 4 2
♥ 7 5
♦ 10 8 5 4 3 2
♣ A 5

PLAY HANDS FOR SOUTH

(After each hand, the dealer is given, followed by the vulnerability, e.g., S/E-W means Dealer South, East-West vulnerable.)

1 N/Nil	2 E/N-S	3 S/E-W	4 W/Both	5 N/N-S	6 E/E-W
♠ A962	♠ J8	♠ AQJ	♠ K106	♠ J108	♠ A532
♥ K862	♥ 107	♥ J875	♥ 109	♥ AK5	♥ QJ5
◇ 72	◇ QJ432	◇ AKJ3	◇ QJ74	◇ 109	◇ A8
♣ J64	♣ AJ102	♣ J5	♣ 7532	♣ KQ432	♣ AQJ6

7 S/Both	8 W/Nil	9 N/E-W	10 E/Both	11 S/Nil	12 W/N-S
♠ KQ8	♠ 954	♠ QJ542	♠ K1065	♠ ---	♠ KQ1043
♥ A9532	♥ 7	♥ AQJ3	♥ J10732	♥ J8762	♥ 7
◇ J963	◇ A96532	◇ 84	◇ 8	◇ QJ103	◇ KJ103
♣ 9	♣ K73	♣ 97	♣ 1087	♣ 9832	♣ 765

13 N/Both	14 E/Nil	15 S/N-S	16 W/E-W	17 N/Nil	18 E/N-S
♠ J86543	♠ 107	♠ A7	♠ A52	♠ 984	♠ 93
♥ 632	♥ 83	♥ AK3	♥ Q87	♥ AJ9642	♥ K1063
◇ 107	◇ K965	◇ QJ43	◇ 953	◇ Q	◇ 10873
♣ 94	♣ A10972	♣ AKJ2	♣ AKJ4	♣ A92	♣ KQ5

19 S/E-W	20 W/Both	21 N/N-S	22 E/E-W	23 S/Both	24 W/Nil
♠ 1043	♠ AQ105	♠ QJ10	♠ AJ1084	♠ KQ874	♠ 10543
♥ A93	♥ J2	♥ Q103	♥ A6	♥ J742	♥ A742
◇ A8742	◇ Q10954	◇ K105	◇ K3	◇ J9	◇ 9853
♣ AQ	♣ 105	♣ 8643	♣ J872	♣ Q10	♣ 4

25 N/E-W	26 E/Both	27 S/Nil	28 W/N-S	29 N/Both	30 E/Nil
♠ 943	♠ 4	♠ KQ3	♠ K853	♠ AJ1053	♠ KQ84
♥ AK93	♥ J10974	♥ KJ1093	♥ 103	♥ KJ7	♥ 6
◇ KJ93	◇ Q108	◇ A543	◇ 6532	◇ K4	◇ 954
♣ K5	♣ 9863	♣ 4	♣ A63	♣ 762	♣ KQ1085

31 S/N-S	32 W/E-W	33 N/Nil	34 E/N-S	35 S/E-W	36 W/Both
♠ Q103	♠ AQ65	♠ A85432	♠ 87	♠ QJ	♠ 53
♥ 843	♥ 64	♥ Q10	♥ AK873	♥ AK6	♥ QJ10632
◇ QJ4	◇ KQ72	◇ A8	◇ 9863	◇ 10853	◇ KJ3
♣ J762	♣ 1043	♣ A85	♣ K4	♣ 10832	♣ K2

37 N/N-S	38 E/E-W	39 S/Both	40 W/Nil	41 N/E-W	42 E/Both
♠ J10653	♠ J3	♠ 83	♠ Q10942	♠ J6543	♠ 9643
♥ J5	♥ A9	♥ 87	♥ 6	♥ 7542	♥ 87654
◇ KJ6	◇ AKQJ72	◇ AK	◇ 542	◇ 1043	◇ K7
♣ A105	♣ AK3	♣ AKQ9874	♣ 10942	♣ 6	♣ A4

43 S/Nil	44 W/N-S	45 N/Both	46 E/Nil	47 S/N-S	48 W/E-W
♠ AKJ6	♠ 10	♠ A942	♠ 109	♠ ---	♠ 2
♥ A	♥ 1082	♥ 6	♥ Q108	♥ KQ8653	♥ K6432
◇ Q53	◇ KQJ6	◇ A7	◇ J9864	◇ 974	◇ Q107
♣ AKQJ3	♣ Q10543	♣ AKQ965	♣ K105	♣ 10976	♣ AK93

PLAY HANDS FOR SOUTH

(After each hand, the dealer is given, followed by the vulnerability, e.g., W/Both means Dealer West, both sides vulnerable.)

49 N/Nil	50 E/N-S	51 S/E-W	52 W/Both	53 N/N-S	54 E/E-W
♠ A J 8 3	♠ J 10 9 6	♠ K 9 8 5 2	♠ K 10 8 6 2	♠ A K Q 6 2	♠ K 9 4 2
♥ 7 4 3	♥ - - -	♥ A K Q 6 2	♥ 7	♥ Q	♥ Q J 5
♦ 6 5 3	♦ Q 10 7 4 3	♦ 3	♦ 6 5 3	♦ 6 4 2	♦ 7
♣ K 8 7	♣ J 9 5 4	♣ K 9	♣ J 8 4 3	♣ A K 8 6	♣ A K Q 9 6

55 S/Both	56 W/Nil	57 N/E-W	58 E/Both	59 S/Nil	60 W/N-S
♠ - - -	♠ 9 6 3	♠ K Q J 6 5	♠ K J 5 3	♠ 9 6 4 2	♠ 8
♥ J 10 7 3	♥ - - -	♥ Q 9	♥ A 9 5	♥ A K 3	♥ Q J 10 9 2
♦ 10 9 6 5 2	♦ K Q 9 7 4	♦ J 8 7 2	♦ 4 2	♦ A K 4	♦ 9 8
♣ A Q 10 8	♣ J 9 8 7 4	♣ A 9	♣ J 10 9 5	♣ K J 8	♣ K 7 6 4 3

61 N/Both	62 E/Nil	63 S/N-S	64 W/E-W	65 N/Nil	66 E/N-S
♠ 8 5	♠ K 7 5	♠ A Q 10	♠ 7	♠ A Q	♠ 5
♥ 6 2	♥ Q 10 8 2	♥ A K J 7 6	♥ 10 7 5	♥ 6 5	♥ J 10 5 4
♦ 7 3 2	♦ J 5	♦ K 9	♦ Q J 10 5 3	♦ Q J 8 6	♦ J 10 9 5
♣ A K Q 7 4 2	♣ J 10 9 4	♣ Q 4 3	♣ K Q 7 6	♣ Q 7 6 5 4	♣ A Q 7 2

67 S/E-W	68 W/Both	69 N/N-S	70 E/E-W	71 S/Both	72 W/Nil
♠ 7 4 3 2	♠ J 9 6 4	♠ A 8 3	♠ 9 3	♠ 10 7 5	♠ 7 6 5 4 2
♥ A J 9 8 6	♥ A Q 7 2	♥ 10 7 5 4	♥ K J 10 5 2	♥ K 8 4 3	♥ 8 2
♦ J 6 2	♦ 7 5	♦ K 5 4 2	♦ 6 5	♦ 9 8 6	♦ 9 8 4 2
♣ J	♣ J 10 9	♣ 10 9	♣ A Q 7 4	♣ Q 8 7	♣ A 7

73 N/E-W	74 E/Both	75 S/Nil	76 W/N-S	77 N/Both	78 E/Nil
♠ A 9 8 3	♠ 8 6	♠ 10	♠ K 3 2	♠ A 10 8 7 4	♠ A K 9 7 5
♥ A 8 4 3	♥ J 10 7	♥ A Q 8 7 4	♥ A 9 7 4	♥ 4 3	♥ K 3
♦ 4	♦ 10 8 4 2	♦ A 7 2	♦ K 10 2	♦ 4	♦ 6 4 3
♣ A K J 5	♣ 9 6 5 4	♣ K J 6 2	♣ 6 5 3	♣ Q J 10 9 3	♣ Q 9 6

79 S/N-S	80 W/E-W	81 N/Nil	82 E/N-S	83 S/E-W	84 W/Both
♠ A 5	♠ 2	♠ Q J 6 2	♠ K J 10 7 6 5 2	♠ K 8 5 2	♠ Q 8
♥ A 6 4	♥ J 6 2	♥ 5 3 2	♥ A 10	♥ 8 3 2	♥ K Q J 10 9 4
♦ K Q 7	♦ 4 3	♦ A K	♦ 10 8 5	♦ A J 4	♦ Q J 10 5
♣ A Q 10 4 2	♣ A J 10 8 7 6 2	♣ A K 9 7	♣ 7	♣ Q 10 5	♣ 2

85 N/N-S	86 E/E-W	87 S/Both	88 W/Nil	89 N/E-W	90 E/Both
♠ 10 4	♠ K 3	♠ Q J 10 8 6 4	♠ A 10 4 3	♠ K J 7 3	♠ A 8 7 5 2
♥ Q 9 7 3	♥ A 7 3	♥ K 9	♥ 8 2	♥ 9	♥ 10 7 4
♦ J 9 5 3	♦ K 10 3	♦ J 10 3	♦ K Q 7 3	♦ 8 7 4	♦ K 10
♣ 10 6 5	♣ K Q J 5 3	♣ 7 6	♣ A Q J	♣ K 8 6 5 2	♣ 6 5 3

91 S/Nil	92 W/N-S	93 N/Both	94 E/Nil	95 S/N-S	96 W/E-W
♠ K 7	♠ A J 10 2	♠ 4	♠ K 9 5 4 3	♠ 7 2	♠ A 9 3
♥ A 10 9 8 5 3	♥ 10	♥ Q 8	♥ A Q 10	♥ K 8 3 2	♥ K Q J 2
♦ J 7 6 5	♦ A 10 3 2	♦ Q J 10 6 5	♦ 6 2	♦ K 9 6 5	♦ A Q J 9
♣ J	♣ Q J 10 6	♣ K Q 10 9 4	♣ A 7 3	♣ A 9 4	♣ J 9

PLAY HANDS FOR WEST

(After each hand, the dealer is given, followed by the vulnerability, e.g., S/E-W means Dealer South, East-West vulnerable.)

1 N/Nil	2 E/N-S	3 S/E-W	4 W/Both	5 N/N-S	6 E/E-W
♠ 8 3	♠ A K Q 4	♠ K 9 7 3 2	♠ 9 5	♠ K 7 6 5 4 2	♠ K Q 10
♥ 10 9 5 4	♥ K J 8 4	♥ 9 3 2	♥ 8 6 4 2	♥ 8 7 3	♥ 8 4
◇ J 8 5	◇ A 8 5	◇ 10 9 7	◇ A K 9 8	◇ 5	◇ Q 7 6 4
♣ A 10 5 2	♣ 8 6	♣ Q 9	♣ Q J 9	♣ 9 8 5	♣ K 9 8 4

7 S/Both	8 W/Nil	9 N/E-W	10 E/Both	11 S/Nil	12 W/N-S
♠ 7 6 4	♠ J 6	♠ 9 8	♠ J 3 2	♠ 5 3 2	♠ A 6 5
♥ - - -	♥ Q J 10 8	♥ 10 5 4	♥ 9	♥ A Q 4 3	♥ J 8 6 2
◇ Q 7 5 4	◇ Q J 10	◇ K 9 5	◇ A K Q 5 3	◇ K 8 5	◇ 7 6 4
♣ J 10 8 7 3 2	♣ 10 9 5 4	♣ K Q 10 8 5	♣ 9 5 4 2	♣ A K Q	♣ K 8 4

13 N/Both	14 E/Nil	15 S/N-S	16 W/E-W	17 N/Nil	18 E/N-S
♠ K 10 7	♠ A Q J 5	♠ Q 4 2	♠ K Q	♠ Q 7	♠ A K Q 7 2
♥ J 10	♥ A Q J 9	♥ 5	♥ A K 6 2	♥ K 8 7 5	♥ Q 7
◇ K J	◇ A 4	◇ A 10 8 7 6	◇ A K Q J	◇ J 9 4 3	◇ 6 5
♣ 10 8 7 6 3 2	♣ K J 6	♣ Q 8 6 3	♣ 9 8 3	♣ Q J 8	♣ 10 7 4 2

19 S/E-W	20 W/Both	21 N/N-S	22 E/E-W	23 S/Both	24 W/Nil
♠ 7 2	♠ 8 4 3	♠ A 8 3	♠ 9 6	♠ J 3 2	♠ - - -
♥ 10 5 4	♥ Q 8 6 4	♥ K 9 8 5 2	♥ Q 10 5 2	♥ A K 10 9 6 5	♥ J 10 9 8 6 5
◇ K Q 10 6	◇ J 6	◇ 6	◇ Q 9 7 5	◇ A 8	◇ A K 6
♣ 10 8 7 5	♣ A K Q J	♣ K J 7 2	♣ Q 9 6	♣ 8 6	♣ 9 8 6 3

25 N/E-W	26 E/Both	27 S/Nil	28 W/N-S	29 N/Both	30 E/Nil
♠ Q 7 6	♠ J 8 5 3 2	♠ J 10 9 7	♠ Q J 6	♠ Q 9 2 9 3	♠
♥ 7	♥ K 8	♥ 2	♥ K Q 9 6 5	♥ 9 5 3 2	♥ Q 9 7 3
◇ Q 7 5 2	◇ K J 2	◇ J 10 8 6	◇ Q J	◇ A J 8 6 3	◇ A K Q
♣ 8 7 4 3 2	♣ K J 10	♣ A Q 10 5	♣ Q 10 2	♣ 5	♣ 7 6 4 3

31 S/N-S	32 W/E-W	33 N/Nil	34 E/N-S	35 S/E-W	36 W/Both
♠ 8 7 2	♠ 9 3	♠ Q 10	♠ K 9 2	♠ A K 10 6 5 3	♠ A K 7 2
♥ Q J 2	♥ K J 10 7 2	♥ 6 4	♥ J 10	♥ 7 4 2	♥ 7 5 4
◇ K 10 6 5	◇ J 10 4	◇ 7 6 5 4 3	◇ A J 2	◇ J 7 2	◇ 9 6 2
♣ A 10 5	♣ K Q 5	♣ K Q 10 9	♣ A Q 10 8 7	♣ 9	♣ A 6 3

37 N/N-S	38 E/E-W	39 S/Both	40 W/Nil	41 N/E-W	42 E/Both
♠ 7	♠ K Q 8 7 2	♠ A Q 7 6 2	♠ A K 3	♠ A 10 8 7	♠ A K J 2
♥ 6 4 2	♥ K 4 2	♥ 5 3	♥ A Q J 10 8 7	♥ A 6	♥ 3
◇ 10 8 7 5	◇ 9 8 4	◇ 8 7 6 4	◇ A J 8	◇ K 5 2	◇ 4 2
♣ J 9 8 3 2	♣ 7 5	♣ 10 3	♣ 6	♣ 10 9 5 3	♣ 10 9 8 7 6 3

43 S/Nil	44 W/N-S	45 N/Both	46 E/Nil	47 S/N-S	48 W/E-W
♠ 9 8 2	♠ A K Q 8 7 6	♠ - - -	♠ 3	♠ K Q 7 3	♠ 8 6
♥ K Q 7 5 2	♥ A K Q 9 3	♥ K Q 10 5	♥ K J 7 6 2	♥ A J	♥ Q 10 8 7
◇ 10 9 8 7 4	◇ 2	◇ 9 8 5 3 2	◇ 10 7 2	◇ A J 8 6 2	◇ K J 3
♣ - - -	♣ A	♣ 10 7 4 2	♣ A Q 9 3	♣ 4 3	♣ J 10 8 4

PLAY HANDS FOR WEST

(After each hand, the dealer is given, followed by the vulnerability, e.g., W/Both means Dealer West, both sides vulnerable.)

49 N/Nil	50 E/N-S	51 S/E-W	52 W/Both	53 N/N-S	54 E/E-W
♠ Q 10 9	♠ K Q 5	♠ Q J 10	♠ - - -	♠ 7 4	♠ - - -
♡ J 10	♡ J 5 4 3	♡ J 9 3	♡ A K Q 6 4	♡ A J 3	♡ 10 9 4
◊ 8 7 4	◊ A 8 5	◊ A J 7 6 2	◊ 10 9 7 4 2	◊ J 10 7 3	◊ J 8 6 5
♣ J 9 6 4 2	♣ A K 7	♣ Q 4	♣ A 7 6	♣ Q J 10 9	♣ 10 7 5 4 3 2

55 S/Both	56 W/Nil	57 N/E-W	58 E/Both	59 S/Nil	60 W/N-S
♠ A K Q 8 5	♠ J 10 2	♠ 10	♠ Q 4	♠ - - -	♠ A 5 3
♡ A Q 8 6 2	♡ K J 2	♡ J 6 4 3	♡ 4	♡ 7 6 5 4	♡ A K
◊ - - -	◊ A J 8 5	◊ K Q 10 4	◊ A K 10 9 8 7 3	◊ Q J 8 6 3	◊ Q 4 2
♣ J 9 6	♣ K 3 2	♣ J 8 4 3	♣ A 8 6	♣ 10 7 6 5	♣ Q J 10 9 8

61 N/Both	62 E/Nil	63 S/N-S	64 W/E-W	65 N/Nil	66 E/N-S
♠ J 10 9 4 2	♠ A J	♠ K J 6	♠ A 9 6 4 3	♠ 10 9 7	♠ Q 7 6 2
♡ Q 9 5	♡ A 9 6 5	♡ 9 4	♡ K Q 2	♡ K J 9 4	♡ K Q
◊ J	◊ A Q 6	◊ J 8 4 2	◊ K 6 4	◊ A 9 2	◊ 8 4 2
♣ J 10 6 5	♣ A K 7 6	♣ J 10 9 6	♣ A 8	♣ J 10 9	♣ J 10 6 3

67 S/E-W	68 W/Both	69 N/N-S	70 E/E-W	71 S/Both	72 W/Nil
♠ J 10	♠ A 7 3 2	♠ 10 9 4	♠ A Q J 4 2	♠ A Q 9 8 3	♠ Q
♡ 10 7	♡ 9	♡ 9 3	♡ 6 4 3	♡ A Q 7	♡ A J 10
◊ A Q 10 3	◊ Q 9 8 4 3	◊ J 10 9	◊ J 8 7	◊ 7	◊ Q 7 6 3
♣ Q 10 9 5 3	♣ K 8 5	♣ A J 6 3 2	♣ J 10	♣ A 10 6 5	♣ K Q 10 3 2

73 N/E-W	74 E/Both	75 S/Nil	76 W/N-S	77 N/Both	78 E/Nil
♠ 10	♠ A Q 10 5 4	♠ K 8 7 4	♠ J 7 4	♠ 9	♠ 3
♡ Q 7 2	♡ 8 6 5 4	♡ J 5 3	♡ Q 10 8 3	♡ K 10 7	♡ A Q J 7 2
◊ Q J 5 2	◊ 6 3	◊ 10 8 6 4 3	◊ Q 9 7 6	◊ K Q 10 9 5	◊ K Q 10 9 7 2
♣ Q 9 7 4 2	♣ J 8	♣ 4	♣ J 8	♣ A 8 6 4	♣ A

79 S/N-S	80 W/E-W	81 N/Nil	82 E/N-S	83 S/E-W	84 W/Both
♠ 10 9 7 6 4 2	♠ 5 4	♠ 3	♠ Q 4	♠ Q 10 9 6 4	♠ J 6
♡ K Q 8 7 2	♡ A Q 9 8 5 4	♡ K Q J 10 9	♡ 9 8 7 6 4	♡ 9 4	♡ A 8 5 2
◊ 6	◊ A 2	◊ J 7	◊ Q 9 6 4	◊ 7 5 2	◊ 6 3
♣ 3	♣ K 5 4	♣ 10 8 6 5 4	♣ A Q	♣ K 6 4	♣ A 6 5 4 3

85 N/N-S	86 E/E-W	87 S/Both	88 W/Nil	89 N/E-W	90 E/Both
♠ 7 6 2	♠ A 6	♠ 7	♠ Q 8 7	♠ A Q 10 5	♠ - - -
♡ J 10 8 6 4 2	♡ 8 4 2	♡ A Q 7 5 3	♡ A	♡ 4	♡ 6 5 2
◊ 7 4	◊ 7 6 5 2	◊ A K 4	◊ 9 8 6 5 4	◊ K 6 3 2	◊ Q J 9 8 5 2
♣ Q 8	♣ A 10 8 6	♣ A K J 2	♣ 10 7 3 2	♣ A Q J 9	♣ K J 9 7

91 S/Nil	92 W/N-S	93 N/Both	94 E/Nil	95 S/N-S	96 W/E-W
♠ A J 6 5 4	♠ Q 4	♠ Q 9 6 2	♠ A Q 8 7 2	♠ Q J 10 6 5	♠ K J 10 6 5
♡ 6 4	♡ J 8 4 2	♡ A K 9	♡ J 4	♡ 9	♡ 6 4 3
◊ Q 10	◊ 7 6 5	◊ A 8 3 2	◊ J 8 7 4 3	◊ A J 10 8 4 3	◊ - - -
♣ Q 9 8 6	♣ K 8 5 3	♣ 7 6	♣ J	♣ 5	♣ K Q 10 8 6

WHERE TO FROM HERE?

You have come this far and you want to go further. What should you do?

1. Your partner : Find a partner whose company you enjoy and who is as keen and as ambitious as you are. There is no future if one partner is eager to work and practise and try new material and the other is happy playing the same methods that were in vogue thirty years ago. By all means enjoy a social game with social partners but if you want to do better, find an enthusiastic partner.

2. Your tournaments : Play in as tough company as you can. The harder the games, the more you will meet the methods and style that are needed for winning. Pay attention to what happens when you play against the top players. Note how they compete constantly and the actions they take. The more pleasant experts will not mind if you ask them questions about their decisions. The secure experts will even acknowledge that their decision may have been a mistake. (The theory goes that no expert ever makes a mistake : they take a 'wrong view'.)

Whether it is a club championship or a national tournament, always go over the boards after the session. Study in particular the boards on which you did badly. Never let animosity enter your post mortems. The aim should be to fix the mistake, not fix the blame. Both partners should approach these discussions in the spirit of 'How could we have done better? Could I have helped you more?' and not 'You botched that one, didn't you?'

3. Your bidding system : Whatever system and conventions you and partner play, make sure you know them thoroughly and that you and partner play them the same way.

4. Your practise sessions : A serious partnership puts in considerable time in bidding practise sessions normally involving just the two partners. The Bidding Challenge features in various magazines are a good source of material, although some of these focus on trap hands rather than the regular routine hands which you need to handle well.

For slam bidding practise, remove twenty low cards (10 or lower) randomly from the pack. That leaves 32 cards which are shuffled and 13 are dealt to each partner. Do not look at the 6 cards left over. With so many high cards around, you will have game, small slam or grand slam decisions every hand. Write your auction down and each partner should describe the other's hand after the auction is over. If a misunderstanding has occurred, this is a golden opportunity to sort out the problem.

For slam, game and partscore practise, remove only 13 low cards and deal three hands of 13 cards each. Bid two of these and when finished, retain the stronger of these two and bid the third hand with this hand. This allows you to see two sets of possible problems for each of the stronger hands.

For minor suit practise, remove 13 low major suit cards and vice versa for major suit bidding practise.

5. Your behaviour at the table : This should always be impeccable. The game is tough enough without the added pressure of a critical, bickering partner. If you have such partners, get rid of them. If divorce is out of the question, arrange some other partner for your spouse.

It is best not to have any post mortem discussions at the table. Reserve these for later when passions have cooled. The less said during the session, the better. Do not try to teach partner at the table and never rebuke or criticise partner. You may well find later that you were the one in the wrong.

Always maintain your composure and have a bright and cheerful disposition. It is in your best interests to be supportive of partner. No one else is on your side and a happy, confident partner will play better. Isn't that what you want?.

6. Your personal habits : You need to find the conditions under which you perform best. Most people play better without the effect of alcohol in the bloodstream. Try to have at least an hour's break after a solid meal before the next session. Playing on a full stomach often leads to drowsiness and careless mistakes. Sleep and fitness are also important factors for producing your best efforts.

Suggestions for further reading :

This selection is totally biased, but the following are worth reading if you have not already done so :
The Modern Losing Trick Count
50 Winning Duplicate Tips
World Championship Pairs Bridge
Bridge Conventions, Defenses and Countermeasures
The Power System (for a very keen partnership)
Guide To Better Card Play
Guide To Better Bridge
Cue Bidding To Slams
100 Winning Bridge Tips

My favourite authors are Kelsey, Kantar and Lawrence. You will hardly go wrong with any of their books. There are many bridge magazines around. Subscribe to as many as you can afford.

Well worth studying are the annual world championship books, an excellent source of material on the methods and styles of the world's top players.